Fundamentals of Marketing

Paul Baines, Chris Fill,
Sara Rosengren, and Paolo Antonetti

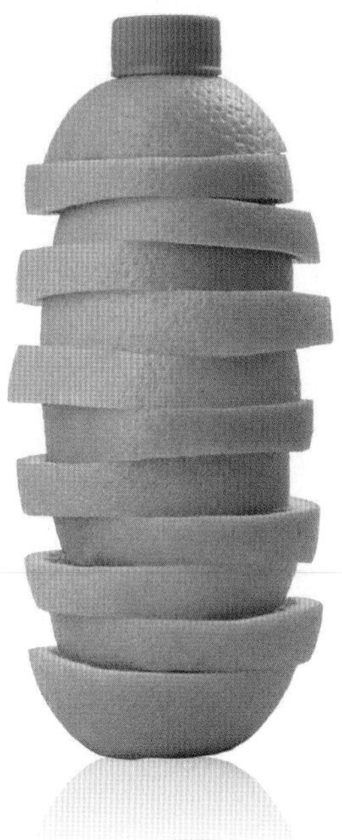

OXFORD
UNIVERSITY PRESS

Great Clarendon Street, Oxford, OX2 6DP,
United Kingdom

Oxford University Press is a department of the University of Oxford. It furthers the University's objective of excellence in research, scholarship, and education by publishing worldwide. Oxford is a registered trade mark of Oxford University Press in the UK and in certain other countries

Impression: 4

Published in the United States of America by Oxford University Press
198 Madison Avenue, New York, NY 10016, United States of America

British Library Cataloguing in Publication Data
Data available

Library of Congress Control number: 2016961446

ISBN 978–0–19–874857–1

Printed in Great Britain by
Bell & Bain Ltd, Glasgow

Fundamentals of Marketing

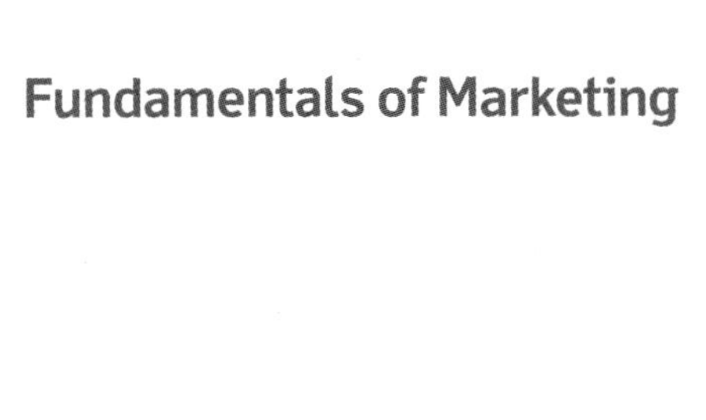

To Ning, for your constant support and generous love.
Paul Baines

To Karen, my loving companion in life.
Chris Fill

To Olof, Alma, and Moa—my own dream team.
Sara Rosengren

To Qianni, my everyday joy.
Paolo Antonetti

Brief Contents

Detailed Contents

Part 2 Designing and Delivering the Market Strategy

Part 3 Implementing the Marketing Mix

Case Insights

Case Insight 1.1 Aldoraq Water

Established in 1994 by Khaled A. Almaimani, Aldoraq Water Bottling Plant was one of the first water bottling factories in Madinah, Saudi Arabia. We speak to Abdurahman Almaimani, general manager, to find out more about how the company seeks to compete with well-known international brands.

Case Insight 2.1 Holdz®

Founded in 2000, Holdz® is an online climbing holds and accessories firm. We speak to Steve Goodair, managing director, to find out more about how the firm meets its customers' needs.

Case Insight 3.1 MESH Planning

How should organizations measure the effectiveness of all touchpoints in interactions with customers, not only marketing communications? We speak to Fiona Blades, MESH Planning's chief experience officer, to find out more.

Case Insight 4.1 3scale

Through its staff and offices in Barcelona and San Francisco, 3scale helps organizations to open, manage, and use application programming interfaces (APIs). We speak to Manfred Bortenschlager, API market development director, to find out how the company competes in its marketplace.

Case Insight 5.1 Lanson International

Founded in 1760, Champagne Lanson is one of the oldest existing champagne houses in France, making some of the world's finest champagnes. We speak to Paul Beavis, managing director of Lanson International, to find out more about how the company looks to further develop its presence in international markets, including the UK.

Case Insight 6.1 Aston Martin

The Aston Martin brand, founded in 1913, is synonymous with hand-crafted luxury, peerless beauty, incredible performance, and international motorsport glory. We speak to Simon Sproule, director of global marketing and communications, to find out how the brand is promoted in China.

Case Insight 7.1 Simply Business

Founded in 2005, Simply Business is an online insurance broker. We speak to its director of strategy and pricing, Philip Williams, to find out more about how the company has developed its pricing strategy.

Case Insight 8.1 *The Guardian*

How could an organization realize its objective not only to shift audience perceptions, but also to also change behaviours? We speak to Agathe Guerrier, strategy director at advertising agency Bartle Bogle Hegarty (BBH), to find out more about the work it undertook for its client *The Guardian*.

Case Insight 9.1 Budweiser Budvar

How should a heritage brand in the Czech Republic design a campaign to reposition itself against competing foreign brands? We speak to Lubos Jahoda, account director of Budweiser Budvar's advertising agency, to find out more.

Case Insight 10.1 Åhléns

As shopper behaviour turns increasingly digital, established retailers are having to adapt their channel strategies. We talk to Lotta Bjurhult, business developer, retail operations, at Sweden's largest department store chain Åhléns, to find out what it takes to add an online channel to an existing network of department stores.

Case Insight 11.1 Spotify

What role does social media play and how should organizations incorporate it into their communication campaigns? We talk to Chug Abramowitz, vice-president of global customer service and social media at Spotify, to find out more.

Case Insight 12.1 Withers Worldwide

Founded in London in 1896, Withers Worldwide has global revenues of over US$200 million, 163 partners, employs more than 1,000 people, has clients in more than 80 countries, and has acted for 42 per cent of the top 100 *Sunday Times* Rich List and 20 per cent of the top 100 of the *Forbes* Rich List. We speak to Laura Boyle, head of EU marketing and business development, to explore how Withers works to improve the quality of its client relationships.

About the Authors

Paul Baines is Professor of Political Marketing and Director of the Executive MBA programme at Cranfield University. He is author, co-author, and editor of more than 100 published articles, book chapters, and books on marketing issues. Among others, his work has been published in the *European Journal of Marketing*, *Marketing Theory*, and *Psychology & Marketing*. Over the last 20 years, Paul's research has particularly focused on political marketing, public opinion, and propaganda. He is Fellow of the Chartered Institute of Marketing (CIM), the Market Research Society (MRS), and the Institute of Directors (IoD), and a member of ESOMAR and the Academy of Marketing. Paul's consultancy experience includes work for various UK government departments on strategic communication research projects, as well as many small, medium, and large private enterprises, including Saint Gobain Glassolutions, IBM, 3M, and many more. Paul is Director of Baines Associates Ltd.

Chris Fill is Director of Fillassociates, which develops and delivers learning materials related to marketing and corporate communications (see http://www.chrisfill.com). Formerly Principal Lecturer at the University of Portsmouth, Chris now works with a variety of private and not-for-profit organizations, including several publishers. He is Fellow of the CIM, where he was the senior examiner responsible for the marketing communications modules and, more recently, the Professional Postgraduate Diploma module 'Managing Corporate Reputation'. In addition to numerous papers published in a range of academic journals, Chris has written or contributed to more than 40 books, including his market-leading and internationally recognized textbook, *Marketing Communications*, now in its seventh edition.

Sara Rosengren is Professor of Marketing at Stockholm School of Economics, where she is Head of Research at the Center for Retailing. She is also a board member of the European Advertising Academy (EAA). Sara's research on creative marketing communications has been published in leading academic journals such as the *Journal of Advertising*, *Journal of Advertising Research*, and *Journal of Brand Management*. She is especially renowned for her work on advertising equity. Sara is passionate about bridging the gap between the marketing academics and practitioners. She is frequently invited to speak at academic institutions, industry seminars, and company get-togethers, and regularly comments on marketing-related phenomena in Swedish media.

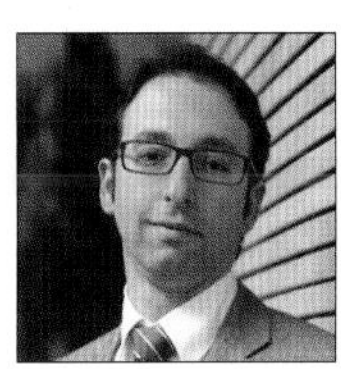

Paolo Antonetti is Lecturer (Assistant Professor) in Marketing and Director of the MSc in Marketing in the School of Business and Management at Queen Mary University of London. His research focuses predominantly on the interface between corporate social responsibility (CSR) and marketing, with a specific interest in the influence of emotions in decision-making and persuasion. Paolo's articles have appeared in several leading international publications, such as the *British Journal of Management*, *Journal of Business Ethics*, *European Journal of Marketing*, and *Psychology & Marketing*. He is a member of the Academy of Marketing and on the editorial board of the *International Journal of Market Research* and *Frontiers in Psychology*.

Acknowledgements

Course textbooks are substantial writing and research projects, resulting from the sweat and toil of numerous people in the design, development, and production of the text, and in the sales, marketing, and distribution tasks associated with it. Some of those people are outlined below, others are not, but their contributions should be acknowledged anonymously nonetheless.

We would like to thank our colleagues and former colleagues at Cranfield University, the Portsmouth Business School, the Stockholm School of Economics, and Queen Mary University of London for their support and discussions, all of which have in some way made their way into the book. We would like to thank Dr Ning Baines, at Birkbeck College, University of London, for contributions to the extensive online resources developed for the text.

This work is the result of a co-production between the academic authors and Oxford University Press editors and staff. Consequently, we would like to thank Antony Hey, our Commissioning Editor, for his support at various stages of the commissioning and development processes. Thanks are also due to Alexandra McGregor, our Development Editor, and Kate Gilks, our Publishing Editor, especially for help in incorporating the comments of many reviewers, in managing the development process expertly, and in helping to iron out any wrinkles in the final manuscript. We would like to thank Sal Moore, Production Editor, for her role in shaping the final design of the book and bringing it out on schedule with the help of the Designer, Elisabeth Heissler. We would also like to thank our colleagues at Oxford Digital Media, particularly James Tomalin, Sam Cooper, Matt Greetham, and the rest of the team, for their help to substantially improve our online resources proposition with their great video production work. We would also like to thank Vanessa Plaister and Joy Mellor for their superb proofreading efforts.

Unless our customers, students, and lecturers seek to use this book, there's no point writing and producing it, so we also recognize the efforts of the marketing team, Marianne Lightowler, Head of Marketing, and Tristan Jones, Marketing Manager, in developing and implementing the sales and marketing plans for the book.

The authors and publishers would like to thank the following people, for their comments and reviews throughout the process of developing the text and the online resources:

Dr Norin Arshed, *Heriot-Watt University*, UK
Dr Marija Banovic, *Aarhus University*, Denmark
David Brown, *Northumbria University*, UK
Dr Polymeros Chrysochou, *Aarhus University*, Denmark
Ruth Gosnay, *Leeds Beckett University*, UK
Dr Jialin Hardwick, *University of Lincoln*, UK
Dr Erik Jacobi, *University of Essex*, UK
Dr Mihalis Kavaratzis, *University of Leicester*, UK
Marnie de Koning, *Hogeschool Utrecht*, The Netherlands
Ariane Lengyel, *University Of West London*, UK
Adrian McGrath, *Liverpool John Moores University*, UK

Wybe Popma, *University of Brighton*, UK
Dr S. van Renssen, *Saxion University of Applied Sciences*, The Netherlands
Dr Neil Richardson, *Leeds Metropolitan University*, UK
Fiona Syson, *Edge Hill University*, UK
Judy Taft, *Nottingham Trent University*, UK
Robert Warmenhoven, *Van Hall Larenstein*, The Netherlands
Dr Nick K.T. Yip, *University of East Anglia*, UK

We would particularly like to thank the following lecturers, students, and practitioners who have contributed market insights to this edition.

Dr Ning Baines, *Birkbeck, University of London*, UK
Dr Ethel Claffey, *Waterford Institute of Technology*, Republic of Ireland
Will Leach, *VP, BrainJuicer Behavioural Activation Unit*
Ashwien Bisnajak, *Market Intelligence Manager, Hunkemöller*
Dr Rajiv Maher, *Post-Doctoral Researcher at the Pontifical Catholic University of Chile*
Dr Fredrik Törn, *Head of Insight, Analytics, and Intelligence, Coop Sweden*
Dr Jonas Gunnarsson, *Market and Consumer Research Manager at ICA AB*, Sweden
Jenny Li, *Senior Retail Analyst, IGD UK*
Dr Danae Manika, *Queen Mary University of London*, UK
Karl Wikström, *Planner, TBWA Stockholm*, Sweden
Dr Jonas Colliander, *Stockholm School of Economics*, Sweden
Dr Angela R. Dobele, *RMIT University*, Australia
Dr Erik Modig, *Stockholm School of Economics*, Sweden

We've also incorporated a series of practitioner marketing 'problems' within the text. This requires a considerable commitment from practitioners in developing the marketing 'problem' with the authors and in filming the 'solution'. Consequently, we would like to thank the following practitioners for their time, effort, and commitment to this project.

Chug Abramowitz, *VP Global Customer Service and Social Media, Spotify*, Sweden/USA
Abdurahman Almaimani, *General Manager, Aldoraq Water Bottling Plant*, Saudi Arabia
Paul Beavis, *Managing Director, Champagne Lanson UK/International Markets*, UK
Lotta Bjurhult, *Business Developer Retail Operations, Åhléns*, Sweden
Fiona Blades, *CEO, MESH Planning*, UK
Manfred Bortenschlager, *API Market Development Director, 3scale.net*, Spain
Laura Boyle, *Head of EU Marketing and Business Development, Withers Worldwide*, UK
Steve Goodair, *Managing Director, Holdz®*, UK
Agathe Guerrier, *formerly Strategy Director, Bartle Bogle Hegarty*, UK, now at Tiny Warrior
Lubos Jahoda, *Advertising Agency Account Director, Budweiser Budvar*, Czech Republic
Simon Spoule, *Director of Marketing and Communications, Aston Martin Lagonda*, UK
Philip Williams, *Director of Strategy and Pricing, Simply Business*, UK

Numerous reviewers have chosen to remain anonymous but contributed considerably to the final proposition. We would like to thank them for taking time to comb over various draft chapters of the book and provide us with valuable feedback. The publishers would be pleased to clear permission with any copyright holders that we have inadvertently failed, or been unable, to contact.

Preface

Welcome to the first edition of *Fundamentals of Marketing*. The aim of this book is to provide an engaging and comprehensive text that covers all of the fundamental areas of marketing knowledge in a concise manner. Our research suggests that students need:

- a rigorous textbook offering contemporary marketing insights that is suitable for courses running over a single semester;
- an inspirational book, able to pique your curiosity and inspire the next generation of marketers to excel in this exciting and fast-moving discipline;
- to be able to link marketing theory to marketing practice better—and, accordingly, the textbook offers several student-friendly 'market insight' vignettes in each chapter;
- a book that recognizes the need to go beyond the conventional '4Ps', and to offer extended insights on services, and digital and social marketing; and
- to recognize the importance of ethical issues in marketing—an area given special attention in this text, with the introduction of one market insight in each chapter to deal with matters of ethics, corporate social responsibility (CSR), or sustainable marketing.

We have included several international case insights, including, among others, Aldoraq Water from Saudi Arabia, Lanson from France, Spotify from Sweden, Aston Martin, and Withers Worldwide, to help to illustrate how real-life practitioners tackle marketing problems.

Fundamentals of Marketing starts with a look at classical marketing perspectives, and contrasts these with contemporary perspectives from the services and societal schools of marketing, helping you to develop your knowledge and understanding of marketing. To recognize the importance of the service-dominant logic perspective now so prevalent in marketing, we have integrated content on services marketing into one chapter, although there remain a large number of case and market insights throughout the book that make use of services examples.

In the online resources, we also provide you with web-based research activities, abstracts from seminal papers, study guidelines, multiple-choice questions, and a flashcard glossary to help you to broaden and reinforce your own learning. We aim to provide powerful learning insights into marketing theory and practice through a series of 'insight' features—that is, case, market, and research insights.

Who Should Use this Book?

The main audiences for this book are as follows.

- *Undergraduate students in universities and colleges of higher and further education, who are taught in English, around the world*—The case material and the examples within the text are global and international in scale, so that international students can benefit from the text.

- *Postgraduate students on MBA and MSc/MA courses with a strong marketing component*—It is hoped that such readers will find this text useful for pre-course and background reading, particularly because of the real-life case studies presented at the beginning of each chapter, accompanied by audiovisual material presenting the solution(s) available in the online resources.
- *Professional students studying for marketing qualifications through the Chartered Institute of Marketing (CIM), the Direct Marketing Association (DMA), and other professional training organizations and trade bodies*—The extensive use of examples of marketing practice from around the world make this text relevant for those working in a marketing or commercial environment.

How to Use this Textbook

We have tried to make your learning fun and meaningful by including a multitude of real-life cases. If there is a seminal article associated with a particular concept, try to get hold of the article through your university's electronic library resources and read it. Reflect on your own experience, if possible, around the concepts you are studying. Above all, recognize that you are not on your own in your learning: you have your tutor, your classmates, and us to help you to learn more about marketing.

This textbook includes not only explanatory material and examples of the nature of marketing concepts, but also a holistic learning system designed to aid you, as part of your university or professional course, to develop your understanding through reading the text and working with the materials available in the online resources. Work through the examples in the text and the review questions; read the seminal articles that have defined a particular subdiscipline in marketing; use the learning material on the website. This textbook aims to be reader-focused, designed to help you to learn marketing for yourself.

To help your learning experience, we strongly suggest that you complete the exercises, visit the web links, and conduct the Internet activities and worksheets at the end of each chapter, and other activities available in the online resources, to improve your understanding and your course performance.

Learning such an exciting discipline as marketing should be both fun and challenging. We hope that this textbook and its associated resources bring the discipline alive for you and pique your curiosity about how the marketing world works.

Good luck with your learning and in your career!

Sustainable Printing

Sustainability, a central focus of this book, is of ever-increasing importance in our world today, not only in marketing but in all business processes. To reflect this concern and take a responsible approach to our environment, Oxford University Press and the authors have elected to print *Fundamentals of Marketing* on Carbon Capture paper. Through the Woodland Carbon scheme, the carbon footprint created from the production and distribution of the paper for this book will be measured, charged for, and the charges will be paid to the Woodland Trust to fund the planting of further trees at one of their accredited woodland creation sites across the UK. By contributing to this programme we hope to reduce the effect of carbon produced by printing, and support a sustainable paper source.

How to Use this Book

This book comes equipped with a range of carefully designed learning features to help you get to grips with marketing and develop the essential knowledge and skills you'll need for your future career.

IDENTIFY & REVIEW *through* Learning Outcomes

Introducing you to every chapter, Learning Outcomes outline the main concepts and themes that will be covered to clearly identify what you can expect to learn. These bullet-pointed lists can also be used to review your learning and effectively plan your revision.

Learning Outcomes

After reading this chapter, you will be able to:

- define the marketing concept;
- explain how marketing developed over the twentieth century and into the twenty-first century;
- understand the exchange and marketing mix

LEARN & EVALUATE *through* Case Insights

Learn from the professionals with real-life case studies from leading marketers at organizations including Aston Martin, Budweiser Budvar, and Spotify. Discover what their businesses aim to do, what their jobs involve, and what kinds of challenges they face, before evaluating your own response to tackling their marketing problems. In the online resources you can find bespoke video interviews with all these professionals, and gain insights into how they ultimately resolved their marketing dilemmas.

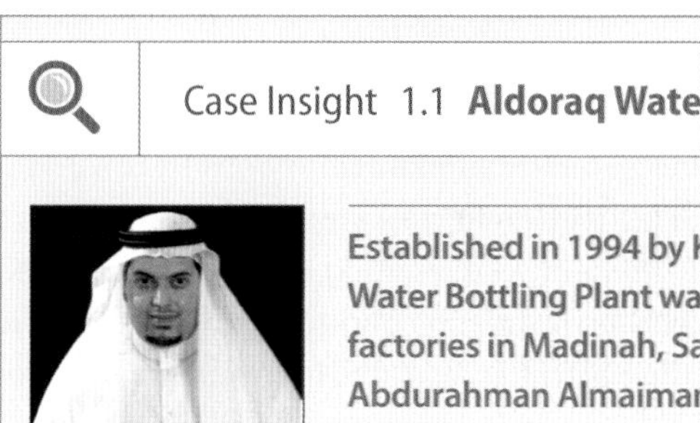
Case Insight 1.1 **Aldoraq Wate**

Established in 1994 by
Water Bottling Plant wa
factories in Madinah, Sa
Abdurahman Almaimai

ANALYSE & APPLY *through* Market Insights

Contemporary and varied examples from the business world illustrate the concepts discussed in the chapter, prompting you to analyse the marketing practices and apply the marketing theory to practical examples from a huge range of companies, with accompanying questions reinforcing your learning.

Market Insight 2.1 **Easy Purcha**

Car manufacturer Peugeot, with operational headquarters in Sochaux, France, sold 11,563 new cars in in the UK in 2015, taking a 4.0 per cent share of the market, way behind more popular brands in the UK such as Ford, Vauxhall, Volkswagen, Audi, BMW, Nissan, and Mercedes-

RESEARCH & PROGRESS *through* Research Insights

Take your learning further with the key books and journal articles highlighted in Research Insights, to aid your research and progress your understanding of key topics.

Research Insight 1.1

To take your learning further, you might wish to read this influentia

Borden, N. H. (1964) 'The concept of the marketing mix', *Journal of Adv*

RECAP & CONSOLIDATE *through* Chapter Summaries

Recap the core themes and ideas of the chapter to consolidate and review your learning in these handy Chapter Summaries.

Chapter Summary

To consolidate your learning, the key points from this chapter are summarized b

- **Define the marketing concept.**

  Marketing is the process by which organizations anticipate and satisfy their parties' benefit. It involves mutual exchange. Over the last 25 years, the marke

REVIEW & REVISE *through* Review Questions

Stimulating questions at the end of every chapter will review your knowledge and highlight any areas that need further revision ahead of the exam.

Review Questions

1. **How do we define the 'marketing' concept?**
2. **How do the AMA and the CIM definitions of marketing differ?**
3. **What is the difference between customers and consumers?**

PRACTICE & UNDERSTAND *through* Worksheet Summaries

These useful summaries signpost to Worksheets available for each chapter in the online resources. Visit the Worksheets to put your new marketing knowledge into practice and reinforce your understanding.

Worksheet Summary

To apply the knowledge you have gained from this chapter and to test y marketing principles and society, visit the **online resources** and compl

CHALLENGE & REFLECT *through* Discussion Questions

Develop your analytical and reasoning skills by challenging the theory and reflecting on key issues with these stimulating Discussion Questions, designed to create lively debate.

Discussion Questions

1. Having read Case Insight 1.1 at the beginning of this chapter, how wo attempts to differentiate itself from national and international brands
2. Read the section on 'The Marketing Mix and the 4Ps' and draw up mar organizations and their target customers.

LOOK UP & CHECK *through* Key Terms and Glossaries

Key Terms are highlighted in blue when they first appear and are collated into Glossaries at the end of each chapter, designed for you to look up terms and check your understanding of essential definitions.

Glossary

advertising a form of non-personal communication, by an identified sponsor, transmitted through the use of paid-for media.
American Marketing Association (AMA) a

based in the UK, around the worl
circular economy linear economy

How to Use the Online Resources

 **www.oup.com/uk/baines_fundamentals/**

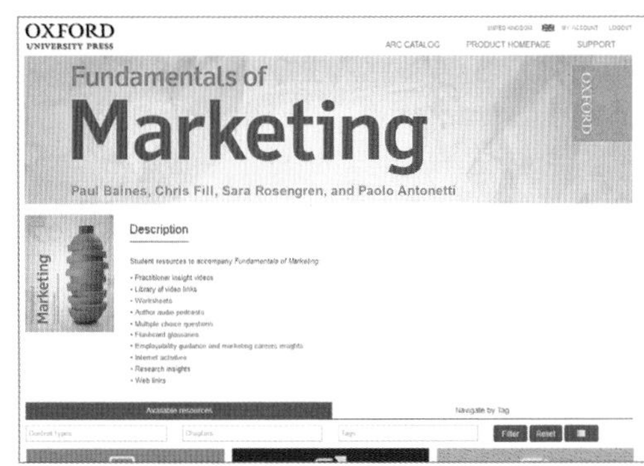

The online resources are signposted throughout chapters and provide you with access to the following specialized resources:

Student Resources—Free and open-access material available for users of the book.

Case Insight Videos

Watch the book's authors in discussion with the leading marketing practitioners featured in the chapter-opening Case Insights as they expand on the marketing challenges they face and what strategies they use to tackle them. Transcripts of each video are also available.

Worksheets

Task-focused Worksheets provide the opportunity to apply and reinforce your understanding of the key marketing frameworks and theories.

Worksheet 1.1: Marketing Principles

Chapter Reference
Chapter 1: Marketing Principles & Society

Overview
This activity introduces you to two frameworks that help us to understand how managers can market their goods and services.

Learning Outcomes
After completing this worksheet you should be able to:
- apply McCarthy's 4P's to a good;
- apply Bitner and Boom's 7P's to a service;
- describe the exchange process;
- discuss the differences and similarities between a good and a service.

Worksheet

Choose a brand of soft drink you are familiar with and apply McCarthy's 4P's framework to this Fast

Author Audio Podcasts

Short audio summaries of each chapter from the authors, to listen to on the go and help you revise.

Library of Video Links

A bank of links to marketing videos designed to demonstrate key principles and themes in practice.

Library of video links

A bank of links to marketing videos designed to demonstrate key principles and themes in practice

Resource Title: What is marketing?
Brand and/or Topic: Marketing
Resource Description: Professor of the Department of Marketing Management. Director of ESADE's Chair of Design Management
Channel: esade
Link (URL): http://www.youtube.com/watch?v=h7FIWC2NdEM

Resource Title: Evolution of Marketing
Brand and/or Topic: Marketing Evolution
Resource Description: Marketing is constantly changing - thanks to the internet. Check out the evolution of marketing from Austin Internet Marketing Agency - Three Sixty Solutions
Channel: Sherfben
Link (URL): http://www.youtube.com/watch?v=mR5x9QPzCSM&NR=1

Multiple-Choice Questions

Test your knowledge of the chapter and receive instant results with these interactive questions. References to page numbers in the book accompany every question to help you navigate to the topics that need further study.

Multiple choice questions

Which of the following statements is correct?

- Marketing is the term used to refer only to the sales fu
- Marketing managers don't usually get involved in prod decisions.

Flashcard Glossary

Learning the jargon associated with the range of topics in marketing can be a challenge, so this online glossary has been designed to help you understand and memorize the key terms in the book.

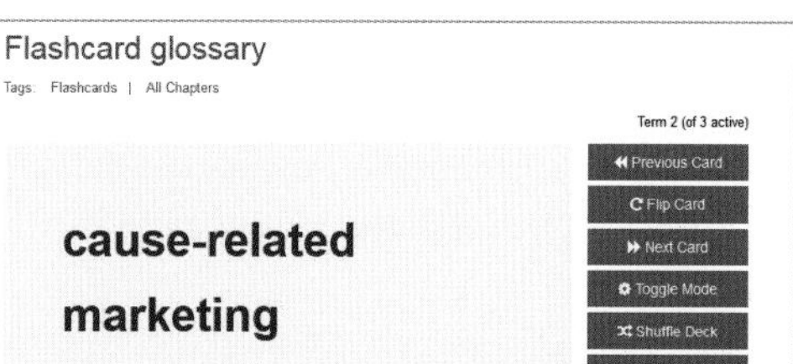

Employability Guidance and Marketing Career Insights

Listen to students and graduates talk about the skills they've developed at university, and also hear from graduate employment and recruitment specialists about the skills and attributes you'll need to succeed in your job applications and future career.

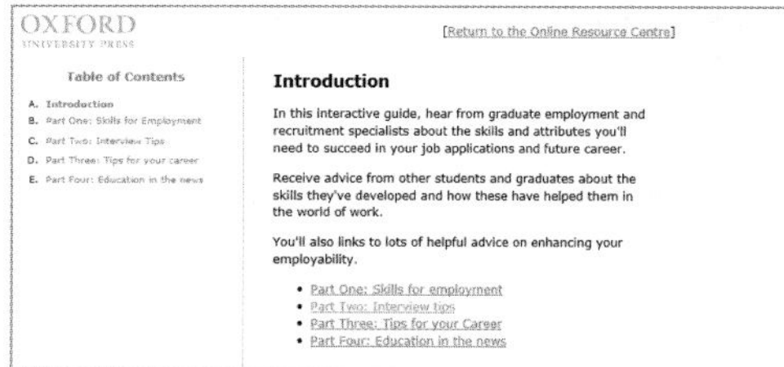

Internet Activities

Arranged by chapter, these Internet Activities help you develop your knowledge and improve your understanding of the topic through online research.

Chapter Reference
Chapter 1: Marketing Principles and Society

Overview
This activity will introduce you to leading professional marketing associations servic marketing industry around the world.

Activity Description
Visit the following websites for the professional marketing associations around the v and compare and contrast them.
Consider the following:

Research Insights

Follow the links to access the seminal academic papers suggested in the book's Research Insights.

Source: Borden, N. H. (1964), 'The concept of the marketing mix', *Journal of Advertising Research*, 4, 2–7.

Insight: This easy-to-read early article explains how marketing managers act as 'mixers of ingredients' when developing marketing programmes. The marketing mix, popularized as the 4Ps, remains popular today, although the advent of relationship marketing challenged the impersonal notion of marketers as manipulators of marketing policies, and focused more on the need to develop long-term interpersonal relationships with customers.

Abstract:
The abstract for this article can be accessed at the following link: http://search.ebscohost.com/login.aspx?direct=true&db=bth&AN=6630137&site=ehost-live (requires institutional access via EBSCO)

URL: http://search.ebscohost.com/login.aspx?direct=true&db=bth&AN=6630137&site=ehost-live (requires institutional access via EBSCO)

Web Links

Annotated Web Links allow you easy access to up-to-date and reliable marketing-related sites.

Lecturer Resources—For all registered adopters of the book.

VLE Content

To make your teaching more efficient and learning more effective, import all the material available in this online resource into your VLE.

PowerPoint Slides

A suite of fully customizable PowerPoint slides for use in lecture presentations accompanies each chapter.

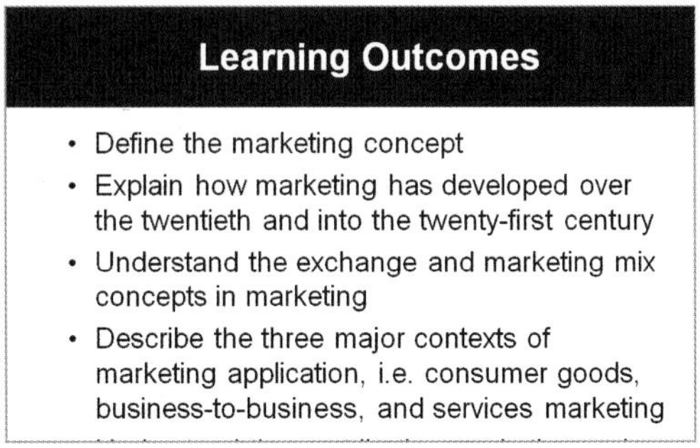

Essay Questions

Provided for each chapter, these stimulating essay questions are accompanied by clear and detailed answer guidance.

Test Bank

A ready-made interactive testing resource, fully customizable for your teaching and featuring built-in feedback for students, to save you time when creating assessments.

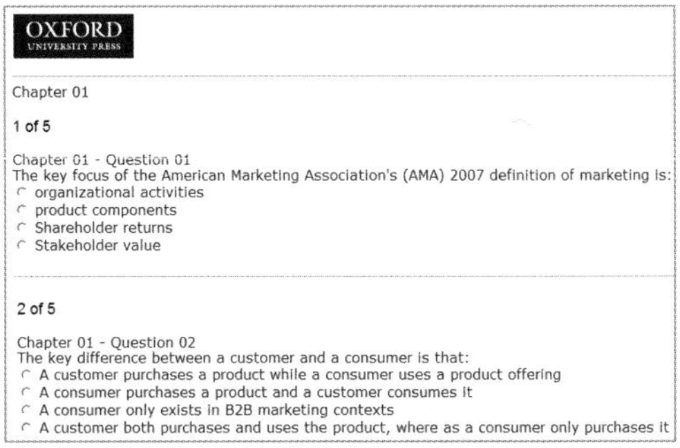

Tutorial Activities

Designed for use in seminars and tutorials, and to reinforce practical marketing skills, these activities are directly related to concepts and companies in the book. They offer a range of suggested ideas for easily integrating the book and its resources with your teaching.

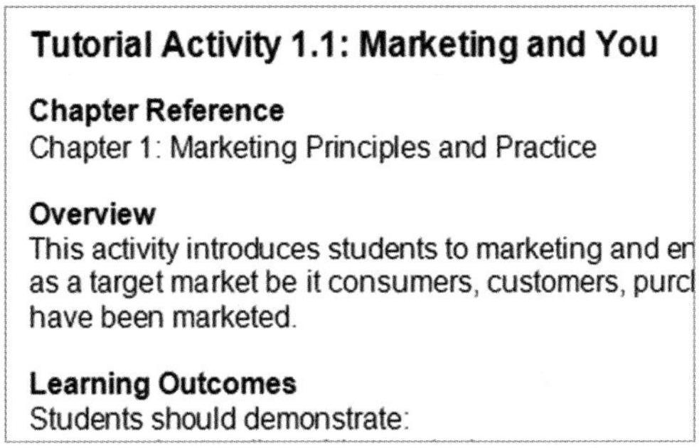

Marketing Resource Bank

A suite of interactive and multimedia marketing tools accompanied by detailed teaching notes provide a diverse collection of practical examples to use in your teaching.

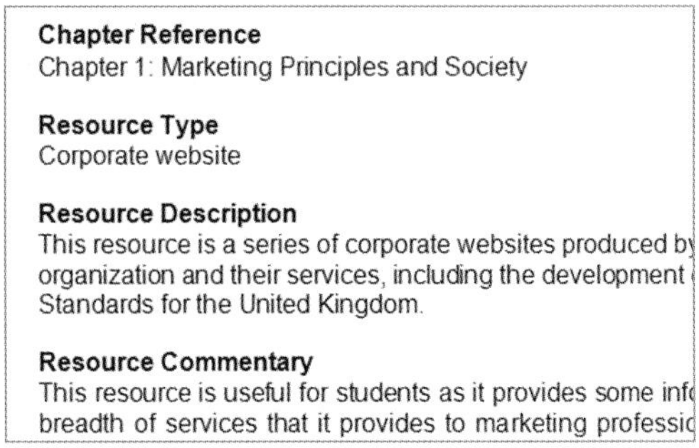

Pointers on Answering Discussion Questions

Possible points for inclusion when answering the Discussion Questions at the end of each chapter of the textbook.

Figures and Tables from the Book

Available for downloading into presentation software or for use in assignments and exam material.

Learning Outcomes

- Define the marketing concept
- Explain how marketing has developed over the twentieth and into the twenty-first century
- Understand the exchange and marketing mix concepts in marketing
- Describe the three major contexts of marketing application, i.e. consumer goods, business-to-business, and services marketing

OXFORD UNIVERSITY PRESS

Chapter 01

1 of 5

Chapter 01 - Question 01
The key focus of the American Marketing Association's (AMA) 2007 definition of marketing is:
- organizational activities
- product components
- Shareholder returns
- Stakeholder value

2 of 5

Chapter 01 - Question 02
The key difference between a customer and a consumer is that:
- A customer purchases a product while a consumer uses a product offering
- A consumer purchases a product and a customer consumes it
- A consumer only exists in B2B marketing contexts
- A customer both purchases and uses the product, where as a consumer only purchases it

Tutorial Activity 1.1: Marketing and You

Chapter Reference
Chapter 1: Marketing Principles and Practice

Overview
This activity introduces students to marketing and en as a target market be it consumers, customers, purcl have been marketed.

Learning Outcomes
Students should demonstrate:

Chapter Reference
Chapter 1: Marketing Principles and Society

Resource Type
Corporate website

Resource Description
This resource is a series of corporate websites produced by organization and their services, including the development Standards for the United Kingdom.

Resource Commentary
This resource is useful for students as it provides some inf breadth of services that it provides to marketing professio

Dashboard

Simple. Informative. Mobile.

Dashboard is a cloud-based online assessment and revision tool. It comes pre-loaded with test questions for students, a homework course if your module leader has adopted Dashboard, and additional resources as listed below. If your lecturer has adopted Dashboard and you have purchased the Dashboard Edition of the book, your standalone access code should be included and will provide instructions on how to sign up for the platform. If you have not purchased the Dashboard Edition or if you have purchased a second-hand copy, you can purchase standalone access online—visit **www.oxfordtextbooks.co.uk/dashboard** for more information.

SIMPLE: With a highly intuitive design, it will take you less than fifteen minutes to learn and master the system.

INFORMATIVE: Your assignment and assessment results are automatically graded, giving your instructor a clear view of the class's understanding of the course content.

MOBILE: You can access Dashboard from every major platform and device connected to the Internet, whether that's a computer, tablet, or smartphone.

Student Resources

Dashboard offers all the features of the online resources, but comes with additional questions to take your learning further.

Lecturer Resources

A preloaded homework course structured around the book is available, supported by a test bank containing additional multiple-choice questions. Your students can follow the preloaded course, or you can customize it, allowing you to add questions from the test bank or from your existing materials to meet your specific teaching needs. Dashboard's Gradebook will automatically grade the homework assignments that you set for your students. The Gradebook also provides heat maps for you to view your students' progress, which helps you to quickly identify areas of the course where your students may need more practice, as well as the areas they are most confident in. This feature helps you focus your teaching time on the areas that matter.

The Gradebook also allows you to administer grading schemes, manage checklists, and administer learning objectives and competencies.

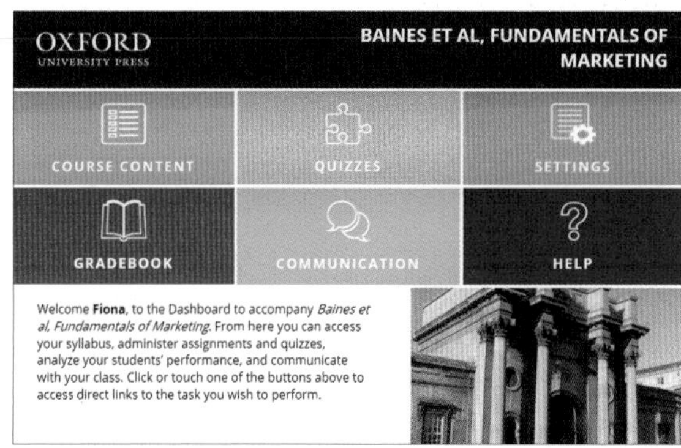

Part 1

Understanding Customers

Chapter 1
Marketing Principles and Society

Learning Outcomes

After reading this chapter, you will be able to:

- define the marketing concept;
- explain how marketing developed over the twentieth century and into the twenty-first century;
- understand the exchange and marketing mix concepts in marketing;
- understand the positive contribution that marketing makes to society;
- assess the negative impact that marketing has on society; and
- define sustainable marketing and its implications for marketing practice.

Case Insight 1.1
Aldoraq Water

Market Insight 1.1
V&D Goes Bust!

Market Insight 1.2
Servitization at Rolls-Royce

Market Insight 1.3
Insomnia: Brewing a New Customer Experience

Market Insight 1.4
Desso: Customer Orientation and Sustainability

Case Insight 1.1 **Aldoraq Water**

Established in 1994 by Khaled A. Almaimani, Aldoraq Water Bottling Plant was one of the first water bottling factories in Madinah, Saudi Arabia. We speak to Abdurahman Almaimani (pictured), general manager, to find out more about how the company seeks to compete with well-known international brands.

Aldoraq, headquartered in Madinah, Saudi Arabia, distributes its natural mineral water **products** throughout the Kingdom, and particularly in Madinah, Makkah, and Yanbu. It is one of the biggest factories in the Middle East, and a member of one of the oldest and largest family-owned businesses in Saudi Arabia. The company produces purified drinking water in different bottle sizes and capacities (from 250 ml to 5 gallon containers) and was the first water company in Saudi Arabia to join the International Bottled Water Association (IBWA) The water produced by Aldoraq contains a good percentage of fluoride, is derived from natural water bore-wells, and is purified by ozone. In 2015, sales of the company's 250 ml, 375 ml, and 600 ml products were increasing strongly on 2014 sales, but falling slightly in the 2 litre, 1 gallon, 5 litre, and 5 gallon bottle categories. The 5 gallon refill category, however, saw a slight gain.

The future looks bright for bottled water in the Kingdom, with population growth expected at 20 per cent per year until 2019, growing retail infrastructure, and an increasing number of *baqalah* (small independent stores). Aldoraq's **customers** are mostly hypermarkets, supermarkets, and medium and small stores that distribute or sell bottled waters to **consumers** (restaurants, fast-food stores, canteens, hospitals, households, etc.). Other customers include catering companies, hotels, airport retail outlets, and corporate offices. Often, such customers are looking for **price** discounts, longer terms of payment, and even coolers in which to store the water. Distributors decide to buy bottled drinking water from the factory based on which products are available in time and can steadily be supplied to customers' volume requirements, and the terms of deals and consignments, including beneficial payment terms. Of particular importance to customers is their ability to buy all of the products they need from one location. Because there are more than 30 water distributors in Medinah, many customers base their decision on the price they pay.

To promote awareness of the brand, Aldoraq recommends that customers display the product prominently in their stores, in potential customers' line of sight, and Aldoraq offers volume discounts to its largest distributors accordingly. In addition, it supports the community by giving free water to charities, and discounted water to the mosques and other religious places. Nevertheless, more recently, some large hotels and stores have started to purchase only premium water from companies selling international brands, such as Evian, Nestlé, and Aquafina, making it hard for Aldoraq to compete with them. These big brands are competing by trying to dominate the supply chain system. For example, Aquafina, owned by PepsiCo, is pushing its water product alongside other products such as Pepsi cola. When Aquafina first entered the market, PepsiCo gave away free samples of water with Pepsi product and then pushed customers to buy the Aquafina water brand from them at the same time as buying Pepsi. Coca-Cola also competed in this way with Arwa, its water product.

How should Aldoraq seek to differentiate itself, and thereby compete against both local and international brands?

Introduction

How have companies marketed their offerings to you in the past? Consider the last smartphone you bought, the music you stream, and the airlines on which you have flown. Why did you decide to purchase these offerings? Each one has been marketed to you to cater for a particular need that you have. Consider how the offering was distributed. What physical and service-based components is it made of? What societal contributions, if any, positive or negative, do these offerings make? Are other versions of these offerings available that meet your needs and the needs of society better? These are some of the questions that marketers should ask themselves when designing, developing, and delivering offerings to the customer.

This chapter develops our understanding of marketing principles and marketing's impact on society by defining 'marketing'. We consider the origins and development of marketing throughout the twentieth and into the twenty-first centuries. The core principles of marketing, incorporating the **marketing mix**, the principle of marketing exchange, **market orientation**, **relationship marketing**, and **service-dominant logic**, are all considered. Finally, we review the positive and negative impacts that marketing has on society, and consider the implications for companies.

What is Marketing?

There are numerous definitions of 'marketing', but we present three for easy reference in Table 1.1.

Visit the **online resources** and follow the web links to the **Chartered Institute of Marketing (CIM)** and **American Marketing Association (AMA)** websites to read more about their views on 'What is Marketing?'

The CIM and AMA definitions recognize marketing as a 'management process' and an 'activity', although many firms organize marketing as a discrete department, rather than as a service across departments (Sheth and Sisodia, 2005). Nike, for example, uses a regional matrix organizational structure, enabling marketing to operate within and across departments, such as apparel, footwear (Brenner, 2013).

What all of these definitions display is how the concept of marketing has changed over the years, from including only transactional concepts such as pricing, **promotion**, and distribution, to encompassing relationship concepts as well, such as the importance of customer trust, risk, commitment, and co-creation.

In addition, the nature of the relationships between an organization and its customers, in its offerings and its mission, are different in not-for-profit and for-profit organizations. Nevertheless, the broad principles of how marketing is used remain the same. All definitions recognize this widened concept of the wider societal applicability of marketing.

Visit the **online resources** and complete Internet Activity 1.1 to learn more about the professional marketing associations around the world.

Table 1.1	Definitions of marketing
Defining institution/author	**Definition**
Chartered Institute of Marketing (CIM)	The management process responsible for identifying, anticipating, and satisfying customer requirements profitably. (CIM, 2015: 2)
American Marketing Association (AMA)	Marketing is the activity, set of institutions, and processes for creating communicating, delivering, and exchanging offerings that have value for customers, clients, partners, and society at large. (AMA, 2013)
A French perspective	*Le marketing est la stratégie d'adaptation des organisations à des marchés concurrentiels, pour influencer en leur faveur le comportement des publics dont elles dépendent, par une offre dont la valeur perçue est durablement supérieure à celle des concurrents. Dans le secteur marchand, le rôle du marketing est de créer de la valeur économique pour l'entreprise en créant de la valeur perçue par les clients.* (Lendrevie and Lévy, 2014: 5) [Broadly translated:] Marketing is the adaptation strategy of organizations to competitive markets so that they can influence the behaviour of the publics on which they depend, through an offering whose perceived value is durably superior to that of competitors. In the commercial sector, the role of marketing is to create economic value for the company by creating value as perceived by customers.

What's the Difference Between Customers and Consumers?

What is the difference between a 'customer' and a 'consumer'? The difference is subtle, but real. A customer is a buyer, a purchaser, a patron, a client, or a shopper, and therefore someone who buys from a shop, a website, a business, or, in the sharing economy, another customer (for example via Airbnb or eBay). The consumer is someone who uses the offering (or eats it, in the case of food).

To illustrate, consider Mondelez International's Dairylea Dunkers, dairy food designed to be a good source of calcium, with each pack contributing at least 26 per cent of the daily reference intake of calcium. In this case, the customer is the chief shopper, the parent or guardian, and the consumer is the child. Sometimes, the customer and consumer can be the same person, for example the girl buying cinema tickets for herself and a friend online.

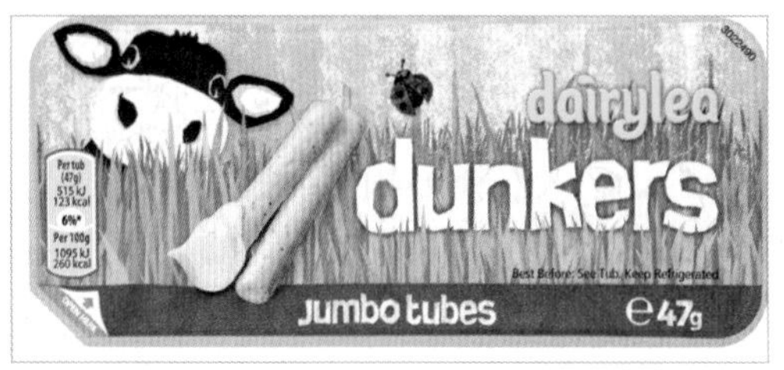

Dairylea Dunkers, the 'moo-vellous' snack for children.
Source: Reproduced with kind permission of Mondelez International.

Market Orientation

The concept of market orientation (Kohli and Jaworski, 1990) lies at the heart of marketing. Developing a market orientation makes organizations more profitable in both the long and short runs (Kumar et al., 2011). In a meta-analysis of market orientation studies, Kirca and colleagues (2005) conclude that market orientation may be imperative for survival in service firms and the source of competitive advantage in manufacturing firms.

But developing a market orientation is not the same as developing a market*ing* orientation. So what is the difference? A company with a marketing orientation would be a company that recognizes the importance of marketing within the organization, for example by appointing a marketing person as chief executive officer (CEO), or to chair its board of directors (or trustees in the case of a charity), or to the executive team more generally in a limited company or partnership.

Developing a market orientation refers to 'the organization-wide generation of market intelligence pertaining to current and future customer needs, dissemination of the intelligence across the departments, and organization-wide responsiveness to it' (Kohli and Jaworski, 1990: 3). So a market orientation not only involves marketing, but also requires a focus on:

- *customer orientation*, which is concerned with creating superior **value** by continuously developing and redeveloping offerings to meet customer needs;
- *competitor orientation*, which requires an organization to develop an understanding of its competitors' short-term strengths and weaknesses, and its own long-term capabilities and strategies (Slater and Narver, 1994); and
- *interfunctional coordination*, which requires all functions of an organization to work together for long-term profit growth.

A Brief History of Marketing

Marketing developed in a four-stage sequence, as follows.

1. *Production period, 1890s–1920s*—The period was characterized by a focus in the firm on physical production and supply, where demand exceeded supply, there was little competition, and the range of products was limited. This phase came after the Industrial Revolution.
2. *Sales period, 1920s–50s*—The second period was characterized by a focus in the firm on personal selling supported by market research and **advertising**. This phase took place after the First World War.
3. *Marketing period, 1950s–80s*—Next came a more advanced focus in the firm on the customer's needs. This phase came after the Second World War.
4. *Societal marketing period, 1980s–Present day*—Marketing then came to be characterized by a stronger focus on social and ethical concerns in marketing in the firm and recognition that not-for-profits could also undertake marketing. This phase took place during the 'information revolution' of the late twentieth century (Enright, 2002).

Marketing, as a discipline, has developed as a result of the influence of its practitioners, as well as developments in related disciplines, including the areas of industrial economics, psychology, sociology, and anthropology, as follows.

- *Industrial economics influences*—Our knowledge of the matching of supply and demand, within industries, owes much to the development of microeconomics. For instance, the economic concepts of 'perfect competition' and the 'matching of supply and demand' underlie the marketing concept, particularly in relation to the concepts of the price at which offerings are sold and the quantity distributed (see Chapter 7). Theories of income distribution, scale of operation, monopoly, competition, and finance all derive from economics (Bartels, 1951), although the influence of economics over marketing is declining (Howard et al., 1991).
- *Psychological influences*—Our knowledge of consumer behaviour derives principally from psychology, especially in the early days, motivation research (see Chapter 2) in relation to consumer attitudes, perceptions, motivations, and information processing (Holden and Holden, 1998), and our understanding of persuasion, consumer personality, and customer satisfaction (Bartels, 1951).
- *Sociological influences*—Knowledge of how groups of people behave derives from sociology, with insights into areas such as how people from similar gender and age groups behave (demographics), how people in different social positions within society behave (class), why we do things in the way that we do (motivation), general ways that groups behave (customs), and culture (Bartels, 1951, 1959). Our understanding of what society thinks as a whole (that is, public opinion), how communications pass through opinion leaders (Katz, 1957), and how we influence the way in which people think and to adopt our perspective (for example propaganda research—see Lee, 1945; Doob, 1948) have all informed marketing practice.
- *Anthropological influences*—Our debt to **social anthropology** increases as we use qualitative approaches such as **ethnography**, **netnography**, and **observation** in researching consumer behaviour (see Chapter 3), particularly the behaviour of subgroups and cultures (such as **tweenagers**, **haul girls**).

What Do Marketers Do?

To answer this question, the British government—in the shape of Skills CFA (formerly the Council for Administration, or CfA)—has worked with relevant stakeholders to map out how the marketing function operates. The consultation indicated that the job covered eight functional areas (see Figure 1.1), each of which is interlinked with stakeholder requirements.

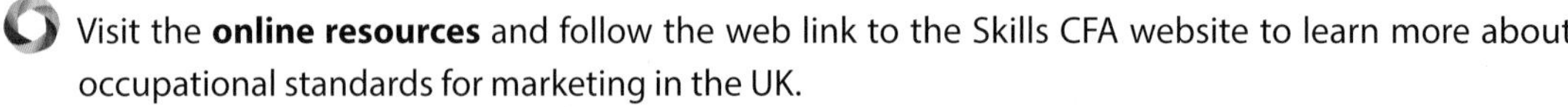

Visit the **online resources** and follow the web link to the Skills CFA website to learn more about occupational standards for marketing in the UK.

It is important to stress that marketing is present in all aspects of an organization, since all departments have some role to play with respect to creating, delivering, and satisfying customers. Employees in the research and development (R&D) department designing new products to meet existing customer needs are performing a marketing role. Similarly, members of the **procurement** department buying components for a new product or service must purchase those components of a specific quality and at a certain cost that will meet customer needs. In fact, we can go through

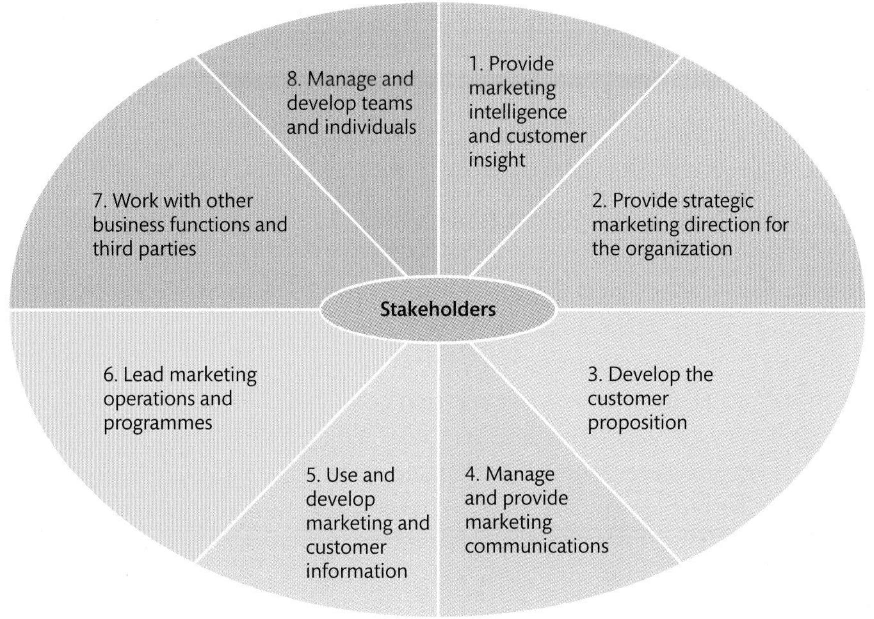

Figure 1.1 A functional map for marketing

Source: The Marketing and Sales Standards Setting Body (2010). Reproduced with the kind permission of Dr Chahid Fourali.

all departments of a company and find that, in each department, there is a marketing role to be played to some extent. In other words, marketing is distributed throughout the organization and all employees can be considered to be part-time marketers (Gummesson, 1990).

The Principal Principles of Marketing

Marketing involves a series of highly complex interactions between individuals, organizations, society, and government. Consequently, it is difficult to develop general principles that apply to all contexts. However, we can make at least some law-like generalizations. According to Leone and Shultz (1980), these include the following.

- *Generalization 1*—Advertising has a direct and positive influence on total industry (market) sales: all advertising done at industry level serves to increase sales within that industry.
- *Generalization 2*—Selective advertising has a direct and positive influence on individual company (brand) sales: advertising undertaken by a company tends to increase the sales of the particular brand for which it was spent.
- *Generalization 3*—The **elasticity** of selective advertising on company (brand) sales is low (inelastic): for frequently purchased goods, advertising has only a very limited effect in raising sales.
- *Generalization 4*—Increasing store shelf space (display) has a positive impact on sales of **non-staple** grocery items, such as products bought on impulse (for example ice cream, chocolate bars) rather than those that are planned purchases, which are less important, but perhaps more

luxurious, types of good (for example gravy mixes, cooking sauces). For impulse goods, the more shelf space you give an item, the more likely you are to sell it.

- *Generalization 5*—Distribution, defined by the number of outlets, has a positive influence on company sales (market share): setting up more retail locations has a positive influence on sales.

Marketing as Exchange

Marketing is a two-way exchange process. It is not solely about the marketing organization doing the work; the customer inputs also—sometimes extensively. Customers specify how we might satisfy their needs, because marketers cannot read their minds. Customers must then pay for the offering. In the mid-1970s, there was an increasing belief that marketing centred on the exchange process between buyers and sellers, and associated supply chain intermediaries. Exchange relationships were seen to be economic (for example a consumer buying groceries) and social (for example the service provided by the police on behalf of society paid for by government) (Bagozzi, 1975). There are numerous types of buyer–seller exchange in marketing. Figure 1.2 illustrates some

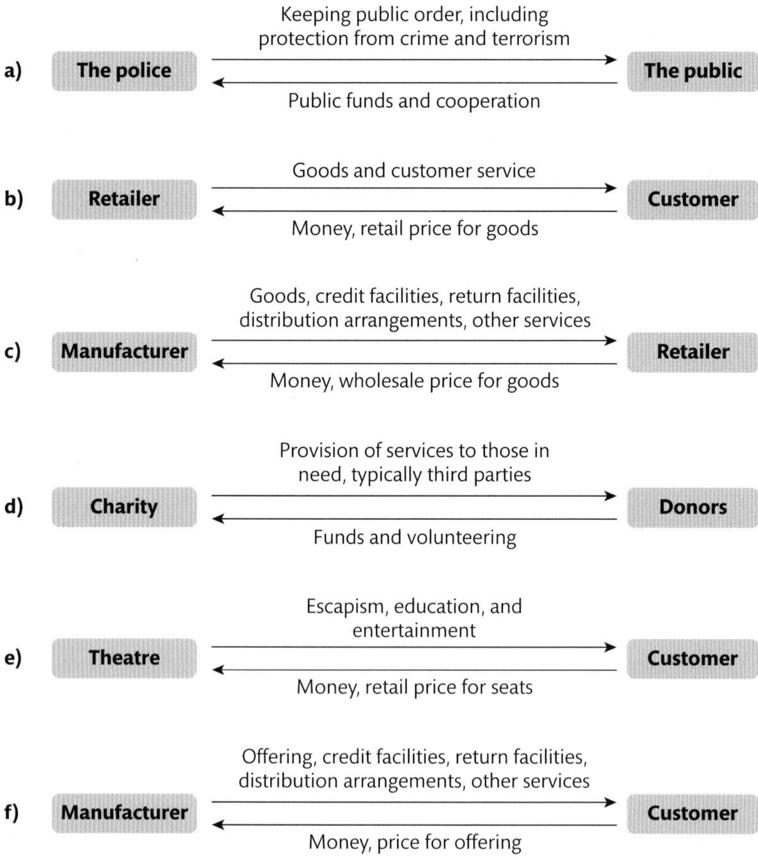

Figure 1.2 Examples of marketing exchange processes

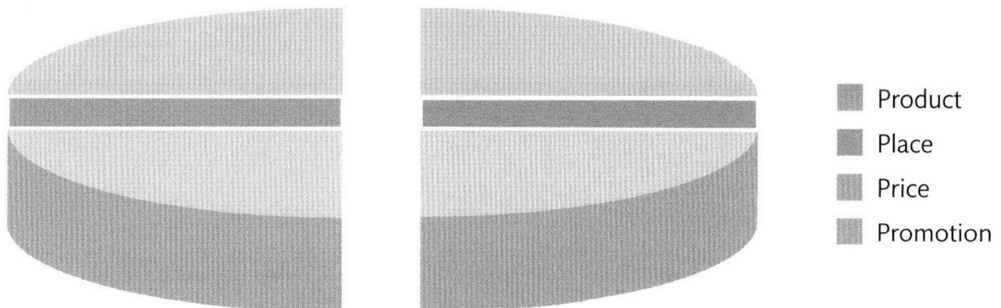

Figure 1.3 The 4Ps of the marketing mix

examples of two-way (**dyadic**) exchanges and the resources exchanged in these interactions. By understanding how exchanges take place between members of the supply chain, we can determine where to add value to the customer experience.

The Marketing Mix and the 4Ps

Neil Borden originally developed the concept of the 'marketing mix' in his teaching at Harvard University in the 1950s. His idea was that marketing managers were 'mixers of ingredients'—that is, chefs who concoct a unique marketing recipe to fit the requirements of customers' needs at any particular time. He composed a 12-item list of elements that the manufacturer should consider when developing marketing mix policies and procedures (Borden, 1964). This list was simplified and amended by Eugene McCarthy (1960) to become the more memorable, but rigid, '4Ps' (see Figure 1.3)—that is:

- *Product*—for example the offering and how it meets the customer's need, its packaging, and its labelling (see Chapter 6);
- *Place (distribution)*—for example the way in which the offering meets customers' needs (see Chapter 10);
- *Price*—for example the cost to the customer and the cost plus profit to the seller (see Chapter 7); and
- *Promotion*—for example how the offering's benefits and features are conveyed to the potential buyer (see Chapters 8 and 9).

The intention was to create a simpler framework around which managers could develop their planning. Although there was recognition that all of these elements might be interlinked (for example promotion based on the price paid by the consumer), such interplay between these mix components was not taken into account by McCarthy's framework. (See Market Insight 1.1 for an example of why the V&D department store offering in Holland and the marketing mix more generally needs redeveloping.)

Research Insight 1.1

To take your learning further, you might wish to read this influential paper.

Borden, N. H. (1964) 'The concept of the marketing mix', *Journal of Advertising Research*, 4: 2–7.

This easy-to-read, early article explains how marketing managers act as 'mixers of ingredients' when developing marketing programmes. The marketing mix, popularized as the '4Ps', remains popular today, although the advent of relationship marketing challenged the impersonal notion of marketers as manipulators of marketing policies and focused more on the need to develop long-term interpersonal relationships with customers.

Visit the online resources to read the abstract and access the full paper.

Market Insight 1.1 **V&D Goes Bust!**

On New Year's Eve, 2015, Dutch department store Vroom & Dreesman (V&D), owned by US private equity firm Sun Capital, declared itself insolvent after suffering poor sales, a loss of €49m on sales of €604m in 2014, and a year of conflict with unions and landlords. The company was finding it difficult to compete with new entrants to the market and the shift to online purchasing. The company, first established in 1887, had more than 10,000 staff and 62 stores across the Netherlands, selling items such as designer clothing and shoes, jewellery, home electric appliances, furniture, china, stationery, books and CDs, and much more. It also owned the La Place restaurant chain in 250 locations. In early 2016, bankruptcy administrators began trying to find a buyer for parts of the business.

The V&D works council (that is, the employees) wrote to the bankruptcy administrators, Kees van de Meent and Hanneke de Coninck-Smolders, to request that the owners Sun Capital not be allowed involvement in the future activities of the company should it emerge from its financial difficulties. However, after suggestions of up to 70 candidate buyers for the business, the administrators invited ten candidates to submit bids.

Iconic Dutch department store V&D shuts its doors after 128 years of service.

Source: © iStock.com/Poulssen.

1. **If you were a senior executive at a company that acquired the V&D business from bankruptcy specialists Kees van de Meent and Hanneke de Coninck-Smolders, how would you seek to use the 4Ps to revive the company's marketing to appeal to more consumers? Why might its marketing mix strategy have failed?**
2. **Why do you think V&D has found it so difficult to alter its business model?**
3. **What other companies can you think of that need to revive their marketing mixes?**

Source: Anon. (2015a); BBC News (2015); Pieters (2015).

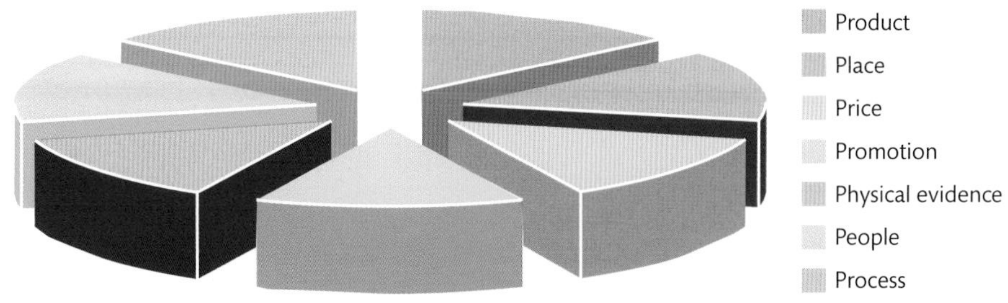

Figure 1.4 The amended marketing mix for services: The 7Ps

The Extended Marketing Mix

It might seem that what is exchanged in a service context (such as purchasing a holiday) is different from what is exchanged in a goods context (such as buying a car). Two American scholars (Booms and Bitner, 1981) suggested an extension to the original model and incorporated a further three 'Ps' into the marketing mix to reflect the need to market services differently, as follows (see Figure 1.4).

- *Physical evidence*—The aim here is to emphasize that the tangible components of services are strategically important: potential university students, for example, might assess whether or not they want to attend a university and a particular course by requesting a copy of brochures or by visiting the campus to assess the **servicescape** for themselves.
- *Process*—This aims to emphasize the importance of the service delivery. When processes are standardized, it is easier to manage customer expectations: DHL International GmbH, the German international express, transport, and air freight company, is a master at producing a standardized menu of service options, such as track-and-trace delivery services, which are remarkably consistent around the world.
- *People*—This emphasizes the importance of customer service personnel, sometimes experts and often professionals interacting with the customer. How they interact with customers, and how satisfied customers are as a result of their experiences, is of strategic importance. For example, McKinsey & Company prides itself on the quality of its more than 9,000 consultants, and its 2,000 research and information specialists as an integral part of its offering (McKinsey & Co., 2016).

Table 1.2 applies the marketing mix for the airline industry.

Relationship Marketing, Service-Dominant Logic, and Co-creation

If marketing is about exchange, should marketing not also be concerned with relationships between those parties that are exchanging value? This was the principal idea behind the development of 'relationship marketing' in the 1990s. The concept spawned further evolution of marketing's conceptual foundations. There was a shift from the need to engage in transactions towards the

Table 1.2 The marketing mix: The airline industry

Marketing aspect	Airline industry
Basic customer need	Safe long- and short-haul transportation, domestic and international
Target market	Mass consumer market (economy class), the discerning traveller (economy plus), business people (business class), and high-net-worth individuals (HNWIs) (first class)
Offering	Typically, differentiated based on class of passenger, with seat size increasing, check-in and boarding times reducing, quality of food increasing, and levels of ancillary services (e.g. limousine service) increasing as we move from economy through business to first class Some carriers focus on 'no-frills' basic services (e.g. EasyJet, Ryanair, Air Asia)
Price	Substantial difference depending on class of service, type of carrier, and purchasing approach (e.g. cheaper via Internet)
Principal promotional tools	(1) the Internet; (2) press, magazine, and radio advertising; (3) billboards
Distribution	Increasingly purchased via mobile apps and the Internet, including third-party brokerages such as Expedia, as well as (to a lesser degree in many countries) through physical travel agents
Process	Self-service via mobile phone or Internet, or aided by travel agent in retail location Travel options increasingly customized to the customer's needs, including size of baggage allowance, class of travel, and increasing availability of alternative and multi-centre locations Customer and organization use of social media to air and resolve problems now very important
Physical evidence	Airline loyalty cards and souvenirs, in-flight magazines, in-flight entertainment services, food and snack meals, grooming and toiletry products provided On some flights, depending on class purchased, suites, bars, and shower facilities offered
People	Combination of check-in staff, customer service personnel, baggage handlers, and cabin crew/pilot teams, all of whom interface with the customer or their belongings at different points in the experience

need to develop long-term customer relationships, including relationships with other stakeholders (Christopher et al., 2002), including:

- suppliers;
- potential employees;
- recruiters;

- referral markets—where they exist, for example retail banks partly relying on professional services organizations, including estate agents, for mortgage referrals;
- influence markets—such as regulatory authorities, politicians, and civil servants (see also Viney and Baines, 2012); and
- internal markets, for example existing employees.

Companies employing a relationship marketing approach stressed customer retention over customer acquisition. Customer retention is an important activity in marketing, with research demonstrating that when a company retains loyal customers, it is more likely to be profitable compared with competitors who do not, because loyal customers:

- will increase their purchases over time;
- are cheaper targets for promotion;
- who are happy with their relationship with a company are happy to refer it to others; and
- are often prepared to pay a (small) price premium (Reichheld and Sasser, 1990).

More recently, there has been a realization that marketing needed to shift beyond a goods-based paradigm towards a service-dominant logic (Vargo and Lusch, 2004). This new marketing paradigm sees service as *the* fundamental basis of exchange (see Research Insight 1.2). In that sense, for physical goods offerings, the good is simply the distribution mechanism.

To understand this concept better, consider the difference between purchasing a music CD from a shop (such as HMV) versus streaming a music file from Spotify's subscription service. The knowledge and technologies embedded in the offering by the company to meet the customers' needs are the source of competitive advantage. Because offerings are inherently service-based, customers become co-creators of the service experience. Therefore, in the end, the ultimate value-in-use of the offering is specified by the customer, often after the sale has taken place.

Research Insight 1.2

To take your learning further, you might wish to read this influential paper.

Vargo, S. L., and Lusch, R. F. (2008) 'Service-dominant logic: Continuing the evolution', *Journal of the Academy of Marketing Science*, 36(1): 1–10.

This article builds on, and updates, the authors' original ground-breaking article (Vargo and Lusch, 2004), which redefined how marketers should think about offerings, arguing that it was necessary to move beyond the idea of tangible versus intangible goods, embedded value and transactions, and other outmoded concepts derived from economics towards the notion of intangible resources and the co-creation of value and relationships. The article asserts that service is the fundamental basis of all exchanges in marketing and that value is always determined by the beneficiary.

 **Visit the online resources to read the abstract and access the full paper.**

Market Insight 1.2 **Servitization at Rolls-Royce**

Rolls-Royce is a global provider of integrated power systems and services to the civil and defence aerospace, marine, nuclear, and power systems markets. However, Rolls-Royce plc (which no longer owns the Rolls-Royce motor car brand) has completely redefined itself since the early 1970s, when it was nationalized by the then Conservative government after running into financial problems. In 2014, it had underlying revenues of £14.6 billion, down 6 per cent on 2013, with an order book of £73.7 bn. Product–service revenue ratios in 2014 were 48:52 in civil aerospace, 39:61 in defence aerospace, 63:37 in the marine sector, and 70:30 in power systems and 37:63 in the nuclear business. By comparison, after-market sales, as they were then known, were only 20 per cent of the civil aerospace division's revenues in 1981.

Rolls Royce wins contract to supply IAG with Trent XWB engines and long-term TotalCare® service support.
Source: © Airbus S.A.S. 2011. Photo by exm company/H. Goussé.

Since then, Rolls-Royce has transformed its business model from selling engines and aftercare (to ensure that the engines work properly and are maintained) to selling its customers 'power by the hour', recognizing that it is not in the engine manufacturing business; rather, it is in the power-generation integrated solutions business. In the civil aerospace sector, Rolls-Royce sells its engines with TotalCare®. With TotalCare®, a customer enters into an overall agreement with Rolls-Royce that provides visibility of cost and a guarantee of product reliability. It was first introduced in the 1990s and charges airline customers based on the total number of hours flown. By collecting data from aircraft engines in flight worldwide on a continuous basis, Rolls-Royce maintains those engines better, predicts engine failures, optimizes engine maintenance programmes, and improves future engine design. Service looks set to become more important than ever with Rolls-Royce's product market opportunities likely to be worth around £1.79 trillion, and the services market opportunities worth £1.38 trillion between 2012 and 2032.

1. **Why do you think Rolls-Royce has been so successful in selling the service concept?**
2. **Check out the websites of Rolls-Royce's competitors, Pratt & Whitney and GE. How do their service offerings in their civil aerospace divisions compare with that of Rolls-Royce?**
3. **Can all manufacturers' products be servitized, do you think?**

Sources: Rolls-Royce (2014); Ryals and Rackham (2012); http://www.rolls-royce.com/about.aspx.

(Read Market Insights1.2 and 1.3 to learn about examples of companies that are switching to a relationship marketing approach, focusing more on service experience.)

According to Prahalad and Ramaswamy (2004a, 2004b), organizations should use co-creation to differentiate their offerings, given that value is tied up inside the customer's experience with the organization. The co-creation experience is about *joint* creation of value, in which customers take part in an active dialogue and co-construct personalized experiences. Therefore organizations wishing to enhance customer input to co-creation should map supplier and customer processes

Market Insight 1.3 **Insomnia: Brewing a New Customer Experience**

Since its establishment in 1997, Insomnia has grown to become Ireland's leading coffee-focused chain, despite Starbucks and Costa entering the Irish market in 2005. In 2016, Insomnia was estimated to be worth €25 million—50 per cent more than it had been valued at in 2008. Plans to open additional outlets in both Ireland and the UK are expected to be implemented in 2017. The company recognizes the importance of focusing on the consumer experience and value that is created through interaction and dialogue in service systems. The Insomnia brand is not only about the consumption of coffee, but also about providing the consumer with a range of experiences, from a convenient access point to pick up a coffee through to offering an affordable indulgent treat in a relaxed atmosphere. Supplementing the in-house experience, Insomnia's technology focus is constantly evolving to bring new experiences to the consumer. For example, Insomnia has harnessed the power of engaging its consumers online by providing an engagement platform that allows consumers to share experiences, advice, support, questions, and knowledge with other consumers, which has provided the firm with a direct engagement tool.

Another innovative offering is the Insomnia customer loyalty programme, which allows customers to register for 'treats' as they consume the company's products. For example, Insomnia offers every tenth coffee free or, on special occasions such as birthdays, it provides free drinks or other seasonal items. Recent research has shown that approximately a third of Insomnia's customers use the loyalty card system, which is high by general industry standards. Insomnia's most loyal customers visited more than once a day and, on average, 16 times per month.

Insomnia recently introduced mobile payments via a loyalty app. This is a significant step forward in the Irish retail space, with a double effect in increasing footfall in Insomnia stores. Consumers can purchase a coffee or something else regardless of whether they have cash or credit cards, greatly increasing the convenience factor. But this kind of frictionless payment also directly eases the 'pain of paying' experienced by many consumers. With this kind of technology, it is not only the coffee that is smooth.

1. **Is it a good idea for Insomnia to focus on value that is created through the customer experience rather on than its products?**

Insomnia focuses on customer experience to stay ahead in a fiercely competitive industry.

Source: Courtesy of Insomnia.

2. **What would you consider to be the next technical step forward for Insomnia to enhance the customer experience further?**
3. **Insomnia is rolling out coffee services in petrol forecourts across Ireland. However, it has yet to integrate its loyalty scheme with in-garage coffee vending machines. Why do you think the company has adopted this approach?**

Sources: http://www.insomnia.ie; Mulligan (2016); Murphy and Garavan (2011).

This case was kindly contributed by Dr Ethel Claffey, Waterford Institute of Technology, Republic of Ireland.

to identify how to design their services accordingly (Payne et al., 2008). The process of co-creation therefore potentially shifts value creation from value-in-exchange, at the point of purchase, to value-in-use, after purchase (Grönroos and Voima, 2013). For example, airplane manufacturer Boeing incorporated feedback from both airline companies and passengers into its Dreamliner plane design before final production.

Marketing's Positive Impact on Society

Marketing impacts both positively and negatively on society. Wilkie and Moore (1999) describe the complexities of what they call the 'aggregate marketing system'. The distributive capacity of the aggregate marketing system is amazing, especially when we consider that there were around 514 million people in the European Union in 2015, each of whom is brought his or her own unique mixture of breakfast offerings each morning (CIA, 2015). Broadly, the aggregate marketing system in most countries works well. We are not all starving and we do not have to ration our food to preserve the amount we eat. There are parts of certain countries in Africa, North Korea, and parts of China where people are dying of hunger, but these countries often experience imperfections in supply and demand because of political (such as war, dictatorship, famine) and environmental circumstances (such as drought). Thus marketing plays an important role in developing and transforming society.

Some of the world's most important inventions have come to us through the aggregate marketing system. Consider how some of the offerings outlined in Table 1.3 have affected your own life. What would we do without these inventions today? We enjoy them because innovative individuals and companies brought these to us.

The aggregate marketing system also impedes offerings that do not meet consumer needs. Hence it provides a number of benefits to society, including the following (Wilkie and Moore, 1999):

- the promotion and delivery of desired offerings;
- the provision of a forum for market learning (that is, we can see what does and what does not get through the system);
- the stimulation of market demand;
- the provision of a wide scope of choice of offerings by providing a close or customized fit with consumer needs;
- the facilitation of purchases (or acquisitions generally, for example if no payment is made directly, as in the case of public services);
- time savings and the promotion of efficiency in customer requirement matching;
- new offerings, and improvements, to meet latent and unserved needs; and
- the pursuit of customer satisfaction for repeat purchases.

Visit the **online resources** and complete Internet Activity 1.2 to learn more about how marketing innovation impacts upon society.

Table 1.3	Some modern consumer products and their dates of invention			
Consumer product	**Product attribute**	**Consumer need**	**Inventors/ pioneers***	**Year of invention**
Breakfast cereals	Cereals that, when added to milk, provide a healthy meal	Quick and easy-to -prepare foodstuff that was rapidly adopted as a breakfast meal	W. K. Kellogg Foundation, United States	1906
Television	Transmission of moving images	Information, entertainment, and education	Baird Television Development Company, UK/ Telefunken, Germany	1929/1932
Carton	Cardboard liquid storage device	Allows liquid foodstuffs to be stored, packaged, and distributed in an environmentally friendly way	TetraPak, Sweden	1951
Artificial sweeteners	Xylitol (as the sweetener is known) used to sweeten food products such as sugar-free chewing gum and toothpastes	Sweetens food products without damaging teeth	Cultor, Finland	1969
Mobile phone	Hand-held device for making telephone calls whilst in motion	Ability to stay in telephone contact with others regardless of location	NTT, Japan	1979
Personal computer	Machine allowing users to play electronic games, perform calculations, and write word-processed documents and other applications	Time-saving device, simplifying complex writing/arithmetic tasks, offering recreational possibilities, i.e. game-playing	IBM, United States	1980

*The named companies are not always the inventors per se; they often acquired the patents from the inventor, and so were licensed to produce and distribute the invention.

Sources: Various, including http://www.inventors.about.com and manufacturers' websites.

Unsustainable Marketing: The Critical 'Turn'

Marketing does not always serve the common good. Marketing is frequently criticized for doing precisely the opposite—for being unethical in nature, manipulative, and creating wants and needs where none previously existed (Packard, 1960). We agree that not all of marketing's contributions to society are good; consequently, there is a need to develop a critical approach to understanding marketing practice. To truly understand the discipline, we need to study both mainstream and critical marketing, given their interdependence (Shankar, 2009).

Critical marketing analysis helps in 'problematizing hitherto uncontentious marketing areas to reveal underlying institutional and theoretical dysfunctionalities' (Saren, 2011: 95). A critical approach to marketing suggests that we consider.

- the need to (re-)evaluate marketing activities, categories, and frameworks, and to improve them so that marketing operates in a desirable manner within society;
- the extent to which marketing knowledge is developed based on our contemporary social world—for example the implications that the fact that much current marketing knowledge encompasses American (and Western) practice and research has for the rest of the world;
- how the historical and cultural conditions in which we operate, as consumers and as students of marketing, impact on how we see marketing as a discipline; and
- how marketing can benefit from other intellectual perspectives such as social anthropology, social psychology, linguistics, philosophy, and sociology (Burton, 2001).

Some key topics in critical marketing include the notions of marketing as manipulation, commodity fetishism, and the nature of need versus choice (see Tadajewski, 2010). We consider each of these topics next.

Marketing as Manipulation

Packard (1960) critiqued marketing by explaining that it beguiled its target audiences, often covertly, and frequently without people even understanding that they were being manipulated.

Marketers and public relations officers certainly do 'frame' their communications to make them more persuasive. **Framing** is the action of presenting persuasive communication and the action of audiences in interpreting that communication to assimilate it into their existing understanding (Scheufele and Tewksbury, 2007). The framing takes place via the framing of situations (such as by highlighting sales promotions available for a fixed time only), attributes (such as by highlighting usage features of, say, a smartphone), choices (such as by showing a potential car buyer options across the range), actions (such as 'buy now, pay later' schemes), issues (for example Asda explaining why it boycotted the 2015 UK Black Friday sales promotion), responsibilities (for example Save the Children explaining why African children need help to elicit donations), and news (for example Volkswagen explaining why its chief executive was replaced after the emissions scandal).

The problem arises when framing becomes 'spin', because 'marketing promotion' then becomes corporate propaganda. For example, some photographic tricks to make food offerings look great in print adverts include using motor oil as syrup or honey, or glue or shampoo as milk in cereals. For hotels and resorts, photos are frequently doctored to remove unwanted elements or wide-angle lens are used to make scenes look expansive. In the United States, while adverts are generally fairly trusted, adverts for diet offerings, financial services, and prescription drugs are far less so (Anon., 2014).

Visit the **online resources** and complete Internet Activity 1.3 to learn more about manipulative practices in marketing.

Commodity Fetishism

'Commodity fetishism' is a critical perspective, derived from Marxist economic theory (Marx, 1867 [1990]), that proposes that society is overly dominated by consumption, hence fetishizes it (that is, places supreme importance on it). Marx suggested that, prior to industrialization, goods were produced for their use-value: a producer manufactured a product for a user and exchanged it with the customer. After industrialization, the social relationship between producer and user changed. Marx argued that workers were exploited for their labour, because they became removed from the product they produced and were paid a piece rate rather than a share of the financial return generated as a result of their labour. In the process, the commodity produced acquired exchange-value, becoming tradable with other commodities within the capitalist market system, benefiting the capitalist (that is, the investor). Marx felt that the rigid pursuit of capitalism was so doctrinal that it represented a religious ideology. Commodities produced as a result of capitalist endeavour took on a religious aura, worshipped by those seduced by their perceived value (Sherover, 1979). The idea that we are worshipping consumption raises the question of whether marketers meet our wants or needs, or neither.

Need and Choice

The received wisdom is that marketing works to meet the needs of customers and consumers. However, Alvesson (1994), coming from outside the marketing discipline, rejects this notion. He argues that people in affluent societies seek more without gaining any further long-term satisfaction from such consumption, because much of the consumption is superficial anyway, and because appealing to people's fantasies and highlighting their imperfections (to encourage them to reduce these feelings of inadequacy by buying a particular offering) leads to narcissistic tendencies. Inherently, the notion is that more choice is good—but is it so, when more choice can lead to customer confusion and a decline in trust (Newman, 2001)? Some customers are persuaded and manipulated into purchasing offerings that they do not want or which are unfit for their requirements: financial services companies in the UK have been charged with mis-selling payment protection insurance (PPI), for example. By 2015, British banks had had to put aside £27 billion for extra administration and to settle customers' compensation claims to cover the claims of 16.5 million people, with a further 5.5 million still yet to claim (Treanor, 2015).

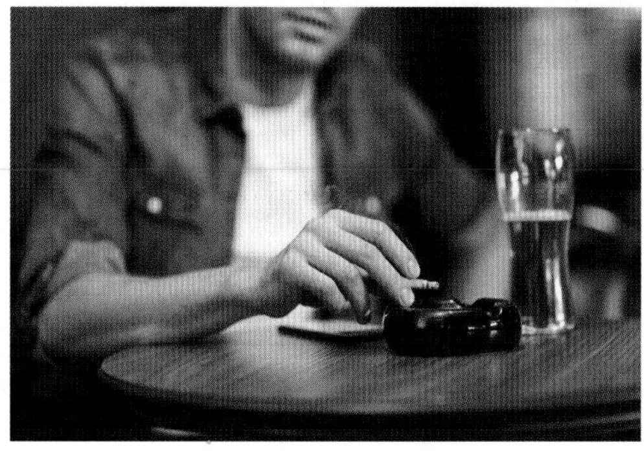

The marketing system sometimes provides consumers with choices that are not in their long-term interests. What are the implications for marketers?

Source: © Syda Productions/Shutterstock.

Although the aggregate marketing system (Wilkie and Moore, 1999) distributes life-saving medicines, food, and important utilities (such as heat and light), it also distributes alcohol, tobacco, and gambling products, among other things. These are products that most would regard as dangerous to our health and well-being. While in many cultures around the world, people enjoy drinking, smoking, and gambling, if we use these to excess, all three can have addictive properties to varying degrees.

If prostitution and soft drugs, such as cannabis, were to be made legal in the UK, the aggregate marketing system would distribute them. It already does this in the Netherlands, for instance, where these practices are not illegal. The aggregate marketing system is amoral—that is, not *im*moral (designed to harm), but designed without any care as to whether it harms or not. The system is made moral by the decisions taken by government and other institutional actors regulating the aggregate marketing system.

Sustainable Marketing

Supporters of **sustainable marketing** accept the limitations of marketing philosophy and acknowledge the need to impose regulatory constraints on marketing (van Dam and Apeldoorn, 1996), particularly concerning its impact on the environment. Sustainable economic development—that is, development that meets the needs of current generations without imposing constraints on the needs of future generations—was first proposed at a United Nations Conference in Stockholm in 1972 (WCED, 1987). To understand why a policy on sustainable development is necessary, consider the following two examples of companies causing catastrophic environmental impacts.

- *BP, 2010*—More than 200 million gallons of oil were spilled into the Gulf of Mexico after an oil rig explosion killed 11 people. The oil spill affected 1,000 miles of shoreline, killing thousands of birds, around 153 dolphins, and other local wildlife. The disaster caused BP to initially lose half its share value and total costs (including fines, compensations, legal fees, and other costs) for the disaster were US$53.8 billion in 2015 (Bryant, 2011; Anon., 2015b). BP's contractor, Transocean, shared some blame for the incident, receiving a fine of $1.4 billion from the US authorities (BBC News, 2013). Another contractor, Halliburton, was also found to be partly liable for some of the damage caused by the incident and reached a $1.1 billion settlement in 2014 (Rushe, 2014).

A view from space of the consequences of the 2010 Gulf of Mexico oil spill.

Source: NASA/GSFC, MODIS Rapid Response.

- *Tokyo Electric Power (Tepco), 2011*—Three former executives at Tepco were charged with professional negligence contributing to death and injury from the meltdown in 2011 at the Fukushima Daiichi nuclear plant (McCurry, 2016). The meltdown was caused after a magnitude-9 earthquake caused a massive tsunami, flooding the nuclear reactors. The men were charged with failing to take measures to defend the plant, despite knowing the risks of a tsunami. More than 300,000 people were made homeless and 20,000 killed as a result of the earthquake and the tsunami across Japan (Conca, 2015). In Fukushima Prefecture alone, a further 1,656 people died as a result of post-disaster health conditions occurring after the government-enforced evacuation of everyone living within 20 km of the site—that is, as a result of stress from the evacuation, transfer trauma in relation to the infirm, and those with chronic illnesses unable to access medical treatments (World Nuclear Association, 2016).

Sustainable marketers attempt to broaden sustainable development to the practice of marketing, beyond simple economic development. They introduce the following maxims, known as the 'three Es of sustainability'.

- *Ecological*—Marketing should not negatively impact upon the environment.
- *Equitable*—Marketing should not allow or promote inequitable social practices.
- *Economic*—Marketing should encourage long-term economic development as opposed to short-term economic development.

Sustainable marketing is the 'third age' of green marketing (Peattie, 2001). In the 'first age', ecological green marketing (*c.*1960s–70s) was concerned with automobile, oil, and agrichemical companies that encountered environmental problems in the production process. In the 'second age', environmental green marketing (*c.*1980s), we saw the development of the green consumer—that is, the person who purchased offerings to avoid negative environmental impacts (for example cosmetic products that had not been tested on animals). But green marketing was too heavily focused on the purchasing element of consumption (Peattie and Crane, 2005), perhaps because the sustainability debate did not consider the business-to-business (B2B) dimension sufficiently.

The 'third age' of green marketing is sustainable green marketing. Sustainable marketers should focus on **positioning** and demand stimulation for recycled/remanufactured products and build-to-order offerings, as well as consider **supply chain management** issues, such as enabling materials recovery from end-consumers, designing offerings to enable their dismantlement, enabling **reverse logistics** for recycling and remanufactured offerings, and reducing supply by offering build-to-order offerings (Sharma et al., 2010). In the third age, companies also need to lengthen the time horizons within which they achieve investment returns, requiring also emphasis on the full costs of purchase rather than simply the price paid. Proposition development activities should fully consider, equitably, inputs and cooperation from all members of the supply chain. Companies need to adopt environmental auditing methods (such as including costs for disposal, as well as development, delivery, and consumption) and organizations may actually discourage consumption in certain cases (Bridges and Wilhelm, 2008)—or at least encourage more mindful consumption and temperance, rather than acquisitive, repetitive, or aspirational overly consumptive behaviour (Sheth et al., 2011). For example, in 2013, Coca-Cola launched a worldwide campaign on obesity, partnering in the UK until 2015 with StreetGames, a sport participation charity, by introducing smaller bottles (375 ml) and by displaying detailed calorie content on packs (Mintel, 2013). But Coca-Cola has not always been consistent: in 2012, the company was said to have used more water than had a quarter of the world's population—that is, 79 billion gallons to dilute its syrup and an extra 8 trillion gallons in other elements of production (Gwyther, 2015). In 2014, The Body Shop—to maintain its own strict policy against animal testing—removed all products from duty-free shelves in airports in China after consumer watchdog, Choice, revealed that the Chinese government conducted post-market testing of Body Shop products on animals (Davidson, 2014).

Such longer-term thinking led to the development of the **circular economy**: Vodafone, for example, runs a 'Red Hot' deal whereby customers lease a phone and return the old one for an upgrade. Airbnb—founded in 2008, but valued at $25.5 billion in 2015—is another example of a company encouraging the sharing, swapping, and renting of possessions (that is, **collaborative consumption**), specifically in the spare-room business (Alba, 2015).

Corporate Social Responsibility

Corporate social responsibility (CSR) initiatives are increasingly common. Many companies publish annual CSR or sustainability reports, for example British American Tobacco (BAT) and GlaxoSmithKline (GSK). Governments and supranational organizations such as the United Nations' Global Compact project actively encourage CSR initiatives, and CSR practitioners and academics continue to try to demonstrate the commercial effectiveness of such programmes to explain why being 'good' translates into being profitable.

Despite any obvious return, business people and companies have given to charity for centuries. Famous cases include the John Paul Getty Foundation in the United States (built on oil industry profits), which funds art and social projects, and Anglo American, the mining conglomerate that provides welfare support for its employees living with HIV/AIDS in Africa. The rationale for developing CSR initiatives, irrespective of their financial contribution, is based around the following ideas (Buchholz, 1991: 19).

- Corporations have responsibilities going beyond the production of their offerings at a profit.
- These responsibilities involve helping to solve important social problems—especially those that they have helped to create.

Market Insight 1.4 **Desso: Customer Orientation and Sustainability**

For some companies, the focus on sustainability and CSR does not have to represent a trade-off in terms of their financial performance: some firms really can do well by doing good. An example is Dutch carpet manufacturer Desso. In 2007, the company started an internal revolution that focused on both being more environmentally friendly and improving its customer orientation. Desso adopted the 'Cradle-to-Cradle' (C2C) philosophy—that is, a set of design principles focused on maximizing the recycling and remanufacture of all carpets to reduce the environmental impact of its operations. The goal of the organization is to achieve 100 per cent recycling and reprocessing of its carpets by 2020. The organization has achieved Cradle-to-Cradle certification on a number of products.

Desso developed its marketing strategy around this bold environmental goal because it could see a synergy between trying to become greener and trying to become closer to its customers and/or key stakeholders. The market for carpets was already interested in sustainability and C2C offered Desso the opportunity of adopting a unique positioning. Architects and designers across Europe are interested in environmentally friendly solutions, and Desso's strong environmental credentials helped the brand. Its focus on the environment also led it to consider the health implications of carpets and to a focus on sustainable innovations. The C2C design

Certain Desso products have been certified C2C. Cradle to Cradle Certified™ is a third-party certification program that assesses products for safety to human & environmental health, design for future use cycles, and sustainable manufacturing.

Source: Courtesy of C2C Certified.

Market Insight 1.4 (continued)

philosophy requires a careful examination of all manufacturing processes and drove Desso to the development of new products (such as the Ecobase®, the AirMaster®) that offered better environmental performances, while offering new solutions to customers (for example the AirMaster® guarantees better air quality than traditional carpets, which is a feature appreciated by many potential customers). Finally, C2C represented a revitalizing element for corporate culture. The commitment to a circular business model required re-examining the way in which products are used and helped the company to abandon a product-focused mentality to become more customer-oriented.

Desso's market share in its key European market grew more than 20 per cent thanks, among other things, to its focus on sustainability. While sustainability is often perceived as a potential cost by many organizations, Desso shows that this does not have to be the case.

1 **What are the factors that facilitate the adoption of sustainable marketing and/or CSR programmes by corporations?**

2 **What are the major challenges faced by manufacturers like Desso when trying to move towards a circular economy? What (if any) are the financial advantages of moving towards a circular economy?**

3 **What industries are more likely to adopt a circular approach to their business models? What industries are more likely to resist?**

Sources: Confino (2011); Kranendijk (2012); http://www.c2ccertified.org/.

Research Insight 1.3

To take your learning further, you might wish to read this influential paper.

Maignan, I., Ferrell, O. C., and Ferell, L. (2005) 'A stakeholder model for implementing social responsibility in marketing', *European Journal of Marketing*, 39(9–10): 956–77.

This is a frequently cited, readable paper providing a managerial framework to help marketers to orient stakeholders' needs when designing CSR programmes. The authors provide a series of eight steps outlining how to implement CSR, including:

1 **discovering organizational norms and values;**

2 **identifying stakeholders;**

3 **identifying stakeholder issues;**

4 **assessing the meaning of CSR;**

5 **auditing current practices;**

6 **implementing CSR initiatives;**

7 **promoting CSR; and**

8 **gaining stakeholder feedback.**

 Visit the **online resources** to read the abstract and access the full paper.

- Corporations have a broader constituency of stakeholders than shareholders alone.
- The impacts of corporations go beyond simple marketplace transactions.
- Corporations serve a wider range of human values, not captured solely by a focus on economic values.

Ethics and Marketing

Ethics, a subdiscipline of philosophy, is over 2,000 years old. It can be defined as 'moral principles that govern a person's behaviour or the conducting of an activity' and 'the branch of knowledge that deals with moral principles' (Oxford Dictionaries, 2016). Marketing, like any other area of business, is affected by ethical norms that relate to how we *should* behave. Professional marketing organizations have a code of professional practice that requires members to behave and act in a certain manner, as do many companies and organizations. For example, the AMA requires the following of its members (AMA, 2014):

1. **Do no harm.** This means consciously avoiding harmful actions or omissions by embodying high ethical standards and adhering to all applicable laws and regulations in the choices we make.
2. **Foster trust in the marketing system.** This means striving for good faith and fair dealing so as to contribute toward the efficacy of the exchange process as well as avoiding deception in product design, pricing, communication, and delivery of distribution.
3. **Embrace ethical values.** This means building relationships and enhancing consumer confidence in the integrity of marketing by affirming these core values: honesty, responsibility, fairness, respect, transparency and citizenship.

Chapter Summary

To consolidate your learning, the key points from this chapter are summarized below.

- **Define the marketing concept.**

  Marketing is the process by which organizations anticipate and satisfy their customers' needs to both parties' benefit. It involves mutual exchange. Over the last 25 years, the marketing concept has changed to recognize the importance of long-term customer relationships to organizations.

- **Explain how marketing has developed over the twentieth and into the twenty-first century.**

  There have been four main phases in the history of marketing: the production era; the sales era; the marketing era; and the societal marketing era.

- **Understand the exchange and marketing mix concepts in marketing.**

  The concept of exchange is important: empathizing with customers to understand what they want and determining how sellers seek to provide what buyers want is a central concept in marketing. The marketing mix comprises *product* (the offering), *place* (the distribution mechanism), *price* (the value placed on the offering), and *promotion* (how the company communicates that value). For services marketing, because of the intangible nature of the service, marketers consider an extra 3Ps, including *physical evidence* (how cues are developed for customers to recognize quality), *process* (how the experience is designed to meet customers' needs), and *people* (the training and development of those delivering the customer experience).

- **Understand the positive contribution that marketing makes to society.**

  The aggregate marketing system delivers to us a wide array of offerings, either directly or indirectly through business markets, to serve our wants and needs. There is much that is positive about the aggregate marketing system and it has served to improve the standard of living for many people around the world.

- **Assess the negative impact that marketing has on society.**

  The critical marketing perspective suggests that marketing impacts negatively on society. The perspective calls for the (re-)evaluation of marketing activities, categories, and frameworks to improve them, so that marketing can operate in a more desirable manner within society. It critiques the nature of marketing knowledge, and questions in whose interests existing frameworks, approaches, and techniques operate.

- **Define sustainable marketing and its implications for marketing practice.**

  Sustainable marketing has been termed the 'third age' of green marketing, and is concerned with the ecological, equitable, and economic impacts of marketing practice. Sustainable marketers seek to meet the needs of existing generations while not compromising those of future generations. Consequently, companies are reimagining marketing practices, for example by recovering the costs of investment financing over longer payback periods, by emphasizing the full costs of purchase to customers, by considering all members of the supply chain and ensuring that they are paid equitably, and by demarketing consumption to vulnerable groups or those overconsuming.

Review Questions

1. **How do we define the 'marketing' concept?**
2. **How do the AMA and the CIM definitions of marketing differ?**
3. **What is the difference between customers and consumers?**
4. **How has marketing developed historically?**
5. **What is the marketing mix?**
6. **What positive contributions does marketing make to society?**
7. **Name the key concepts in critical marketing.**
8. **How will sustainable marketing impact on marketing practice?**
9. **How do we define 'marketing ethics'?**
10. **How should marketers behave according to the AMA?**

Worksheet Summary

To apply the knowledge you have gained from this chapter and to test your understanding of marketing principles and society, visit the **online resources** and complete Worksheet 1.1.

Discussion Questions

1 Having read Case Insight 1.1 at the beginning of this chapter, how would you advise Aldoraq as it attempts to differentiate itself from national and international brands?

2 Read the section on 'The Marketing Mix and the 4Ps' and draw up marketing mixes for the following organizations and their target customers.

A Streaming video company Netflix and its audiences
B A luxury hotel group and its wealthy clientele
C Pharmacies (such as Boots UK Ltd, Sweden's Apoteket AB, Holland's Etos BV) and their consumers
D A company supplying glass to construction companies

3 Go online to find examples of companies with a strong stance on sustainable marketing. Are there any common characteristics across these companies? (**Hint:** Take a look at any of the following companies' websites and search for their sustainability credentials: the UK's Marks and Spencer; Sweden's SCA; France's Danone; Nigeria's Guaranty Trust Bank.)

4 Consider whether or not it is unethical to act in the following ways in the following circumstances.

A You are a salesperson working for a South African construction company trying to secure a road-building contract in Nigeria. You know that if you do not pay a 'commission' to the public official in charge of tendering for the project, you will not win the contract. Should you pay the 'commission' or do you have other choices of action?
B You are a Dubai-based banker. A potential new client in Dubai insists on taking you to a very exclusive restaurant at the Burj al Arab to discuss a loan she requires to purchase a new building for her rapidly expanding business. Should you accept?
C You are a farmer supplying a large chain supermarket in Copenhagen with selected prime cuts of meat products. The supermarket requests an upfront 'listing' fee of 170,000 Danish krone before it can accept you as a supplier; you can then expect high-value orders worth millions of krone. Should you pay the 'listing fee'? What other courses of action do you have?

Visit the **online resources** and complete the multiple-choice questions to assess your knowledge of this chapter.

Glossary

advertising a form of non-personal communication, by an identified sponsor, transmitted through the use of paid-for media.

American Marketing Association (AMA) a professional body for marketing professionals and marketing educators based in the United States, operating principally there and in Canada.

Chartered Institute of Marketing (CIM) a professional body for marketing professionals based in the UK, with study centres and members around the world.

circular economy an alternative to a traditional linear economy (make—use—dispose) in which we keep resources in use for as long as possible, extract the maximum value from them while in use, and then recover and regenerate products and materials at the end of each service life.

collaborative consumption the trend towards the sharing, swapping, and renting of possessions.

consumer the user of a product, service, or other form of offering.

corporate social responsibility (CSR) typically, a programme of social and/or environmental activities undertaken by a company on behalf of one or more of its stakeholders to develop sustainable business operations, foster goodwill, and develop the company's corporate reputation.

customer the person who purchases and pays for (or initially requests and specifies, in the case of a non-financial transaction) a product, service, or other form of offering from a company or organization.

dyadic essentially meaning 'two-way'; a dyadic commercial relationship is an exchange between two people—typically, a buyer and a seller.

elasticity an economic concept associated with the extent to which changes in one variable are related to changes in another, for example if a price increase in a good causes a decline in volume of sales of that good, we say the good is 'price elastic' and specify by how much; if it causes no change or very little change, we say it is 'price inelastic'.

ethnography a subdiscipline derived from cultural anthropology as an approach to research, which emphasizes the collection of data through participant observation of members of a specific subcultural grouping and observation of participation of members of a specific subcultural grouping.

framing the dual action by which communicators present ideas and concepts, and members of an audience interpret those concepts by assimilating them into their pre-existing cognitive schema.

haul girls women who go shopping for clothes or beauty products, then make a YouTube video showing viewers what they have bought, item by item.

market orientation refers to the development of a whole-organization approach to the generation, collection, and dissemination of market intelligence across different departments, and the organization's responsiveness to that intelligence.

marketing mix the list of items that a marketing manager should consider when devising plans for marketing products, including product decisions, place (distribution) decisions, pricing decisions, and promotion decisions; later extended to include physical evidence, process, and people decisions, to account for the lack of physical nature in service products.

netnography the branch of ethnography that seeks to analyse Internet users' behaviour.

non-staple in the grocery context, grocery products that are not a main or important food.

observation a research method that requires a researcher to watch, and record, how consumers or employees behave, typically in relation to either purchasing or selling activities.

place (distribution) essentially about how you can place the optimum amount of goods and/or services before the maximum number of members of your target market, at times and locations that optimize the marketing outcome—that is, sales.

positioning the way in which an audience of consumers or buyers perceives a product or service, particularly as a result of the marketing communications process aimed at a target audience.

price the amount that the customer has to pay to receive a good or service.

procurement the purchasing (buying) process in a firm or organization.

product anything that is capable of satisfying customer needs.

promotion the use of communications to persuade individuals, groups, or organizations to purchase products and services.

relationship marketing the development and management of long-term relationships with customers, influencers, referrers, suppliers, recruiters, and employees.

reverse logistics the process of returning goods in a physical distribution channel, which might be a flow from customer to manufacturer via a retailer (for example for repair or replacement).

service-dominant logic asserts that organizations, markets, and society are concerned fundamentally with exchange of service, based on the application of knowledge and skills; rejects the notion of dualism between goods and services marketing by arguing that all offerings provide a service.

servicescape the physical environment in which a service takes place, such as a stadium for a football game.

social anthropology the scientific discipline of observing and recording the way in which humans behave in their different social groupings.

supply chain management the management and coordination of supply-side activities (including planning, sourcing, making, and delivering) from production to consumption to enhance customer value.

sustainable marketing marketing activities undertaken to meet the wants or needs of present customers without compromising the wants or needs of future customers, particularly in relation to negative environmental impacts on society.

tweenagers pre-adolescent children, typically taken to be between the ages of 9 and 12, who are hence about to enter their teenage years.

value the regard that something is held to be worth, typically, although not always, in financial terms.

References

Alba, D. (2015) 'Airbnb confirms $1.5bn funding round, now valued at $25.5bn', *Wired*, 17 July. Available online at http://www.wired.com/2015/12/airbnb-confirms-1-5-billion-funding-round-now-valued-at-25-5-billion/ [accessed 29 March 2016].

Alvesson, M. (1994) 'Critical theory and consumer marketing', *Scandinavian Journal of Marketing*, 10(3): 291–313.

American Marketing Association (AMA) (2013) 'About AMA'. Available online at https://www.ama.org/AboutAMA/Pages/Definition-of-Marketing.aspx [accessed 27 December 2015].

American Marketing Association (AMA) (2014) *Statement of Ethics*. Available online at https://archive.ama.org/archive/AboutAMA/Pages/Statement%20of%20Ethics.aspx [accessed 29 March 2016].

Anon. (2014) 'The art of deceptive advertising: From brown shoe polish on burgers to hairspray for brighter ingredients, how commercials trick us into buying their products', *Mail Online*, 11 June. Available online at http://www.dailymail.co.uk/femail/article-2655351/The-art-deceptive-advertising-From-brown-shoe-polish-burgers-hairspray-brighter-ingredients-commercials-trick-buying-products.html [accessed 29 March 2016].

Anon. (2015a) 'V&D on brink of bankruptcy as warm winter hits sales', *DutchNews.nl*, 23 December. Available online at http://www.dutchnews.nl/news/archives/2015/12/vd-on-brink-of-bankruptcy-as-warm-winter-hits-sales/ [accessed 17 January 2016].

Anon. (2015b) 'BP and Deepwater Horizon: A costly mistake', *The Economist*, 2 July. Available online at http://www.economist.com/news/business-and-finance/21656847-costly-mistake [accessed 28 March 2016].

Bagozzi, R. P. (1975) 'Marketing as exchange', *Journal of Marketing*, 3(4): 32–9.

Bartels, R. D. W. (1951) 'Can marketing be a science?' *Journal of Marketing*, 15(3): 319–28.

Bartels, R. D. W. (1959) 'Sociologists and marketologists', *Journal of Marketing*, 24(2): 37–40.

BBC News (2013) 'Transocean agrees to pay $1.4bn oil spill fine', 3 January. Available online at http://www.bbc.co.uk/news/business-20905472 [accessed 28 March 2016].

BBC News (2015) 'Dutch V&D department store business goes bust', 31 December. Available online at http://www.bbc.co.uk/news/business-35208209 [accessed 17 January 2016].

Booms, B. H., and Bitner, M. J. (1981) 'Marketing strategies and organisation structures for service firms', in J. H. Donnelly and W. R. George (eds) *Marketing of Services*, Chicago, IL: AMA, 47–52.

Borden, N. H. (1964) 'The concept of the marketing mix', *Journal of Advertising Research*, 4: 2–7.

Brenner, B. (2013) *Inside the NIKE Matrix*, Wirtschafts Universität Wien Case Series No. 0001/2013. Available online at http://epub.wu.ac.at/3791/1/Nike__WU-CaseSeries.pdf [accessed 28 December 2015].

Bridges, C. M., and Wilhelm, W. B. (2008) 'Going beyond green: The "why" and "how" of integrating sustainability into the marketing curriculum', *Journal of Marketing Education*, 30(1): 33–46.

Bryant, B. (2011) 'Deepwater Horizon and the Gulf oil spill: The key questions answered', *The Guardian*, 20 April. Available online at http://www.theguardian.com/environment/2011/apr/20/deepwater-horizon-key-questions-answered [accessed 5 April 2016].

Buchholz, R. A. (1991) 'Corporate responsibility and the good society: From economics to ecology—Factors which influence corporate policy decisions', *Business Horizons*, 34(4): 19–31.

Burton, D. (2001) 'Critical marketing theory: The blueprint?', *European Journal of Marketing*, 35(5–6): 722–43.

Central Intelligence Agency (CIA) (2015) *The World Factbook: European Union*. Available online at https://www.cia.gov/library/publications/the-world-factbook/geos/ee.html [accessed 18 January 2014].

Chartered Institute of Marketing (CIM) (2015) *Marketing and the 7Ps*. Available online at http://www.cim.co.uk/files/7ps.pdf [accessed 27 December 2015].

Christopher, M., Payne, A., and Ballantyne, D. (2002) *Relationship Marketing: Creating Stakeholder Value* (2nd edn), Oxford: Butterworth Heinemann.

Conca, J. (2015) 'The Fukushima disaster wasn't disastrous because of the radiation', *Forbes*, 16 March. Available online at http://www.forbes.com/sites/jamesconca/2015/03/16/the-fukushima-disaster-wasnt-very-disastrous/#4d68476951e7 [accessed 28 March 2016].

Confino, J. (2011) 'Cradle to cradle: How Desso has adapted to birth of new movement', *The Guardian*, 1 September. Available online at https://www.theguardian.com/sustainable-business/cradle-to-cradle-desso-carpet-tiles-innovation [accessed 29 March 2016].

Davidson, H. (2014) 'Body Shop removes all its products from Chinese duty free stores', *The Guardian*, 12 March. Available online at http://www.theguardian.com/world/2014/mar/12/body-shop-removes-products-from-chinese-duty-free-stores [accessed 28 March 2016].

Doob, L.W. (1948) *Public Opinion and Propaganda*, Oxford: Henry Holt.

Enright, M. (2002) 'Marketing and conflicting dates for its emergence: Hotchkiss, Bartels and the fifties school of alternative accounts', *Journal of Marketing Management*, 18(5–6): 445–61.

Grönroos, C., and Voima, P. (2013) 'Critical service logic: Making sense of value creation and co-creation', *Journal of the Academy of Marketing Science*, 41(2): 133–50.

Gummesson, E. (1990) 'Marketing orientation revisited: The crucial role of the part-time marketer', *European Journal of Marketing*, 25(2): 60–75.

Gwyther, M. (2015) 'The real thing: Ain't what it used to be', *Management Today*, 42(3): 45–6.

Holden, A. C., and Holden, L. (1998) 'Marketing history: Illuminating marketing's clandestine subdiscipline', *Psychology and Marketing*, 15(2): 117–23.

Howard, D. G., Savins, D. M., Howell, W., and Ryans, J. K., Jr (1991) 'The evolution of marketing theory in the United States and Europe', *European Journal of Marketing*, 25(2): 7–16.

Katz, E. (1957) 'The two-step flow of communication: An up-to-date report on an hypothesis', *Public Opinion Quarterly*, 21(1): 61–78.

Kirca, A. H., Jayachandran, S., and Bearden, W. O. (2005) 'Market orientation: A meta-analytic review and assessment of its antecedents and impact on performance', *Journal of Marketing*, 69(2): 24–41.

Kohli, A. K., and Jaworski, B. J. (1990) 'Market orientation: The construct, research propositions and managerial implications', *Journal of Marketing*, 54(2): 1–18.

Kranendijk, S. (2012) 'I got my strategy from Greenpeace', *Harvard Business Review Blog*, 21 March. Available online at https://hbr.org/2012/03/i-got-my-strategy-from-greenpe [accessed 29 March 2016].

Kumar, V., Jones, E., Venkatesan, R., and Leone, R. P. (2011) 'Is market orientation a source of sustainable competitive advantage or simply the cost of competing?' *Journal of Marketing*, 75(1): 16–30.

Lee, A. M. (1945) 'The analysis of propaganda: A clinical summary', *American Journal of Sociology*, 51(2): 126–35.

Lendrevie, J., and Lévy, J. (2014) *Mercator: Tout le Marketing à l'Ère Numérique* (11th edn), Paris: Dunod.

Leone, R. P., and Shultz, R. L. (1980) 'A study of marketing generalisations', *Journal of Marketing*, 44(Winter), 10–18.

Maignan, I., Ferrell, O. C., and Ferell, L. (2005) 'A stakeholder model for implementing social responsibility in marketing', *European Journal of Marketing*, 39(9–10): 956–77.

Marketing and Sales Standards Setting Body (MSSSB) (2010) *Developing World-Class Standards for the Marketing Profession*. Available online at http://www.msssb.org/marketing.htm [accessed 17 September 2010].

Marx, K. (1990 [1867]) *Capital: Critique of Political Economy, Vol. 1*, London: Penguin.

McCarthy, E. J. (1960) *Basic Marketing*, Homewood, IL: Irwin.

McCurry, J. (2016) 'Former Tepco bosses charges over Fukushima meltdown', *The Guardian*, 29 February. Available online at http://www.theguardian.com/environment/2016/feb/29/former-tepco-bosses-charged-fukushima [accessed 29 March 2016].

McKinsey & Co. (2016) 'About us'. Available online at http://www.mckinsey.com/about_us/who_we_are [accessed 17 January 2016].

Mintel (2013) 'Coca-Cola brings anti-obesity push to the UK', 11 April. Available online at http://www.mintel.com [accessed 5 April 2016].

Mulligan, J. (2016) 'Insomnia coffee shop chain slashes its losses', *The Independent*, 17 June. Available online at http://www.independent.ie/business/irish/insomnia-coffeeshop-chain-slashes-its-losses-26787378.html [accessed 17 June 2016].

Murphy, A., and Garavan, T. N. (2011) 'Insomnia case study: Bobby Kerr from RTE's Dragon's Den', 11 February. Available online at http://www.bobbykerr.com/insomnia-case-study/ [accessed 17 June 2016].

Newman, K. (2001) 'The sorcerer's apprentice? Alchemy, seduction and confusion in modern marketing', *International Journal of Advertising*, 20(4): 409–29.

Oxford Dictionaries (2016) 'Ethics'. Available online at http://oxforddictionaries.com/definition/english/ethics?q=ethics [accessed 30 March 2016].

Packard, V. O. (1960) *The Hidden Persuaders*, Harmondsworth: Penguin.

Payne, A., Storbacka, K., and Frow, P. (2008) 'Managing the co-creation of value', *Journal of the Academy of Marketing Science*, 36(1): 83–96.

Peattie, K. (2001) 'Towards sustainability: The third age of green marketing', *Marketing Review*, 2(2): 129–46.

Peattie, K., and Crane, A. (2005) 'Green marketing: Legend, myth, farce or prophesy?' *Qualitative Market Research*, 8(4): 357–70.

Pieters, J. (2015) 'Dutch department store V&D declared bankrupt; some 10,000 job losses', *NLtimes*, 31 December. Available online at http://www.nltimes.nl/2015/12/31/dutch-dept-store-v-some-10000-job-losses/ [accessed 17 January 2016].

Prahalad, C. K., and Ramaswamy, V. (2004a) 'Co-creation experiences: The next practice in value creation', *Journal of Interactive Marketing*, 18(3): 5–14.

Prahalad, C. K., and Ramaswamy, V. (2004b) 'Co-creating unique value with customers', *Strategy and Leadership*, 32(3): 4–9.

Reichheld, F. F., and Sasser, W. E., Jr (1990) 'Zero defections: Quality comes to services', *Harvard Business Review*, 68(5): 105–11.

Rolls-Royce (2014) *Rolls-Royce Holdings plc Annual Report 2014*. Available online at http://ar.rolls-royce.com/2014/ [accessed 18 January 2016].

Rushe, D. (2014) 'Halliburton reaches $1.1bn settlement over Deepwater Horizon spill', *The Guardian*, 2 September. Available online at http://www.theguardian.com/environment/2014/sep/02/halliburton-11bn-settlement-deepwater-horizon-spill [accessed 28 March 2016].

Ryals, L., and Rackham, N. (2012) *Sales Implications of Servitization*. Available online at http://www.som.cranfield.ac.uk/som/dinamic-content/media/Sales%20Implications%20of%20Servitization%20White%20Paper%20Feb%202012%20v2.pdf [accessed 10 April 2013].

Saren, M. (2011) 'Critical marketing: Theoretical underpinnings', in G. Hastings, K. Angus, and C. Bryant (eds) *The Sage Handbook of Social Marketing*, London: Sage, 95–107.

Scheufele, D. A., and Tewksbury, D. (2007) 'Framing, agenda setting and priming: The evolution of three media effects models', *Journal of Communication*, 57(1): 9–20.

Shankar, A. (2009) 'Reframing critical marketing', *Journal of Marketing Management*, 25(7–8): 681–96.

Sharma, A., Gopalkrishnan, I. R., Mehotra, A., and Krishnan, R. (2010) 'Sustainability and business-to-business marketing: A framework and implications', *Industrial Marketing Management*, 39(2): 330–41.

Sherover, E. (1979) 'The virtue of poverty: Marx's transformation of Hegel's concept of the poor', *Revue Canadienne de Théorie Politique et Sociale* [*Canadian Journal of Political and Social Theory*], 3(1): 53–66.

Sheth, J. N., and Sisodia, R. J. (2005) 'A dangerous divergence: Marketing and society', *Journal of Public Policy and Marketing*, 24(1): 160–2.

Sheth, J. N., Sethia, N. K., and Srinivas, S. (2011) 'Mindful consumption: A customer-centric approach to sustainability', *Journal of the Academy of Marketing Science*, 39(2): 21–39.

Slater, S. F., and Narver, J. C. (1994) 'Market orientation, customer value and superior performance', *Business Horizons*, 37(2): 22–8.

Tadajewski, M. (2010) 'Towards a history of critical marketing studies', *Journal of Marketing Management*, 26(9–10): 773–824.

Treanor, J. (2015) 'FCA unable to estimate future PPI cost to banks', *The Guardian*, 26 November. Available online at http://www.theguardian.com/money/2015/nov/26/fca-unable-to-estimate-future-ppi-cost-to-banks [accessed 30 March 2016].

van Dam, Y. K., and Apeldoorn, P. A. C. (1996) 'Sustainable marketing', *Journal of Macromarketing*, 16(2): 45–56.

Vargo, S. L., and Lusch, R. F. (2004) 'Evolving to a new service-dominant logic for marketing', *Journal of Marketing*, 68(1): 1–17.

Vargo, S. L., and Lusch, R. F. (2008) 'Service-dominant logic: Continuing the evolution', *Journal of the Academy of Marketing Science*, 36(1): 1–10.

Viney, H., and Baines, P. (2012) 'Engaging government: Why it's necessary and how to do it', *European Business Review*, Sept–Oct: 9–13.

Wilkie, W. L., and Moore, E. S. (1999) 'Marketing's contributions to society', *Journal of Marketing*, 63(3–4): 198–218.

World Commission on Environment and Development (WCED) (1987) *Our Common Future: The Brundtland Report*, Oxford: University Press.

World Nuclear Association (2016) 'Fukushima incident'. Available online at http://www.world-nuclear.org/information-library/safety-and-security/safety-of-plants/fukushima-accident.aspx [accessed 28 March 2016].

Chapter 2
Understanding Customer Behaviour

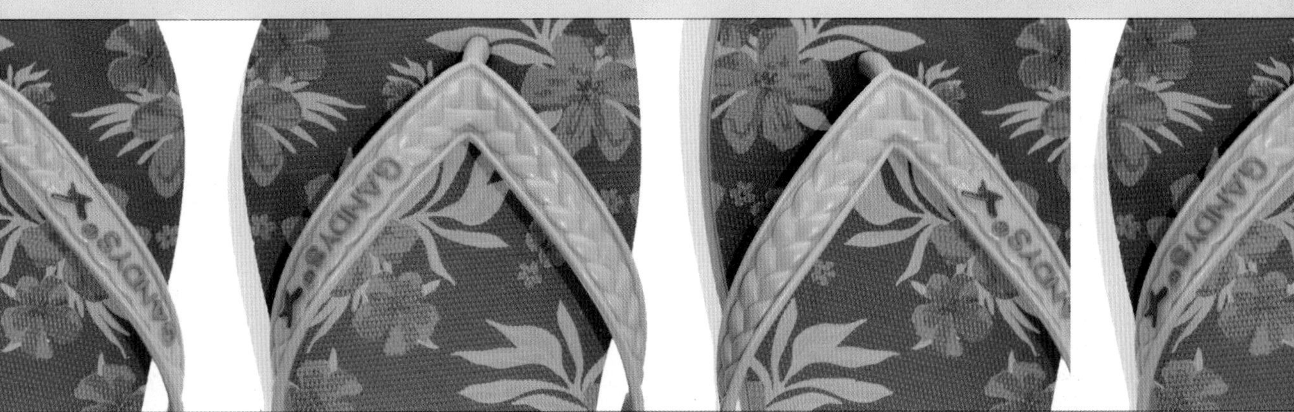

Learning Outcomes

After studying this chapter, you will be able to:

- explain the consumer product acquisition process;
- explain the processes involved in human perception, learning, and memory in relation to consumer choice;
- understand the importance of personality and motivation in consumer behaviour; and
- set out the main processes and stages associated with organizational buying and purchasing.

Case Insight 2.1
Holdz®

Market Insight 2.1
Easy Purchasing at Peugeot in 2015

Market Insight 2.2
Guilt Appeals: How Do They Change Behaviour?

Market Insight 2.3
Consumer Reactions to Tax Avoidance

Market Insight 2.4
Connecting Buyers and Suppliers

Case Insight 2.1 **Holdz®**

Founded in 2000, Holdz® is an online climbing holds and accessories firm. We speak to Steve Goodair (pictured), managing director, to find out more about how the firm meets its customers' needs.

'Holdz® is a small-to-medium-sized enterprise specializing in making the polyurethane resin holds that screw onto climbing walls to allow climbers to practise indoors in a safe, but natural-looking, environment. Our holds are expertly crafted in all shapes and sizes to resemble real rock features, from cracks to crimpz and sloperz to smoothies. We also produces bouldering mats, chalk bags, and clothing.

'Typical customers include climbing centres (which simulate climbing on rock faces), bouldering centres (which simulate climbing on large boulders), and serious individual climbers who have built climbing walls in their own homes to allow them to train even harder. Where climbing walls are owned by local councils, they tend to try to buy in volume, because they are less interested in the shape of hold they are getting and more interested in obtaining a volume discount. I sometimes have to point out to them that I can make holds for low prices, but that the holds would be so small that they'd be useless! So, we sometimes have to educate our customers about product and typical industry prices. Top route-setters (the people who put the holds on the wall) buy based on the shapes of the holds. This is so that they can make specific climbing route 'problems' requiring climbers to ascend a route in a certain way with different degrees of difficulty ranging from 'easy', through hard and very severe, through to 11 grades of 'extremely severe'. Home wall users tend to buy a pack of holds to get them started, but they also tend to return for more after a few months—both for variety, and because they have mastered those holds and got stronger.

'Because climbers sometimes fall when they ascend difficult routes, we produce heavy-duty matting, which allows climbers to fall more safely and with less likelihood of injury. We have manufactured our matting for 15 years, during which time it has become an industry best-seller. We are so confident of its quality that we offer a five-year quality guarantee. Overall, we cater for serious climbers, keen on the high product quality that we provide. We have a lot of repeat customers—especially with home walls—and we work hard to look after them. We know that our customers find holds quite expensive, so we put one or two free holds in with their order as a surprise. Lots of our customers share images of their purchases on social **media**, which is a great way of spreading positive word-of-mouth.

'To raise awareness of the Holdz® brand, we have, in the past, sponsored climbing and bouldering competitions, including the International Federation of Sport Climbing World Cup. Whenever the Federation holds a competition, it brands the wall and competitors' vests with sponsors' logos. We engage with our customers mainly by means of social media and face-to-face, when we're on the road selling to climbing centres or installing holds. But we also engage with customers in another unique way: all of our products display our logo, and climbers subconsciously note the Holdz® name and the hold's product type name when they're hanging onto it for dear life! This means that they recall these details when they are looking for the same type of hold when setting their own routes.

Case Insight 2.1 (continued)

'In 2006, there were no bouldering centres anywhere in the world; there were only climbing centres with small bouldering walls. A friend opened the world's first bouldering-only centre in Sheffield and asked us to provide the crash mats. No one knew how many visitors the centre would receive per day or if a bouldering-only venue would take off, but it did. For its crash mats, we used foam and PVC (polyvinyl chloride), but the sheer amount of traffic that this centre was receiving was phenomenal and it became very popular. If 150 climbers were completing an average of 30 climbing "problems" per session, the mats were being hammered 4,500 times per day. Multiply that by a year and that's 1.64 million feet-first landings onto the matting. Over time, our customers noticed that this force was damaging the matting, because the seams and materials became stressed from the landings, requiring its constant replacement. Our customers did not want to have to replace the crash matting continually, because this was expensive in terms of both materials and labour.'

The problem that Holdz® faced was how to develop a matting solution for its customers that was both durable and affordable, but still allowed the company to generate a reasonable profit?

Introduction

What process did you go through when deciding which university course to study? After reading this chapter, you will understand why consumers think and behave as they do. You will also understand how organizations make purchasing decisions, and that there are differences between consumer behaviour and business-to-business (B2B) buying behaviour. We start with the former, considering **cognition** (thoughts), **perception** (how we see things), and learning (how we memorize techniques and knowledge). These are processes that are fundamental in explaining how consumers think and learn about offerings.

We also discuss **personality** and motivation to illustrate how these psychological concepts affect how we buy. Because marketing comes alive when it is woven into the fabric of our social lives, we consider how **social class**, life cycles, and lifestyles influence consumer behaviour. We then examine the characteristics of organization buyer behaviour, focusing on the processes that allow companies to purchase the products they need to operate successfully.

Consumer Proposition Acquisition

The consumer proposition acquisition process consists of six distinct stages (see Figure 2.1). The process model is useful, because it highlights the importance and distinctiveness of proposition selection and re-evaluation phases in the process. In Figure 2.1, the buying process is iterative—that is, each stage can lead back to previous stages or move forward to the next.

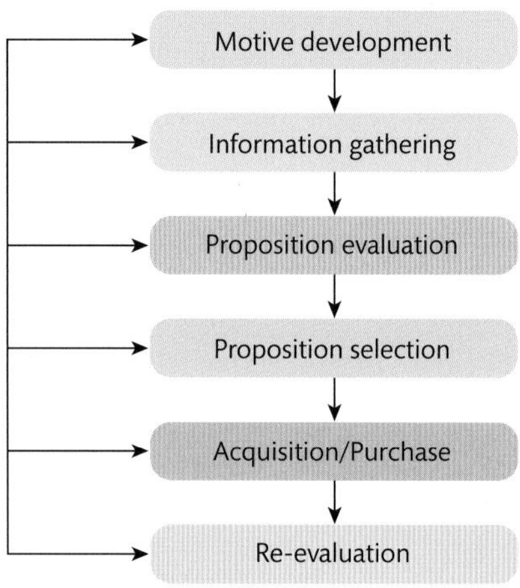

Figure 2.1 The consumer proposition acquisition process

Motive Development

The process begins when we decide that we wish to obtain an offering. This involves the initial recognition that a problem needs solving. To solve the problem, we must first become aware of it. A consumer may decide that she needs to buy a new dress for a party, for example; perhaps she has grown tired of the old one, or she thinks it is out of fashion, or decides to cheer herself up, or wants to buy for a special occasion (such as an engagement or hen party), or wants to buy it for a whole host of other reasons.

Information Gathering

In the next stage, we seek alternative ways of solving our problems. Our dress buyer might ask herself where she bought her last dress, how much dresses typically cost, what different retail outlets stock dresses, and where those retailers are located. She might ask herself where she normally buys party dresses (online or in-store), what kinds of dresses are in fashion, perhaps which retailers have sales on, which store staff treat her well if she shops in-store, and what the returns policies are of various online and high-street retailers. Our search for a solution may be active, an **overt search**, or passive. In other words, we are open to ways of solving our problem, but we are not actively looking for information to help us (Howard and Sheth, 1969). The search for information may be internal—that is, we may consider what we already know about the problem and the offerings that we might buy to solve our problem. Alternatively, it might be

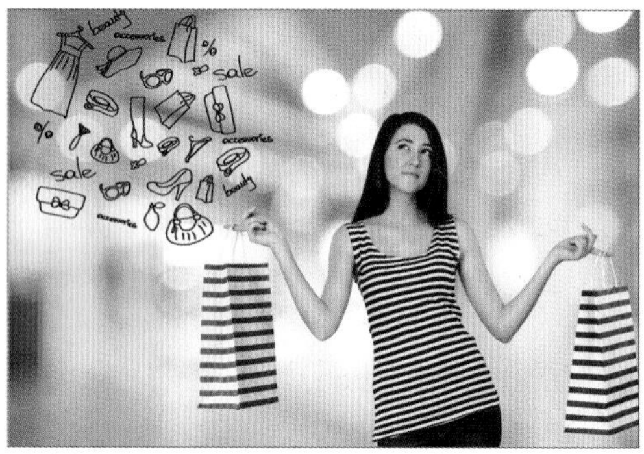

Shopping is influenced by a myriad personal and social variables: it might be a much more complex process than you ever imagined.

Source: © Billion Photos/Shutterstock.

external—that is, when we do not know enough about our problem and so we seek advice or supplementary information. At this stage, we build our awareness by increasing our knowledge both of an offering and of the competitors making that offering available.

Proposition Evaluation

Once we have all of the information necessary to make a decision, we evaluate alternative propositions. But, first, we must determine the criteria used to rank the various offerings. These might be rational (for example based on cost) or irrational (for example based on desire or intuition). The dress buyer might ask herself which website or retail outlet is the best **value** for money and which is the most fashionable. Consumers are said to have an **evoked set** of products in mind when they come to evaluate which particular product, brand, or service they want to solve a particular problem. An evoked set for the dress buyer might include Zara, H&M, Mango (MNG elsewhere in the world other than the UK), ASOS, or Net-a-Porter, for instance. The more affluent buyer might visit a department store (such as Harrods or Selfridges in the UK), or the websites of DKNY or Gucci, for example. This stage might also be termed the 'consideration' stage.

Proposition Selection

Typically, the offering that we eventually select is that which we evaluate as fitting our needs more closely. However, we might select a particular offering at some distance from where we actually buy or acquire it. For example, the dress buyer may have checked online to make her selection (intending to go to the shop to try it on), but turns up at the retailer only to find that the dress she wants is not available, so decides on an alternative on impulse at the point of purchase. Proposition selection is therefore a separate stage in the proposition acquisition process, distinct from proposition evaluation, because there are times when we must re-evaluate what we buy or acquire because what we want is not available, for example buying a cinema ticket for one film because the seats for another are sold out.

Acquisition/Purchase

Once selection has taken place, different approaches to purchasing might exist. For example, our dress buyer may make a routine purchase: a dress for work. A routine purchase is a purchase made regularly. Because the purchase is regular, we do not get too involved in the decision-making process; we simply buy the offering that we bought previously unless new circumstances arise. The purchase may be specialized, conducted on a one-off or infrequent basis, for example an evening gown for a ball or a formal work event. In this case, we may become much more involved in the decision-making process to ensure that we understand what we are buying and that we are happy it will satisfy our needs (to look classy, perhaps, and not cheap). For routine purchases, we might use debit cards or cash; for infrequent purchases, we might use a credit or store card. With infrequent purchases, the marketer might ease the pain of payment by offering credit or generous warranties. Our dress buyer might be intending to purchase the dress, but the store's policy on returns (that is, whether it allows this or not over what period of time) may have an impact on whether or not she actually buys a dress from that particular shop.

Re-evaluation

The theory of **cognitive dissonance** (Festinger, 1957) suggests that we are motivated to re-evaluate our beliefs, **attitudes**, **opinions**, or values if the position we hold on them at one time is not the same as the position we held at an earlier period owing to some intervening event, circumstance, or action. This difference in evaluations, termed 'cognitive dissonance', is psychologically uncomfortable (that is, it causes anxiety). For example, we may feel foolish or regretful about a purchasing decision (perhaps we spent too much on a night out or on a meal at a slightly too fancy restaurant). Therefore we are motivated to reduce our anxiety by redefining our beliefs, attitudes, opinions, or values to make them consistent with our circumstances (by not going to that particular bar as often or to that particular restaurant again). We will also actively avoid situations that might increase our feeling of dissonance.

To reduce dissonance, we might try to neutralize it by:

- selectively forgetting information;
- minimizing the importance of an issue, decision, or act;
- selectively exposing ourselves only to new information consonant with our existing view (rather than information that is not); and/or
- reversing a purchase decision, for instance by taking an offering back or selling it for what it was worth.

The concept of cognitive dissonance has significant application in marketing. Industrial or consumer purchasers are likely to feel cognitive dissonance if their expectations of proposition performance are not met in reality. This feeling of dissonance may be particularly acute in a high-**involvement** purchase, such as a car, house, holiday, or high-value investment product. (See Market Insight 2.1 on Peugeot's 0 per cent interest scheme aiming to minimize customer cognitive dissonance.) We are also likely to search out information to reinforce our choice of offering.

Market Insight 2.1 **Easy Purchasing at Peugeot in 2015**

Car manufacturer Peugeot, with operational headquarters in Sochaux, France, sold 11,563 new cars in in the UK in 2015, taking a 4.0 per cent share of the market, way behind more popular brands in the UK such as Ford, Vauxhall, Volkswagen, Audi, BMW, Nissan, and Mercedes-Benz. Market share was down 1.1 per cent over the period 2009–15. Worldwide, PSA Peugeot Citroën, the brand's owner, saw sales increase 1.2 per cent in 2015. In Europe, group sales rose 5.9 per cent to 1,864,000 units. Peugeot made up the bulk of the sales, seeing sales in Europe (particularly in The Netherlands, Spain, Italy, and France) increase 9.4 per cent to 1,086,000 units. The 308 model was in the top three in the small family car segment. The Peugeot brand also saw success in other overseas markets, including China (up 6 per cent to 408,000 units), the Middle East and Africa (up 2.3 per cent to 117,000 units), Mexico (up 34 per cent), Chile (up 4 per cent), and India-Pacific, including India, South Korea, and Japan (up 6.5 per cent to 23,800 units).

Market Insight 2.1 (continued)

Given relatively sluggish economic growth and the low rates of wage inflation in many countries, vehicle manufacturers and dealership sales personnel understand the psychological anxiety that car buyers feel when purchasing new cars, especially after the purchase. The buyer's key consideration is ensuring that they obtain value for money and that they do not feel they have spent their money badly. The problem is particularly acute when customers buy new cars, because new cars are significantly more expensive than second-hand cars.

Considering that cars lose 15–35 per cent of their value in depreciation the moment they leave the showroom and up to 50 per cent by the third year, we can see why new car buyers feel vulnerable. Of course, there are benefits: new cars look better, incorporate the latest design features, and have reduced maintenance costs.

Car dealers work hard to reinforce the purchase decisions made by buyers of new cars by sending customers newsletters and offering efficient (or free three-year warranty) after-sales service to ensure that there are no, or few, maintenance problems. In many cases, new vehicles are sold with free insurance, 0 per cent finance deals, or 'buy now, pay later' schemes, all designed to reduce the post-purchase cognitive dissonance car buyers naturally feel after their purchase.

In 2015, Peugeot sweetened the sales with its Just Add Fuel® deal on the 308 model, by offering a time-limited offer of 0 per cent financing over 37 months, three years' free insurance, and three years' servicing (including warranty, car tax, and roadside assistance), with only £500 deposit contribution at participating dealers.

The Peugeot 308: even more attractive when it comes interest-free with free insurance and deposit contribution.

Source: © Dong liu/Shutterstock.

But, in the UK in 2016, Skoda, Seat, Nissan, Mazda, Jeep, and Hyundai were also all offering 0 per cent finance deals on selected models. The question for Peugeot, therefore, is whether the promotion on the 308 will help to turn the tide of negative sales growth in the UK and result in an increase in market share for Peugeot?

1. **What else could Peugeot do to reduce the cognitive dissonance felt by its customers?**
2. **Do you think that cognitive dissonance would increase or decrease during an economic downturn?**
3. **Consider a time when you purchased something that left you feeling anxious afterwards. What were you purchasing and why did it make you feel anxious?**

Sources: Mintel (2016); Peugeot (2016).

On the other hand, if we are happy with our purchase, we might decide to repurchase it, thereby displaying some degree of behavioural loyalty to a particular brand. This stage is termed the 'loyalty stage'. If we really like our purchase, we might also encourage others to buy the brand—the so-called advocacy stage. Such advocacy is common in the user-generated content (UGC) developed online.

In Figure 2.1, the buying process is iterative (that is, it occurs in steps), particularly at the re-evaluation phase of the acquisition process. This is because the re-evaluation of the offering leads us back to any, or all, of the previous phases in the proposition acquisition process as a result of experiencing cognitive dissonance. For example, we may have bought a games console (Xbox One), but not be completely happy with it (perhaps we think it has poor picture quality or sound). If it were covered under warranty, this would lead us to the acquisition phase, where a new perfect product should be provided by the retailer. If the product were delivered in perfect working order, but we simply did not enjoy using it, we might revisit the original alternatives we selected (for example PS4, Wii U) and pick one of the other alternatives (perhaps one that might offer a larger variety of games). If we were really not sure about which games console to buy after this initial purchase, we might re-evaluate the alternatives we originally selected and then decide. If we were to really dislike our original purchase and if this were to shake our belief in what we thought was important in selecting a games console, we might go back to the information-gathering phase to get more of an idea about the offerings available. Finally, if we were extremely disappointed, we might decide that our original motive—the need to play, to relax, and to have fun—can best be solved by purchasing something other than a games console, which will still meet the same need, such as membership of a sports club.

Perceptions, Learning, and Memory

Often, consumers do not understand the messages that marketers convey, either because they have not received, comprehended, or remembered those messages, or because the messages were unclear. Consumer understanding depends on how effectively the message is transmitted and perceived. Consumers receive thousands of messages every day. Human perception, learning, and memory processes must be used to attend to, filter, and store so many messages.

Perceptions

The American Marketing Association (AMA, 2016) defines 'perceptions' as:

> . . . based on prior attitudes, beliefs, needs, stimulus factors, and situational determinants, individuals perceive objects, events, or people in the world about them. Perception is the cognitive impression that is formed of 'reality' which in turn influences the individual's actions and behaviour toward that object.

As consumers, we are interested in certain types of offering that are relevant to us when we receive marketing messages. So, men would not usually be interested in adverts about handbags (as opposed to 'man-bags') unless they were to want to buy one as an anniversary, birthday, or travel gift for a special woman in their lives. We avoid exposure to certain messages and actively seek out others. We may also expose ourselves selectively to particular messages through the media we choose to read (such as certain newspapers, magazines, ezines, Facebook pages, Twitter feeds) or watch (for example certain terrestrial, cable, satellite, or Internet television channels). It is therefore important to determine which media channels customers use.

Advertisers label this concept of representing the personal importance that a person attaches to a given communication message as 'involvement'. This is important because it explains a person's receptivity to communications, and people can therefore be segmented into high, medium, and low involvement groups (Michaelidou and Dibb, 2008). We are interested in consumers' receptivity because we are interested in changing or altering their perceptions of particular offerings.

An interesting way of displaying how people think about particular offerings uses perceptual mapping, a technique dating back to at least the early 1960s (Mindak, 1961). People view champagne brands differently in the UK, for example, using (brand) personality keywords 'zesty' vs 'mellow' and 'fresh fruit' vs 'baked fruit'. Lanson is associated with zesty and fresh fruit; Moët et Chandon is associated with mellow and baked fruit. Organizations deliberately seek to position themselves in the minds of specific target audience groups. To do this properly, they must understand the nature of the group's subculture.

Learning and Memory

How do consumers continually learn about new offerings, their relative performance, and new trends? The answer is by learning. Learning is the process by which we acquire new knowledge and skills, attitudes and values, through study, experience, or modelling others' behaviour. Theories of human learning include **classical conditioning**, **operant conditioning**, and **social learning**.

- *Classical conditioning* occurs when the unconditioned stimulus becomes associated with the conditioned stimulus. In other words, we learn by associating one thing with another. This approach to learning is frequently used in marketing. For example, perfume and aftershave manufacturers (such as L'Oréal) place free samples of products in sachets in magazines so that, when readers see an advert for a particular brand of perfume or aftershave, they associate the image they see with the smell and so are more likely to purchase the product when they see its image in the future.
- *Operant conditioning* is learning through behavioural reinforcement. Skinner (1954) termed this 'reinforcement', because the behaviour would occur more readily in connection with a particular stimulus if the required resulting behaviour had been reinforced through punishment or reward. In marketing, consider the typical in-store sales promotion, perhaps of a new yoghurt brand offered in a supermarket. If we do not normally eat this brand and we are curious, we might try it, because there are no costs in terms of time, effort, or money in having a taste. The sales promotion provides the stimulus, the trial behaviour occurs, and if the consumer likes the yoghurt and is rewarded with a money-off coupon, the behaviour of purchasing that particular yoghurt brand is reinforced. Supermarkets reinforce our loyalty by providing reward cards and points for purchasing particular items, for example the Nectar card in the UK or the stamps system used by the retailer 7-Eleven in its convenience stores worldwide.
- *Social learning* was proposed by the psychologist Albert Bandura (1977), who argued that humans can delay gratification and dispense our own rewards or punishment. As a result, we have more choice over how to react to stimuli; we can reflect on our own actions and change future behaviour. This led to the idea that humans learn not only from how they respond to situations, but also from how other humans respond to situations. Bandura (1977) called this 'modelling'. In social learning, we learn by observing others' behaviour. The implications for marketers are profound. For adolescents, role models include parents, athletes, and entertainers, but parents are the most influential (Martin and Bush, 2000). Parents socialize their children into purchasing and consuming the same brands that they buy, actively teaching them consumer skills—materialistic values and

consumption attitudes—in their teenage years. Interaction with peers also makes adolescents more aware of different offerings (Moschis and Churchill, 1978). Companies have long recognized the power of peers, particularly in the social media world, encouraging purchasers to leave reviews of products that they have previously bought, 'like' their Facebook pages, and retweet their messages. Research indicates that those who read reviews are twice as likely to select a product compared with those who do not (Senecal and Nantal, 2004).

But what happens once consumers have learnt information? How do they retain it—that is, what stops them from forgetting such information? Knowledge develops with familiarity, repetition of marketing messages, and a consumer's acquisition of product or service information. Marketing messages need to be repeated often, because people forget them over time—particularly the specific arguments or message presented. The general substance or conclusion of the message is marginally more likely to be remembered (Bettinghaus and Cody, 1994: 67).

We enhance memorization through the use of symbols, such as corporate identity logos, badges, and signs. Shapes, creatures, and people carry significant meanings, as seen in badges, trademarks, and logos. Airlines around the world have adopted symbols, such as the kangaroo of Australian airline Qantas. Well-recognized symbols worldwide include the KFC 'Colonel' symbol, Intel's symbol, Apple's bitten apple logo, Coca-Cola's ubiquitous script logo, and Google's multi-coloured script symbol.

Our memories—as a system for storing perceptions, experience, and knowledge—are highly complex (Bettman, 1979). A variety of memorization processes affect consumer choice, including the following.

- *Factors affecting* **recognition** and **recall**—Less frequently used words in advertising are recognized more and recalled less.
- *The importance of context*—Memorization is strongly associated with the context of the stimulus, so information available in memory will be inaccessible in the wrong context.
- *The form of object coding and storage*—We store information in the form it is presented to us, either by object (brand) or dimension (offering attribute), but there is no evidence that one form is organized into memory more quickly, or more accurately than the other (Johnson and Russo, 1978).

Five of the world's most iconic logos.

Sources: Google and the Google logo are registered trademarks of Google Inc., used with permission; McDonald's logo used with permission from McDonald's Corporation; Facebook logo © Facebook; Nike logo © Nike; LG logo © LG.

- *Load processing effects*—We find it more difficult to process information into our short-term and long-term memories when we are presented with a great deal of information at once.
- *Input mode effects*—Short-term recall of sound input is stronger than short-term recall of visual input where the two compete for attention, for example in television and YouTube advertising.
- *Repetition effects*—Recall and recognition of marketing messages or information increase the more a consumer is exposed to them, although later exposures add less and less to memory performance.

Market Insight 2.2 **Guilt Appeals: How Do They Change Behaviour?**

Marketers often use messages based on guilt to influence consumer behaviour. Whether it is a charity asking for donations or a gym promoting a new exercise plan, messages aimed at eliciting guilt to change behaviour are very common. How do these messages work and are they really effective? Let us consider each question in turn.

Marketers used to think that the learning from guilt appeals was based mostly on motivation and the negative feeling that consumers experience. Because feeling guilty about one's lack of exercise is unpleasant, consumers would decide to exercise more to feel better about themselves. In most cases, however, this view is flawed, because when we see an advert, we do not change our behaviour straight away; the idea is that the message will influence our decision at a later point in time. Recent research suggests that guilt does not work simply by making people feel bad, but influences consumers because it engages them more deeply with the message (what researchers call 'transportation'). Feelings of guilt favour persuasion because they make us pay much more attention to the message and make us feel that the message is really relevant to us. Through this process, people internalize the information communicated more effectively.

Some remain sceptical about the effectiveness of guilt and other negative messages. So what is the evidence? The reality is that guilt and other negative emotions can be effective when used appropriately. However, guilt messages can also backfire, because consumers can resent advertisers who try to manipulate them through the use of negative emotions. To avoid such negative reactions, marketers need to make sure that (a) their target audience will be predisposed to accept a message based on guilt, and (b) the message is not too explicit and assertive. The most effective campaigns use mild messages to elicit guilt.

Guilt is often used in persuasive messages to trigger consumer responses.

Source: Courtesy of Greenpeace.

1. **What are the implications for advertisers of the findings discussed?**
2. **Find an advertisement containing a guilt appeal (that is, a message based on guilt) and evaluate its effectiveness based on the information noted here.**
3. **What product categories might be promoted effectively using guilt appeals? Why would these product categories be suitable for this form of communication?**

Sources: Antonetti and Baines (2016); research funded by the British Academy Small Research Grant SG142942.

Personality

How and what we buy is also based on our personalities. Personality is that aspect of our psyche that determines how we respond to our environment in a relatively stable way over time. There are various theories of personality. One popular approach categorizes people into different personality types or so-called traits (pronounced 'trays'). Researchers characterize personalities using bipolar scales, including the following traits:

- sociable–timid;
- action-oriented–reflection-oriented;
- stable–nervous;
- serious–frivolous;
- tolerant–suspicious;
- dominant–submissive;
- friendly–hostile;
- hard–sensitive;
- quick–slow; and/or
- masculine–feminine.

Researchers frequently talk about the 'big five' personality dimensions (McRae and Costa, 1987):

- extraversion (sociable, fun-loving, affectionate, friendly, and talkative);
- openness (original, imaginative, creative, and daring);
- conscientiousness (careful, reliable, well-organized, and hard-working);
- neuroticism (worrying, nervous, highly strung, self-conscious, and vulnerable); and
- agreeableness (soft-hearted, sympathetic, forgiving, and acquiescent).

Certain types of personality prefer certain brands, for example 'conscientious' people prefer 'trusted' brands, while extroverts prefer 'sociable' brands. There are also gender differences, for example neurotic male and conscientious females prefer 'trusted brands' (Mulyanegara et al., 2009). An understanding of personality types therefore helps marketers to segment customer groups using personality dimensions.

Various companies use personality as a segmentation criterion, for example car manufacturers link personality to particular car attributes (such as safety features, aesthetics, handling). Makers of running shoes and mobile phones are interested in two personality traits in particular, extraversion and openness to experience, because these traits link to attitudinal and purchase loyalty displayed towards those brands (Matzler et al., 2006).

Visit the **online resources** and complete Internet Activity 2.1, an online quiz, to learn more about your own personality across a number of key personality traits.

Self-actualization needs
Psycho-transformative: the need to fulfill our potential

Esteem needs
Socio-psychological: valued and respected by self and others

Belongingness needs
Socio-cultural: affection, attachment, friendship

Safety needs
Physical and psychological: a predictable, non-threatening environment

Physiological needs
Primitive and biological: food, water, oxygen, sex, and shelter from the elements

Figure 2.2 Maslow's hierarchy of needs

Source: Adapted from Maslow (1943). This content is in the public domain.

Motivation

Abraham Maslow (1943) suggested a hierarchical order of human needs, as outlined in Figure 2.2. According to Maslow, we satisfy lower-order physiological needs first, before safety needs, then belongingness needs and esteem needs, before finally addressing the need for self-actualization. There is little research evidence to confirm Maslow's hierarchy, but the concept possesses logical simplicity, making it a useful tool for understanding how we prioritize our own needs and therefore why we might buy what we buy.

Theory of Planned Behaviour

Theories of motivation in marketing help us to understand why people behave as they do. The theory of planned behaviour explains that behaviour is brought about by our **intention** to act in a certain way. This intention to act is affected by the attitude that a subject has towards a particular behaviour, encompassing the degree to which the subject has favourable or unfavourable evaluations or appraisals of the behaviour in question. Intention to act is also affected by the subjective norm, which is perceived social pressure to perform or not perform a particular behaviour. Finally, intention to act is affected by perceived behavioural control, referring to the perceived ease or difficulty of performing the behaviour, based on a reflection on past experience and future obstacles. Figure 2.3 provides a graphical illustration.

For example, if we consider cigarette use, we might have different attitudes towards smoking based on our geographical location, for example whether we live in France or China versus the UK or New Zealand. We might think we cannot give up smoking because we need a cigarette to calm our nerves

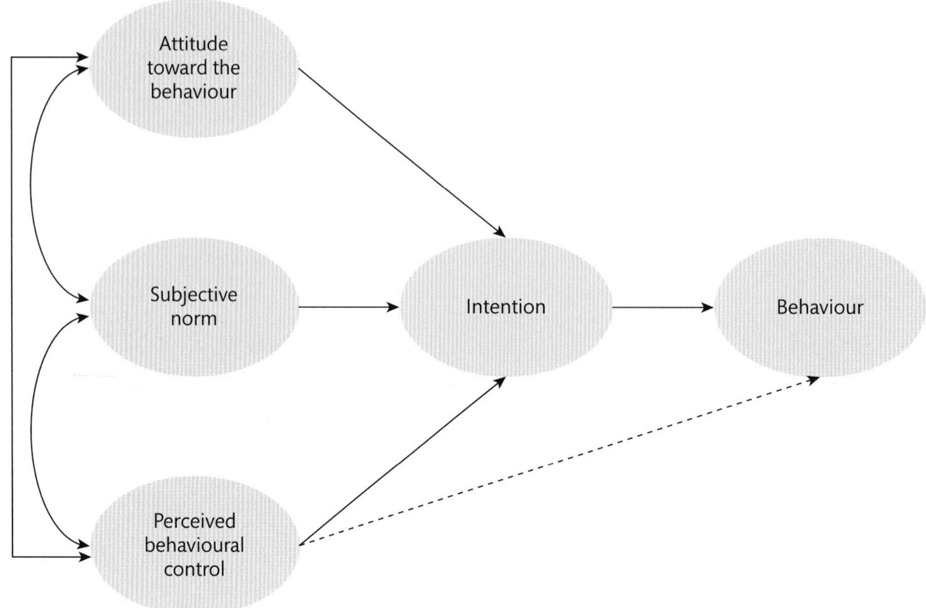

Figure 2.3 Theory of planned behaviour

Source: Ajzen (1991).

(perhaps we have a stressful job). Equally, we might also consider the opinions that significant others (our spouses, our children, or our friends) have towards smoking cigarettes. If we place ourselves in the mind of government (de)marketers, the key elements of the theory of planned behaviour (that is, attitudes, subjective norms, and perceived behavioural control) can help us to understand how to discourage smoking. For example, we could either (a) try to alter subjects' attitudes towards smoking, (b) change their views on how others see them as smokers, or (c) change their perceptions of how they perceive their own ability to give up. An advertising campaign called 'smokefree' from Public Health England, running in late 2015, actively discouraged smoking by showing 'disgusting' images of 'rotting' entrails in roll-up cigarettes. The idea is to make people realize that smoking roll-ups is just as dangerous as smoking manufactured cigarettes (Siciliano, 2014).

Public Health England uses a 'disgust' appeal to discourage 'roll-up' smoking.

Source: Image courtesy of DARE and Public Health England. Photography by Nick Georghiou.

Research Insight 2.1

To take your learning further, you might wish to read this influential article.

Ajzen, I. (1991) 'The theory of planned behaviour', *Organisational Behaviour and Human Decision Processes*, 50(2): 179–211.

In this highly cited seminal article, the author outlines how behaviour and behavioural intention to act in a certain way are affected by the attitude the subject has towards a particular behaviour, the subjective norm, and perceived behavioural control. The author developed our understanding of the fact that how humans intend to act may not be how they end up acting in a given situation. Intention, perception of behavioural control, attitude toward the behaviour, and subjective norm all reveal different aspects of the target behaviour and serve as possible directions for attack in attempts to alter particular behaviours, making this a powerful motivational theory in marketing.

 **Visit the online resources to read the abstract and access the full paper.**

Social Grade

In marketing, the term **social grade** refers to a system of classification of consumers based on their socio-economic grouping. NRS Ltd—the successor to the Joint Industry Committee for National Readership Surveys (JICNARS)—provides social grade population estimates, not only for the National Readership Survey, but also for a number of other major industry surveys (see Table 2.1). There is a widely held belief that consumers make purchases based on their socio-economic position within society, and that different social classes have different self-images, social horizons, and consumption goals (Coleman, 1983).

Lifestyle

Marketers increasingly target consumers on the basis of their lifestyles. The AMA (2016) defines 'lifestyle' as 'the manner in which the individual copes and deals with his/her psychological and physical environment on a day-to-day basis', 'as a phrase describing the values, attitudes, opinions, and behaviour patterns of the consumer', and 'the manner in which people conduct their lives, including their activities, interests, and opinions'. For example, a segmentation of the South Australian wine market reveals the following lifestyle types (Bruwer and Li, 2007).

- *Conservative, knowledgeable wine drinkers* (19.2 per cent of the population)—More likely to be male (57 per cent), well educated, and well remunerated, this segment drinks wine frequently (particularly red), displaying connoisseur qualities when buying wine.
- *Enjoyment-oriented, social wine drinkers* (16.2 per cent of the population)—More likely to be female and younger, this segment likes white and sparkling wine, and has an eye for value for money.
- *Basic wine drinkers* (23.5 per cent of the population)—This is a predominantly male segment, as happy drinking beer as wine, depending on what is available.

Table 2.1 Social grading scale

Social grade	Social status	Occupational status	Population estimate, UK, age 15+ (July 2014–June 2015) (%)	Population estimate, UK, age 15+ (July 1984–June 1985) (%)
A	Upper middle class	Higher managerial, administrative, and professional	4	3
B	Middle class	Intermediate, managerial, administrative, and professional	23	14
C1	Lower middle class	Supervisory, clerical, and junior managerial, administrative, and professional	27	22
C2	Skilled working class	Skilled manual workers	22	29
D	Working class	Semi-skilled and unskilled manual workers	15	18
E	Those at lowest levels of subsistence	State pensioners; casual and lowest grade workers; unemployed with state benefits only	9	14

Source: Reproduced with the kind permission of the National Readership Survey.

- *Mature, time-rich wine drinkers* (18.2 per cent of the population)—This older, male segment displays connoisseur tendencies and is interested in the provenance of the wine.
- *Young, professional wine drinkers* (22.9 per cent of the population)—This segment is predominantly female and employed in the professions. They tend to drink red wine, mainly at business functions.

Life Stage

Marketers frequently hypothesize that people at certain stages of life purchase and consume similar kinds of offerings. Most market research agencies routinely measure attitudes and purchasing patterns based on life stage to determine differences among groups. Table 2.2 indicates that there is a difference in the types of offering purchased as a result, with solitary survivors far more likely to purchase funeral plans, nursing home care, and cruise holidays, and bachelors more likely to spend their income on package and long-haul holidays and educational service products, for instance.

Visit the **online resources** and complete Internet Activity 2.2 to learn more about how Volkswagen uses the family life cycle to communicate its brand values to its target audience.

Table 2.2 The life stage concept

Bachelor (young, single person not living with parents/guardians)	Newly married or long-term cohabiting (young, no children)	Full nest I (youngest children under age of 6)	Full nest II (youngest children aged 6 or over)	Full nest III (older, married couples, with dependent children)	Empty nest I (older, married couples, no children living at home, chief income earner or both in work)	Empty nest II (older, married couples, no children living at home, chief income earner or both retired)	Solitary survivor, in work	Solitary survivor, retired
Few financial burdens Fashion opinion leaders Recreation-oriented Buy: basic kitchen equipment; basic furniture; cars; package and long-haul holidays; education	Better off financially, because of dual wages High purchase rate of consumer durables Buy: cars; refrigerators; package holidays	Home purchasing at peak Low level of savings Buy: washer-dryers; TV; baby food and related products; vitamins; toys	Financial position better Sometimes both parents in work Buy: larger-sized family food packages; cleaning materials; pianos; child-minding services	Financial position better still Both parents more likely to be in work Some children will have part-time jobs High average purchase of consumer durables Buy: better homeware and furniture products; magazines; non-essential home appliances	Home ownership at peak Most satisfied with savings and financial position Interested in travel, recreation, self-education More likely to give gifts and make charitable contributions Less interested in new products Buy: luxurious holidays; meals out; home improvements	Drastic cut in household income More likely to stay at home Buy: medical appliances and private health care; sleep aids; digestive aids	Medical needs depend on age Buy: financial, healthcare, and retirement plans; meals for one	Same medical needs as other retired group Drastic cut in income Buy: household staples; cruise holidays; nursing home services; funeral plans

Source: Adapted from Wells and Gubar (1966). Published by the American Marketing Association.

Ethnic Groups

In a globalized society, marketers are increasingly interested in how to market offerings to ethnic groups within particular populations. For example, in the United States, the Hispanic population—often immigrants from Mexico—and the black population together represent a sizeable proportion of the total population. France and the UK both have large Muslim populations. In Sweden, there are large groups of Finns, former Yugoslavs, Iraqis, and Iranians. Multicultural consumers spent about US$3.4 trillion in the United States in 2015 and, importantly, ethnic groups behave differently (Gil and Rosenberg, 2015). Cui (1997) proposes that in any country in which there are ethnic marketing opportunities, a company has four main strategic options, as follows.

Have a break, have a green tea KitKat!

Source: © Paul Baines.

1 *Total standardization*—Use the existing marketing mix without modification to the ethnic market. This is very difficult to do. Even Coca-Cola, well known for its ardent approach to standardization, adapts its cola around the world (for example by adding pineapple in Indonesia to cater for local tastes).

2 *Product adaptation*—Use the existing marketing mix, but adapt the product to the ethnic market in question (for example Nestlé selling green-tea-flavoured KitKats in Thailand).

3 *Advertising adaptation*—Use the current marketing mix, but adapt the advertising, particularly the use of foreign languages, to the target ethnic market by promoting the product using different associations that are more resonant with ethnic audiences (for example stores in some parts of Finland advertising in Swedish and Finnish to cater for the minority Swedish population, and in the United States, in Spanish).

4 *Ethnic marketing*—Use a totally new marketing mix (for example Bollywood films aimed at audiences in the Indian subcontinent and in diaspora around the world using strong love and ethical themes, and a musical format).

Market Insight 2.3 **Consumer Reactions to Tax Avoidance**

There has been significant media attention recently on companies engaging in tax avoidance. Giant corporations such as Google, Amazon, and Starbucks having been accused of exploiting loopholes in international laws to minimize their tax burden very aggressively. For example, Amazon had revenues in the UK of £3.35 billion in 2011, but paid only £1.8 million in tax (roughly equal to a tax rate of 0.05 per cent). Although tax avoidance is not illegal, most consumers consider it immoral, leading to what some have called the 'tax shaming' of multinationals. Investors have started to consider whether the savings from tax avoidance are actually worth the trouble considering the global backlash around these practices.

Market Insight 2.3 (continued)

There is, in fact, research showing that consumers have a negative view of companies that engage in tax avoidance and are likely to engage in negative word-of-mouth against these organizations. Paying a fair share of taxes, according to this view, is considered a moral responsibility (see Chapter 1), and companies that fail to comply will be punished by consumers and other stakeholders. However, how people react to tax avoidance might also be influenced by their social context. Recent findings suggest that, at least in the United States, consumers who agree with right-wing political views do not see tax avoidance as immoral and are less likely to react negatively to it; consumers on the left of the political spectrum tend to react very strongly to news about companies engaging in aggressive tax decisions. This suggests that our political views influence how we judge companies' practices. Interestingly, things change when we consider a company to which we feel very close: when the corporation engaging in tax avoidance is such a brand, both right-wingers and left-wingers feel betrayed and react very negatively. This suggests that tax avoidance is indeed a risky strategy, because it could alienate a company's best customers.

1. **What are the implications of this research for marketers?**
2. **What factors beyond political identification can affect how people react to information about tax avoidance?**
3. **Why do you think most consumers seem to consider tax avoidance unethical even when it complies with national and international laws? (See Chapter 1 on ethical decision-making and corporate social responsibility, or CSR.)**

Sources: Barford and Holt (2013); Marriage (2014); Antonetti and Anesa (2016).

Organizational Buyer Behaviour

Parkinson and Baker (1994: 6, cited by Ulkuniemi, 2003) state that organizational buying behaviour concerns 'the purchase of a product or service to satisfy organisational rather than individual goals'. This makes the point that **organizational buyer behaviour** is about satisfying organization-wide needs and hence requires marketers to adopt processes that take into account the needs of different people, not a single individual.

The buying processes undertaken by organizations differ in a number of ways from those used by consumers. These differences are a reflection of the potential high financial value associated with these transactions, the product complexity, the relatively large value of individual orders, and the nature of the risk and uncertainty. As a result, organizations have developed particular processes and procedures that often involve a large number of people. What is central, however, is that the group of people involved in organizational purchasing processes are referred to as a **decision-making unit**, that the types of purchase they make are classified as **buyclasses**, all of which are made in various **buyphases**.

Characteristics of the Decision-Making Unit

The group of people tasked with buying decisions is referred to as either the 'decision-making unit' (DMU) or the **buying centre**. In many circumstances, these are informal groupings of people who come together in varying ways to contribute to the decision-making process. Certain projects,

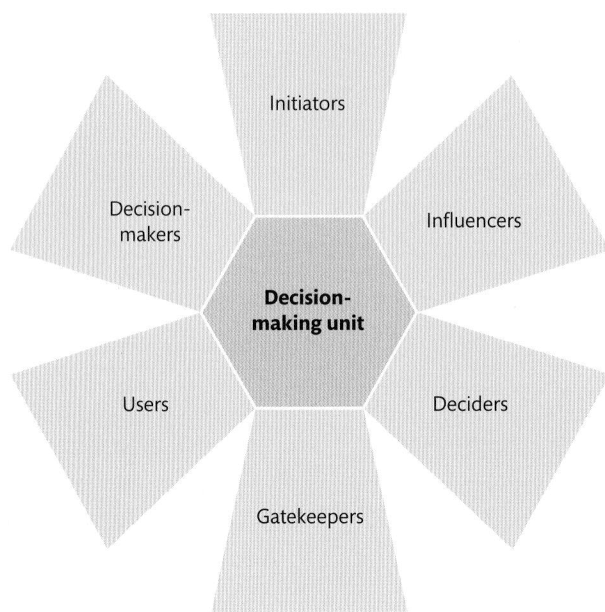

Figure 2.4 Membership of the decision-making unit

Source: Fill and McKee (2012). Reproduced with the kind permission of Goodfellow Publishers.

usually of major significance or value, require a group of people to be formally constituted with the responsibility for overseeing and completing the purchase of a stipulated item or products and services relating to a specific project.

Decision-making units vary in composition and size according to the nature of each individual purchasing task. Webster and Wind (1972) identified a number of people who undertake different roles within buying centres, and these are set out in Figure 2.4.

- **Initiators** start the whole process by requesting the purchase of an item. They may also assume other roles within the DMU or wider organization.
- **Users** literally use the product once it has been acquired and they will also evaluate its performance. Users may not only initiate the purchase process, but also sometimes be involved in the specification process. Their role is continuous, although it may vary from the highly involved to the peripheral.
- **Influencers** very often help to set the technical specifications for the proposed purchase and assist the evaluation of alternative offerings by potential suppliers. These may be consultants hired to complete a particular project. An office furniture manufacturer, for example, will regard office managers as key decision-makers, but understand that specifiers, such as office designers and architects, influence the office manager's decision about furniture decision.
- **Deciders** are those who make purchasing decisions and they are the most difficult to identify. This is because they may not have formal authority to make a purchase decision, yet are sufficiently influential internally that their decision carries the most weight. In repeat-buying activities, the buyer (see below) may also be the decider. However, it is normal practice for a senior manager to authorize expenditure decisions involving sums over a certain financial limit.

- **Buyers** or *purchasing managers* select suppliers and manage the process whereby the required products are procured. Buyers may not decide which product is to be purchased, but they influence the framework within which the decision is made. They will formally undertake the process whereby products and services are purchased once a decision has been made to procure them. They may be formal buyers, for example, and kick-start the purchase of a type of lubricant because the stock figures have fallen to a threshold level that indicates that current supplies will be exhausted within three weeks. They will therefore assume the role of both an initiator and a buyer.
- **Gatekeepers** have the potential to control the type and flow of information to the organization and the members of the DMU. These gatekeepers may be assistants, technical personnel, secretaries, or telephone switchboard operators.

Processes of the Decision-Making Unit

There are three main types of buying situation. Referred to by Robinson and colleagues (1967) as 'buyclasses', these are: **new task**; **modified rebuy**; and **straight rebuy**. These are summarized in Table 2.3.

Buyclasses

New Task

As the name implies, the 'new task' buyclass sees the organization faced with a first-time buying situation. Risk is inevitably large at this point, because there is little collective experience of the product or service or of the relevant suppliers. As a result of these factors, there are normally a large number of decision participants. Each participant requires a lot of information, and a relatively long period of time is needed for the information to be assimilated and a decision to be made.

Table 2.3 Main characteristics of the buyclasses

Buyclass	Degree of familiarity with the problem	Information requirements	Alternative solutions
New buy	Problem fresh to decision makers	Great deal of information required	Alternative solutions unknown; all considered new
Modified rebuy	Requirement not new, but different from previous situations	More information required, but past experience of use	Buying decision needs new solutions
Rebuy	Problem identical to previous experiences	Little or no information required	Alternative solutions not sought or required

Source: Fill and Turnbull (2016). Reproduced with the kind permission of Pearson Education Ltd.

Modified Rebuy

Having purchased a product, uncertainty is reduced, but not eliminated, so the organization may request through its buyer(s) that certain modifications be made to future purchases, such as adjustments to the specification of the product, further negotiation on price levels, or perhaps an arrangement for alternative delivery patterns. Fewer people are involved in the 'modified rebuy' decision-making process than in the new task situation.

Straight Rebuy

In the 'straight rebuy' situation, the purchasing department reorders on a routine basis, very often working from an approved list of suppliers. These may be products that an organization consumes to keep operating (for example office stationery), or may be low-value materials used within the operational, value-added part of the organization (for example the manufacturing processes). No other people are involved with the exercise until different suppliers attempt to change the environment in which the decision is made. For example, a new supplier may interrupt the procedure with a potentially better offer. This may stimulate the emergence of a modified rebuy situation.

Straight rebuy presents classic conditions for the use of automatic reordering systems. Costs can be reduced, managerial time redirected to other projects, and the relationship between buyer and seller embedded within a stronger framework. One possible difficulty is that both parties perceive the system to be a significant exit barrier should conditions change and this may deter flexibility or restrict opportunities to develop the same or other relationships.

Visit the **online resources** and follow the web link to Electronic Commerce Europe, the biggest online trade network in the world, for more information on the use of electronic B2B purchasing.

Buyphases

Organizational buyer behaviour (OBB) consists of a series of sequential activities through which organizations proceed when making purchasing decisions. Robinson and colleagues (1967) referred to these as 'buying stages' or 'buyphases'. The following sequence of buyphases is particular to the new task situation just described. Many of these buyphases can be ignored or compressed according to the complexity of the offering and when either a modified rebuy or straight rebuy situation is encountered.

Need/Problem Recognition

The need/problem recognition phase is about the identification of a gap between the benefits an organization is experiencing now and the benefits it would like to experience. For example, when a new product is to be produced, there is an obvious gap between having the necessary materials and components and being out of stock and unable to build. The first decision is therefore about how to close this gap and there are two broad options: outsourcing the whole or parts of the production process; or building or making the objects in-house. Thus the need has been recognized and the gap identified.

The rest of this section is based on a build decision being taken.

Product Specification

As a result of identifying a problem and the size of the gap, influencers and users can determine the desired characteristics of the product needed to resolve the problem. This may take the form of either a general functional description or a much more detailed analysis and the creation of a detailed technical specification for a particular product. What sort of photocopier is required? What is it expected to achieve? How many documents should it copy per minute? Is a collator or tray required? This is an important part of the process, because if it is executed properly, it will narrow the supplier search and save on the costs associated with evaluation prior to a final decision. The results of the functional and detailed specifications are often combined within a purchase order specification.

Supplier and Product Search

At the supplier and product search stage, the buyer actively seeks suppliers who can supply the necessary product(s). There are two main issues at this point: first, will the product match the specification and the required performance standards; and second, will the potential supplier meet the other organizational requirements such as experience, reputation, accreditation, and credit rating? In most circumstances, organizations review the market and their internal sources of information, then arrive at a decision that is based on rational criteria.

Evaluation of Proposals

Depending on the complexity and value of the potential order(s), the proposal is a vital part of the process and should be prepared professionally. The proposals from the shortlisted organizations are reviewed in the context of two main criteria: the purchase order specification; and the evaluation of the supplying organization. If the potential supplier is already a part of the network, little search and review time is needed. If the proposed supplier is not part of the network, a review may be necessary to establish whether it will be appropriate (in terms of price, delivery, and service) and whether there is the potential for a long-term relationship or whether this is a single purchase that is unlikely to be repeated.

Supplier Selection

The DMU will normally undertake a supplier analysis and use a variety of decision criteria, according to the particular type of item sought. A further useful perspective is to view supplier organizations as a continuum, from reliance on a single source through to the use of a wide variety of suppliers for the same product. Some companies maintain a range of multiple sources (a practice of many government departments). The major disadvantage is that this approach fails to drive cost as low as possible, because the discounts derived from volume sales are not achieved. The advantage to the buying centre is that a relatively small investment is required and little risk is entailed in following such a strategy. At the other end of the continuum are organizations that use only a single-source supplier. All purchases are made from the single source until circumstances change to such a degree that the buyer's needs are no longer being satisfied. An increasing number of organizations are choosing to enter alliances with a limited number of, or even single-source, suppliers. The objective is to build a long-term relationship, to work together to build quality, and for each to help the other to achieve its goals. Outsourcing manufacturing activities for non-core activities has increased considerably.

Evaluation

The order is written for the selected supplier, which is then monitored and evaluated against such diverse criteria as responsiveness to enquiries, modifications to the specification, and timing of delivery. When the product is delivered, it may reach the stated specification, but fail to satisfy the original need. In this case, the specification needs to be rewritten before any future orders are placed. Developments in the environment can impact on organizational buyers, changing both the nature of decisions and the way in which they are made. The decision to purchase new plant and machinery, for example, requires consideration of the future cash flows generated by the capital item. Many people will be involved in the decision and the time necessary for consultation may mean that other parts of the decision-making process are completed simultaneously.

Visit the **online resources** and complete Internet Activity 2.3. This will help you to learn about the seven buying phases through which organizations go when purchasing industrial goods and services.

Market Insight 2.4 **Connecting Buyers and Suppliers**

A B2B online marketplace enables exporters, importers, brokers, and retailers from across the globe to interact with a view to developing buying and selling opportunities. The platform can have a huge influence on purchase decisions.

Alibaba.com is perhaps the world's leading platform for global wholesale trade. The portal brings together sellers, by giving them the tools necessary to reach a global audience for their products, and buyers, by helping them to find products and suppliers quickly and efficiently.

'Gandys', established in 2011 by brothers Rob and Paul Forkan, is a footwear brand based on stylish and fun flip-flops. Orphaned by the 2004 tsunami, the brothers decided to set up a social enterprise to make a range of authentic flip-flops. To find the right manufacturer, they used Alibaba.com. After entering their requirements in the online system, they were provided with a list of suitable product manufacturers. Following discussions with several nominated suppliers, a few prototypes were developed. By 2013, more than 100 UK boutiques were selling Gandys. To grow, Rob and Paul needed investment, and they achieved this through a reverse *Dragons' Den* type of process. This involved inviting several potential wealthy investors to a

Rob and Paul founded Gandys to support their Orphans for Orphans foundation by donating 10 per cent of their profits to help underprivileged children who were affected by the 2004 tsunami.

Source: Courtesy of Gandys.

Market Insight 2.4 (continued)

Imprinted into each design are a myriad travel experiences combined to express Rob and Paul's unique upbringing and adventurous nature.

Source: Courtesy of Gandys.

Brixton pub and asking them to compete for the chance to invest.

The Alibaba.com platform also supplies a range of added-value services designed to support the primary transactional processes. These include training, finance, inspection, and logistics.

1 **Make a list of the efficiencies that an online platform can bring to buyer–seller transactions.**

2 **How does this type of platform assist the relationships between buyers and sellers?**

3 **Visit Alibaba.com, then list the advantages and disadvantages of using the site from a marketing perspective.**

Sources: Plummer (2014); Seager (2014); http://www.alibaba.com; http://www.gandysflipflops.com.

Research Insight 2.2

To take your learning further, you might wish to read this influential paper.

Johnston, W. J., and Lewin, J. E. (1996) 'Organizational buying behavior: Toward an integrative framework', ***Journal of Business Research*****, 35(1): 1–15.**

Although written in 1996, this paper is important, because it includes critical contributions by the leading researchers, including the work of Robinson and colleagues (1967), Webster and Wind (1972), and Sheth (1973). The paper concludes by developing a model of buying behaviour drawing on a number of constructs developed since these three leading models were published.

 **Visit the online resources to read the abstract and access the full paper.**

Purchasing in Organizations

All organizations have to buy a variety of products and services to operate normally and achieve their performance targets. What we have set out so far are the general principles, types, and categories associated with organizational buying. The way in which organizations buy products and services, however, varies considerably and does not always fit neatly with the categories presented here. Professional purchasing is not only an important (if not critical) feature, but also, for many organizations, an integral part of their overall operations and strategic orientation (Ryals and Rogers, 2006; Pressey et al., 2007).

A common approach is to reduce the number of suppliers, sometimes to only one, and to use **strategic procurement** (as it is often termed) to negotiate with suppliers on a cooperative basis, to help to build long-term relationships. Purchasing has become an integral and strategic part of an organization's operations, and managing a smaller number of suppliers can improve performance considerably. For example, Senn and colleagues (2013: 27) report that Airbus reduced its supplier portfolio by over 80 per cent, from 3,000 to 500.

There are several strategic issues related to the purchasing activities undertaken by organizations. First, there is the 'make or buy' decision. Should organizations make and/or assemble products for resale, or outsource or buy in particular products, parts, services, or sub-assemblies, and concentrate on what is referred to as 'core' activities or competences? Second, the benefits that arise through closer cooperation with suppliers and the increasing influence of buyer–seller relationships and 'joint value creation' have inevitably led to a tighter, more professional, and integrated purchasing function. The third strategy-related issue concerns the degree to which the purchasing function is integrated into the organization. New information technology (IT) systems have raised the level of possible integration of purchasing and operations to the extent that the competitive strength of the organization is enhanced (Hemsworth et al., 2008). As though to highlight the variation in approaches to purchasing behaviour, Svahn and Westerlund (2009) identify six principal purchasing strategies used by organizations, as follows.

- The *price minimizer* purchasing strategy refers to a buyer's efficiency orientation whereby the main purchasing goal is to seek the lowest price for the offering. To help to achieve this, the buyer actively promotes competition among several potential suppliers.
- The *bargainer* purchasing strategy focuses on a dyadic buyer–seller relationship. Here, the buyer's strategy is to achieve operational efficiency through long-term collaboration with a selected supplier (Håkansson and Snehota, 1995).
- The *clockwiser* purchasing strategy refers to network relationships that function predictably and precisely, just as a clock works. Again, the goal is strict efficiency, achieved through the vigilant integration of production-based integrated control systems and IT, and the careful coordination of the value activities performed by each supply network partner (Glenn and Wheeler, 2004).
- The *adaptator* purchasing strategy focuses on adapting the manufacturing processes between the exchange parties. This can arise during the purchase of one major product or service when the seller is required to accommodate its offering to the particular needs of the buyer.
- The *projector* purchasing strategy occurs between buyers and sellers who are development partners. This can occur during projects when partners develop their offerings in close collaboration, after which the joint-development project is completed and the parties continue the development work independently. As an example of this strategy, we could explore the collaboration between Nokia and Skype. These major players in the information and communication technology (ICT) industry joined their development efforts to develop a radically novel type of mobile phone that utilizes the Voice-over-Internet Protocol (VoIP) service (the free call system created by Skype).

- The *updater* purchasing strategy is based on collaboration in research and development. Here, collaboration between partners is continuous and the nature of the relationship is not a dyad, but a supply network. This collaboration is intentional, as demonstrated by Intel and various personal computer (PC) manufacturers, who produce updated versions of PCs based on constant co-development.

Chapter Summary

To consolidate your learning, the key points from this chapter are summarized here.

- **Explain the consumer product acquisition process.**

  The consumer product acquisition model has six key stages: motive development; information gathering; product evaluation; product selection; acquisition; and re-evaluation.

- **Explain the processes involved in human perception, learning, and memory in relation to consumer choice.**

  The human perception, learning, and memory processes involved in consumer decision-making are complex. When designing advertising, developing distribution strategies, designing new offerings, and implementing other marketing tactics, marketers should (repeatedly) explain the information associated with these actions to consumers. Such an approach is necessary to encourage consumers to engage with, remember, and learn about different offerings, which in turn influences consumers' buying decisions.

- **Understand the importance of personality and motivation in consumer behaviour.**

  Consumers are motivated differently in their purchasing behaviours depending on their personalities and social identities, and, to some extent, how they feel their personality or social identity fits with particular offerings. Maslow's (1943) seminal work on human needs helps us to understand how we are motivated to satisfy five key human desires. From the theory of planned behaviour (Ajzen, 1991), we know that how we intend to behave is not always how we actually behave, because this is affected by our attitudes towards the behaviour in question, subjective norms (how we think others perceive that behaviour), and our own perceptions of how we can control our behaviour.

- **Set out the main processes and stages associated with organizational buying and purchasing.**

  Organizational buying behaviour can be understood to be a group buying activity in which a number of people with differing roles make purchasing decisions that affect the organization and the achievement of its objectives. Buying decisions can be understood in terms of different types of decision (buyclasses) and different stages (buyphases).

Review Questions

1. **What is the process through which consumers go when buying offerings?**
2. **How are the psychological concepts of perception, learning, and memory relevant to understanding consumer choice?**

3 **How are concepts of personality relevant to understanding consumer behaviour?**

4 **How are concepts of motivation relevant to understanding consumer behaviour?**

5 **What is the theory of planned behaviour?**

6 **What are opinions, attitudes, and values, and how do they relate to consumer behaviour?**

7 **How does lifestyle and ethnicity influence how we buy?**

8 **Name four of the different types of person that make up a decision-making unit.**

9 **Distinguish clearly between buyphases and buyclasses.**

10 **What are the main purchasing strategies adopted by organizations?**

Worksheet Summary

To apply the knowledge that you have gained from this chapter and test your understanding of customer buying behaviour, visit the **online resources** and complete Worksheet 2.1.

Discussion Questions

1 Having read Case Insight 2.1 at the beginning of this chapter, how should Holdz® develop its matting solution for its bouldering centre corporate customers to take account of the considerable volumes of feet-first falls from climbers, but still allow Holdz® to generate a reasonable profit?

2 Describe the purchasing process that you would use in the following instances using the consumer product acquisition model shown in Figure 2.1.

- A A chocolate bar, for example a Snickers or Cadbury's Dairy Milk in the UK, Plopp in Sweden, or Droste in the Netherlands
- B A flight to the Caribbean from your home country
- C A tablet computer to help you to write essays and complete group work for your marketing course
- D A dishwasher
- E Refuse collection services from the local council (paid for indirectly through local taxes)

3 Use the theory of planned behaviour to explain consumer motivations to pursue the following behaviours.

- A A purchase of a room at Raffles Hotel, Singapore
- B A visit to the Abba Museum in Stockholm
- C Voting during an election in France
- D Sky diving in California

4 Using PowerPoint, prepare a short presentation in which you explain the meaning of 'decision-making unit', 'buyclasses', and 'buyphases'.

Visit the **online resources** and complete the multiple-choice questions to assess your knowledge of this chapter.

Glossary

attitudes refers to the mental states of individuals that underlie the structuring of perceptions and guide behavioural response.

buyclasses the different types of buying situation faced by organizations.

buyers also known as 'purchasing managers', these people select suppliers and manage the process whereby the required products are procured.

buying centre *see* **decision-making unit**

buyphases the series of sequential activities or stages through which organizations proceed when making purchasing decisions.

classical conditioning a theory of learning propounded by Russian physiologist Ivan Pavlov, who carried out a series of experiments with his dogs. He realized that if he were to ring a bell before serving food, the dogs would automatically associate the sound of the bell (the conditioned stimulus) with the presentation of the food (the unconditioned stimulus), and begin salivating. Classical conditioning occurs when the unconditioned stimulus becomes associated with the conditioned stimulus.

cognition a psychological term relating to the action of thinking about something. Our opinions are cognitive—that is, mental structures formed about something in our minds.

cognitive dissonance a psychological theory proposed by Leon Festinger in 1957, which states that we are motivated to re-evaluate our beliefs, attitudes, opinions, or values if the position we hold on them at one point in time does not concur with the position held at an earlier period owing to some intervening event, circumstance, or action.

deciders people who make organizational purchasing decisions; often very difficult to identify.

decision-making unit a group of people who make purchasing decisions on behalf of an organization.

evoked set a group of goods, brands, or services for a specific item brought to mind in a particular purchasing situation and from which a person makes a decision as to which product, brand, or service to buy.

gatekeepers people who control the type and flow of information into an organization, and in particular to members of the decision-making unit.

influencers people who help to set the technical specifications for a proposed purchase and assist the evaluation of alternative offerings by potential suppliers.

initiators people who start the organizational buying decision process.

intention in the consumer context, linked to whether or not we are motivated to purchase a good or service.

involvement the greater the personal importance people attach to a given communication message, the more involvement they are said to have with that communication.

media facilities used by companies to convey or deliver messages to target audiences; plural of medium.

modified rebuy the organizational processes associated with the infrequent purchase of products and services.

new task the organizational processes associated with buying a product or service for the first time.

operant conditioning a learning theory developed by B. F. Skinner, which suggests that when a subject acts on a stimulus from the environment (antecedents), this is more likely to result in a particular behaviour (behaviour) if that behaviour is reinforced (consequence) through reward or punishment.

opinions refers to observable verbal responses given by individuals to an issue or question; easily affected by current affairs and discussions with significant others.

organizational buyer behaviour the characteristics, issues, and processes associated with the behaviour of producers, resellers, government units, and institutions when purchasing goods and services.

overt search the point in the buying process at which a consumer seeks further information in relation to a product or buying situation, according to the Howard–Sheth model of buyer behaviour.

perception a mental picture based on existing attitudes, beliefs, needs, stimulus factors, and factors specific to our situation, which governs our attitudes and behaviour towards objects, events, or people in the world about us.

personality that aspect of our psyche which determines the way in which we respond to our environment in a relatively stable way over time.

recall a measure of advertising effectiveness based on what an individual is able to remember about an advert.

recognition refers to the process whereby new images and words are compared with existing images and words in memory and a match is found.

social class a system of classification of consumers or citizens, based on the socio-economic status of the chief income earner in a household, typically into various subgroupings of middle class and working class.

social grade a system of classification of people based on their socio-economic group, usually based on the household's chief income earner.

social learning a theory, advocated by Albert Bandura, which suggests that we can learn from observing the experiences of others, and that, in contrast with operant conditioning, we can delay gratification and even administer our own rewards or punishment.

straight rebuy the organizational processes associated with the routine reordering of good and services, often undertaken from an approved list of suppliers.

strategic procurement an approach used to negotiate with suppliers on a cooperative basis, to help to build long-term relationships.

users people or groups who use business products and services once they have been acquired, and who then evaluate the performance of the products or services.

value the regard in which something is held, typically, although not always, expressed in financial terms.

References

Ajzen, I. (1991) 'The theory of planned behaviour', *Organisational Behaviour and Human Decision Processes*, 50(2): 179–211.

American Marketing Association (AMA) (2016) 'Dictionary'. Available online at https://www.ama.org/resources/Pages/Dictionary.aspx? [accessed 22 February 2016].

Antonetti, P., and Anesa, M. (2016) Consumer reactions to corporate tax strategies: The role of political ideology. Working paper on file with the author.

Antonetti, P., and Baines, P. (2016) Guilt trips: An integrated model of longitudinal persuasion through transportation. Working paper on file with the author.

Bandura, A. (1977) *Social Learning Theory*, Englewood Cliffs, NJ: Prentice-Hall.

Barford, V., and Holt, G. (2013) 'Google, Amazon, Starbucks: The rise of "tax shaming"', *BBC News*, 21 May. Available online at http://www.bbc.co.uk/news/magazine-20560359 [accessed 30 June 2016].

Bettinghaus, E. P., and Cody, M. J. (1994) *Persuasive Communication* (5th edn), London: Harcourt Brace.

Bettman, J. R. (1979) 'Memory factors in consumer choice: A review', *Journal of Marketing*, 43(2): 37–53.

Bruwer, J., and Li, E. (2007) 'Wine-related lifestyle (WRL) market segmentation: Demographic and behavior factors', *Journal of Wine Research*, 18(1): 19–34.

Coleman, R. P. (1983) 'The continuing significance of social class to marketing', *Journal of Consumer Research*, 10(3): 265–80.

Cui, G. (1997) 'Marketing strategies in a multi-ethnic environment', *Journal of Marketing Theory and Practice*, 5(1): 122–35.

Festinger, L. (1957) *A Theory of Cognitive Dissonance*, Palo Alto, CA: Stanford University Press.

Fill, C., and McKee, S. (2012) *Business Marketing*, Oxford: Goodfellow.

Fill, C., and Turnbull, S. (2016) *Marketing Communications* (7th edn), London: Pearson.

Gil, M., and Rosenberg, S. (2015) *The Multicultural Edge: Rising Super Consumers*. Available online at http://www.nielsen.com/content/dam/corporate/us/en/reports-downloads/2015-reports/the-multicultural-edge-rising-super-consumers-march-2015.pdf [accessed 2 March 2016].

Glenn, R. R., and Wheeler, A. R. (2004) 'A new framework for supply chain manager selection: Three hurdles to competitive advantage', *Journal of Marketing Channels*, 11(4): 89–103.

Håkansson, H., and Snehota, I. (1995) *Developing Relationships in Business Networks*, London: Routledge.

Hemsworth, D., Sánchez-Rodríguez, C., and Bidgood, B. (2008) 'A structural model of the impact of quality management practices and purchasing-related information systems on purchasing performance: A TQM perspective', *Total Quality Management & Business Excellence*, 19(1–2): 151–64.

Howard, J. A., and Sheth, J. N. (1969) *The Theory of Buyer Behavior*, New York: John Wiley.

Johnson, E. J., and Russo, J. E. (1978) 'The organisation of product information in memory identified by recall times', in K. Hunt (ed.) *Advances in Consumer Research, Vol. V*, Chicago, IL: Association for Consumer Research, 79–86.

Johnston, W. J., and Lewin, J. E. (1996) 'Organizational buying behavior: Toward an integrative framework', *Journal of Business Research*, 35(1): 1–15.

Marriage, M. (2014) 'Aggressive tax avoidance troubles large investors', *Financial Times*, 2 November. Available online at https://www.ft.com/content/e56ca00c-6010-11e4-98e6-00144feabdc0 [accessed 28 June 2016].

Martin, C. A., and Bush, A. J. (2000) 'Do role models influence teenagers' purchase intentions and behavior?', *Journal of Consumer Marketing*, 17(5): 441–54.

Maslow, A. H. (1943) 'A theory of motivation', *Psychological Review*, 50(4): 370–96.

Matzler, K., Bidmon, S., and Grabner-Kräuter, S. (2006) 'Individual determinants of brand affect: The role of the personality traits of extraversion and openness to experience', *Journal of Product and Brand Management*, 15(7): 427–34.

McRae, R. R., and Costa, P. T. (1987) 'Validation of the five-factor model of personality across instruments and observers', *Journal of Personality and Social Psychology*, 52(1): 81–90.

Michaelidou, N., and Dibb, S. (2008) 'Consumer involvement: A new perspective', *Marketing Review*, 8(1): 83–99.

Mindak, W. A. (1961) 'Fitting the semantic differential to the marketing problem', *Journal of Marketing*, 25(4): 29–33.

Mintel (2016) *Car Review: UK*, February. Available online at http://reports.mintel.com/display/747599/ [accessed 25 February 2016].

Moschis, G. P., and Churchill, G. A., Jr (1978) 'Consumer socialisation: A theoretical and empirical analysis', *Journal of Marketing Research*, 15(4): 599–609.

Mulyanegara, R. C., Tsarenko, Y., and Anderson, A. (2009) 'The Big Five and brand personality: Investigating the impact of consumer personality on preferences towards particular brand personality', *Journal of Brand Management*, 16(4): 234–47.

Parkinson, S. T., and Baker, M. J. (1994) *Organizational Buying Behaviour: Purchasing and Marketing Management Implications*, London: Macmillan.

Peugeot (2016) 'PSA Peugeot Citroën worldwide sales up 1.2% in 2015', 12 January. Available online at http://www.peugeot.co.uk/news/psa-peugeot-citroen-worldwide-sales-up-in-2015/ [accessed 25 February 2016].

Plummer, R. (2014) 'Gandys Flip Flops: Footwear with soul', *BBC News*, 15 June. Available online at http://www.bbc.co.uk/news/business-27638426 [accessed 22 January 2016].

Pressey, A., Tzokas, N., and Winklhofer, H. (2007) 'Strategic purchasing and the evaluation of "problem" key supply relationships: What do key suppliers need to know?', *Journal of Business & Industrial Marketing*, 22(5): 282–94.

Robinson, P. J., Faris, C. W., and Wind, Y. (1967) *Industrial Buying and Creative Marketing*, Boston, MA: Allyn & Bacon.

Ryals, L. J., and Rogers, B. (2006) 'Holding up the mirror: The impact of strategic procurement practices on account management', *Business Horizons*, 49(1): 41–50.

Seager, C. (2014) 'Five minutes with . . . Gandys flip flops' co-founders, Rob and Paul', *The Guardian*, 9 January. Available online at http://www.theguardian.com/social-enterprise-network/2014/jan/09/gandys-flip-flops-orphans-for-orphans-social-enterprise [accessed 23 January 2016].

Senecal, S., and Nantal, J. (2004) 'The influence of online product recommendations on consumers' online choices', *Journal of Retailing*, 80(2): 159–69.

Senn, C., Thoma, A., and Yip, G. S. (2013) 'Customer-centric leadership: How to manage strategic customers as assets in B2B markets', *California Management Review*, 55(3): 27–59.

Sheth, J. N. (1973) 'A model of industrial buyer behavior', *Journal of Marketing*, 37(4): 50–6.

Siciliano, L. (2014) 'Watch: Graphic anti-smoking ad shows father rolling and smoking rotting flesh', *The Telegraph*, 29 December. Available online at http://www.telegraph.co.uk/news/health/11315959/Watch-Graphic-anti-smoking-ad-shows-father-rolling-and-smoking-rotting-flesh.html [accessed 28 February 2016].

Skinner, B. F. (1954) 'The science of learning and the art of teaching', Harvard Educational Review, 24(2): 88–97.

Svahn, S., and Westerlund, M. (2009) 'Purchasing strategies in supply relationships', Journal of Business & Industrial Marketing, 24(3–4): 173–81.

Ulkuniemi, P. (2003) Purchasing Software Components at the Dawn of Market. Available online at http://herkules.oulu.fi/isbn9514272188/ [accessed 5 September 2006].

Webster, F. E., and Wind, Y. (1972) *Organizational Buying Behaviour*, Englewood Cliffs, NJ: Prentice Hall.

Wells, W. D., and Gubar, G. (1966) 'Life cycle concept in marketing research', *Journal of Marketing Research*, 3(4): 355–63.

Chapter 3
Market Research and Customer Insight

Learning Outcomes

After studying this chapter, you will be able to:

- define the terms 'market research', 'marketing research', and 'customer insight';
- describe the customer insight process and the role of marketing research within it;
- explain the role of marketing research and list the range of possible research approaches;
- define the term 'big data' and describe its role in marketing;
- discuss the importance of ethics and the adoption of a code of conduct in marketing research; and
- understand the concept of 'equivalence' in relation to obtaining comparable data.

Case Insight 3.1
MESH Planning

Market Insight 3.1
Customer Insight at Royal Bank of Scotland

Market Insight 3.2
How Scent Sells Lingerie at Hunkemöller

Market Insight 3.3
Is Facebook Manipulating You?

Case Insight 3.1 MESH Planning

How should organizations measure the effectiveness of all touchpoints in interactions with customers, not only marketing communications? We speak to Fiona Blades (pictured), MESH Planning's chief experience officer, to find out more.

MESH Planning, an innovative market research agency, was set up in 2006. Fiona Blades had worked previously as an advertising planning director, seeing at first hand how organizations were seldom able to get the data they needed from traditional campaign evaluation, since these were often overly focused on television advertising. There was also a tendency to believe that because advertising effectiveness questions were added to **brand health** monitoring, it was advertising that caused changes in brand health, when this is often not the case. In fact, MESH data shows that usage is the most influential **touchpoint** for almost all categories of offering. Results of traditional campaign analysis were always reported well after the campaign, making it too late to make interim changes. MESH Planning's response was to develop a research process to measure touchpoint effectiveness using a process called 'real-time experience tracking' (RET). This focuses on experiences that capture the essence of what brands are made of, not interim measures.

Real-time experience tracking fuses a number of different data sources, using traditional survey data, as well as analysing experiences quantitatively, and then applying statistical measurements to them and viewing qualitative comments. Because MESH has planners (account planners and media planners), as well as researchers, the output for the client is more recommendation/action-focused than findings/ research-focused.

Clients come to MESH because RET collects people's responses to different touchpoints, including those that they have not been able to get before (such as seeing whether it is television, online, or retail activity that drives brand consideration). The approach is faster and more cost-effective than previous tools, such as **market mix modelling.** Beyond marketing campaigns, clients want to understand the impact of retail activity and the path to purchase. MESH clients have reported good results with RET: Energizer executives calculated that the new measures led to a threefold improvement in advertising cost-effectiveness, increasing Energizer's revenue in the razor category by 10 per cent in less than four months; LG Electronics won the coveted POPAI award for retail marketing effectiveness and attributed this to working with MESH; and BSkyB re-evaluated how to spend £150 million per annum using RET analytics.

Gatorade, another client, decided to reposition its offering from the sports drink category to sports nutrition. Its launch in Mexico included television advertising, sponsorship, and an innovative channel strategy that used experiential channels such as gyms, fitness centres, and parks.

How might MESH design research to determine, if people were to experience an experiential touchpoint, whether having this experience impacted positively on their perceptions of the brand and, specifically, those related to Gatorade's sports nutrition attributes?

Introduction

How do companies develop their successful offerings? More often than not, companies develop propositions using research programmes designed to identify customers' changing needs.

Contemporary **marketing research** is very much affected by technology. Digitization has led to a proliferation of information and data being available to marketers. This shift in availability, often referred to as 'big data', is currently transforming the market research industry. Traditional market research companies, such as Gallup and A.C. Nielsen, are under pressure from large tech firms, such as IBM and Adobe, as well as fast-growing analytic companies, such as Brainjuicer and Qualtrics, offering a wide range of tools with which to track customer behaviours in real time (ESOMAR, 2015).

We begin this chapter by defining the difference between 'marketing research' and 'market research'. Whereas market research is conducted to understand markets—customers, competitors, and industries—marketing research also determines the impact of marketing strategies and tactics. Marketing research thus subsumes market research. 'Customer insight' refers to actionable knowledge about customers gained through research. We then introduce the different steps through which marketers need to go when conducting research. We also introduce big data, which is increasingly being used to generate insights that lead to strategic marketing decisions. Finally, we consider the challenges of conducting international marketing research.

The Customer Insight Process

In Chapter 2, we examined the fundamentals of customer behaviour. The customer insight process allows organizations to generate knowledge about consumers that is relevant to their specific circumstances. Market research is work undertaken to determine the structural characteristics of the industry of concern (for example demand, market share, market volumes, customer characteristics, and segmentation), whereas marketing research is work undertaken to understand how to make specific marketing strategy decisions (for example for pricing, sales forecasting, proposition testing, and promotion research). Marketing research is further characterized by being systematic, meaning that the procedures followed in each step of the research process are methodologically sound, well documented, and, as far as possible, planned in advance (Malhotra, 2010).

In contrast, customer insights are generated based on the knowledge gained by different research activities. Information requires transformation to generate insight. Customer insights are thus distinct from customer information: they are an acquired, deeper understanding of customers. 'Marketing analytics' refers to the mathematical and statistical analytical procedures used to distil insights out of high-volume, high-velocity, and/or high-variety information, typically denoted as 'big data'. We will discuss this further in the section 'Big Data and Marketing Analytics', but before doing so we will look at different steps in the insight generation and market research processes, respectively.

Visit the **online resources** and follow the web links to the Market Research Society (MRS) and ESOMAR to learn more about these professional marketing research associations.

A customer insight is of value if it is rare, difficult to imitate, and of potential use to formulate management decisions (Said et al., 2015). Cowan (2008) suggests that if organizations are to genuinely make use of insights:

- chief executive officers (CEOs) and/or chief marketing officers (CMOs) should recognize the importance of supporting the insight process, ask 'helicopter' (that is, wide-ranging) questions, not try to guess the answers to strategic problems, demand evidence-based answers, and provide the necessary resources;
- researchers should view themselves as problem-solvers, not reporters, focus on trying to gain a causal understanding, not only describing attitudes, and focus on changing the marketing situation; and
- insight managers should challenge the strategy assumptions that the organization is making, challenge the 'obvious' solution, since it is often wrong, analyse and combine all existing relevant data, and devote greater resources to extracting insight.

Market Insight 3.1 **Customer Insight at Royal Bank of Scotland**

The Royal Bank of Scotland (RBS) Group is a British company operating a number of leading brands in banking and insurance. After the financial crisis of 2007–08, which severely affected its financial viability and required a significant injection of capital from the British government, RBS has focused on improving its customer insight processes towards delivering a superior customer experience to that of its competitors. (See Chapter 12 for more information on customer experience.)

RBS puts customer insight at the heart of its service delivery.

Source: © chrisdorney/Shutterstock.

Over the last six years, RBS has developed a unique approach that involves systematically collecting information from employees, customers, and internal accounting systems. The objective is to match, for each service developed by the bank, employee perceptions, customer feedback, and data about the cost to serve of a certain activity to the bank. The RBS customer insight process therefore usually follows four phases.

1 Internal workshops are conducted to determine the key phases of service delivery for any product offered by the bank. In the case of a mortgage, for example, the workshops will focus on detailing all of the steps that the customer takes, from the initiation of the application down to the management of the mortgage.

2 Marketing research is conducted with customers to evaluate the feedback on each of these dimensions. For example, customers are asked to evaluate their satisfaction with the application process, the management of the mortgage, the clarity of RBS' procedures, etc.

Market Insight 3.1 (continued)

3 RBS links customer feedback to information about the cost of each service. In this way, the company knows how different satisfaction judgments relate to the current level of spending. Is poor performance justified by low spending or is the company getting poor customer feedback in an area that is actually attracting significant resources?

4 Finally, once all of this information has been collated, managers can make strategic decisions about internal priorities for investment in relation to the bank's own positioning, as well as additional insight on its competitors.

The systematic application of this approach has yielded significant benefits for the company. Considering only the retail banking division of the company, the improvement in satisfaction is estimated to have generated around £50 million in additional revenues. Perhaps even more strikingly, the unique ability to link customer satisfaction with internal data about cost has allowed savings of around £150 million, while at the same time improving customer satisfaction.

1. **What functions of a company should be measured?**
2. **Data collection can be expensive. Is it necessary to collect feedback from customers, employees, and the general public?**
3. **What are the main strengths and weaknesses of RBS's approach?**

Source: Maklan et al. (2017).

Research Insight 3.1

To take your learning further, you might wish to read this influential paper:

Said, E., Macdonald, E. K., Wilson, H. N., and Marcos, J. (2015) 'How organisations generate and use customer insight', *Journal of Marketing Management*, 31(9–10): 1158–79.

In this article, the authors investigate how organizations generate and use customer insights. Based on case studies of four organizations in different sectors—charity, telecoms, training, and information technology (IT)—they develop a framework for insight generation and insight use. The results show that insight generation requires alignment between market research providers, internal insight specialists, and internal insights users. What is more, the authors highlight the role of insights in aiding interpretation of research results, as well as dealing with information overload. This framework provides a starting point for (re)designing processes within and beyond the firm to optimize insight generation and use.

 Visit the **online resources** to read the abstract and access the full paper.

Commissioning Market Research

Much market research is not conducted in-house by marketers. When commissioning research, a client determines whether or not it wants to commission an agency, a consultant, a field and tabulation (tab) agency, or a data preparation and analysis agency. Typically, a consultant might do a job that does not require extensive fieldwork; a field and tab agency is used when the organization can design its own research, but not undertake the data collection; a data preparation and analysis agency, when it can both design and collect the data, but does not have the expertise to analyse it; and a **full-service agency**, when it does not have the expertise to design the research and collect or analyse the data.

Agencies are shortlisted according to criteria and asked to make a presentation of their services. Visits are made to their premises to check the quality of agency staff and facilities, and previous reports are considered to assess the quality of the agency's work. Permission to interview or obtain references from an agency's clients is usually requested. Each agency is evaluated based on its ability to undertake work of an acceptable quality at an appropriate price. The criteria used to evaluate an agency's suitability (after proposal submission) includes:

- the agency's reputation;
- the agency's perceived expertise;
- whether the study offers value for money;
- the time taken to complete the study; and
- the likelihood that the research design will provide insights into the **management problem**.

Shortlisted agencies are given a preliminary outline of the client's needs in a **research brief**, and asked to provide proposals on research methodology, timing, and costs. After this, an agency is selected to undertake the work required. In the long term, clients are most satisfied with flexible agencies that avoid rigid research solutions and demonstrate professional knowledge of the industry, an ability to focus on the management problem, and provide solutions, and consistent service quality (Cater and Zabkar, 2009).

The Marketing Research Process

There are numerous basic stages that guide a marketing research project (see Figure 3.1). The first, most crucial, stage involves problem definition and setting the information needs of the decision-makers. The client organization explains the basis of the problem(s) it faces to the market researcher. This might be the need to understand market volumes in a potential new market or the reason for an unexpected sudden increase in uptake of an offering. Problem definition does not always imply that threats face the organization. The initial stage allows the organization to assess its current position, define its information needs, and make informed decisions about its future.

Stage 1: Problem Definition

The first step in a market research project is defining the management problem and writing the research brief. It is important that these are not expressed in vague terms, because organizations

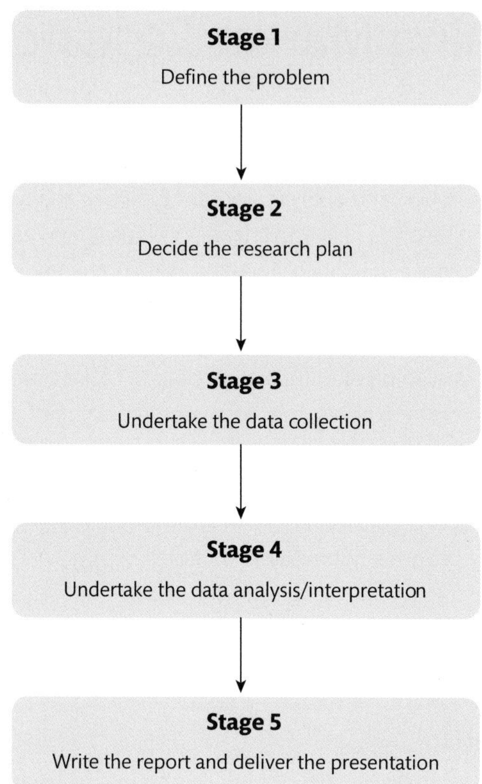

Figure 3.1 The marketing research process

Source: Baines and Chansarkar (2002). © John Wiley & Sons. Reproduced with permission.

are not always sure what information they require. An example might be Carrefour, the supermarket chain, explaining that sales are not as strong as expected in its Czech Republic stores and wondering whether or not this is a result of the emergence of a competitor supermarket (see Figure 3.2).

Carrefour, the French supermarket chain, operates globally.

Source: © PhotoStock10/Shutterstock.

The problem description provides the researcher with relatively little depth of understanding of the situation in which the supermarket finds itself, so the researcher needs to discuss the problem with the staff commissioning the study to investigate further. This allows the researcher to translate the management problem into a marketing research question. Typically, this question may include a number of sub-questions for further exploration. An example of a marketing research question and a number of more specific sub-questions is shown in Figure 3.3.

Management problem

Sales at the new store have not met management expectations, possibly owing to the emergence of a new competitor

Figure 3.2 Example of a management problem

The marketing research question transforms the management problem into a question while trying to remove any assumptions made by the organization's management. The more clearly the commissioning organization defines the management problem, the easier it is for the agency to design the research to solve that problem. Once the agency discusses the brief with the client, the agency provides a detailed outline of how it will investigate the problem. This document is called the **research proposal**. Figure 3.4 briefly outlines a typical marketing research proposal.

Stage 2: Decide the Research Plan

Once the marketing research question(s) have been decided, it is time to develop a research plan. At this stage, the framework for conducting the project is developed. In developing this framework, marketing researchers need to consider what type of research is needed. The market research need can be specified based on objective (exploratory, descriptive, or causal research), as well as source (primary vs secondary data) and methodology (qualitative vs quantitative). The research need will have implications for the design of the research plan.

Type of Market Research Based on Objectives

There are three types of research depending on the management problem that the research should solve. These include the following:

1 **Exploratory research** is used when little is known about a particular management problem and it needs to be explored further. Exploratory designs enable the development of hypotheses or help in developing new concepts.

2 **Descriptive research** focuses on accurately describing the variables being considered, such as market characteristics or spending patterns in key customer groups. Examples are consumer profile studies, usage studies, attitude surveys, and media research.

Marketing research question

Why are sales levels not meeting management expectations?

1. Sub-question: Has customer disposable income in the area declined over the last six months?
2. Sub-question: Is a new competitor, Tesco, taking away customers?
3. Sub-question: Are customers tired/bored of the current product range in the existing supermarket?
4. Sub-question: Are customers conducting more of their shopping online?
5. Sub-question: Were management expectations set too high and/or market potential overestimated?

Figure 3.3 Example of a marketing research question

The basic structure and contents of a typical research proposal should include the following.

- **Executive Summary**—A brief summary of the research project including the major outcomes and findings. Rarely more than one page in length. It allows the reader to obtain a summary of the main points of the project without having to read the full report.
- **Background to the Research**—An outline of the problem or situation and the issues surrounding this problem. This section demonstrates the researcher's understanding of the management problem.
- **Research Objectives**—An outline of the objectives of the research project, including the data to be generated and how this will be used to address the management problem.
- **Research Design**—A clear, non-technical description of the research type adopted and the specific techniques to be used to gather the required information. This will include details of data-collection instruments, sampling procedures, and analytical techniques.
- **Personnel Specification**—The details of the people involved in the collection and analysis of the data, providing a named liaison person and outlining the company's credibility in undertaking the work.
- **Time Schedule**—An outline of the time requirements with dates for the various stages to completion and presentation of results.
- **Costs**—A detailed analysis of the costs involved in the project is usually included for large projects or simply a total cost for the project.
- **References**—Typically, three references are outlined, so that a client can be sure that an agency has the requisite capability to do the job in hand.

Figure 3.4 A marketing research proposal outline

3 **Causal research** is used to determine whether or not one variable causes an effect in another variable. To determine causality, experimental or longitudinal studies are needed. Experimental studies are characterized by the marketing researchers manipulating a specific variable (cause) thought to influence important outcomes (effect), thereby allowing them to carefully test causation. Longitudinal studies, on the other hand, track the effect of a certain variable (cause) over time. Examples of causal research are studies of customer satisfaction and advertising effectiveness, which typically set out to understand what factors of an offer or an advert impact on consumer evaluations.

Type of Market Research Based on Source

When conducting market research, we can either use what is already known or devise research that creates new knowledge. **Primary research** is research conducted for the first time, involving the collection of data for the purpose of a particular project. Secondary data is second-hand data, collected for someone else's purposes. **Secondary research** (also known as **desk research**) involves gaining access to the results of previous research projects. This method can be a cheaper and more efficient process of data collection. Common sources of secondary data include:

- government sources, such as export databases, government statistics, social trend databases, and other resources;
- the Internet, including sources identified using search engines, blogs and microblogs, and discussion groups;
- company internal records, including information housed in a marketing information or customer relationship management (CRM) system or published in reports;

- professional bodies and trade associations, which frequently have databases available online for research purposes, and may also publish industry magazine articles and research reports; and
- market research companies, which frequently undertake research into industry sectors or specific product groups and can be highly specialized, for example Mintel, Euromonitor, ICC Keynote, and Google.

Visit the **online resources** and follow the web links to learn more about market research organizations.

In practice, most research projects involve both secondary and primary research, with desk research occurring initially to ensure that a company does not waste money. Once this initial insight is gleaned, the decision is made on whether or not it is necessary to commission a primary data study. Assuming that primary research needs to be undertaken, researchers usually design their research by considering what type of research to employ. Marketing directors should understand what types of study can be conducted, because this impacts on the type of information collected and hence the data that they receive to solve the management problem.

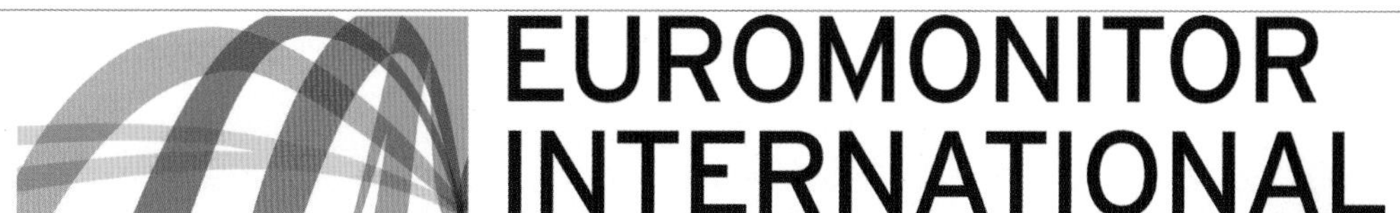

Euromonitor is well known for its in-depth industry reports, which can provide useful secondary data to inform marketing decision-making.

Source: Courtesy of Euromonitor.

Type of Market Research Based on Methodology

At the outset of a research project, we might consider whether to use **qualitative research** or **quantitative research**, or a combination of both.

- *Qualitative* research denotes research methodologies relying on small samples, using open and probing questions that set out to uncover underlying motives and feelings. The data gathered is then interpreted focusing on meanings and is typically quite hard to replicate. Typically, qualitative research is intended to provide insights and understanding of the problem setting, and thus it is frequently used in exploratory market research. The main methods for collecting qualitative data are individual interviews, focus groups, and observations.
- *Quantitative* research methods are used to elicit responses to predetermined standardized questions from many respondents. This involves collecting information, quantifying the responses as frequencies or percentages and descriptive statistics, and analysing them statistically. Quantitative research is thus commonly used in descriptive and causal marketing research, and replication is a highly desirable trait of the outcome of such research. Thus quantitative data collection methods are much more structured than qualitative data collection methods. Common methods include different types of surveys (online, offline), face-to-face or telephone interviews, and longitudinal studies.

Table 3.1 summarizes the key differences between qualitative and quantitative research methods. In many cases, qualitative and quantitative methods can be combined to generate insights from different perspectives.

Table 3.1	Qualitative and quantitative research methods compared

Characteristic	Qualitative	Quantitative
Purpose	Oriented towards discovery and exploration	Oriented towards cause and effect
Procedure	Emergent design; merges data collection and analysis	Predetermined design; separates data collection and analysis
Emphasis	Meaning and interpretation	What can be measured
Role of researcher	Involved; used as a 'research instrument'	Detached; uses standardized research instruments
Unit of analysis	Analyses a holistic system	Analyses specific variables
Size of sample	Involves a small number of respondents, typically fewer than 30	Involves a large number of respondents, more than 30
Sampling approach	Uses purposively selected samples	Tends to use **probability sampling** techniques

The client (or in-house research client) may also have specific budget constraints or know which particular approach it intends to adopt. However, the choice primarily depends on the circumstances of the research project and its objectives. If there is little advance understanding of the management problem, it would be better to explore the problem using qualitative research to gather insights. Globally, 73 per cent of marketing research investments is spent on quantitative research. In Portugal (95 per cent), Finland, and Sweden (both 92 per cent), the share is even higher, whereas it is typically lower in developing countries (ESOMAR, 2015). Industry surveys also indicate that marketers increasingly combine both qualitative and quantitative methods (Murphy, 2015).

Designing the Research Project

Once we know what type of research to conduct, we should consider:

- who to question and how (the sampling plan and procedures to be used);
- what methods to use (for example discussion groups or an experiment);
- which types of question are required (open questions for qualitative research or closed questions for a survey); and
- how the data should be analysed and interpreted (for example what approach to data analysis should be undertaken).

Research methods describe the techniques and procedures used to obtain the necessary information. We might use a survey or a series of in-depth interviews. We might use observation to see how

Market Insight 3.2 How Scent Sells Lingerie at Hunkemöller

Behavioural economics explores why people sometimes make irrational decisions and why their behaviour does not follow traditional economic models. It has produced hundreds of fascinating academic case studies, but many businesses find it hard to apply it in a way that produces real business advantage.

One exceptional example was when BrainJuicer and lingerie retailer Hunkemöller worked to create and test interventions, based around behavioural economic designs, in Hunkemöller stores in the Netherlands. Why did Hunkemöller want to use behavioural economics? There is a growing body of evidence of the immense importance of context to decision-making. This means that small interventions in the environment can have a small, but significant, impact on customer behaviour and sales. For instance, in a related study for a separate BrainJuicer client, introducing a brand logo at the point of sale was associated with a 4 per cent increase in purchases for that brand. Context—for example music, scent, and emotion—plays a huge part in shopper decisions, but shoppers hardly notice some of the most important factors, so researching it can be very difficult. The study explained how using scent in Hunkemöller stores led to a striking gain in average customer value.

BrainJuicer began by undertaking a behavioural audit of the retail environments of Hunkemöller stores, and consumers' behaviour within them, to design appropriate in-store interventions designed to increase sales. The experiment was designed using an alternating experimental and control store run over six weeks, alternating week on week, to measure the effect of using scent in stores as a 'prime'—that is, to make customers feel happy and romantic before buying Hunkemöller's lingerie. Store sales data were used for effectiveness data. This work was supplemented with a short questionnaire when customers exited the store, which was designed to uncover the extent to which they had enjoyed their visit and noticed the intervention (the scent prime).

BrainJuicer is an innovative UK-based market research agency.

Source: © BrainJuicer.

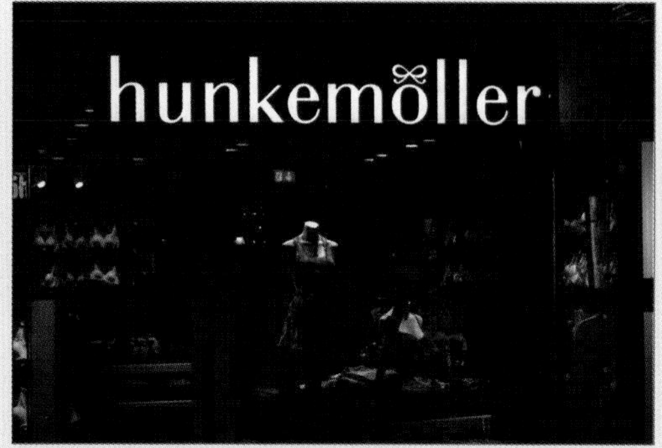

Hunkemöller uses behavioural economics to create and test interventions in its stores.

Source: © 360b/Shutterstock.

The experiments showed that in-store scent increased average customer basket value for Hunkemöller by 20 per cent. Hunkemöller would later roll out scent in all new and refurbished stores. The research also helped the company to develop protocols for undertaking behavioural economic research—running audits, creating interventions, and working with a research agency to make the interventions happen, and to understand how to prime customer emotion and satisfaction. The results of the research offered a strong argument for continuing the experimental, hands-on research approach rooted in behavioural science, backed up with traditional data. It is a method pointing to the future of research—away from what customers say and towards what they do.

Market Insight 3.2 (continued)

1 **Why do you think it was necessary to use a behavioural experimental approach?**

2 **Why is it necessary to use a control group in an experiment?**

3 **What other decision-making scenarios can you think of that might use the experimental approach?**

Sources: Goyal (2013); Leach and Bisnajak (2013); http://www.brainjuicer.com/html/stream/labs; http://www.Hunkemöller.com/en/about-us/corporate-info.html.

This case was kindly contributed by Orlando Wood, BrainJuicer, and Ashwien Bisnajak, Market Intelligence Manager, Hunkemöller.

consumers purchase goods online or how employees greet consumers when they enter a particular shop (that is, mystery shopping). We could use consumer panels whereby respondents record their weekly purchases or their television viewing habits over a specified time period. Nielsen Homescan is a service whereby consumers use specially developed barcode readers to record their supermarket purchases in return for points, which are redeemed for household goods. Nowadays, companies increasingly use online methods. According to a 2015 survey of CMOs, many marketers reported relying on digital online technology for understanding consumer needs: 40 per cent used online customer surveys; 26 per cent used online customer observations; 19 per cent used online customer experiments; and 6 per cent studied the online use of words of pictures by customers to gain insights (Moorman, 2015).

Figure 3.5 indicates the key considerations when designing qualitative and quantitative research projects. The design of marketing research projects involves determining how each of these components interrelates with the others. The components comprise:

- research objectives;
- the sampling method;
- the interviewing method to be used;
- the research type and methods undertaken;
- question and questionnaire design; and
- data analysis.

When designing research projects, we must first determine the type of approach to use for a given management problem (for example exploratory, descriptive, or causal). We then determine which techniques are most capable of producing the desired data at the least cost and in the minimum time period.

Generally, certain types of research (exploratory, descriptive, causal) use certain methods or techniques. Exploratory research studies, for example, use qualitative research methods, non-probability sampling methods, and non-statistical data analysis methods. Descriptive research projects often adopt survey interviews using quota or random sampling methods and statistical analysis techniques. Causal researchers use experimental research designs using convenience or probability sampling methods and statistical data analysis procedures.

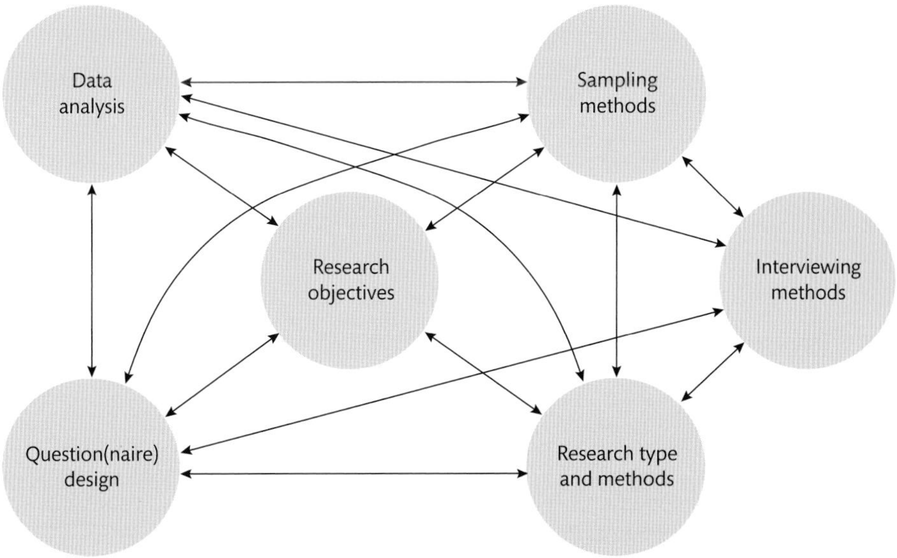

Figure 3.5 The major components of research design

Source: Baines and Chansarkar (2002). © John Wiley & Sons Ltd. Reproduced with permission.

Stage 3: Data Collection and Sampling

The third stage involves the conduct of fieldwork and the collection of data. At this stage, we send out questionnaires, or run the online focus group sessions, or conduct a netnographic study, depending on the decisions taken in the first design stage of the fieldwork. The procedures undertaken when conducting the fieldwork might relate to how to ask the questions of the respondents—whether this involves using the Internet, telephone, (e)mail, or in person—and how to select an appropriate sample, how to **pre-code** the answers to a questionnaire (quantitative research), or how to code the answers arising out of open-ended questions (particularly with qualitative research).

The market research manager might be concerned about whether or not to conduct the research in-company or to commission a field and tab agency. Other issues concern how to ensure high data quality. When market research companies undertake shopping mall intercept interviews, they usually re-contact a proportion of the respondents to check their answers to ensure that the interviews have been conducted properly.

In qualitative research, samples are often selected on a convenience or judgmental basis. In quantitative research, we might use either probability or non-probability methods, including:

- *simple random sampling*, whereby the population elements are accorded a number and a sample is selected by generating random numbers that correspond to the individual population elements;
- *systematic random sampling*, whereby population elements are known and the first sample unit is selected using random number generation, but after that each of the succeeding sample units is selected systematically on the basis of an *n*th number, where *n* is determined by dividing the population size by the sample size; or

- *stratified random sampling*, whereby a specific characteristic(s) is used (such as gender, age) to design homogeneous subgroups from which a representative random sample is drawn.

Non-random methods include:

- *quota sampling*, whereby criteria such as gender, ethnicity, or some other customer characteristics are used to restrict the sample, but the selection of the sample unit is left to the researcher's discretion;
- *convenience sampling*, whereby no such restrictions are placed on the selection of the respondents and anybody can be selected;
- *snowball sampling*, whereby respondents are selected from rare populations (such as buyers of high-performance cars), perhaps from among responses to newspaper adverts, and then further respondents are identified using referrals from the initial respondents, thereby 'snowballing' the sample.

With the growth of online market research, the reliance on Internet panels has become increasingly common. Two types of panel are used in online research (Miles, 2004).

- *Access panels*, which provide samples for survey-style information, are made up of targets especially invited by email to take part, with a link to a web survey.
- *Proprietary panels*, set up or commissioned by a client firm, are usually made up of that company's customers.

To encourage survey participation, the researchers use incentives (for example a prize draw).

Visit the **online resources** and complete Internet Activity 3.1 to learn more about Market Research Portal, a useful source of online research resources.

Stage 4: Data Analysis and Interpretation

The fourth stage comprises data input, analysis, and interpretation. Data input depends on the type of data collected. Increasingly, computer software applications are used for analysis of both qualitative and quantitative data (for example NVivo and **SPSS**, respectively). With

Research Insight 3.2

To take your learning further, you might wish to read the following influential paper.

Evans, J. R., and Mathur, A. (2005) 'The value of online surveys', *Internet Research*, 15(2): 195–219.

This highly cited paper outlines the strengths and weaknesses of undertaking online research. The article also compares online survey approaches with other survey formats, making it a particularly useful paper for those undertaking online research.

Visit the online resources to read the abstract and access the full paper.

online questionnaires, the data are automatically entered into a database, saving time and ensuring a higher level of data quality. If **computer-assisted personal interviewing** (CAPI) or **computer-assisted telephone interviewing** (CATI) methods are used, analysis can also occur instantaneously as the interviews are undertaken. **Computer-assisted web interviewing** (CAWI) techniques allow the researcher to read the questions from a computer screen and directly enter the responses of the respondents. Using the Internet, CAWI techniques can also allow the play-back of video and audio files.

Market research methods are used to aid managerial decision-making. Information obtained needs to be valid and reliable, because company resources are deployed on the basis of the information gleaned. **Validity** and **reliability** are important concepts, particularly in quantitative market research. They aid researchers in understanding the extent to which the data obtained from the study represent reality and 'truth'. Quantitative research methods rely on the degree to which the data elicited might be reproduced in a later study (that is, reliability) and the extent to which the data generated are bias-free (that is, valid).

'Validity' is defined as 'a criterion for evaluating measurement scales; it represents the extent to which a scale is a true reflection of the underlying variable or construct it is attempting to measure' (Parasuraman, 1991: 441). One way of measuring validity is for researchers to use their subjective judgment to ascertain whether an instrument is measuring what it is supposed to measure (content validity): a question asked about job satisfaction, for instance, does not necessarily infer loyalty to the organization.

'Reliability' is defined as 'a criterion for evaluating measurement scales; it represents how consistent or stable the ratings generated by a scale are' (Parasuraman, 1991: 443). Reliability is affected by the concepts of time, analytical bias, and questioning error. We can also distinguish between two types of reliability—that is, internal and external reliability (Bryman, 1989). To determine how reliable the data are, we conduct the study again over two or more time periods to evaluate the consistency of the data. This is known as the 'test–retest method' and measures external reliability. Another method used involves dividing the responses into two random sets and testing both sets independently, using ***t*-tests** or ***z*-tests**. This would illustrate internal reliability. The two different sets of results are then correlated. This method is known as 'split-half reliability testing'. These methods are more suited to testing the reliability of rating scales than data generated from qualitative research procedures. The results of a quantitative marketing research project are reliable if we conduct a similar research project within a short time period and the same or similar results are obtained in the second study. For example, if the marketing department of a travel agency chain were to interview 500 of its customers and discover that 25 per cent were in favour of a particular resort (perhaps a particular Greek island), and then repeat the study the following year and discover that only 10 per cent of the sample were interested in the same resort, the results of the first study could be said to be unreliable and chain's procurement department should not base its purchase of package holidays purely on the previous year's finding.

In qualitative research, concepts of validity and reliability are generally less important, because the data are not used to imply representativeness. Qualitative data are more about the generation of ideas and the formulation of hypotheses. Validity can be assured by sending out transcripts to respondents and/or clients for checking, to ensure that what they have said in in-depth interviews or focus groups was properly reproduced for analysis. When analysts read the data from a critical perspective to determine whether or not this fits with their expectations, this constitutes what is termed a '**face validity** test'. Reliability is often achieved by checking that similar statements are made by the range of respondents both across and within the interview transcripts. Interviewees' transcripts are checked to assess whether or not the same respondent, or other respondents, have made the discussion point.

Stage 5: Report Preparation and Presentation

The final stage of a research project involves reporting the results and the presentation of the findings of the study to the external or in-house client. The results should be presented free from bias. Marketing research data are of little use unless translated into a format that is meaningful to the manager or client who initially demanded the data. Senior people within the commissioning organization who may or may not have been involved in commissioning the work often attend presentations. Usually, agencies and consultants prepare their reports using a basic prewritten template.

Market and Advertisement Testing

Marketing research reveals attitudes to a campaign, brand, or some other aspect of the exchange process, whereas market testing, by comparison, measures actual behaviour. Market testing studies use **test markets** to carry out controlled experiments in specific country regions, where specific adverts can be shown before exposing the 'new feature' (offering, campaign, distribution, etc.) to a full national, or even international, launch. Another region or the rest of the market may act as the control group against which results can be measured. As an example, films are often test-screened before release because of the substantial cost of producing the film in the first place.

Marketing research is used to test advertisements, whether these are in print, online, or broadcast via radio or television. Research company Millward Brown International is renowned for this type of research. A variety of methods are used to test adverts. Typically, quantitative research is undertaken to test customer attitudes before and after exposure to see whether the advert has had a positive impact or not. In addition, research occurring after exposure to the advert tests the extent to which audiences can recognize a particular advert (for example by showing customers a copy of a still from a television advert, a print advert, or a photo online) or recall an advert without being shown a picture (that is, unaided recall). Qualitative research identifies and tests specific themes that might be used in the adverts, and tests **storyboards** and **cuts** of adverts (before they are properly produced). More recently, advances in technology have allowed us to evaluate visual imagery more objectively, without relying on respondents' opinions: technology company 3M, for example, offers a service named '3M VAS' (standing for 'Visual Attention Service'), which allows users to test communications material to see whether specific sections of the communication will be noticed and in what order, using algorithms based on sophisticated eye-tracking research. Another approach to proposition and marketing communication testing uses facial coding analysis.

Big Data and Marketing Analytics

The term 'big data' refers to a more comprehensive set of data than that traditionally used to provide marketing information and customer insights. More specifically, 'big data' refers to the volume, velocity, and variety of data used (McAfee and Brynjolfsson, 2012; Erevelles et al., 2016).

- *Volume* denotes the shear amount of information used. As an illustration, Wal-Mart collected more than 2.5 petabytes of data every hour in 2012. A petabyte is 1 quadrillion bytes—or the equivalent of about 20 million filing cabinets' worth of text.
- *Velocity* refers to the fact that data is recorded in real time. For example, using location data from mobile phones, Google is able to offer up-to-date information about travelling time adjusted for traffic.
- *Variety* denotes that big data analytics combines data from several different sources. For example, combining customer databases with social media and mobile data can give a more comprehensive understanding of shopper behaviours than what was possible before.

With increasing digitization of business and consumers in everyday life, the availability of such varied information is growing rapidly. The different sources employed in big data analysis can be divided into five categories: public data; private data; data exhaust; community data; and self-quantification data (George et al., 2014).

- *Public data* refers to information held by governments or local communities, for example with regards to incomes, transportation, or energy use, which are accessed under certain restrictions, to guard individual privacy.
- *Private data* refers to data held by private organizations or individuals that cannot be readily be imputed from public sources. Examples are customer database information or browsing behaviours online.

Research Insight 3.3

To take your learning further, you might wish to read the following influential paper.

Erevelles, S., Fukawa, N., and Swayne, L. (2016) 'Big data consumer analytics and the transformation of marketing', *Journal of Business Research*, 69(2): 897–904.

This paper introduces a theoretical framework for when and how big data can lead to sustainable competitive advantage. More specifically, it discusses how three resources—physical, human, and organizational capital—moderate the processes of (a) collecting and storing evidence of consumer activity as big data, (b) extracting consumer insight from big data, and (c) utilizing consumer insight to enhance dynamic or adaptive capabilities.

 **Visit the online resources to read the abstract and access the full paper.**

- *Data exhaust* refers to data that are passively collected—that is, non-core data with limited or zero value to the original data-collection partner. When individuals adopt and use new technologies (such as mobile phones), they generate ambient data as a by-product of their everyday activities. These data can be recombined with other data sources to create new insights. Another source of data exhaust is information-seeking behaviour, such as online search and call centre calls, which can be used to infer people's needs, desires, or intentions.
- *Community data* refers to distilled, unstructured data, such as consumer reviews on products or 'liking' pages on social media, which is combined into dynamic networks that capture social trends.
- Individuals using technology to quantify their own personal actions and behaviours reveal *self-quantification data*, for example through the fitness bands worn on users' wrists that monitor their exercise and movement.

Marketing Research and Ethics

Marketing research should be carried out in an objective, unobtrusive, and honest manner. Researchers are also concerned about the public's increasing unwillingness to participate in marketing research and the problem of recruiting suitable interviewers. The apathy among interviewees is probably associated with the amount of research conducted, particularly through intrusive telephone interviewing, which is increasing, and door-to-door survey interviewing, which is declining. Marketing research is increasingly conducted online, creating its own set of ethical concerns. How can we verify that someone online is who they say they are? Is it acceptable to observe and analyse customer blogs and conversations on social networking sites? In social media research, ethical problems include the need to be open and transparent when conducting research within communities, and anonymizing and paraphrasing comments (since verbatim comments can often be tracked back to a particular user). Clear ethical codes for conducting social media research are, however, still in development. Consequently, key organizations such as ESOMAR and the MRS are devising clear policies on the topic.

Marketing research neither attempts to induce sales nor attempts to influence customer attitudes, intentions, or behaviours. The MRS (2014: 3) requires the following of its members:

1 Researchers shall ensure that participation in their activities is based on voluntary informed consent.
2 Researchers shall be straightforward and honest in all their professional and business relationships.
3 Researchers shall be transparent as to the subject and purpose of data collection.
4 Researchers shall respect the confidentiality of information collected in their professional activities.
5 Researchers shall respect the rights and well being of all individuals.
6 Researchers shall ensure that participants are not harmed or adversely affected by their professional activities.
7 Researchers shall balance the needs of individuals, clients, and their professional activities.
8 Researchers shall exercise independent professional judgment in the design, conduct and reporting of their professional activities.

9 Researchers shall ensure that their professional activities are conducted by persons with appropriate training, qualifications and experience.

10 Researchers shall protect the reputation and integrity of the profession.

The MRS Code of Conduct, based on the ESOMAR Code, is binding on all members of the MRS. Members of the general public are entitled to assurances that no information collected in a research survey will be used to identify them, or be disclosed to a third party, without their consent. Data in European countries are also subject to the Data Protection Directive, implemented in the UK as the Data Protection Act 1998. Respondents must be informed of the purpose of the research and the length of time for which they will be involved in it. Research findings must also be reported accurately and not used to mislead. In conducting marketing research, researchers have responsibility for themselves, their clients, and their respondents or participants.

The results of research studies should remain confidential unless otherwise agreed by the client and agency, and the agency should provide detailed accounts of the methods employed to carry out the research project, where their clients request this.

Visit the **online resources** and complete Internet Activity 3.2 to learn more about ESOMAR's Marketing Research Code of Practice.

Market Insight 3.3 **Is Facebook Manipulating You?**

In 2014, a research paper was published in a prestigious scientific journal reporting the results of a massive experimental study conducted on Facebook. The researchers manipulated the emotional tone of the posts appearing to a random selection of 689,003 Facebook users. Some of the participants were exposed to more positive emotions and others, to posts containing more negative emotional information. The objective was to monitor the posts that the different groups of participants would subsequently share. Researchers found that emotions are contagious: people exposed to positive stories are more likely to share posts containing positive emotions, while individuals exposed to more negative emotions will tend to communicate more negative emotions in their own posts.

Beyond the academic results, however, the research sparked significant interest from an ethical perspective. Many have branded the research unethical because participants had not expressed explicit consent to the manipulation of their feeds for the purposes of this study. Some contend that vulnerable participants might have been harmed by being exposed to too many negative stories. The study nonetheless respected all relevant regulations because the manipulation of the news feed is part of Facebook's terms and conditions, and consequently has been accepted by all users. Most online companies routinely run this type of experiment, evaluating how consumers react to changes in the

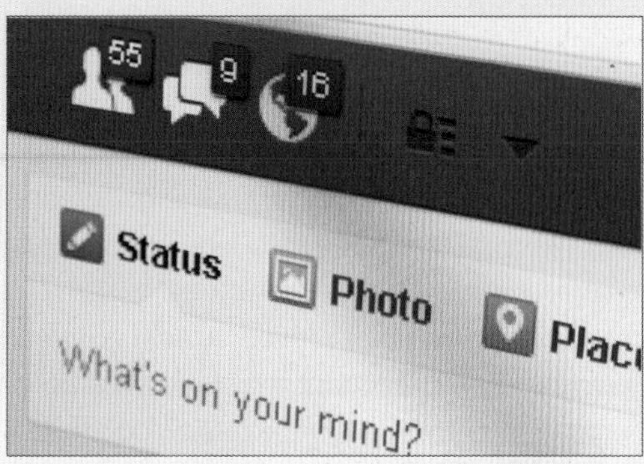

Why are you seeing what you are seeing? Social media research poses new and thorny ethical challenges.

Source: © JaysonPhotography/Shutterstock.

Market Insight 3.3 (continued)

information provided. The researchers claim that this type of research is necessary to improve the user experience. Specifically, Facebook has justified the project claiming that it wanted to find out how potentially seeing certain stories on the website could affect users emotionally.

Beyond the specific research, the incident has focused attention on the terms of service adopted by companies such as Facebook, Twitter, and Google. Is it fair for users to be forced into participating in experiments? Should these companies require explicit written agreement before enrolling users into their research projects? How can researchers evaluate the potentially harmful consequences of experimental manipulations for participants in such an uncontrolled research environment?

As the case demonstrates, it is not easy to find a definite answer to these questions. Online research—and especially this type of large-scale experiment—poses difficult ethical challenges, because researchers need to define the boundaries between legitimate scientific research and the protection of privacy rights.

1 **Would you consider Facebook's experiment ethical? Why or why not?**
2 **What could online companies do to minimize concerns regarding the ethicality of their research?**
3 **How would Facebook's project fare when compared to the MRS Principles?**

Sources: BBC News (2014); Goel (2014).

International Marketing Research

Often, marketers wish to promote their offerings internationally and to develop global brands (see Chapter 6). Marketing researchers, however, find it challenging to understand how culture operates in international markets and how it affects research design. Complexity in the international business environment makes international marketing research more complex, because it affects the research process and design. Key decisions include whether to customize the research to each of the separate countries in a study using differing scales, sampling methods, and sizes, or to try to use a single method for all countries, adopting an international **sampling frame**.

International researchers try to ensure that comparable data are collected despite differences in sampling frames, technological developments, availability of interviewers, and the acceptability of public questioning. Western approaches to marketing research, data collection, and culture might be inappropriate in some research environments because of variations in economic development and consumption patterns. How comparable are the data related to the consumption of Burger King's offerings collected through personal interviews in the United Arab Emirates (UAE), telephone interviews in France, and shopping mall intercept questionnaires in Sweden? Might an online panel be used instead across all countries? Ensuring comparability of data in research studies of multiple markets is not simple: concepts could be regarded differently; the same offerings could have different functions; language may be used differently, even within a country; offerings might be measured differently; the sample frames might be different; and the data collection methods adopted might differ because of variations in infrastructure.

Table 3.2 outlines three types of equivalence: **conceptual equivalence**; **functional equivalence**; and **translation equivalence**. All three types of equivalence impact on the semantics (that is, the meaning) of words used in different countries, for example in developing the wording for questionnaires or in focus groups. Getting the language right is important because it affects how respondents perceive the questions and structure their answers.

When designing international research programmes, we need to consider how the meaning of words is different and how the data should be collected. Different cultures have different ways of measuring concepts. They also live their lives differently, meaning that it may be necessary to collect the same or similar data in a different way. Table 3.3 outlines how measurement, sampling, and data collection equivalence impacts on international research.

As we can see from Table 3.3, achieving comparability of data when conducting international surveys is difficult. Usually, the more countries that are included in an international study, the more likely it is that errors will be introduced, and that the results and findings will be inaccurate and liable

Table 3.2 Types of semantic equivalence in international marketing research

Type of equivalence	Explanation	Example
Conceptual equivalence	When interpretation of behaviour, or objects, is similar across countries, conceptual equivalence exists.	Conceptual equivalence should be considered when defining the research problem, in wording the questionnaire, and determining the sample unit, e.g. there would be less need to investigate 'brand loyalty' in a country where competition is restricted and product choice limited.
Functional equivalence	Functional equivalence relates to whether a concept has a similar function in different countries.	Purchasing a bicycle in India, perhaps for transport to and from work, or France, perhaps for shopping, is a different concept from purchasing a bike in Norway, perhaps for mountain biking. Functional differences can be determined using focus groups before finalizing the research design by ensuring that the constructs used in the research measure what they are supposed to measure.
Translation equivalence	Translation equivalence is an important aspect of the international research process. Words in some languages have no real equivalent in other languages.	The meaning associated with different words is important in questionnaire design, since words can connote a different meaning from that intended when directly translated into another language. To avoid translation errors of these kinds, the researcher can adopt one of the following two methods. • *Back translation*—A translator fluent in the language into which the questionnaire is to be translated is used, then another translator whose native language is the original language translates it back again. Differences in wording can thus be identified and resolved. • *Parallel translation*—A questionnaire is translated using different translators fluent in the languages into which the questionnaire is to be translated, as well as from, until a final version is agreed upon.

to misinterpretation. International research requires local and international input; therefore the extent to which one can internationalize certain operations of the research process depends on the objectives of the research.

Table 3.3 Types of measurement and data collection equivalence

Type of equivalence	Explanation	Example
Measurement equivalence	The extent to which measurement scales are comparable across countries	Surveys are conducted in the United States using imperial systems of measurement, whilst the metric system is used in Europe. Clothing sizes adopt different measurement systems in Europe, North America, and South East Asia. Multi-item scales present challenges for international researchers, because dissatisfaction might not be expressed in the same way in one country compared with another. Some cultures are more open in expressing opinions or describing their behaviour than others.
Sampling equivalence	Determining the appropriate sample to question may provide difficulties when conducting international marketing research projects.	The respondent profile for the same survey could vary from country to country, e.g. different classification systems are in existence for censorship of films by age shown at the cinema in France compared with the UK.
Data collection equivalence	When conducting research studies in different countries, it may be appropriate to adopt different data collection strategies.	Typically, data collection methods include (e)mail, telephone or CATI, or personal or CAPI. • *(E)Mail*—Used more where literacy or Internet access is high and where the (e)mail system operates efficiently. Sampling frames can be compiled from electoral registers, although it is now illegal in some countries to use these lists. European survey respondents can be targeted efficiently and accurately because international sampling frames do exist. • *Telephone/CATI*—In many countries, telephone penetration may be limited and CATI software, using random digit dialling, more limited still. • *Personal interviews/CAPI*—Used most widely in European countries favouring the door-to-door and shopping mall intercept variants. Shopping mall intercept interviews are not appropriate in Arab countries in which women must not be approached in the street; here, comparability is achieved using door-to-door interviews. In countries in which it is rude to openly disagree with someone (e.g. China), it is best to use in-depth interviews.

With international projects, the key decision is to determine to what extent to centralize and to what extent to delegate work to local agencies. There is, throughout this process, ample opportunity for misunderstanding, errors, and lack of cultural sensitivity. To proceed effectively, the central agency should identify a number of trusted local market research providers on a variety of continents. Typically, an international agency will have a network of trusted affiliates, whom it will monitor on a continual basis.

Chapter Summary

To consolidate your learning, the key points from this chapter are summarized below.

- **Define the terms 'market research', 'marketing research', and 'customer insight'.**

  'Market research' is research undertaken about markets (for example customers, channels, and competitors), whilst 'marketing research' is research undertaken to understand the efficacy of marketing activities (for example pricing, supply chain management policies). 'Customer insight' derives from knowledge about customers, which can be turned into an organizational strength.

- **Describe the customer insight process and the role of marketing research within it.**

  Understanding customers is at the core of the marketing concept and the basic idea with these systems is that marketing information should be used for timely, continuous information to support decision-making. Customer insight is typically derived from fusing knowledge generated from a range of sources, including industry reports, sales force data, **competitive intelligence**, CRM data, employee feedback, social media analysis data, and managerial intuition. A customer insight is of value if it is rare, difficult to imitate, and of potential use in formulating management decisions.

- **Explain the role of marketing research and list the range of possible research approaches.**

  Marketing research plays an important role in the decision-making process and contributes through ad hoc studies, as well as continuous data collection, through industry reports and from secondary data sources, as well as through competitive intelligence either commissioned through agencies or conducted internally, with data gathered informally through sales forces, customers, and suppliers. What methodologies are used depends on the type of research problem (exploratory, descriptive, causal) and the availability of data (primary or secondary sources), as well as the type of insights sought (qualitative or quantitative).

- **Define the term 'big data' and describe its role in marketing.**

  'Big data' can be defined as the systematic gathering and interpretation of high-volume, high-velocity, and/or high-variety information using cost-effective, innovative forms of information processing to enable enhanced insight, decision-making, and process automation. 'Big data' thus refers to a more comprehensive set of data than that traditionally used to provide marketing information and customer insights.

- **Discuss the importance of ethics and the adoption of a code of conduct in marketing research.**

  Ethics is an important consideration in marketing research because consumers and customers either provide personal information about themselves or personal information is collected from them. Their privacy needs to be protected through observance of a professional code of conduct and the relevant laws in the country in which the research is conducted.

- **Understand the concept of 'equivalence' in relation to obtaining comparable data.**

  International market research is complex because of the differences in language, culture, infrastructure, and other factors that intervene in the data collection process, meaning that obtaining comparable equivalent data is more difficult.

Review Questions

1. **How do we define 'market research'?**
2. **How do we define 'marketing research'?**
3. **How do we define 'customer insight'?**
4. **What is 'big data'?**
5. **What are the different types of research that can be conducted in marketing research?**
6. **What are the main differences between qualitative and quantitative marketing research?**
7. **Why is a marketing research code of conduct important?**
8. **What is a marketing information system and how is it used in the customer insight process?**
9. **What is the concept of 'equivalence' in relation to obtaining comparable data from different countries?**
10. **How are the different aspects of the research process affected by differences in equivalence between countries?**

Worksheet Summary

To apply the knowledge you have gained from this chapter, and to test your understanding of marketing research and customer insight, visit the **online resources** and complete Worksheet 3.1.

Discussion Questions

1. Having read Case Insight 3.1, how would you advise MESH Planning to develop a suitable research proposal for Gatorade to evaluate the effectiveness of its marketing activities? Use the outline proposal in Figure 3.4 to help you to design the research.

2. Orange, the telecoms company, wants to conduct a market research study aimed particularly at discovering what market segments exist across Europe, and how customers and potential customers view the Orange brand.

   A. Draft a market research question and a number of sub-questions for the study.
   B. How would you go about selecting the particular countries in which to conduct the fieldwork?
   C. What process would you use when conducting the fieldwork for this multi-country study?

3 **What type of research (that is, descriptive, exploratory, or causal) should be commissioned in each the following contexts? Why.**

A The management of UAE airline Etihad wants to measure passenger satisfaction with the flight experience.

B Nintendo wants new ideas for new online games for a youth audience.

C Spanish fashion retailer Zara wants to know what levels of customer service are offered at its flagship stores.

D Procter & Gamble (P&G), makers of Ariel detergent, wants to test a new packaging design for six months to see if it is more effective than the existing version. Fifty supermarkets have been selected from one key P&G account: the new design is used in one half (25) of the supermarkets and the existing version in the other.

4 **You have recently won the research contract to evaluate customer satisfaction for Prêt A Manger, the food retail chain specializing in sandwiches, soups, and coffee. Your key account manager wants to increase customer satisfaction further using the knowledge gained from the study to identify potential new food offerings. Suggest a suitable research design for the following purposes. (Hint: You can recommend the use of more than one type of study.)**

A To collect information about levels of customer satisfaction

B To decide what new food offerings customers might like to see

In addition, your account manager asks you to outline what secondary data you can find in the area, detailing market shares, market structure, and other industry information, identifying specific secondary data sources and reports.

Visit the **online resources** and complete the multiple-choice questions to assess your knowledge of the chapter.

Glossary

behavioural economics the study of the psychology of consumer decision-making, particularly seeking to explain irrational decision-making and behaviour.

brand health the overall condition of a brand relative to the context in which it operates.

causal research a technique used to investigate the relational link between two or more variables by manipulating the independent variable(s) to see the effect on the dependent variable(s) and comparing effects with a control group within which no such manipulation takes place.

competitive intelligence the organized, professional, systematic collection of information, typically through informal mechanisms, used for the achievement of strategic and tactical organizational goals.

computer-assisted personal interviewing (CAPI) an approach to personal interviewing using a handheld computer or laptop to display questions and record the respondents' answers.

computer-assisted telephone interviewing (CATI) an approach to telephone interviewing using a laptop or desktop computer to display the questions to the interviewer, who reads them out and records the respondent's answers.

computer-assisted web interviewing (CAWI) an approach to online interviewing whereby the respondent uses a laptop or desktop computer to access questions in a set location, with questions automatically set based on the respondent's answers.

conceptual equivalence the degree to which interpretation of behaviour, or objects, is similar across countries.

control group a sample group used in causal research, which is not subjected to manipulation of some sort

cuts adverts initially produced in cartoon format, complete with dialogue, before they are produced, filmed, and edited.

descriptive research a research technique used to test, and confirm, hypotheses developed from a management problem.

desk research *see* **secondary research**

exploratory research a research technique used to generate ideas to develop hypotheses based around a management problem.

face validity the use of the researcher's or an expert's subjective judgment to determine whether an instrument is measuring what it is designed to measure.

full-service agency an advertising agency that provides its clients with a full range of services, including strategy and planning, designing the advertisements, and buying the media.

functional equivalence relates to whether or not a concept has the same function in different countries.

management problem a statement that outlines a situation faced by an organization, requiring further investigation and subsequent organizational action.

market mix modelling a research process that uses multiple-regression analysis based on customer survey data to ascertain the relative contributions of different promotional techniques on a customer-based dependent variable (such as awareness, intention to buy).

marketing research the design, collection, analysis, and interpretation of data collected for the purpose of aiding marketing decision-making.

pre-code the assignation, in surveys, of a unique code (for example male = 1, female = 2) to answers to questions, to speed up data processing and to aid data analysis.

primary research a technique used to collect, for the first time, data which has been specifically collected and assembled for the current research problem.

probability sampling a sampling method used where the probability of selection of the sample elements from the population is known. Typical examples include simple random, stratified random, and cluster sampling methods.

qualitative research a type of exploratory research using small samples and unstructured data collection procedures, designed to identify hypotheses, possibly for later testing in quantitative research. The most popular examples include in-depth interviews, focus groups, and projective techniques.

quantitative research research designed to provide responses to predetermined, standardized questions from a large number of respondents, involving the statistical analysis of the responses.

reliability the degree to which the data elicited in a study are replicated in a repeat study.

research brief a formal document prepared by the client organization and submitted to either an external market research provider (such as a market research agency or consultant) or an internal research provider (such as in-house research department) outlining a statement of the management problem and the perceived research needs of the organization.

research proposal a formal document prepared by an agency, consultant, or in-house research manager and submitted to the client to outline what procedures will be used to collect the necessary information, including timescales and costs.

sampling frame a list of population members from which a sample is generated (for example a telephone directory or membership list).

secondary research also known as 'desk research', a technique used to collect data that has previously been collected for a purpose other than the current research situation.

SPSS short for Statistical Package for the Social Sciences, a software package used for statistical analysis marketed by SPSS, a company owned by IBM.

storyboards an outline of the story that an advertisement will follow prepared before its production, showing its key themes, characters, and messages.

t-test a statistical test of difference used for small randomly selected samples with a size of fewer than 30.

test market region within a country used to test the effects of the launch of a new product or service, typically using regional advertising to promote the service and pre- and post-advertising market research to measure promotional effectiveness.

touchpoint an occasion on which a consumer engages with a brand, including those occasions not directly associated with advertising activities.

translation equivalence the degree to which the meaning of one language is represented in another after translation.

validity the ability of a measurement instrument to measure exactly the construct that it is attempting to measure.

z-test a statistical test of difference used for large randomly selected samples with a size of 30 or more.

References

Baines, P., and Chansarkar, B. (2002) *Introducing Marketing Research*, Chichester: John Wiley.

BBC News (2014) 'Facebook emotion experiment sparks criticism', 30 June. Available online at http://www.bbc.co.uk/news/technology-28051930 [accessed 7 August 2016].

Bryman, A. (1989) *Research Methods and Organization Studies*, London: Unwin Hyman.

Cater, B., and Zabkar, V. (2009) 'Antecedents and consequences of commitment in marketing research services: The client's perspective', *Industrial Marketing Management*, 38(7): 785–97.

Cowan, D. (2008) 'Forum: Creating customer insight', *International Journal of Market Research*, 50(6): 719–29.

Erevelles, S., Fukawa, N., and Swayne, L. (2016) 'Big data consumer analytics and the transformation of marketing', *Journal of Business Research*, 69(2): 897–904.

ESOMAR (2015) *Global Market Research Report 2015: An Industry Report*. Available online at https://www.esomar.org/uploads/public/publications-store/reports/global-market-research-2015/ESOMAR-GMR2015_Preview.pdf [accessed 2 July 2016].

Evans, J. R., and Mathur, A. (2005) 'The value of online surveys', *Internet Research*, 15(2): 195–219.

George, G., Haas, M., and Pentland, A. (2014) 'From the editors: Big data and management', *Academy of Management Journal*, 57(2): 321–6.

Goel, V. (2014) 'Facebook tinkers with users' emotions in news feed experiment, stirring outcry', *New York Times*, 30 June. Available online at http://www.nytimes.com/2014/06/30/technology/facebook-tinkers-with-users-emotions-in-news-feed-experiment-stirring-outcry.html?_r=0 [accessed 7 August 2016].

Goyal, M. (2013) 'UK-based BrainJuicer finds out how chocolates can boost lingerie sales', *Economic Times of India*, 14 April. Available online at http://media.brainjuicer.com/media/files/The_Economic_Times_India.pdf [accessed 28 May 2013].

Leach, W., and Bisnajak, A. (2013) 'How scent sells lingerie', Paper presented at the ESOMAR Congress, 22–25 September, Istanbul.

Maklan, S., Antonetti, P., and Whitty, S. (2017) 'Think atomistic not holistic: A better way to manage customer experience at Royal Bank of Scotland (RBS)', *California Management Review*, forthcoming.

Malhotra, N. K. (2010) *Marketing Research: An Applied Orientation* (6th edn), Upper Saddle River, NJ: Pearson.

Market Research Society (MRS) (2014) *Code of Conduct*. Available online at https://www.mrs.org.uk/pdf/mrs%20code%20of%20conduct%202014.pdf [accessed 28 December 2015].

McAfee, A., and Brynjulfson, E. (2012) 'Big data: The management revolution', *Harvard Business Review*, 90(10): 60–6.

Miles, L. (2004) 'Online, on tap', *Marketing*, 16 June, 39–40.

Moorman, C. (2015) *CMO Survey Report: Highlights and Insights*. Available online at https://cmosurvey.org/wp-content/uploads/sites/11/2015/09/The_CMO_Survey-Highlights_and_Insights-Aug-2015.pdf [accessed 4 November 2015].

Murphy, L. F. (2015) *The Greenbook Research Industry Trends (GRIT) Report*. Available online at http://www.greenbook.org/pdfs/2015GRIT_WINTER_Q3-4.pdf [accessed 29 January 2016].

Parasuraman, A. (1991) *Marketing Research* (2nd edn), Wokingham: Addison-Wesley.

Said, E., Macdonald, E. K, Wilson, H. N., and Marcos, J. (2015) 'How organisations generate and use customer insight', *Journal of Marketing Management*, 31(9–10): 1158–79.

Designing and Delivering the Market Strategy

Chapter 4
Marketing Environment and Strategy

Learning Outcomes

After studying this chapter, you will be able to:

- describe the key characteristics associated with the marketing environment;
- explain the environmental scanning process and show how PESTLE analysis can be used to understand the external environment;
- analyse the performance environment using the Porter's Five Forces industry analysis model;
- analyse an organization's product/service portfolio to aid resource planning;
- analyse current conditions and formulate marketing strategies; and
- explain the different types of strategic marketing goal and associated growth strategies.

Case Insight 4.1 **3scale**

Through its staff and offices in Barcelona and San Francisco, 3scale helps organizations to open, manage, and use application programming interfaces (APIs). We speak to Manfred Bortenschlager (pictured), API market development director, to find out how the company competes in its marketplace.

Steven Willmott and Martin Tantow founded 3scale in 2007, convinced that the world would become web-enabled, with APIs a critical digital infrastructure requirement. The initial 3scale product focused on an API marketplace, providing a matchmaking service between API providers and API consumers. The company quickly shifted to a more powerful business model: providing management capabilities for API providers. Now, 3scale sells an API management product based on monthly subscriptions with different price plans, starting with a free plan in its basic form: Freemium, also known as the Software-as-a-Service (SaaS) model. This model is successful because it perfectly serves the customers' needs for flexibility and scale. Today, 3scale powers the APIs for close to 700 organizations.

Application programming interfaces are a software technology that provides organizations with a novel and effective way of distributing and leveraging digital assets. Application programming interfaces represent gateways to an organization's data or services (that is, digital assets), which can be programmed and accessed by software increasing automation, scalability, and efficiency. As an analogy, APIs can be seen as an automatic door to a building with a security mechanism (like a pass code or a chip card). Digital transformation and digital strategies are based on APIs. The 3scale API management product provides the essential security, visibility, and control that allows organizations to define and measure their strategies when using APIs. In terms of value chain and customer requirements, the 3scale service follows a business-to-business-to-customer (B2B2C) model: the API provider (owning and providing digital assets) serves a developer (developing and distributing web or mobile apps), who serves the end user (the final consumer of the apps and APIs).

The most important customer requirements from the developer's perspective are, first, the value of the data or service to which the API provides access (the more unique, the higher the value) and, second, the simplicity of access to the API. The most important customer requirement from an end consumer's perspective is added value to an application via additional functionality. This is often achieved via so-called API mashups, whereby a developer combines the APIs of various API providers to create something new for the end consumer. Other requirements include 'user experience', which includes ease of use, clarity, consistency, and speed, for example.

3scale operates in a very fast-moving industry. To be successful, customer focus is essential. 3scale needs constantly to adapt its offering in terms of product features and the pricing model. To achieve that, it needs to integrate engineering, marketing, and sales processes, and to be able to react to change more quickly than can its competitors. 3scale differentiates between 'self-service' and 'enterprise' customers. Self-service customers adopt the 3scale offer almost without any human interaction, whereas customers on enterprise plans get phone support 24 hours a day, seven days a week (24/7) and/or higher guaranteed product reliability.

Case Insight 4.1 **3scale** (continued)

3scale has three main competitive differentiators, as follows.

1 The 3scale product is modular and uses cloud technologies in a unique way. Based on customers' requirements, they can choose to host some of the product modules in 'the cloud' and some on their own IT infrastructure. This gives unmatched availability, scalability, and flexibility.
2 3scale offers the shortest time-to-value in the market, achieved via a comprehensive self-service model and detailed documentation. Customers can adopt 3scale very quickly and leverage the benefits of APIs instantly.
3 The Freemium subscription model is fair and transparent, with very competitive pricing. Customers appreciate the low barrier of entry and the subscription model is easy to understand, with no surprises.

One complex problem was that Amazon Web Services (AWS)—based around cloud technologies—launched the Amazon API Gateway product. This was perceived by many observers in the API management market to be a potential threat. With its size and financial resources, the expectation was that Amazon's offering could substantially impact existing players in the market. The question was: what strategy should 3scale develop to circumvent this competitive threat?

Introduction

How do companies keep up with the many changes that occur in politics, markets, and economics? What processes do they use to try to anticipate changes in technologies? How do they set their competitive positions and strategic marketing objectives? We consider these and other questions in this chapter.

The *external* environment, for example, comprises political, social, and technological factors, and organizations often have very limited, if any, control of these. The **performance environment** consists of competitors, suppliers, and indirect service providers, who shape the way and extent to which organizations achieve their objectives. Here, organizations have a much stronger level of influence. The *internal* environment concerns the resources, processes, and policies with which an organization achieves its goals, which factors it can influence directly. We also discuss how companies assess their competitive positions using strengths-weaknesses-opportunities-threats (SWOT) analysis, and how they set their intended strategic goals and actions and write associated marketing plans.

First, we turn to the concept of analysing the marketing environment (see Figure 4.1).

Understanding the External Environment

To make sense of the external environment, we use the well-known acronym **PESTLE.** The acronym derives from the 'Political, Economic, Socio-cultural, Technological, Legal, and Ecological' factors (see Figure 4.2) that comprise the most popular framework for examining the external environment.

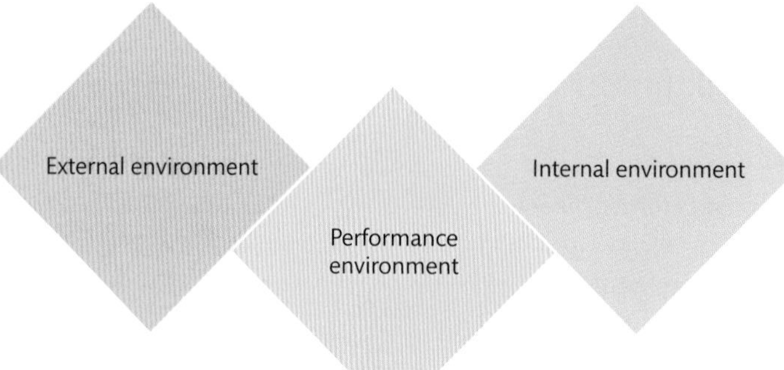

Figure 4.1 The three marketing environments

The Political Environment

The political factors in the external environment relate to the interaction between business, **society**, and **government**. An understanding of the political factors embraces the conditions that exist before laws are enacted, when they are still being formed, or when they are in dispute. Political environmental analysis is important because companies can detect signals concerning potential legal and regulatory changes in their industries, and have a chance to impede, influence, and alter that legislation.

Although the **political environment** is in many ways uncontrollable, there are circumstances in which an organization, or an industry coalition, can affect legislation in its own favour. An organization can outperform other organizations over time if it can manage its relationships with

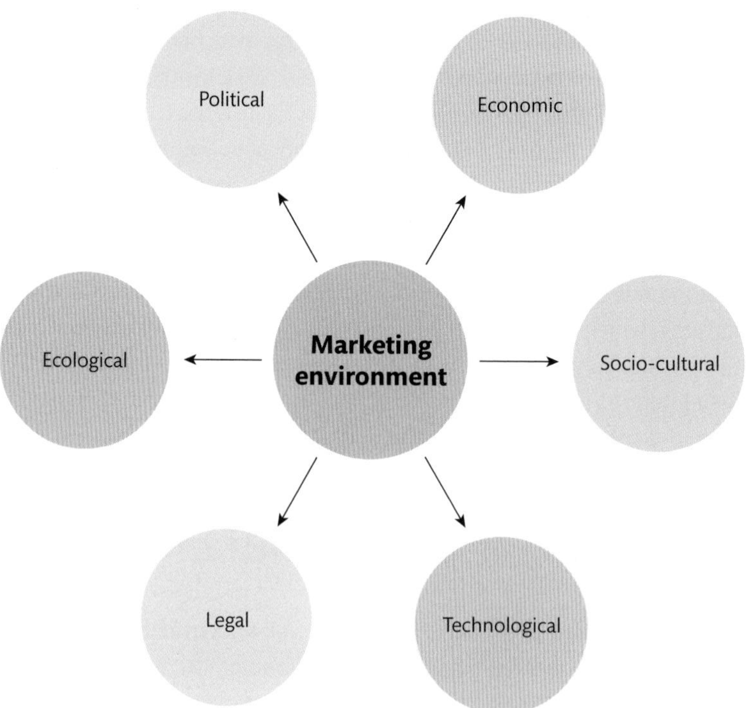

Figure 4.2 The external marketing environment

government and regulatory bodies better than do its competitors (Hillman et al., 2004; Lawton and Rajwani, 2011).

Generally, there are several ways in which marketers might conduct business–government relations in various countries, as follows.

- Lobbyist firms, with key industry knowledge, can be engaged either permanently or as needed.
- **Public relations (PR)** consultancies, such as Weber Shandwick, can be commissioned for their political services, often having members of Parliament (MPs) or others with a high degree of political influence serving as directors and/or advisers, in jurisdictions where this is legal.
- A politician may be paid a fee to give political advice on matters of importance to an organization, where this is legal within that particular jurisdiction and where that politician is not serving directly within the government in question on the same portfolio as that on which he or she is advising.
- An in-house PR manager might handle government relations directly.
- An industry association might be contacted to lobby on behalf of members (for example, in the European financial services industry, the Banking Federation of the European Union).
- A politician may be invited to join the board of directors, board of trustees, or board of advisers of an organization, where this is legal, to aid the company in developing its business–government relations.

Organizations often collaborate to influence governments. This can be achieved by means of industry or trade bodies, or by working with other large companies in their industry. For example, EuropaBio is made up of three main segments of the European biotechnology industry: health care (Red Biotech), industrial (White Biotech), and agri-food (Green Biotech). Experts from member companies actively participate in working groups and taskforces that cover a wide range of issues and concerns particular to their industry in an attempt to influence key **stakeholders**, including national governments and the European legislature.

In industries with significant social and environmental impact (for example oil and gas, transport infrastructures, telecommunications), analysis and management of the political environment is particularly important to allow a company to operate successfully. Read Market Insight 4.1 to learn about the case of a company trying to manage relationships with relevant local stakeholders.

The Economic Environment

Companies and organizations must develop an understanding of the economic factors within the external environment because a country's economic circumstances have an impact on what economists term 'factor prices' within a particular industry for a particular organization.

The economic environment of a firm is affected by the following factors.

- *Wage inflation*—Annual wage increases in a particular sector will depend on the supply of labour in that sector. Where there is scarcity of supply, wages usually increase (doctors being an example).
- *Price inflation*—How much consumers pay for goods and services depends on the rate of supply of those goods and services. If supply is scarce, there is usually an increase in the price of that consumer good or service (as in the case of petrol).

Market Insight 4.1 **Negotiating a Social Licence to Operate**

In 2014, after more than 14 years of local community protests opposing its Pascua Lama gold-mining project in Northern Chile, Canadian mining corporation Barrick Gold (the world's largest miner of gold) celebrated signing an agreement with the local indigenous Diaguita community. The company had obtained signatures from 15 of the 22 local communities. 'We believe this Agreement will form the basis of a new relationship with Diaguita communities, one based on transparency, openness and trust', said Eduardo Flores, Barrick's executive director in Chile.

The Huasco Valley is a green and fertile valley located in the Atacama Desert, the driest in the world. The Valley is home to the Diaguita people, whose main form of livelihood has been grape farming. The community opposition to the Pascua Lama gold mine (designed to be the second largest in South America) was based mainly on the negative impacts that the mining activity would have on local water supplies.

Despite the resistance to the mine, Barrick invested heavily in the local community to obtain a 'social licence to operate'. This term refers to local legitimacy—that is, to being accepted by the local community. A social licence to operate is a matter of great importance for companies extracting natural resources to show a match between their corporate social responsibility (CSR) aspirations and how local communities actually perceive them. In pursuit of this end, by 2007 Barrick claimed to have spent US$16 million on local purchasing, to have paid the Water Vigilance Board (a group of local wealthy farmers) US$60 million compensation for its water supplies, to have offered training courses for farmers, and also in Diaguita pottery and handcraft, and, controversially, to have offered to pay legal fees for those in the local community wishing to obtain official indigenous status from the Chilean state.

Once Barrick Gold reached an agreement with 15 of the 22 communities, it communicated the news on its corporate website. The agreement was said to be centred on how best to mitigate environmental and human rights, and also allows for discussion around potential benefit sharing of mining profits between Barrick and the local community. However, since the signing of the agreement in May 2014 there have continued to be numerous street marches and protests against the Pascua Lama project. For those groups still opposed, the only acceptable solution is no mine and, as such, talk of mitigating impacts and/or compensation is futile.

In a further development, OLCA and MiningWatch Canada, a national and international non-governmental organization (NGO), published a study denouncing the steps taken to obtain the 15 signatures, claiming that the process was illegitimate. Certain local community leaders have also contested the agreement in the Chilean courts. It would therefore appear that there is still much work required if Barrick Gold is to gain a social licence to operate in the region.

1. **Why do you think it is so important for mining companies to gain a social licence to operate?**
2. **What could be the implications for mining companies if they were to fail to secure a social licence to operate?**
3. **Can you think of any flaws with the concept of a social licence to operate?**

Sources: Prno and Slocombe (2012); Barrick Gold (2014); Wiebe (2015).

The case has been kindly contributed by Dr Rajiv Maher, post-doctoral researcher at the Pontifical Catholic University of Chile.

- ***Gross domestic product (GDP)** per capita*—The combined output of goods and services in a particular nation is a useful measure for determining relative wealth between countries when comparisons are calculated per member of the population—that is, as GDP per capita at **purchasing power parity (PPP)**.

- *Income, sales, and corporation taxes*—These taxes, typically operating in all countries around the world, sometimes at different levels, affect substantially how we market different offerings.
- *Exchange rates*—The relative value of a currency vis-à-vis another currency is an important calculation for those businesses operating in foreign markets or holding financial reserves in other currencies.
- *Export quota controls and duties*—There are often restrictions placed on the amounts (quotas) of goods and services that any particular firm or industry can import into a country, depending on to which trading bloc or country a company or firm is exporting. In addition, countries sometimes charge a form of tax on particular items to discourage or encourage imports and to protect their own economies.

Organizations usually have little impact on the wider economic environment, because they have little control over the macroeconomic variables. For example, firms have no control over oil prices, which might affect their business in different ways. The challenge when examining the macroeconomic environment is to foresee changes in the environment and how they might affect the firm's activities.

If **inflation** drives consumer prices higher in a particular country, the price of goods might become more expensive, triggering a fall in sales. Typically, during a **recession**, consumers tend to purchase fewer goods and increase their savings, and prices fall further as producers try to stimulate demand. Economic indicators are frequently available from government central banks.

Visit the **online resources** and complete Internet Activity 4.1 to learn more about how the contribution of service industries to the UK's national economy has changed over the last ten years.

The Socio-Cultural Environment

Lifestyles are constantly changing and, over time, consumers' preferences shift. Companies that fail to recognize changes in the socio-cultural environment and to adapt or change their offerings often fail. For example, the new focus on healthy eating and lifestyles has impacted on two

Research Insight 4.1

To take your learning further, you might wish to read this highly influential paper.

Danciu, V. (2013) 'The future of marketing: An appropriate response to the environment changes', *Theoretical and Applied Economics*, 20(5): 33–52.

This paper looks at trends within different aspects of the marketing environment. It provides a helpful insight into the complexity and diversity of the various environments within which organizations operate.

 **Visit the online resources to read the abstract and access the full paper.**

Too greasy? Fast-food companies need to keep pace with cultural changes and provide healthier alternatives if they wish to remain relevant.

Source: © spflaum1 / iStockphoto.

major brands in particular, McDonald's and Coca-Cola. After several years of falling sales, McDonald's admitted in 2015 that it had failed to keep pace with changing consumer tastes. Its restructuring plan was designed to streamline operations and to discard layers of bureaucracy, aiming to save the company US$300 million in costs.

The socio-cultural factors that companies need to consider comprise the changing nature of households, demographics, lifestyles, and family structures, and the changing **values** prevalent in society.

Demographics and Lifestyles

Changes in population proportions impact on an organization's marketing activity. In the UK (and some other European countries), immigration from Poland after enlargement of the European Union increased, with some supermarkets subsequently specifically targeting Polish customers using adverts in Polish and by stocking products such as borscht, meatballs, pickled vegetables, and sauerkraut (BBC News, 2006).

In addition, there will also be shifts in the proportions of age groups within different populations. Some countries have a relatively large proportion of people in the 'aged 65 or over' age bracket—that is, the 'silver' or 'grey' market, so-called because of the colour of older people's hair. Some countries and regions, such as many African and Middle Eastern countries, have a comparatively high proportion of younger citizens. These shifts in population and the relative differences in age structure in different countries give rise to different-sized markets for brand propositions.

The Technological Environment

The emergence of new technologies has affected most businesses. Examples include technologies that impact productivity and business efficiency, such as changes in energy, transportation, and information and communication technologies (ICT). New technology also changes the way in which companies go to market. Companies are now compelled to use a variety of channels. For example, one unusual app enables shoppers to test whether a melon is ripe: the user rests the microphone of a smartphone on a melon, presses a button, and taps the melon; the app uses an algorithm to determine from the sound whether the melon is ready to eat.

When scanning the technological environment, attention has to be given to research and development (R&D) trends and to competitors' R&D efforts. Strategies to ascertain these involve regular searches of patent registration, trademarks, and copyright assignations, as well as maintaining a general interest in technological and scientific advances. Companies often develop new products based on modifications of patents registered by their competitors. This process, referred to as **reverse engineering**, is often the result of a firm's inability to turn its own technological advances into a **sustainable competitive advantage** (Rao, 2005). As soon

Market Insight 4.2 **Health Issues Slim Down Product Sales**

Sales of store-bought, packaged (sliced) bread fell 8 per cent in the UK in 2014, following a series of external influences. The UK's three biggest sliced-bread brands—Warburtons, Hovis, and Kingsmill, which account for 60 per cent of packaged bread in the UK—collectively lost £121 million in bread sales in 2014. Asda announced that it was losing £500,000 per week in bread sales, or about 5 million loaves.

The reasons for this downward shift include increasing awareness of the need for healthy eating, and a consumer shift towards higher protein products and lower carbohydrates, along with a renewed interest in fresh artisan variants. Television programmes, such as the *The Great British Bake Off*, have spurred interest in home baking to the extent that sales of baking trays at Waitrose soared by 881 per cent and those of bakeware increased by 55 per cent, all during a single week before the 2015 series started.

Food and beverage companies, like their fast-food counterparts, have faced increasing pressure from governments as obesity rates have increased around the world. National governments have begun to scrutinize their public health policies. Several countries, such as Denmark, Finland, Hungary, and France, have introduced a 'fat tax' added to products with high fat content, such as confectionary (including chocolate), dairy products, and sugary foods and drinks, in a bid to reduce public consumption of high-fat foods, the obesity epidemic, and the consequent impact on public health and public healthcare budgets.

A key ethical issue thus arises if you are chief executive officer (CEO) of a major food manufacturer: should you seek to circumvent the obesity issue by reducing the fat content in your products (and by educating consumers to buy healthier options), ignore the obesity issue and simply sell the same product (perhaps even lobbying government not to introduce the tax), or pursue some mixture of these approaches?

The huge success of television programmes such as *The Great British Bake Off* does nothing to encourage healthier eating habits.
Source: © *The Great British Bake Off*/Love Productions & BBC.

As part of Tesco's ten-point plan against obesity, the supermarket decided that it would no longer sell high-sugar drinks targeted at kids in the juice category. As a result, high-sugar drinks such as Ribena, Capri-Sun, and Rubicon fruit juice cartons were delisted from Tesco stores.

1. **What are the advantages and disadvantages to food manufacturers of producing new low-calorie or healthier versions of their existing products?**
2. **How likely do you think it is that the UK government will introduce a 'fat tax' on high-sugar food and drinks such as Ribena? Explain your reasoning.**
3. **Why do you think Tesco decided to delist high-sugar juice drinks, yet still sell other high-sugar and high-calorie products such as Mars bars?**

Sources: Green (2000); Barrie (2015); Davidson (2015); Young (2015).

as a new offering variant is introduced, it is quickly copied. To overcome this, firms attempt to introduce a consistent stream of new propositions and stay as close to the consumer as possible.

The Legal Environment

The legal factors in the external environment span every aspect of an organization's business. Laws and regulation are enacted in most countries, relating to issues ranging from transparency of pricing, through product safety, the promotion of good practice in packaging and labelling, the prevention of restrictive trade practices, and the abuse of a dominant market position, to codes of practice in advertising, to take only a small selection.

In the European Union, for example, product safety is covered under the 2001 General Product Safety Directive which aims to protect consumer health and safety both for EU member states and for importers from third-party countries to the European Union or their EU agents. Where products pose serious risks to consumer health, the European Commission can take action, imposing fines and/or criminal sentences for those contravening the Directive. The General Product Safety Directive does not cover food safety; this is subject to another EU directive, under which are established a European Food Safety Authority and a set of regulations covering food safety. Companies operating in these sectors need to keep up with changes in legislation, because failure might jeopardize the business.

The Ecological Environment

The concept of 'marketing sustainability' is now well established and increasing numbers of consumers express concern about the impact that companies are having on ecological environments.

Fairtrade products aim to guarantee better prices and better working conditions for farmers in developing countries.
Source: © Tracing Tea/Shutterstock.

Sustainability issues embrace the sourcing of products from countries with poor and coercive labour policies. Both Nike and Apple have actively changed parts of their supply chain following investigations. Consumers are also keen to ensure that companies and their products are not damaging the environment or causing harm to consumers. This has been accompanied by a rise in the popularity of Fairtrade products.

How should an organization embrace the changing trend in sustainability? To answer this question, Orsato (2006) suggests four alternative green marketing strategies, as follows.

- *Eco-efficiency*—This strategy involve developing lower costs through organizational processes such as the promotion of resource productivity (for example energy efficiency) and better utilization of by-products. This approach should be adopted by firms that need to focus on reducing the costs and environmental impact of their organizational processes. Supermarket chains in Norway and other Scandinavian countries have long encouraged recycling, for example.
- *Beyond compliance leadership*—This approach involves the adoption of a **differentiation** strategy through organizational processes such as certified schemes to demonstrate ecological credentials and environmental excellence, for example the adoption of the principles outlined in

the United Nations Global Compact or other environmental management system (EMS) schemes and codes. This approach should be adopted by firms that supply industrial markets, such as car manufacturers.

- *Eco-branding*—A firm might differentiate its products or services to promote environmental responsibility. Examples include the British Prince of Wales' food brand Duchy Originals, the late Thai King Bhumipol's Golden Place brand, or the Toyota Prius.
- *Environmental cost leadership*—This strategy is achieved by means of offerings that provide greater environmental benefits at a lower price and particularly suits firms operating in price-sensitive, ecologically sensitive markets, such as the packaging and chemical industries.

Whatever the company and industry, ecological trends in marketing look set to stay, and to develop further, as the sustainability debate rages on and companies use it to develop their own competitive strategies.

Environmental Scanning

Organizations need to monitor all PESTLE elements, but for some industries certain factors are more important than others. Pharmaceutical organizations such as GlaxoSmithKline must take special care to monitor legal and regulatory developments (for example in relation to labelling, patents, and testing); the Environment Agency will monitor political and ecological changes (including such issues as flood plains for housing developments); road haulage companies should watch for changes that impact on transport development (for example congestion charging, diesel duty, toll roads); music distributors should monitor changes in technology and associated socio-cultural developments (for example downloading trends and cloud computing).

To understand changes in their external environment, organizations need to put in place methods and processes to inform them of developments. This process of gathering information about a company's external events and relationships, to assist top management in its decision-making, and the development of its course of action is referred to as **environmental scanning** (Aguilar, 1967). It is the internal communication of external information about issues that may potentially influence an organization's decision-making process, focusing on the identification of emerging issues, situations, and potential threats in the external environment (Albright, 2004).

We can gather information in environmental scanning exercises using company reports, newspapers, industry reports and magazines, government reports, and marketing intelligence reports (for example those published by Datamonitor, Euromonitor, and Mintel).

Visit the **online resources** and follow the web links to learn more about the information and services offered provided by Datamonitor, Euromonitor, and Mintel.

'Soft' personal sources of information obtained through networking, such as contacts at trade fairs, particularly for competitive and legal or regulatory information, are also important. Such verbal, personal sources of information can be critical in fast-changing environments (May et al., 2000), when reports from government, industry, or specific businesses have yet to be written and disseminated.

Visit the **online resources** and complete Internet Activity 4.2 to learn more about a number of sources that can be useful when conducting a scan of the marketing environment.

Research Insight 4.2

To take your learning further, you might wish to read this highly influential paper.

Levitt, T. (1960) 'Marketing myopia', *Harvard Business Review*, 38(4): 45–56.

This is perhaps the most famous and celebrated article ever written on marketing. It won the author the McKinsey Award and has been reprinted twice in the *Harvard Business Review*. The central thesis of the article—as true today as it was in 1960—is that companies must monitor change in the external environment and keep abreast of their customers' needs or else risk decline.

Visit the online resources to read the abstract and access the full paper.

Understanding the Performance Environment

The performance environment, often called the 'microenvironment', consists of those organizations that either directly or indirectly influence an organization's operational performance. There are three main types:

- those companies that compete against the organization in the pursuit of its objectives;
- those companies that supply raw materials, goods, and services and those that act as distributors, dealers, and retailers, further down the marketing channel, all of which have the potential to directly influence the performance of an organization by adding value through production, assembly, and distribution of products prior to reaching the end user; and
- those companies that have the potential to ***indirectly*** influence the performance of the organization in the pursuit of its objectives, which often supply services such as consultancy, financial services, or marketing research or communication agencies.

Analysing Industries

An industry is composed of various organizations that market similar offerings. According to Porter (1979), we should review the 'competitive' environment within an industry to identify the major competitive forces, because this helps us to assess their impact on an organization's present and future competitive positions.

Think of industries such as shipbuilding, car manufacture, coal, and steel, in which levels of profitability have been weak and unattractive to prospective new entrants. Now think of industries such as technology, fashion, airlines, and banking, in which levels of profitability have traditionally been high. The competitive pressures in all of these markets vary quite considerably, but there are enough similarities to establish an analytical framework within which to gauge the nature and intensity of competition.

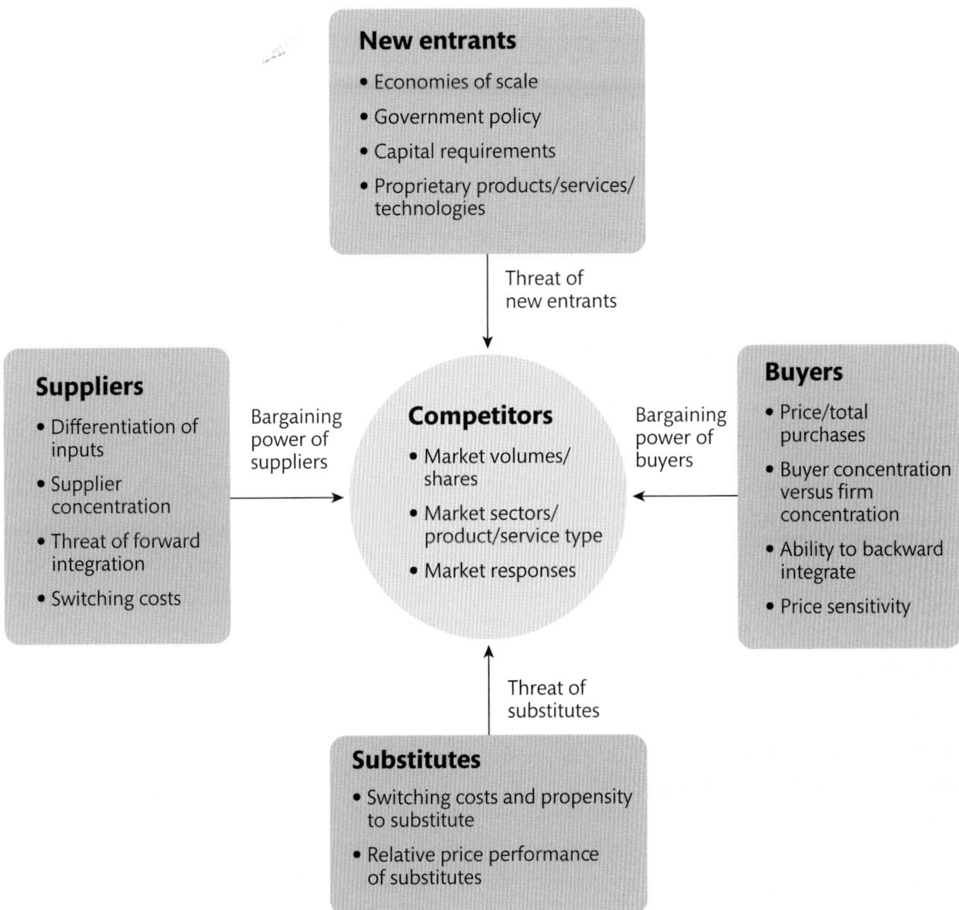

Figure 4.3 Industry analysis: Porter's Five Forces

Source: Adapted from Porter (1979). Reproduced with the kind permission of Harvard Business School Publishing.

Porter suggests that competition in an industry is a composite of five main competitive forces: the level of threat that new competitors will enter the market, the threat posed by substitute products, and the bargaining power of both buyers and suppliers, which in turn affect the intensity of rivalry between the current competitors. Porter called these variables the 'five forces of competitive industry analysis' (see Figure 4.3).

As a general rule, the more intense the rivalry between the industry players, the lower their overall performance. On the other hand, the lower the rivalry, the greater will be the performance of the industry players.

New Entrants

Industries are seldom static: companies and brands enter and exit industries all of the time. Consider the UK beverage industry, which has witnessed the entrance of energy-drink manufacturers such as Red Bull. This company has been competing head-on with industry stalwarts

PepsiCo, Coca-Cola, and GlaxoSmithKline's Lucozade, the original energy drink in the UK beverage market.

New entrants may be restricted through government and regulatory policy or they may be frozen out of an industry because of the capital requirements necessary to set up business. In the oil and gas industry, for example, huge sums of capital are required not only to fund exploration activities, but also to fund the extraction and refining operations.

Companies may otherwise be locked out because companies within a market are using proprietary offerings or technologies. A good example of this is the pharmaceutical industry, in which patents protect companies' investments in new medicines. The cost of developing a new medicine in 2014 was around US$2.56 billion (Edney, 2014). Few companies can afford to compete in a market in which the set-up and ongoing R&D costs are so large.

Substitutes

In any industry, there are usually substitute offerings that perform the same function or meet similar customer needs. Levitt (1960) warned that many companies fail to recognize the competitive threat from newly developing offerings, citing as an example the American railroad industry's refusal to see the competitive threat arising from the development of the automobile and airline industries in the transport sector.

Consumers consider the **switching costs** associated with a purchase decision, which, in turn, affect their propensity to substitute the offering for another. If we were to wish to travel from Amsterdam to Paris, we could fly from Schipol airport to Charles de Gaulle airport, take the train, or drive. We would consider the **relative price** differences (the flight is likely to be the most expensive, but not necessarily so), and we would also factor into this decision how comfortable and convenient these different journeys are likely to be before we finally make our choice. In analysing our place within an industry, we should similarly consider what alternative offerings exist in the marketplace that also meet—to a greater or lesser extent—our customers' needs.

Buyers

Companies should ask themselves what percentage of their sales a single buyer represents. This is an important question because if one buying company purchases a large volume of offerings from the supplying company, as car manufacturers do from steel suppliers, it is likely to be able to demand price concessions (price per total purchase) when there are lots of competing suppliers in the marketplace relative to the proportion of buyers (buyer concentration versus firm concentration).

A factor impacting on a buyer's bargaining power is how price sensitive a particular company is. Depending on their trading circumstances, some companies might be more price-sensitive than others. If such companies are more price-sensitive and yet there are lots of competing suppliers for their business, they are likely to switch suppliers rather than be loyal to one. Most companies try to enhance other factors associated with an offering, such as after-sales service or product/service customization, to try to reduce a client company's **price sensitivity**. When analysing an industry, we should understand the bargaining power that buyers have with their suppliers, because this can impact on the price charged and the volumes sold or total revenue earned.

Suppliers

Any industry analysis should determine how suppliers operate and the extent of their bargaining power. For example, the aircraft manufacture market consists of a small number of major suppliers, such as Boeing and Airbus, and a large number of customers—namely, national airlines and low-cost airline companies; hence the suppliers have the stronger bargaining advantage. Conversely, in the computer gaming industry, there is a large number of suppliers, such as game production companies and gaming console component manufacturers; the few customers, Sony, Nintendo, and Microsoft, hold the bargaining advantage. We should also consider whether or not the suppliers are providing unique components, products, or services that may enhance their bargaining situation.

Competitors

To analyse an industry, we must also understand how the companies within that particular market operate. In the UK cosmetics sector, for example, the market leading cosmetic manufacturers include Avon European Holdings Ltd, Estée Lauder Cosmetics Ltd, L'Oréal (UK) Ltd, Procter & Gamble Ltd, and the Unilever Group, along with large retailers such as Boots Group plc UK Ltd, The Body Shop International plc, and Superdrug Stores plc. In undertaking a competitor analysis, we should outline each company's structure (for example details of the main holding company, the individual business unit, any changes in ownership), current and future developments (which can often be gleaned from reading company prospectuses, websites, and industry reports), and the company's latest financial results. We would be interested in calculating the market volumes and shares for each competitor, because market share is a key indication of company profitability and return on investment (Buzzell et al., 1975).

Competitors provide offerings that attempt to meet the same market need as does our own. There are several ways in which a need might be met, but essentially firms need to be aware of both their direct and indirect competitors. *Direct* competitors provide the same target market similar offerings, for example EasyJet, Flybe, and Ryanair. Direct competitors may also offer a product in the same category, but target different segments. For example, in addition to major global manufacturers Unilever and Nestlé, emerging niche brands such as Jude's (UK), Ciao Bella (US), R&R Ice Cream (Europe), and Mengniu Dairy (China) offer a range of ice creams for different target markets (Hughes Neghaiwi and Geller, 2015). *Indirect* competitors are those who address the same target market, but provide a different offering to satisfy the market need, for example Spotify, Sony, and Apple's iPod.

Suppliers and Distributors

Porter (1979) also realized that suppliers can influence competition and hence built these into his Five Forces model. Transport and delivery services also constitute an important part of the value offered to customers.

It is common to find high levels of integration between a manufacturer and its distributors, dealers, and retailers. Account needs to be taken of the strength of these relationships and consideration given to how market performance might be strengthened or weakened by the capabilities of the channel intermediary. Suppliers and distributors have become central to a firm's ability to develop specific **competitive advantage**. Analysis of the performance environment should therefore incorporate a review of key suppliers and distributors to the firm.

Understanding the Internal Environment

An analysis of the internal environment of an organization is concerned with understanding and evaluating the capabilities and potential of the products, systems, and human, marketing, and financial resources. Attention here is given to two main elements, products and finance, by means of **portfolio analysis.**

Portfolio Analysis

When managing a collection, or 'portfolio', of offerings, we should appreciate that the performance of an individual offering can often fail to give useful insight. What is really important is an understanding of the relative performance of the offerings.

In 1977, the Boston Consulting Group (BCG) developed the original idea of a matrix—the **Boston box**, shown in Figure 4.4—based on two key variables: market growth and relative market share. Market share is measured as a percentage of the share of the product's largest competitor, expressed as a fraction; thus a relative share of 0.8 means that the product achieves 80 per cent of the sales of the market leader's sales volume (or value, depending on which measure is used). This would not be the strongest competitive position, but neither is it a weak position. A relative market share of 1 means that the company shares market leadership with a competitor with an equal share.

When analysed in terms of the Boston box, an offering falls into one of four categories, as follows.

- *Question marks* are offerings that exist in growing markets, but have low market share. As a result, there is negative cash flow and they are unprofitable.
- *Stars* are most probably market leaders, but their growth has to be financed through fairly heavy levels of investment.

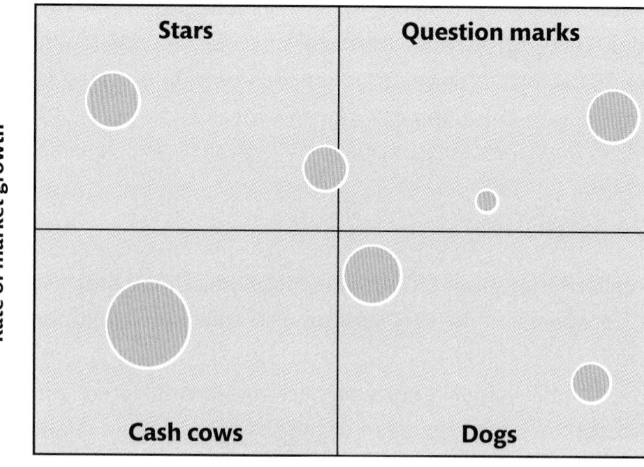

Figure 4.4 The Boston box

Source: Reprinted from B. Hedley, 'Strategy and the business portfolio', ***Long Range Planning***, 10, 1, 12. © 1977, with permission from Elsevier.

- *Cash cows* exist in fairly stable, low-growth markets and require little ongoing investment. Their high market share draws both positive cash flows and high levels of profitability.
- *Dogs* experience low growth and low market share, and generate negative cash flows. These indicators suggest that many of them are operating in declining markets and that they have no real long-term future.

Essentially, excess cash generated by cash cows should be utilized to develop question marks and stars, which are unable to support themselves. This enables stars to become cash cows and self-supporting. Dogs should be retained only as long as they contribute to positive cash flow, and do not restrict the use of assets and resources elsewhere in the business. Once they do so, they should be divested or ejected from the portfolio.

Divestment need not occur only because of low share, however: when pharmaceutical firm Merck sold Sirna Therapeutics to Alnylam Pharmaceuticals, the sale of the drug delivery subsidiary was heralded as enabling Merck to remain consistent with its strategy of reducing its emphasis on platform technologies. Merck's policy is to assess whether particular assets are core to its strategy, whether they provide competitive advantage, and whether they might generate greater value as part of Merck or outside Merck (Zhu, 2014).

By plotting all of a company's offerings within the Boston matrix, it becomes easy to appreciate visually whether a portfolio is well balanced (or otherwise). If offerings are distributed equally—or at least are not clustered in any single area—and market shares and cash flows equate with the offerings' market position, the portfolio is financially healthy and well balanced. An unbalanced portfolio, meanwhile, would see too many offerings clustered in one or two quadrants—and hence portfolio analysis would inform possible strategies to remedy this and allow us to project possible outcomes.

SWOT Analysis

Once the entire operating environment has been examined, it is essential to draw the information together in a form that can be easily understood. Perhaps the most common analytical tool is **SWOT analysis**, the acronym deriving from the Strengths, Weaknesses, Opportunities, and Threats on which the analysis centres. The framework comprises a series of checklists presented as internal strengths and weaknesses, and external opportunities or threats. Strengths and weaknesses relate to the internal resources and capabilities of the organization, as perceived by customers (Piercy, 2002).

- A *strength* is something that an organization is good at doing, or something that gives it particular credibility and market advantage.
- A *weakness* is something that an organization lacks or performs in an inferior way in comparison to others.

Opportunities and threats are externally oriented issues that can potentially influence the performance of an organization or offering.

- An *opportunity* is a potential way in which the organization might advance by developing and satisfying an unfulfilled market need.
- A *threat* is something that, at some time in the future, may destabilize and/or reduce the potential performance of the organization.

SWOT analysis helps us to sort through the information generated in the environmental analysis and to identify the key issues, and prompts us to think about converting weaknesses into strengths and threats into opportunities—that is, about generating conversion strategies.

Once the three or four elements of each part of the SWOT matrix have been derived, then a number of pertinent questions need to be asked, including the following.

1. Does the organization do something far better than its rivals? If it does, this is known as a 'competitive advantage' (or 'distinctive competence', or 'differential advantage'), and this can lead to a competitive edge.
2. Which of the organization's weaknesses does a strategy need to correct and is it competitively vulnerable?
3. Which opportunities can be pursued, and are there the necessary resources and capabilities to exploit them?
4. Which strategies are necessary to defend against the key threats?

Figure 4.5 depicts a SWOT matrix for a small digital media agency. The outcome of a successful SWOT analysis is a series of decisions that help the organization to develop and formulate strategy and goals. (Note that there are no more than four items in any one category, rather than a list of ten or so items. It is important to prioritize and make a judgment about what is really key.)

Strengths	**Weaknesses**
Quick to respond to changes in the marketing environment Flat management encourages fast decision-making Use of contractors enables flexibility—lowers employment costs/finance and improves customers' perception of expertise	Too much work from a few clients and at non-premium rates Few project management skills High office and finance costs Low customer base
Opportunities	**Threats**
Emerging markets such as professional services (e.g. dentists, lawyers, surveyors) New distribution channels Tax incentives to encourage e-commerce	Larger media houses buying business Speed of technological advances Contractors have low levels of loyalty

Figure 4.5 A SWOT analysis for a small digital media agency

Research Insight 4.3

To take your learning further, you might wish to read this influential paper.

Prahalad, C. K., and Hamel, G. (1990) 'The core competence of the organisation', *Harvard Business Review*, 68(3): 79–91.

This paper was incredibly important because it provided a first insight into the critical role of core competencies as a means of developing superior business performance.

 **Visit the online resources to read the abstract and access the full paper.**

Weaknesses need to be addressed, not avoided. Some can be converted into strengths; others, into opportunities. In this example, entering the professional services market would probably increase the number of customers and enable premium rates to be earned.

Threats need to be nullified. For example, by building relationships with key contractors (suppliers) and selected larger media houses, these threats might be dissipated—or even developed into strengths.

Visit the **online resources** and complete Internet Activity 4.3 to learn more about the use of SWOT analysis.

Strategic Marketing Goals

The analysis of the environment and the company's position allows us to determine exactly what the marketing strategy should actually achieve—that is, what the **strategic marketing** goals should be. Strategic marketing is a process that leads to specific decisions on how to compete in the marketplace and how the company should best serve its customers.

There are five strategic objectives, as illustrated in Figure 4.6.

- *Niche* objectives are often the most suitable when firms operate in a market dominated by a major competitor and in which financial resources are limited. A niche can be either a small segment or a small part of a segment. The Australian government identified several **niche markets** when exploring the development of its tourism business. It identified sports, cycling seniors, culture and the arts, backpackers, health, people with disabilities, caravanning and camping, food, wine, and agri-tourism as potential niche markets.
- **Hold** objectives are concerned with defence. They are designed to prevent and fend off attack from aggressive competitors. Market leaders are the most likely to adopt a holding strategy, because they are prone to attack from new entrants and their closest rivals as they strive for the most market share.

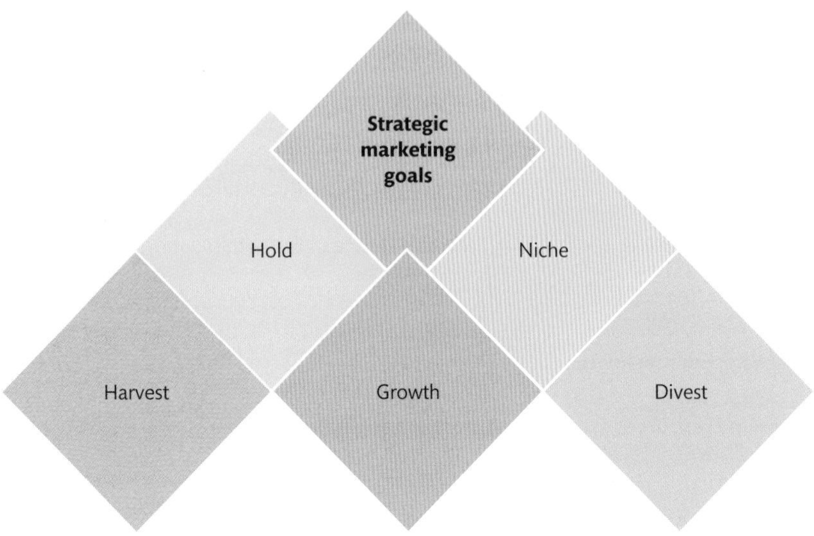

Figure 4.6 Five dimensions of strategic marketing goals

Australia's tourism has been developed around the identification of niche markets.

Source: © James Fisher/Tourism Australia.

- **Harvesting** objectives are often employed in mature markets as firms/offerings enter a decline phase. The goal is to maximize short-term profits and stimulate a positive cash flow.
- *Divest* objectives are sometimes necessary when offerings continue to incur losses and generate negative cash flows, such as when General Motors sold off Saab to sports car manufacturer Spyker (Madslien, 2010).
- *Growth* is an objective that the vast majority of organizations consider to be primary. There are, however, different forms of growth. Ansoff (1957) proposed that organizations should first consider whether new or established products are to be delivered in new or established markets. His product–market matrix (see Figure 4.7) is an important first step in deciding what the marketing strategy should be.

	Present products	**New products**
Present markets	Market penetration	Product development
New markets	Market development	Diversification

Figure 4.7 Ansoff's matrix

Source: Adapted from Ansoff (1957).

Strategic Market Action

An important marketing strategy activity concerns the identification of the most appropriate way of achieving the marketing goals set and putting the plan into action: the implementation phase.

There is no proven formula or toolkit that managers can use simply because of the many internal and external environmental factors. Managers draw upon experience to know which strategies are more likely to be successful than others. Porter (1985) proposed that there are two essential routes to achieving above average performance: to become the lowest cost producer or to differentiate the offering until it is of superior value to the customer. These strategies can be implemented in either broad (mass) or narrow (focused) markets. Porter suggested that these give rise to three generic strategies: overall **cost leadership**; differentiation; and focus strategies.

Cost leadership does not mean a lower price, although lower prices are often used to attract customers. By having the lowest cost structure, an organization can offer standard offerings at acceptable levels of quality, yet still generate above-average profit margins. If attacked by a competitor using lower prices, the low-cost leader has a far bigger cushion than its competitors. Charging a lower price than rivals is not the critical point. The competitive advantage is derived from *how* the organization exploits its cost–price ratio. By reinvesting the profit, for example by improving product quality, investing more in product development, or building extra capacity, long-run superiority is more likely to be achieved.

Differentiation requires that all value chain activities are geared towards the creation of offerings that are valued by, and which satisfy, the needs of particular broad segments. By identifying particular customer groups, each of which has a discrete set of needs, a product can be differentiated from its competitors. Fashion brand Zara differentiated itself by reformulating its value chain so that it became the fastest high-street brand from design, through production and distribution, to delivery of fashion clothing to the customer in store.

Customers are sometimes prepared to pay a higher price—that is, a premium—for offerings that deliver superior or extra value. The Starbucks coffee brand, for example, is strongly differentiated and valued, with consumers willing to pay higher prices to enjoy the Starbucks experience. However, differentiation can equally be achieved by low prices, as evidenced through the success of low-cost airlines such as Ireland's Ryanair.

Focus strategies are used by organizations that seek gaps in broad market segments or find gaps in competitors' ranges. In other words, focus strategies seek out unfulfilled market needs. There are two options for a company wishing to follow a **focus strategy**: one is low cost and the other is differentiation—but both occur within a particular, narrow segment. The difference between a broad differentiator and a focused differentiator is that the former bases its strategy on attributes valued across a number of markets, whereas the latter seeks to meet the needs of particular segments within a market.

Porter argues that, to achieve competitive advantage, organizations must achieve one of these three generic strategies. He argues that to fail to be strategically explicit results in organizations being 'stuck in the middle'—that is, they achieve below-average returns and have no competitive advantage. It has been observed, however, that some organizations have been able to pursue both low-cost and differentiated strategies simultaneously. For example, an organization that develops

Market Insight 4.3 **Discounting Competition**

Over the last 20 years, the rise of 'hard discounters' has significantly affected the competitive dynamic within the retail industry. Leading hard discounters such as Aldi or Lidl have a unique business model that allows them to maintain cost leadership in the industry.

1 They offer fewer categories and carry, on average, 1,400 stock-keeping units (SKUs) compared to the15,000+ SKUs carried by traditional supermarkets.
2 They offer very few manufacturer brands, relying mostly on private labels.
3 They have relatively small stores, being often smaller than 11,000 square feet in terms of trading area.
4 They have minimal customer service and very functional displays.

The combination of these strategic choices allow discounters to be 40–60 per cent cheaper than leading retailers. Such competitive pricing, combined with the tightening effect on family budgets since the global financial crisis of 2007–08 and subsequent economic downturn, has led to significant growth of discounters across Europe. Discounters' market share exceeds 10 per cent in most European countries, and it is above 26 per cent in Norway and 34 per cent in Germany.

This situation has intensified competition within established supermarket chains, which are ill-suited to compete with the discounters' business model purely on price. As a potential retaliation against discounters, large chains have implemented a mixture of two strategies:

- seeking to strengthen their differentiated positioning by focusing on better service and quality; and
- themselves entering the area of retail discounters through the launch of new retail formats.

An attempt at this latter strategy is exemplified by British retailer Sainsbury's, which, in 2014, entered into a joint venture with Danish company Netto to open 20 new stores in the UK. While Sainsbury's is a traditional supermarket, Netto is a hard discounter with a presence in several countries in northern Europe. The joint venture was to allow Netto to enter a market with significant growth potential, while Sainsbury's would benefit from the further success of the discounter model—but the joint venture unravelled in 2016, with Sainsbury's deciding to divest to focus on its core business. This failure stresses further the dominance of Aldi and Lidl, and the challenge they pose to traditional supermarkets in the long term.

Sainsbury's briefly cooperated with Netto in an attempt to respond to the challenge from 'hard discounters'.
Source: © James W. Copeland/Shutterstock.

1 **What strategic objectives are available to Sainsbury's when competing against discounters?**
2 **What are the potential advantages and disadvantages of a collaboration such as that between Sainsbury's and Netto?**
3 **Which types of growth strategy might be available to discounters?**

Source: Cleeren et al. (2010); BBC News (2014); Butler (2016); Trotman (2016).

a large market share through differentiation and by creating very strong brands or through technological innovation may well also become the cost leader.

 Visit the **online resources** and access Internet Activity 4.4 to learn more about business planning in the airline market.

Marketing Planning

The three key activities associated with strategic marketing planning cover strategic market analysis, the setting of strategic marketing goals, and defining strategic marketing action, each area of which we consider in the preceding sections. For organizations to be able to develop, implement, and control these activities at the offering and brand levels, marketing plans are developed. This final section considers the characteristics of the marketing planning process.

Marketing planning is a sequential process involving a series of activities leading to the setting of marketing objectives and the formulation of plans for achieving them (McDonald, 2002: 27). A marketing plan is the key output from the overall strategic marketing planning process. It details a company's or brand's intended marketing activity. Marketing plans can be developed for periods of one, two, or five years—even up to 25 years. Too many organizations, however, regard marketing plans as a development of the annual round of setting sales targets, which are then extrapolated into quasi-marketing plans. In doing so, they fail to take into account the marketplace, customer needs, and resources available.

The first step in the planning process should be a phase of strategic appraisal and evaluation. This will covers a period of between three and five years, and provide a strategic insight into the markets, competitors, and organizational resources that will shape the direction and nature of the way in which the firm has decided to compete. Once agreed, these should be updated on an annual basis, and modified to meet changing internal and external conditions. Only once the strategic marketing plan has been developed should detailed operational or functional marketing plans, covering a one-year period, be developed (McDonald, 2002). This makes marketing planning a continuous process, not something undertaken once a year or, worse, only when a new product is launched.

A marketing plan designed to support a particular offering consists of a series of activities that should be undertaken sequentially. These are presented in Table 4.1.

Many of the corporate-level goals and strategies and internal and external environmental analyses that are established within the strategic marketing planning process can be replicated within each of the marketing plans written for individual products, product lines, markets, or even strategic business units (SBUs). As a general rule, only detail concerning offerings, competitors, and related support resources need change prior to the formulation of individual marketing mixes and their implementation, within functional level marketing plans.

The strategic marketing planning process starts with a consideration of the organization's goals and resources, and an analysis of the market and environmental context in which the organization seeks to achieve its goals. It culminates in a detailed plan, which, when implemented, is measured to determine how well the organization performs against the marketing plan.

Table 4.1 Key activities within a marketing plan

Activity	Explanation
Executive summary	Brief, one-page summary of key points and outcomes
Overall objectives	Makes references to the organization's overall mission and corporate goals—i.e. the elements that underpin the strategy
Product/market background	Summarizes the product and/or market to clarify understanding about target markets, sales history, market trends, main competitors, and the organization's own product portfolio
Marketing analysis	Provides insight into the market, the customers, and the competition; should consider segment needs, current strategies, and key financial data; is supported by the marketing audit and SWOT analysis
Marketing strategies	States the market(s) to be targeted, the basis on which the firm will compete, the competitive advantages to be used, and the way in which the product is to be positioned in the market
Marketing goals	Expresses the desired outcomes of the strategy in terms of the volume of expected sales, the value of sales and market share gains, levels of product awareness, availability, profitability, and customer satisfaction
Marketing programmes	Develops a marketing mix for each target market segment; specifies who is responsible for the various activities and actions, and the resources that are to be made available
Implementation	Sets out: • the way in which the marketing plan is to be controlled and evaluated; • the financial scope of the plan; and • the operational implications in terms of human resources, R&D, and system and process needs
Supporting documentation	Any relevant supporting documentation too bulky to be included in the plan itself, but necessary for reference and detail, e.g. the full PESTLE and SWOT analyses, marketing research data, and other market reports and information, plus key correspondence

Chapter Summary

To consolidate your learning, the key points from this chapter are summarized below.

- **Describe the key characteristics associated with the marketing environment.**

  The marketing environment incorporates the external environment, the performance environment, and the internal environment. The external environment incorporates macro-environmental factors, which are largely uncontrollable and which organizations generally cannot influence. The performance environment incorporates key factors within an industry, impacting on strategic decision-making. The internal environment is controllable and is the principal means, through its resource base, by which an organization influences its strategy.

  The external environment comprises political, social, and technological factors, and organizations often have very limited, if any, control of these. The performance environment consists of competitors, suppliers, and indirect service providers, who shape the way and extent to which organizations achieve their objectives. Here, organizations have a much stronger level of influence. The internal environment concerns the resources, processes, and policies with which an organization achieves its goals, which factors it can influence directly.

- **Explain the environmental scanning process and show how PESTLE analysis can be used to understand the external environment.**

  The environmental scanning process consists of the data-gathering phase, the environmental interpretation and analysis phase, and the strategy formulation phase. The three processes are interlinked, but, over time, more attention is focused on each one more than the others so that at the end of the process, greater effort is expended on using knowledge gleaned from the external and competitive environments to formulate strategy based on changes occurring and identified in the company's environment.

  We considered the various components of the external marketing environment that may impact on any particular organization using the PESTLE framework, which comprises Political, Economic, Socio-cultural, Technological, Legal, and Ecological factors. Some of these factors are more important than others in any particular industry.

- **Analyse the performance environment using the Porter's Five Forces industry analysis model.**

  The most common technique used to analyse the performance environment is Porter's 'Five Forces' model of competitive analysis. Porter concludes that the more intense the rivalry between the industry players, the lower will be their overall performance. On the other hand, the lower the rivalry, the greater will be the performance of the industry players. Porter's Five Forces comprise supplier bargaining power, buyer bargaining power, the threat of new entrants, rivalry among competitors, and the threat of substitutes.

- **Analyse an organization's product/service portfolio to aid resource planning.**

  An organization's principal resources relate to its portfolio of offerings and the financial resources at its disposal. We use portfolio analysis—specifically, the Boston box approach—to determine whether different strategic business units (SBUs) or product/service formulations are 'stars', 'dogs', 'question marks', or 'cash cows', each category characterised by differing levels of cash flow and resource requirements. It is important to undertake a marketing audit as a preliminary measure to allow proper development of marketing strategy.

- **Analyse current conditions and formulate marketing strategies.**

  SWOT analysis is used to determine an overall view of the organization's strategic position, and highlights the need to produce a strong fit between the internal capability (strengths and weaknesses) and the external situation (opportunities and threats). SWOT analysis serves to identify the key issues, and then prompts thought about converting weaknesses into strengths and threats into opportunities.

- **Explain the different types of strategic marketing goal and associated growth strategies.**

  There are several types of strategic objective, but the main ones are niche, hold, harvest, growth, and divest goals. The vast majority of organizations consider growth to be a primary objective.

Review Questions

1. **What are the three main marketing environments?**
2. **How might changes in the political environment affect marketing strategy?**
3. **How might changes in the economic environment affect marketing strategy?**
4. **How might changes in the socio-cultural environment affect marketing strategy?**
5. **How might changes in the technological environment affect marketing strategy?**
6. **How might changes in the legal environment affect marketing strategy?**
7. **How might changes in the ecological environment affect marketing strategy?**
8. **What are Porter's 'Five Forces'?**
9. **Identify the key characteristics of SWOT analysis. What actions should be taken once the SWOT grid is completed?**
10. **List the core parts of a marketing plan.**

Worksheet Summary

To apply the knowledge you have gained from this chapter, and to test your understanding of how the PESTLE framework, Five Forces model, and Boston box can be used to analyse the marketing environment, visit the **online resources** and complete Worksheet 4.1.

Discussion Questions

1. Having read Case Insight 4.1, how would you advise 3scale with regard to Amazon's entry into the market?
2. Read Market Insight 4.2. Search the Internet for further information on the healthy eating debate, obesity, and 'fat taxes', and then answer the following questions.

   A What changes have taken place in the external environment to bring about the introduction of 'fat taxes' in different countries?

B How should Kraft Foods (owner of Cadbury's) ensure that it keeps up to date with trends in consumer lifestyles, government legislation, and competitor new proposition development?

C What strategies in relation to proposition development and promotion could Kraft Foods adopt to ensure that it maintains its market dominance in the chocolate countline market?

3 **Undertake an environmental analysis using PESTLE, by searching the Internet for appropriate information and by using available market research reports, for each of the following markets.**

A The automotive market (for example VW, Renault, BMW, Ford, or Toyota)

B The global multiple retail grocery market (for example Walmart, Carrefour, or Tesco)

C The beer industry (for example InBev, Carlsberg, Heineken, Miller Brands, or Budweiser Budvar)

4 **After a successful period of 20 years' trading, a bicycle manufacturer notices that its sales, rather than increasing at a steady rate, are starting to decline. The company, Rapid Cycles, produces a range of bicycles to suit various segments and distributes them mainly through independent cycle shops. In recent years, however, the number of low-cost cycles entering the country has increased, with many distributed through supermarkets and national retail chains. The managing director of Rapid Cycles feels that he cannot compete with these low-cost imports and asks you for your opinion about what should be done. Discuss the situation facing Rapid Cycles and make recommendations regarding its marketing strategy.**

 Visit the **online resources** and complete the multiple-choice questions to assess your knowledge of the chapter.

Glossary

Boston box a popular portfolio matrix, developed by the Boston Consulting Group, commonly also referred to as the 'BCG matrix'

competitive advantage achieved when an organization has an edge over its competitors on factors that are important to customers.

cost leadership a strategy involving the production of goods and services for a broad market segment, at a cost lower than those of all other competitors.

differentiation a strategy through which an organization offers products and services to broad particular customer groups, who perceive the offering to be significantly different from, and superior to, its competitors.

divestment a strategic objective that involves selling a business or killing a product when that business or product continues to incur losses and generate negative cash flows.

environmental scanning a management process designed to identify external issues, situations, and threats that may impinge on an organization's future and its strategic decision-making.

focus strategy a strategy based on developing gaps in broad market segments or gaps in competitors' product ranges.

government the system of organization of a nation state.

gross domestic product (GDP) a measure of the output of a nation—that is, of the size of its economy; calculated as the market value of all finished goods and services produced in a country during a specified period, typically available annually or quarterly.

harvesting a strategic objective based on maximizing short-term profits and stimulating positive cash flow; often used in mature markets as firms or products enter a decline phase.

hold a strategic objective based on defending against attacks from aggressive competitors.

inflation rising prices.

niche market a small part of a market segment that has specific and specialized characteristics that make it uneconomic for the leading competitors to enter.

performance environment refers to the organizations that directly or indirectly influence an organization's ability to achieve its strategic and operational goals.

PESTLE a framework that examines the external environment, named as an acronym of the Political, Economic, Socio-cultural, Technological, Legal, and Ecological factors on which it focuses.

political environment that part of the macro environment concerned with impending and potential legislation and how it may affect a particular firm.

portfolio analysis an assessment of a company's mix of products, services, investments, and other assets aiming to optimize the use of resources and to assess its suitability, level of risk, and expected financial return.

price sensitivity the extent to which a company or consumer increases or lowers its purchase volumes in relation to changes in price. A company or customer is price *in*sensitive when unit volumes drop proportionately less than increases in prices.

public relations (PR) a non-personal form of communication used by companies to build trust, goodwill, interest, and ultimately relationships with a range of stakeholders.

purchasing power parity (PPP) a way of establishing the relative value of currencies between countries, so that there is an equivalence of purchasing power.

recession a fall in a country's GDP for two or more successive quarters in any one year.

relative price denotes the price of company A's product/service as a proportion of the price of a comparable product/service of company B (typically the market leader) or its nearest competitor (where A is the market leader).

reverse engineering the process of developing a product from the finished version (for example from a competitor's prototype) to its constituent parts rather than the usual approach from components parts to a finished product.

society the customs, habits, and nature of a nation's social system.

stakeholders people with an interest—that is, a 'stake'—in the levels of profit an organization achieves, its environmental impact, and its ethical conduct in society.

strategic marketing the organizational process that leads to decisions on how the company should compete in the marketplace (against its rivals) and how it should serve its customer base.

sustainable competitive advantage when an organization is able to offer a superior product to those of competitors that is not easily imitated and which enjoys significant market share as a result.

switching costs the psychological, economic, time, and effort-related costs associated with substituting one product or service for another, or changing a supplier from one to another.

SWOT analysis a methodology used by organizations to understand their strategic position; involves analysis of an organization's Strengths, Weaknesses, Opportunities, and Threats.

values the standards of behaviour expected of an organization's employees.

References

Aguilar, F. Y. (1967) *Scanning the Business Environment*, New York: Macmillan.

Albright, K. S. (2004) 'Environmental scanning: Radar for success', *Information Management Journal*, May–June: 38–45.

Ansoff, I. H. (1957) 'Strategies for diversification', *Harvard Business Review*, 35(2): 113–24.

Barrick Gold (2014) 'Barrick reaches agreement with Diaguita indigenous communities' 28 May. Available online at http://barrickbeyondborders.com/people/2014/05/barrick-reaches-agreement-with-diaguita-indigenous-communities/ [accessed 9 October 2015].

Barrie, J. (2015) 'Tesco, please don't take away my Ribena!', *The Telegraph*, 27 July. Available online at http://www.telegraph.co.uk/foodanddrink/healthyeating/11766006/Tesco-please-dont-take-away-my-Ribena.html [accessed 10 September 2015].

BBC News (2006) 'Supermarkets covet Polish spend', 10 September. Available online at http://news.bbc.co.uk/1/hi/business/5332024.stm [accessed 11 April 2010].

BBC News (2014) 'Sainsbury's and Netto open first of 15 new discount stores', 6 November. Available online at http://www.bbc.co.uk/news/business-29918179 [accessed 6 November 2016].

Butler, S. (2016) 'Netto's UK stores to close as Sainsbury's calls time on joint venture', *The Guardian*, 4 July. Available online at https://www.theguardian.com/business/2016/jul/04/netto-uk-stores-to-close-as-sainsburys-calls-time-on-joint-venture [accessed 4 July 2016].

Buzzell, R. D., Gale, B. T., and Sultan, R. G. M. (1975) 'Market share: A key to profitability', *Harvard Business Review*, 53(1): 97–106.

Cleeren, K., Verboven, F., Dekimpe, M. G., and Gielens, K. (2010) 'Intra-and interformat competition among discounters and supermarkets', *Marketing Science*, 29(3): 456–73.

Davidson, L. (2015) '*The Great British Bake Off* is killing packaged bread', *The Telegraph*, 12 August. Available online at http://www.telegraph.co.uk/finance/newsbysector/retailandconsumer/11799225/The-Great-British-Bake-Off-is-killing-packaged-bread.html [accessed 10 September 2015].

Danciu, V. (2013) 'The future of marketing: An appropriate response to the environment changes', *Theoretical and Applied Economics*, 20(5): 33–52.

Edney, A. (2014) 'Cost to develop a drug more than doubles to $2.56 billion', *Bloomberg*, 18 November. Available online at http://www.bloomberg.com/news/articles/2014-11-18/cost-to-develop-a-drug-more-than-doubles-to-2-56-billion [accessed 9 October 2015].

Green, J. (2000) 'The role of theory in evidence-based health promotion practice', *Health Education Research*, 15(2): 125–9.

Hedley, B. (1977) 'Strategy and the business portfolio', *Long Range Planning*, 10(1): 9–15.

Hillman, A., Keim, G. D., and Schuler, D. (2004) 'Corporate political activity: A review and research agenda', *Journal of Management*, 30(6): 837–57.

Hughes Neghaiwi, B., and Geller, M. (2015) 'Changing tastes churn up ice cream industry', *Reuters*, 1 September. Available online at http://www.reuters.com/article/2015/09/01/food-icecream-idUSL5N1134KC20150901 [accessed 9 October 2015].

Lawton, T., and Rajwani, T. (2011) 'Designing lobbying capabilities: Managerial choices in unpredictable environments', *European Business Review*, 23(2): 167–89.

Levitt, T. (1960) 'Marketing myopia', *Harvard Business Review*, 38(4): 45–56.

Madslien, J. (2010) 'Spyker boss outlines Saab plans', *BBC News*, 12 February. Available online at http://www.news.bbc.co.uk/1/hi/business/8512224.stm [accessed 25 March 2010].

May, R. C., Stewart, W. H., Jr., and Sweo, R. (2000) 'Environmental scanning behaviour in a transitional economy: Evidence from Russia', *Academy of Management Journal*, 43(3): 403–27.

McDonald, M. (2002) *Marketing Plans and How to Make Them* (5th edn), Oxford: Butterworth-Heinemann.

Orsato, R. J. (2006) 'Competitive environmental strategies: When does it pay to be green?', *California Management Review*, 48(2): 127–43.

Piercy, N. (2002) *Market-Led Strategic Change: Transforming the Process of Going to Market*, Oxford: Butterworth-Heinemann.

Porter, M. E. (1979) 'How competitive forces shape strategy', *Harvard Business Review*, 57(2): 137–45.

Porter, M. E. (1985) *The Competitive Advantage: Creating and Sustaining Superior Performance*, New York: Free Press.

Prno, J., and Slocombe, S. D. (2012). 'Exploring the origins of "social license to operate" in the mining sector: Perspectives from governance and sustainability theories', *Resources Policy*, 37(3): 346–57.

Rao, P. M. (2005) 'Sustaining competitive advantage in a high-technology environment: A strategic marketing perspective', *Advances in Competitiveness Research*, 13(1): 33–47.

Trotman, A. (2016) 'Sainsbury's steps up discount battle with plans for more Netto stores', 8 January. Available online at http://www.telegraph.co.uk/finance/newsbysector/retailandconsumer/12090582/Sainsburys-steps-up-discount-battle-with-plans-for-more-Netto-stores.html [accessed 8 January 2016].

Wiebe, A. (2015) 'A problematic process: The memorandum of understanding between Barrick Gold and Diaguita Communities of Chile', September. Available online at http://miningwatch.ca/sites/default/files/barrick_mou_pascua_lama_eng_15sep1015.pdf [accessed 9 October 2015].

Young, T. (2015) 'A fat tax is not the way to fight obesity', *The Telegraph*, 29 July. Available online at http://www.telegraph.co.uk/news/health/news/11770042/A-fat-tax-is-not-the-way-to-fight-obesity.html [accessed 12 October 2015].

Zhu, K. (2014) 'Top 4 reasons to divest', *Axial*, 12 February. Available online at http://www.axial.net/forum/top-4-reasons-divest/ [accessed 9 October 2015].

Chapter 5
Market Segmentation and Positioning

Learning Outcomes

After studying this chapter, you will be able to:

- describe the principles of market segmentation and the segmentation, targeting, and positioning (STP) process;
- list the characteristics and differences between market segmentation and product differentiation;
- explain consumer and business-to-business (B2B) market segmentation;
- describe different targeting strategies;
- discuss the concept of 'positioning'; and
- consider how the use of perceptual maps can assist in the positioning process.

Case Insight 5.1
Lanson International

Market Insight 5.1
Differentiating Legal Services

Market Insight 5.2
Sustainability Segmentation

Market Insight 5.3
Recapturing Lost B2B Customers

Market Insight 5.4
Positioning Premium Beer

Case Insight 5.1 **Lanson International**

Founded in 1760, Champagne Lanson is one of the oldest existing champagne houses in France, making some of the world's finest champagnes. We speak to Paul Beavis (pictured), managing director of Lanson International, to find out more about how the company looks to further develop its presence in international markets, including the UK.

'Lanson currently operates in more than 30 countries around the world and this has been developed over a number of years, driven by the increase in demand for champagne in the UK, which started more than 15 years ago. Generally, we believe that a company should look at international markets when its appetite for growth supersedes the current in-market capacity. Obviously, however, general economic market conditions apply and these need to be considered before we enter into any new markets. For us, a key success factor for successfully entering a new market is having data, data, and more data! Having the absolute facts about your markets is essential: it's a case of examination (of the market), diagnosis (of the entry method, what channels to use, and how to promote our brand), and prescription (of the operational approach).

'Before we enter a market, we look at the current shape and size of the markets, but also (and this is seldom easy) we try to forecast how the category will be shaped in the next three-to-five years. One key trend that we can see in the global economy today is a concentration of spending power across and within certain markets. To tap into those segments, internationalization has to be a core part of our strategy for the future. So we evaluate a potential market's economic conditions, searching for market data not only about current volumes, but also more about consumer trends, the knowledge gap (what we know versus what we don't know about consumers' attitudes and behaviour), and we look at other drinks categories, such as spirits, and growth in wine consumption generally.

'All of this insight helps us to plan our route-to-market strategy primarily. This also involves ascertaining more generally what strategy we should deploy, in terms of market **positioning**, whether or not we should use a subsidiary brand model or a distributor/agency model, and then considering the financial implications of each of those.

'In the UK, part of the problem is that, as categories get more mature, as the UK is now, there is a real need to be able to explain why your brand is essential in the marketplace. The hardest question any business should ask itself is: what is my true competitive advantage?

'In the UK market, champagne (with sales of £141.3 million in 2014) has generally seen strong competition from sparkling wine brands, particularly prosecco (with sales of £181.8 million in 2014), and especially in the off-licence trade, but Lanson enjoys the position of being the leading rosé brand and the second non-vintage champagne brand. Meanwhile, Spanish cava has seen a recent decline in sales.'

Lanson therefore faced a key question in relation to its international market development strategy: how should a French brand such as Lanson seek to differentiate itself in a category that is dominated, in the UK, by a competitor focus on 'advertising' and the colour of the label?

Introduction

Have you ever wondered how we decide to target certain market segments with our marketing activities? Think about fashion retailers for a moment: how do they identify with which people to communicate about their new ranges? In this chapter, we consider how organizations decide on which segments of a market to concentrate their efforts. This process is known as **market segmentation** and it is an integral part of marketing strategy. After defining 'market segmentation', we explore the differences between market segmentation and **product differentiation**. We consider consumer and **business-to-business (B2B)** market segmentation in detail. The method by which whole markets are subdivided into different segments to allocate marketing programme activity is referred to as the **STP process**, referring to segmentation, targeting, and positioning (see Figure 5.1).

The STP Process

Segmentation, targeting, and positioning is a core component of the strategic marketing process, and the STP process is used because of the prevalence of mature markets and greater diversity in customer needs, and its ability to help us to identify specialized, niche segments. Marketers segment markets and identify attractive segments (that is, who to focus on and why), identify new proposition opportunities, develop suitable positioning and **communication** strategies (that is, what message to communicate), and allocate resources to prioritized marketing activities (that is,

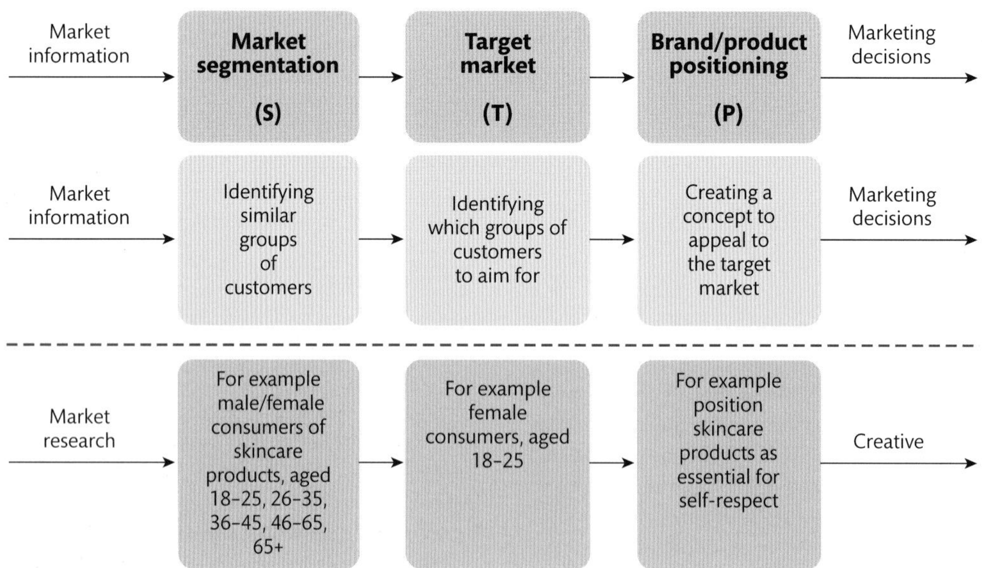

Figure 5.1 The STP process

how much to spend and where). Organizations commission segmentation research to revise their marketing strategies, to investigate a declining brand, to launch a new offering, or to restructure their pricing policies. When operating in highly dynamic environments, segmentation research should be conducted at regular intervals.

The key benefits of the STP process include the following.

Coca-Cola developed Coke Zero to target a specific segment: health-conscious males who enjoy consuming soft drinks.

Source: © Todor Tsvetkov / iStockphoto.

- It enhances a company's competitive position, providing direction and focus for marketing strategies, including targeted advertising, new proposition development, and brand differentiation. For example, Coca-Cola identified that Diet Coke was seen as 'feminine' by male consumers; it consequently developed Coke Zero as a new flavour targeted more generally at the health-conscious segment of the soft drinks market.
- It allows an organization to identify market growth opportunities by means of the identification of new customers, growth segments, or proposition uses, for example when Lucozade repositioned itself away from an offering that sick people used to rebrand itself as an energy drink.
- It allows for the effective and efficient matching of company resources to targeted market segments, promising greater return on marketing investment (ROMI). For example, Asda Wal-Mart uses data-informed segmentation strategies to target direct marketing messages (online and offline) and to offer rewards to customers representing long-term value to the company.

The Concept of Market Segmentation

'Market segmentation' is the division of a mass market into distinct and identifiable groups or segments, within which individuals have common characteristics and needs, and display similar responses to marketing actions.

Market segmentation was first defined as 'a condition of growth when core markets have already been developed on a generalised basis to the point where additional promotional expenditures are yielding diminishing returns' (Smith, 1956: 7). It forms an important foundation for successful marketing strategies and activities (Wind, 1978). The purpose of market segmentation is to ensure that elements of the marketing mix—namely, price, place (or distribution), products, and promotion (plus people, process, and physical evidence for service offerings)—meet different customer groups' needs. Because companies have finite resources, it is not feasible to produce all of the required offerings, for all of the people, all of the time. We cannot be all things to all people; the best that we can do is provide selected offerings for selected groups of people, most of the time. This enables the most effective use of an organization's scarce resources.

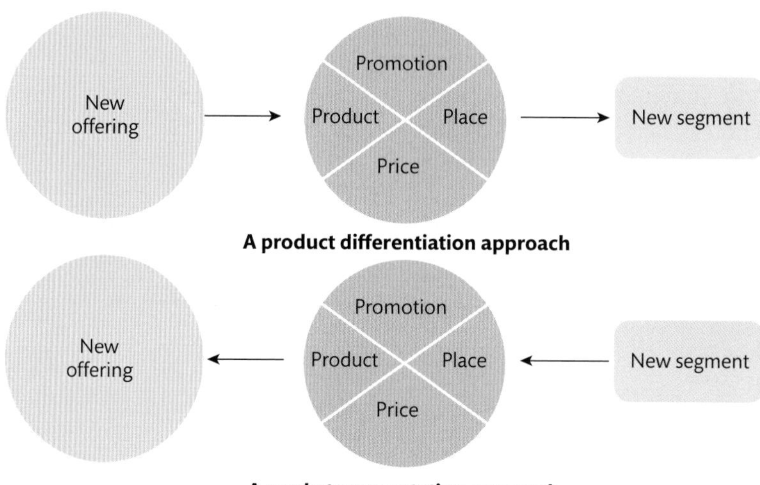

Figure 5.2 The difference between market segmentation and product differentiation

Market segmentation is related to product differentiation (see Figure 5.2). Companies vary their product offering on the basis of the specific needs of the segments they have identified. In fashion retailing, for example, if you adapt your clothing range so that your skirts are more colourful, use lighter fabrics, and have very short hemlines, this styling might appeal to younger women. This is product differentiation—a focus on product offering (see Market Insight 5.1).

Market Insight 5.1 **Differentiating Legal Services**

Complex services are notoriously difficult to differentiate. Successful differentiating strategies need to leverage messages that are relevant to customers and easy to understand. The following four approaches are common sources of differentiation that law firms can implement when promoting themselves to business customers.

- *Industry niche*—Some firms specialize in specific industries. A firm might specialize in legal issues arising in the media (such as defamation law or intellectual property rights), for example. This focus will make the company distinctive in the eyes of potential new clients.
- *Online services*—Some firms specialize in offering to their clients the availability of online services, with databases, videos, and resources that can help them to make legal decisions. This is useful to international corporations, which might be interested in understanding laws regulating business activities across the globe.
- *Ancillary services*—Some clients might value additional services that go beyond legal assistance. Entrepreneurs, for example, might value specialized mentoring and support in the development of their businesses.
- *Emergency team*—Certain businesses will value a quick response to deal with unforeseen circumstances. Law firms can differentiate themselves by offering a team able to respond immediately to the needs of its clients.

1 **Are product/service differentiation strategies an alternative to market segmentation strategies?**

2 **What process should a law firm adopt to choose the right differentiation strategy for it?**

3 **Under what circumstances should market segmentation be used in preference to product/service differentiation?**

Source: McKenna (2013).

The Process of Market Segmentation

There are two main approaches to segmentation. The first adopts the view that markets consist of customers who are similar; the task is to identify groups that share particular differences. This is known as the **breakdown method**. The second approach considers that markets consist of customers who are different; the task is to find similarities. This is known as the **build-up method** (Griffiths and Pol, 1994).

The breakdown method is the most established method for segmenting consumer markets. The build-up method seeks to move from the individual level, at which all customers are different, to a more general level of analysis based on the identification of similarities (Freytag and Clarke, 2001). The build-up method is customer-oriented, seeking to determine common customer needs. The aim of both methods is to identify market segments in which identifiable differences exist between segments—segment heterogeneity—but similarities exist between members within each segment—member homogeneity (see Figure 5.3).

In **business markets**, segmentation should reflect the relationship needs of the organizations involved. However, problems remain concerning the practical application and implementation of B2B segmentation. Managers frequently report that the analytical processes are reasonably clear, but it is unclear how they should choose and evaluate the various market segments (Naudé and Cheng, 2003). Segmentation theory has developed in an era in which a transactional goods-centric approach to marketing was predominant, rather than the service-dominant logic existing today. Under the transactional approach, resources are allocated to achieve designated marketing mix goals. But customers within various segments, have changing needs and therefore these customers may change their segment membership (Freytag and Clarke, 2001). Consequently, market segmentation programmes should use current customer data.

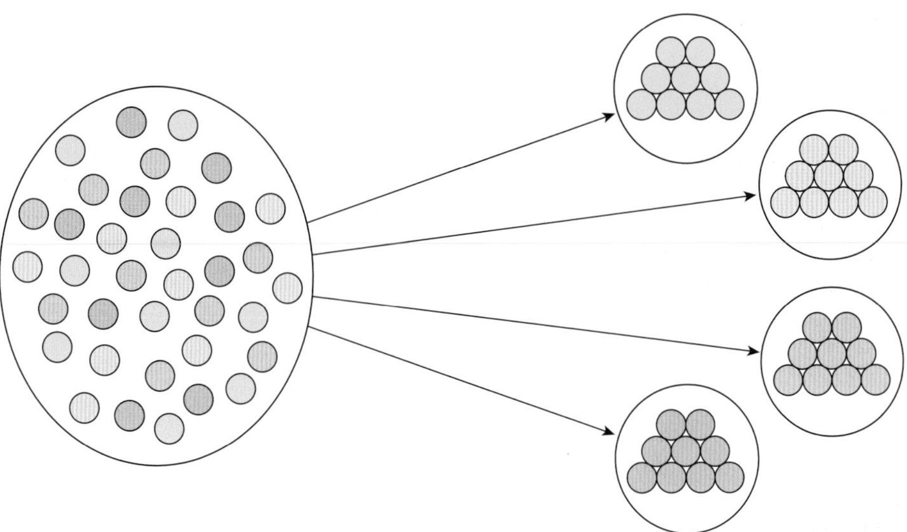

Figure 5.3 Segment heterogeneity and member homogeneity

Market Segmentation in Consumer Markets

To segment consumer markets, we use market information based around key customer-, product-, or situation-related criteria. These are classified as 'segmentation bases' and include profile (for example 'who are my market and where are they?'), behavioural (for example 'where, when, and how does my market behave?'), and psychological criteria (for example 'why does my market behave that way?') (see Figure 5.4). A fourth segmentation criterion is contact data—that is, customers' names and full contact details beyond their postcodes (for example postal and email addresses, and mobile and home telephone numbers). Contact data are useful for tactical-level marketing activities, such as direct and digital marketing.

Table 5.1 illustrates the key characteristics associated with each of the main approaches to consumer market segmentation.

When selecting different segmentation bases, the trade-off between data acquisition costs and the ability of the data to predict customer choice behaviour should be considered. Demographic and geo-demographic data are relatively easy to measure and obtain; however, these bases suffer from low levels of accuracy in predicting consumer behaviour (see Figure 5.5). In contrast, behavioural data (such as product usage, purchase history, and media usage), although more costly to acquire, provide a more accurate means to predict future behaviour: for example, the brand of toothpaste you purchased previously is more likely to be the brand of toothpaste that you purchase in future. However, customer choices are also influenced by susceptibility to marketing communications.

One way of segmenting consumer markets is to use profile criteria to determine who consumers are and where they are located. To do this, we use demographic methods (for example age, gender, race), socio-economics (for example determined by social class or income levels), and geographic location (for example using postcodes). A utility company might segment households based on geographical area to assess regional brand penetration; an insurance company might segment the market

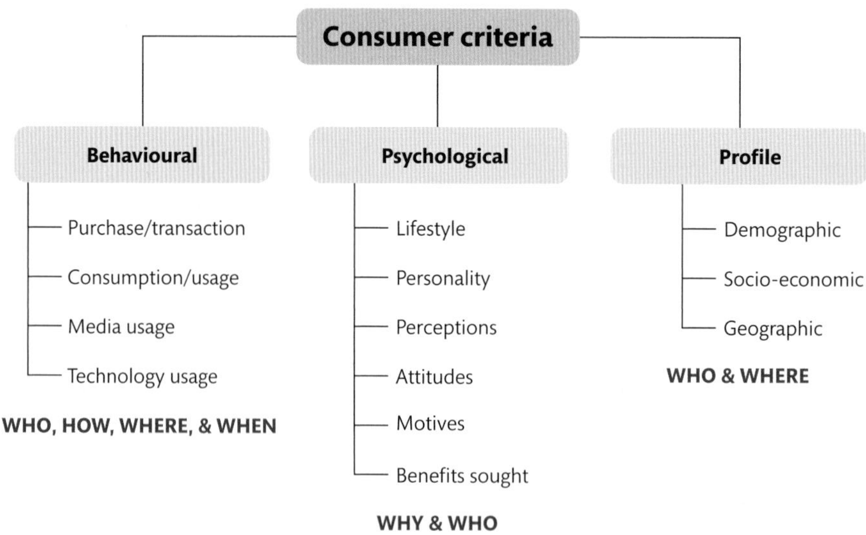

Figure 5.4 Segmentation criteria for consumer markets

Table 5.1	Segmentation criteria	
Base type	**Segmentation criteria**	**Explanation**
Profile	Demographic	Key variables concern age, sex, occupation, level of education, religion, social class, and income characteristics.
	Life stage	This is based on the principle that people need different offerings at different stages in their lives (e.g. childhood, adulthood, young couple, retirement).
	Geographic	The needs of potential customers in one geographic area are often different from those in another area owing to climate, custom, or tradition.
	Geo-demographic	There is a relationship between the type of housing and location in which people live and their purchasing behaviours.
Psychological	Psychographic (lifestyle)	By analysing consumers' activities, interests, and opinions, we can understand individual lifestyles and patterns of behaviour affecting their buying behaviour and decision-making processes. We can also identify similar offering and/or media usage patterns.
	Benefits sought	The motivations customers derive from their purchases provide an insight into the benefits they seek from the use of an offering.
Behavioural	Purchase/transaction	Data about customer purchases and transactions provides scope for analysing who buys what, when, and how often, how much they spend, and through what transactional channel they purchase.
	Product usage	Segments can be derived on the basis of customer usage of the offering, brand, or product category. This may be in the form of usage frequency, time of usage, and usage situations.
	Media usage	What media channels are used, by whom, when, where, and for how long provides useful insights into the reach potential for certain market segments through differing media channels, as well as insight into the segment's media lifestyle.

based on age, employment, income, and asset net worth to identify attractive market segments for a new investment portfolio. These are all examples of segmentation based on profile criteria.

Demographic

Demographic variables relate to age, gender, family size and life cycle, generation (such as 'baby boomers', 'Generation Y'), income, occupation, education, ethnicity, nationality, religion, and social class. They indicate the profile of a consumer and are useful in media planning. For example, gender

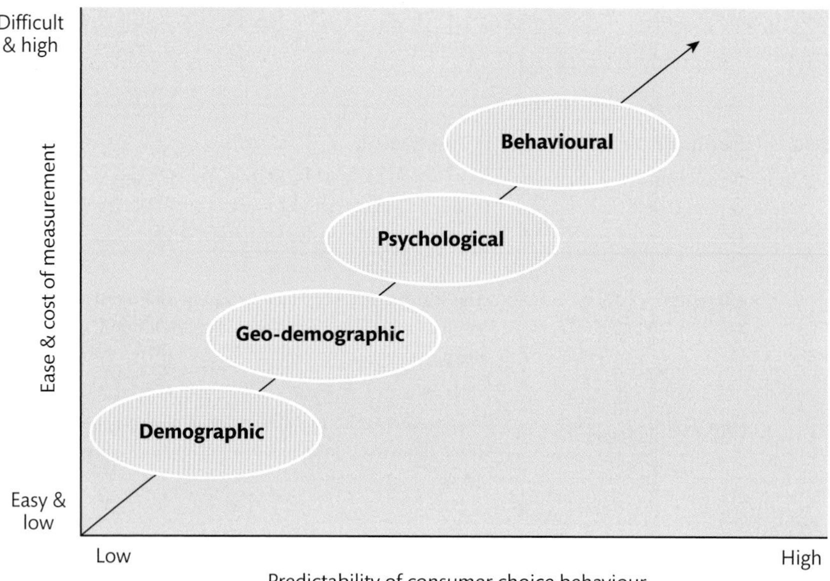

Figure 5.5 Considerations for segmentation criteria accessibility and use

Source: From SHIMP. *Integrated Marketing Communications in Advertising and Promotion®*, International Edition, 7E. ©Profile Criteria.

Advertising campaigns featuring celebrities (as in this case the singer Ellie Goulding for Pantene) can be used to support demographic segmentation.

Source: Courtesy of the Advertising Archives.

differences have spawned a raft of offerings targeted at women, including beauty and fragrance offerings (such as Clinique, Chanel), magazines (such as *Cosmopolitan*, *Heat*), hairdressing (such as Pantene, Clairol), and clothes (such as H&M, New Look). Offerings targeted at men include magazines (such as *GQ*) and beverages (such as Carlsberg, Coke Zero). Some brands develop offerings targeted at both men and women, for example fragrances (such as Calvin Klein) and watches (such as Rolex).

Life cycle

Lifestage analysis posits that people have varying amounts of disposable income and different needs at different times in their lives. Adolescents need different offerings from single 26-year-olds, who need different offerings compared with 26-year-old married people with young children. Major supermarkets (such as Asda Wal-Mart, Tesco) have all invested in the development of offerings targeted at singles with high levels of disposable

Table 5.2 Kantar Media's Target Group Index (TGI) lifestage segmentation groups

Lifestage group	Demographic description
Fledglings	15–34, not married/living as a couple and have no son or daughter; living with own parents
Flown the nest	15–34, not married/living as a couple, do not live with relations
Nest builders	15–34, married/living as a couple, do not live with son/daughter
Mid-life independents	35–54, not married/living as a couple, do not live with relations
Unconstrained couples	35–54, married/living as a couple, do not live with son/daughter
Playschool parents	Live with son/daughter and youngest child 0–4
Primary school parents	Live with son/daughter and youngest child 5–9
Secondary school parents	Live with son/daughter and youngest child 10–15
Hotel parents	35+, live with son/daughter and have no child 0–15
Senior sole decision makers	55+, not married/living as a couple and live alone
Empty nesters	55+, married/living as a couple, and do not live with son/daughter
Non-standard families	Not married/living as a couple, live with relations, do not live with son/daughter, and do not live with parents if 15–34
Unclassified	Not in any group

Source: Reproduced with the kind permission of Kantar Media.

income and busy lifestyles by offering 'meal for one' ranges, which compare with 'family value' and 'multipacks' targeted at families. As families grow and children leave home, the needs of parents change and their disposable income increases (see Table 5.2).

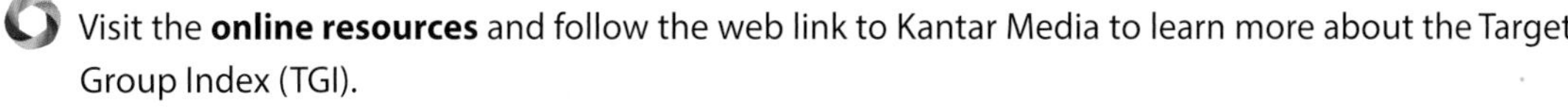

Visit the **online resources** and follow the web link to Kantar Media to learn more about the Target Group Index (TGI).

Geographics

A geographical approach is useful when there are clear locational differences in tastes, consumption, and preferences. These consumption patterns provide an indication of preferences according to differing geographical regions. Markets can be considered by country or region, by size of city or town, by postcode, or by population density, such as urban, suburban, or rural. It is often said that American beer drinkers prefer lighter beers, compared with their UK counterparts, whereas German beer drinkers prefer a much stronger drink.

In addition to proposition selection and consumption, geographical segmentation is important for retail location, advertising and media selection, and recruitment. Direct sales operations (for example catalogue sales) can use census information to develop better customer segmentation and predictive models. Book publishers have long segmented based on geographical markets, frequently charging consumers in developing countries much less for a book than those in the developed world and trying to enforce a non-import policy so that these cheaper books do not enter Western markets.

Geo-demographics

Geo-demographics is a natural outcome when combining demographic and geographic variables. The marriage of geographics and **demographics** has become an indispensable market analysis tool, because it can lead to a rich mixture of who lives where.

Visit the **online resources** and complete Internet Activity 5.1 to learn more about how we use databases compiled with geo-demographic data to profile market segments effectively.

The best-known UK geo-demographic system is A Classification of Residential Neighbourhoods (ACORN). Developed by British market research group CACI, ACORN demonstrates how postcode areas are broken down into 6 categories, 18 groups, and 62 types. ACORN is a geo-demographic tool used to segment the UK population and their demand for a variety of offerings to assist marketers so that they can determine where to locate operations, field sales forces, retail outlets, and so on. ACORN can also be used to determine where to plan marketing communications and social media marketing campaigns.

Visit the **online resources** and follow the web link to CACI to learn more about the ACORN system.

MOSAIC is a geo-demographic segmentation system developed by Experian and marketed globally. The system is based on the classification of 155 person types, aggregated into 67 household types and 15 groups, to create a three-tier classification that can be used at the individual, household, or postcode level.

Visit the **online resources** and follow the web link to Experian to learn more about the MOSAIC system.

Psychological Criteria

Psychological criteria used for segmenting consumer markets include the types of benefit sought by customers from brands in their consumption choices, their attitudes and perceptions (for example their feelings about fast cars), and **psychographics** or the lifestyles of customers (for example extrovert, fashion-conscious, high achiever).

Benefits Sought

The 'benefits sought' approach is based on the principle that we should provide customers with exactly what they want, based on the benefits they derive from use (Haley, 1968). This might sound obvious, but what are the real benefits, both rational and irrational, for the different offerings that people buy, such as mobile phones and sunglasses? Major airlines often segment on the basis of the benefits that passengers seek from transport by differentiating between first-class passengers (given extra luxury benefits in their travel experience), business-class passengers (who get some of the luxury of the first-class passenger), and economy-class passengers (who get none of the luxury of the experience, but enjoy the same flight).

Psychographics

Psychographic approaches rely on analysis of consumers' activities, interests, and opinions to understand their individual lifestyles and behaviour patterns. Psychographic segmentation includes understanding the values that are important to different customer types. A traditional form of lifestyle segmentation is AIO, based on customers' Activities, Interests, and Opinions. Taylor Nelson Sofres (TNS) developed a UK Lifestyle Typology based on lifestyle, comprising 'belonger', 'survivor', 'experimentalist', 'conspicuous consumer', 'social resistor', 'self-explorer', and 'the aimless'.

Fix it quickly: John Deere outperformed rivals thanks to its service network and ability to minimize productivity losses for farmers.

Source: © smereka/Shutterstock.

International Harvester undertook value-based segmentation to discover why farmers consistently rated the equipment of John Deere, its main competitor, as 'more reliable'. International Harvester had invested heavily to minimize breakdowns, but John Deere continued to lead in the reliability rankings. Surveys about repair problems revealed that it was the downtime caused by breakdowns that most affected farmers, because of the days of lost productivity waiting for repairs. John Deere's customers perceived reliability to be much less of a problem because of the company's extensive, service-oriented dealer network, which stocked spare parts and offered temporary tractors that served to get a farmer working again quickly. John Deere was serving a different segment of farmers: those driven by the value of a total-service solution, which John Deere complemented well (Anon., 2013).

Market Insight 5.2 discusses a popular method of segmentation relating to consumers' attitudes and behaviours towards the environment.

Behavioural Criteria

Product-related methods of segmenting consumer proposition markets include using behavioural methods (for example product usage, purchase, and ownership) as bases for segmentation. Observing consumers as they use offerings or consume services can be an important source of ideas for new uses or proposition design and development. Furthermore, new markets for existing offerings can be signalled, as well as appropriate communication themes for promotion. Purchase,

Market Insight 5.2 **Sustainability Segmentation**

Considering the rising social concern over issues of environmental sustainability, marketers have started to examine the potential of the green marketplace. As more and more brands develop 'environmentally friendly' alternatives, there is a need to reliably segment the market and understand the motivations of different groups of consumers. This can be also a tool for policymakers aiming at changing consumer behaviour in more sustainable directions.

The US Natural Marketing Institute (NMI) conducts annual tracking studies to assess peoples' beliefs and lifestyles in relation to the environment. It has conducted analysis on US consumers since 2000 and, from 2005 onwards, has researched sustainability attitudes and behaviours in 23 different countries.

The NMI's research is based on a psychographic approach, focusing on peoples' lifestyles, interests, and behaviours. In the US market, the NMI has identified five different segments, as follows.

- *Unconcerneds* demonstrate very little interest towards sustainability and do not engage in sustainable practices. They represent around 17 per cent of consumers.
- *Conventionals* engage in sustainable behaviour as a way in which to save money. These consumers are likely to recycle or try to reduce energy consumption, but their choices are motivated more by economic concerns than by environmental beliefs. They make up 22 per cent of the population.
- *Drifters* do not hold deep beliefs about sustainability, but are influenced by trends. These consumers will engage with specific issues that become fashionable, but are on the whole not particularly committed. They represent 25 per cent of consumers.
- *Naturalites* are motivated by health beliefs, often associated with environmentally friendly products. They are mostly concerned about pollution and the use of chemicals in household products. Around 17 per cent of consumers belong to this segment.
- *Lifestyles of health and sustainability (Lohas) consumers* are very interested in sustainability, tend to buy environmentally friendly alternatives, and are more likely to support environmental causes in their communities. They make up around 19 per cent of the population.

1. **How could companies use the information provided by sustainability segmentation?**
2. **Why might marketers be interested in understanding the motivations of groups of consumers towards sustainability?**
3. **What criteria could be used to enrich the description of the different segments? Why do you think these criteria would be useful in this context?**

Source: French and Rogers (2010); Ottman (2011).

ownership, and usage are three very different behavioural constructs that can be used to aid consumer market segmentation.

Usage

A company may segment a market based on how often a customer uses its offerings, categorizing these into high, medium, and low users. This allows the development of service specifications or marketing mixes for each user group. For example, heavy users of public transport might be targeted differently from heavy users of private vehicles by a coach-operating company. Consumer usage of offerings can be investigated from three perspectives, as follows.

1. *Social interaction perspective*—This considers the symbolic aspects of usage and the social meanings attached to the consumption of socially conspicuous offerings, such as a car or house (Belk

et al., 1982; Solomon, 1983). For example, Greenpeace launched a television campaign targeting owners of four-wheel drive cars highlighting the environmental social stigma of their car purchase.

2 *Experiential consumption perspective*—This considers emotional and sensory experiences as a result of usage—especially emotions such as satisfaction, fantasies, and fun (Holbrook and Hirschman, 1982). For example, Oxo gravy campaigns have emphasized how usage of Oxo brings families together, and express family values such as love, sharing, and spending time together.

3 *Functional utilization perspective*—This considers the functional usage of products and their attributes in different situations (Srivastava et al., 1978; McAlister and Pessemier, 1982), for example how and when cameras are used, how often, and in what contexts.

Transaction and Purchase

The development of electronic technologies, such as electronic point-of-sale (EPOS) systems, standardized product codes, radio frequency identification (RFID) systems, QR (quick response) codes, and integrated purchasing systems (for example web, in-store, telephone), has facilitated a rapid growth in the collection of consumer purchase and transactional data. Browsing and purchase data allows Amazon to make recommendations of offerings that are more likely to appeal to its consumers; EPOS systems allow retailers to track who buys what, when, for how much, in what quantities, and with what incentives (such as sales promotions). Companies have the ability to monitor purchase patterns in various geographical regions, at different times or seasons of the year, for various offerings, and increasingly for differing market segments. Social media can also be analysed to track what people are saying once they have purchased and used particular offerings.

Transactional and purchase information is very useful for marketers to assess who are their most profitable customers. By analysing the recency, frequency, and monetary (RFM) value of purchases, marketers can identify their most profitable market segments.

Segmentation in Business Markets

Business-to-business market segmentation is the identification of 'a group of present or potential customers with some common characteristic which is relevant in explaining (and predicting) their response to a supplier's marketing stimuli' (Wind and Cardozo, 1974: 155). There are two main groups of interrelated variables used to segment B2B markets (see Table 5.3). The first involves organizational characteristics, such as **organizational size** and location, sometimes referred to as **firmographics**. Those seeking to segment might start with these variables. The second group is based on the characteristics surrounding the decision-making process. Those organizations seeking to establish and develop customer relationships would normally expect to start with these variables.

Organizational Characteristics

The organizational characteristic factors concern the buying organizations that make up a business market. There are a number of criteria that can be used to cluster organizations, including size, geography, market served, value, location, industry type, usage rate, and purchase situation. We discuss the main three categories used in Figure 5.6.

Table 5.3 Segmentation bases used in business markets

Base type	Segmentation base	Explanation
Organizational characteristics	Organizational size	Grouping organizations by relative size (multinational corporations, or MNCs; international corporations; large companies; small and medium-sized enterprises, or SMEs) enables the identification of design, delivery, usage rates or order size, and other purchasing characteristics.
	Geographic location	The needs of potential customers in one geographic area are often different from those in another geographic area.
	Industry type (SIC codes)	**Standard industrial classification (SIC) codes** are used to identify and categorize industries and businesses.
Buyer characteristics	**Decision-making unit** (DMU) structure	Attitudes, policies, and purchasing strategies allow organizations to be clustered.
	Choice criteria	The types of offering bought and the specifications companies use when selecting and ordering offerings form the basis for clustering customers and segmenting business markets.
	Purchase situation	Segments are based on how the company structures its purchasing procedures, the type of buying situation, and whether buyers are involved at an early or late stage in the purchase decision process.

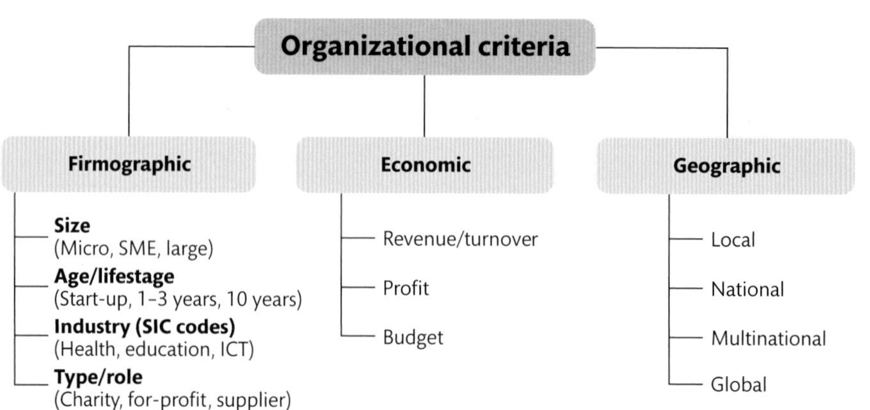

Figure 5.6 Segmentation by organizational characteristic

Organizational Size

By segmenting organizations by size, we can identify particular buying requirements. Large organizations may have particular delivery or design needs based on volume demand. Supermarkets such as France's Carrefour and the UK's Tesco, for example, pride themselves on purchasing goods in sufficiently large quantities to enable them to offer cheaply priced goods. The size of the organization often impacts on the usage rates of an offering, so organizational size is linked to whether an organization is a heavy, medium, or low buyer of a company's offerings.

Geographical Location

Geo-targeting is one of the more common methods used to segment B2B markets and is often used by new or small organizations attempting to establish themselves. This approach is useful because it allows the drawing of sales territories around particular locations that salespersons can service easily (for example Scotland, Scandinavia, Western Europe, the Mediterranean). Alternatively, sales territories may be based on specific regions within a country: in Eastern Europe, for example, they may be based on individual nations (that is, Poland, Czech Republic, Romania, and Hungary). This approach however, becomes less useful as the Internet cuts across geographic distribution channels (see Chapters 10 and 11).

SIC Code

Standard industrial classification (SIC) codes are used to understand market size. They are easily accessible and standardized across most Western regions, for example the UK, Europe, and the United States. However, some marketers have argued that SIC codes comprise categories that are too broad to be useful. Consequently, SIC codes have received limited application, although they do provide an indication of the industrial segments in a market (Naudé and Cheng, 2003). More commonly, companies sometimes segment B2B markets using industry types (so-called verticals). For example, a law firm might segment its customers into, among other sectors, financial services, utilities, transport, and retailing.

Visit the **online resources** and complete Internet Activity 5.2 to learn more about how we use SIC codes to segment business markets.

Customer Characteristics

Customer-specific factors concern the characteristics of buyers within the organizations that make up a business market. Numerous criteria could be used to cluster organizations including by decision-making unit (DMU), by purchasing strategy, by relationship type, by attitude to risk, by choice criteria, and by purchase situation.

Decision-Making Unit

An organization's DMU may have specific requirements that influence purchase decisions in a particular market, for example policy factors, purchasing strategies, a level of importance attached to these types of purchase, or attitudes towards vendors and risk. These characteristics can be used to segregate groups of organizations for particular marketing programmes. Segmentation might be based on the closeness and level of interdependence existing between organizations.

Organizational attitudes towards risk and the degree to which an organization is willing to experiment through the acquisition of new industrial offerings varies. The starting point of any B2B segmentation is a good database or customer relationship management (CRM) system. It should contain customer addresses, contact details, and detailed purchase and transactional history. Ideally, it will also include the details of those buyers present within the customer company's DMU structure.

Market Insight 5.3 **Recapturing Lost B2B Customers**

Customer churn for firms such as FedEx, UPS, and XPO in the logistics industry can reach 20–25 per cent. Customers switch suppliers for a variety of reasons, but some of the more common ones concern core service failures, dissatisfactory service encounters, price, inconvenience in terms of time, location, or delays, poor response to service failure, competition, ethical problems, and involuntary switching. It is therefore important for all firms to understand these switch or defection behaviours to reduce their incidence, retrieve lost customers, and so lower their costs over the long run.

Segmenting B2B markets based on customers who have been lost is not necessarily the same as segmenting to find new customers. One of the reasons for this is that 'lost customers' leave a portfolio of transactions that the sales force can use to leverage a return. Research suggests that five distinct segments of lost customers can be identified and actioned, as follows.

- *Bought-away customers*—Often very price-orientated, these customers are attracted by competitive prices. A decision to regain this segment needs to take into account how easy and profitable it will be to retain them in light of their price vulnerability.
- *Pulled-away customers*—This segment is characterized by buyers seeking better overall value, who will collaborate with suppliers to achieve higher benefits and/or lower costs. The solution to win back these 'lost customers' is thus to co-develop with them value propositions that are unique and sustainable.
- *Unintentionally pushed-away customers*—These customers leave because they perceive that they have been mistreated or neglected. An apology is required, but where there has been service/product failures, service recovery and reacquisition may include compensation, reimbursement, and discounts. In severe cases, often when mistakes have been repeated, customers can be retrieved only after personnel changes in either or both the buying and sales centres.
- *Moved-away customers*—This segment is characterized by customers who no longer need or value the product/service offerings. They might have moved physically or to different markets that the selling company cannot serve. Although lost for good, a positive ending to the relationship is regarded as important to secure referrals and helpful word-of-mouth.
- *Intentionally pushed-away customers*—These problematic or unprofitable customers are deliberately let go because the selling company no longer wants their business. Allowing them to build relationships with competitors should be matched by a positive dissolution to help to maintain a strong reputation and brand image.

1. **Discuss the view that if retrieving lost customers is costly and keeping them problematic, then there is little point in segmenting and actively trying to get them back.**
2. **To what extent is a high churn rate a function of poor customer management?**
3. **Focusing on a different industry, determine how companies try to retain customers.**

Sources: Keaveney (1995); Lopes et al. (2001); Liu et al. (2015).

Choice Criteria

Business markets can be segmented on the basis of the specifications of offerings that they choose. An accountancy practice may segment its clients by those that seek compliance-type offerings, such as audits and tax submission work, companies that require management accounting services, and companies that require a complex mix of both. Companies do not necessarily need to target multiple segments, however; they might simply target a single segment, as RM Education, an information technology (IT) solutions provider, has done successfully in the UK education market.

Purchase Situation

Companies sometimes seek to segment the market on the basis of how organizations buy. There are three questions associated with segmentation by purchase situation that should be considered, as follows.

1. What is the structure of the buying organization's purchasing procedures: centralized, decentralized, flexible, or inflexible?
2. What type of buying situation is present: new task (that is, buying for the first time), modified rebuy (that is, not buying for the first time, but buying something with different specifications from previously), or straight rebuy (that is, buying the same thing again)?
3. What stage in the purchase decision process have target organizations reached? Are they buyers in early or late stages and are they experienced or new?

For example, a large global consulting and IT services company like Infosys from India might segment the market for IT project management services into public and private sectors. The focus might then be on fulfilling large government contracts, which are put out to tender, whereby a group of selected buyers are offered the opportunity to bid for an exclusive franchise to deliver agreed services for a defined period of time.

Research Insight 5.1

To take your learning further, you might wish to read this influential paper.

Beane, T. P., and Ennis, D. M. (1987) 'Market segmentation: A review', *European Journal of Marketing*, 32(5): 20–42.

Beane and Ennis's article provides a useful insight into the main bases for market segmentation, and the strengths and weaknesses of the key statistical methods we use to analyse customer data to develop segmentation models. The article suggests that there are many ways in which to segment a market and that it is important to exercise creativity when doing so.

 Visit the **online resources** to read the abstract and access the full paper.

Target Markets

The second important part of the STP process is to determine which of the segments uncovered should be targeted and made the focus of a comprehensive marketing programme. Ultimately, managerial discretion and judgment determines which markets are selected and exploited. Kotler (1984) suggested that the acronym DAMP should be applied if market segmentation is to be effective—that is, all segments must be the following.

- *Distinct*—Is each segment clearly different from other segments? If so, different marketing mixes may be necessary.
- *Accessible*—Can buyers be reached through appropriate promotional programmes and distribution channels?
- *Measurable*—Is the segment easy to identify and measure?
- *Profitable*—Is the segment sufficiently large to provide a stream of constant future revenues and profits?

Another approach to evaluating market segments uses a rating approach for different segment attractiveness factors, such as market growth, segment profitability, segment size, competitive intensity within the segment, and the cyclical nature of the industry (for example whether or not the business is seasonal, as in retailing). Each of these segment attractiveness factors is rated on a 0–10 scale and loosely categorized in the high, medium, or low columns, based on either set criteria or subjective criteria, dependent on the availability of market and customer data and the approach adopted by the managers undertaking the segmentation programme (see Table 5.4).

Table 5.4 Examples of segment attractiveness factors

Segment attractiveness factors	**Rating**		
	High (10–7)	*Medium (6–4)*	*Low (3–0)*
Growth	2.5%	2.5–2.0%	2.0%
Profitability	15%	10–15%	10%
Size	£5m	£1m–£5m	£1m
Competitive intensity	Low	Medium	High
Cyclicality	Low	Medium	High

Source: McDonald and Dunbar (2004). Reproduced with permission. © Elsevier.

Table 5.5 Example of a segment attractiveness evaluation matrix

Segment attractiveness factors	Weight	Segment 1		Segment 2		Segment 3	
		Score	*Total*	*Score*	*Total*	*Score*	*Total*
Growth	25	6.0	1.50	5	1.25	10	2.50
Profitability	25	9.0	2.25	4	1.00	8	2.00
Size	15	6.0	0.90	5	0.90	7	1.05
Competitive intensity	15	5.0	0.75	6	0.90	6	0.90
Cyclicality	20	2.5	0.50	8	1.60	5	1.00
Total	100	5.9		5.65		7.45	

Source: McDonald and Dunbar (2004). Reproduced with permission. © Elsevier.

Other examples of segment attractiveness factors might include segment stability (that is, stability of the segment's needs over time) and mission fit (that is, the extent to which dealing with a particular segment fits the mission of the company). Once the attractiveness factors have been determined, the importance of each factor can be weighed and each segment rated on each factor. This generates a segment attractiveness evaluation matrix (see Table 5.5).

Decisions need to be made about whether a single offering is made available to a range of segments, a range of offerings is made available to multiple segments or a single segment, or one offering should be presented to a single segment. Whatever the decision, a marketing mix strategy should be developed to meet segment needs that reflects the organization's capabilities and competitive strengths.

Targeting Approaches

Once segments are identified, an organization selects its preferred approach to targeting. Four differing approaches can be used, as follows (see Figure 5.7).

- **Undifferentiated approach**—In this approach to targeting, there is no delineation between market segments and the market is viewed as one mass market, with one marketing strategy for the entire market. Although expensive, this approach is used for markets in which there is limited or no segment differentiation, for example housing offered by local authorities.
- **Differentiated targeting approach**—This is used where there are several market segments to target, each being attractive to the marketing organization. To exploit them, a marketing strategy is developed for each segment. Hewlett Packard, for example, has developed its product range and marketing strategy to target the following user segments of computing

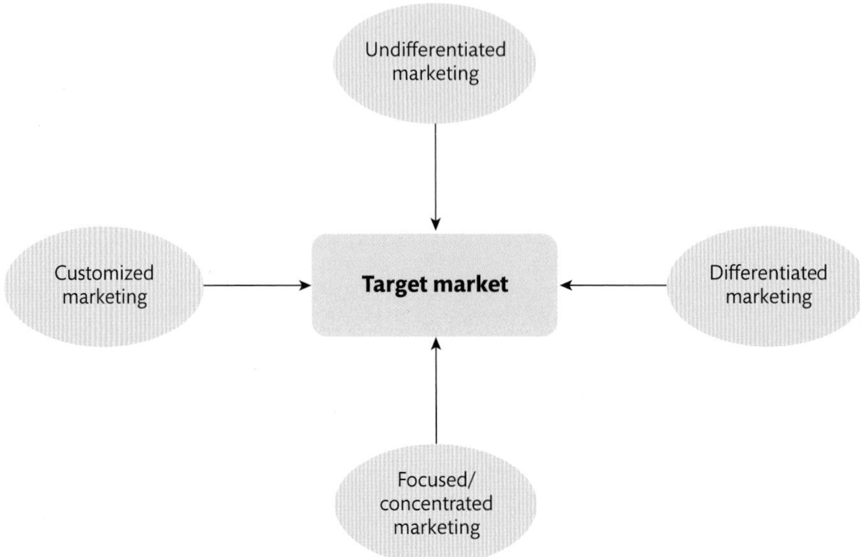

Figure 5.7 Target marketing approaches

equipment: home office users; small and medium-sized businesses; large businesses; and health, education, and government departments. A disadvantage of this approach is the loss of economies of scale owing to the resources required to meet multiple market segments' needs.

- **Concentrated, or niche, marketing strategy**—Where there are only a few market segments, this approach is adopted by firms with limited resources to fund their marketing strategies or which adopt a very exclusive strategy in the market. The UK's Co-operative Bank targets consumers interested in a bank with ethical lending and investment credentials. This approach is used frequently by small-to-medium- and micro-sized organizations with limited resources (for example an electrician, who may focus on local residences).
- **Customized targeting strategy**—This type of marketing strategy is developed for each customer rather than each segment. This approach predominates in B2B markets (for example marketing research or advertising services) or consumer markets with high-value, highly customized products (for example a custom-made car). A manufacturer of industrial electronics for assembly lines might target and customize its offering differently for Nissan, Unilever, and SCA, for example, given the differing requirements in assembly line processes for the manufacture of automobiles, foodstuffs, and hygiene products (such as hand dryers).

Segmentation Limitations

Whilst market segmentation is a useful process for organizations to divide customers into distinct groups, it has been criticized for the following reasons.

- The process approximates offerings to the needs of customer groups, rather than individuals, so there is a chance that customers' needs are not fully met. **Customer relationship marketing (CRM)** processes and software, however, allow companies to develop customized approaches for individual customers.

- There is insufficient consideration of how market segmentation is linked to competitive advantage (Hunt and Arnett, 2004). The product differentiation concept is linked to the need to develop competing offerings, but market segmentation does not stress the need to segment on the basis of differentiating the offering from those of competitors.
- It is unclear how valuable segmentation is to managers. Suitable processes or models to measure market segmentation effectiveness have yet to be developed.

Positioning

Having segmented the market, determined the size and potential of market segments, and selected specific target markets, the third part of the STP process is to position a brand within the target market(s). Positioning is the means by which offerings are differentiated from one another to give customers a reason to buy. It encompasses two fundamental elements. The first concerns the attributes, functionality, and capability that a brand offers (for example a car's engine specification, its design, and carbon emissions). The second positioning element concerns the way in which a brand is communicated and how customers perceive the brand relative to competing brands. This element of communication is important because it is not what you do to an offering that is important, but 'what you do to the mind of a prospect' (Ries and Trout, 1972: 35) that determines how a brand obtains its market positioning (see Market Insight 5.4).

Positioning concerns the overall perception of an offering and not only its features. Positioning is therefore about how customers judge an offering's value relative to those of competitors. To develop a sustainable position, we must understand the market in which the offering is competing.

At a simple level, the positioning process begins during the target market selection process. Key to this process is identifying those attributes considered to be important by consumers. For a car manufacturer, these attributes may be tangible (for example the gearbox, transmission system, seating, and interior design) and intangible (for example the reputation, prestige, and allure that a brand generates). By understanding what customers consider to be the ideal standard that each attribute needs to attain, and how they rate the attributes of each brand in relation to the ideal level and each other, it becomes possible to see how a brand's attributes can be adapted and communicated to become more competitive.

Perceptual Mapping

Understanding the complexity associated with the different attributes and brands can be made easier by developing a visual representation of each market. These are known as 'perceptual maps'. The 'maps' are used to determine how various brands are perceived according to the key attributes that customers value. **Perceptual mapping** allows the geometric comparison of how competing products are perceived (Sinclair and Stalling, 1990). Typically, the closer offerings or brands are clustered on a perceptual map, the greater the competition. The further apart the positions, the greater the opportunity for new brands to enter the market. For example, in the non-vintage champagne market, there are numerous brands competing with each other across differing attributes. Figure 5.8 shows the positioning of key champagne brands in the non-vintage market. Here, the positions

Market Insight 5.4 **Positioning Premium Beer**

The history of Belgian beer brand Leffe can be traced back to 1240. Its current success, however, can be accredited to its positioning and association with contemporary food and lifestyles, rather than its taste and the historic values associated with traditional brewing and ingredients.

Despite its super-premium price, the brand has experienced strong growth in France, nearly doubling its market share between 2008 and 2013.

This growth has been achieved by associating the brand as an 'aperitif'—that is, at a time when social interaction occurs before a meal, normally associated with wine. The brand was positioned as the ideal first drink of the evening, particularly when accompanied by traditional foods such as dry-cured ham and cheese.

The bottle uses foil wrapping around the neck, similar to champagne, reinforcing the premium cue. Rather than using conventional media, Leffe uses an online newsletter called *Leffervescense*. In addition to featuring its own products, Leffe uses the newsletter to introduce readers to celebrity chefs and artisanal food producers. Heineken in the United States has now followed this path by aligning itself with handcrafted products that 'embody Heineken's aspirational and metropolitan essence'.

In Italy, Peroni is priced below the average for mass-market brands. Nastro Azzuro is Peroni's upmarket brand offering, premium priced, and does not carry the Peroni name.

When owner SABMiller launched Peroni in the UK, it recoupled the names and positioned 'Peroni Nastro Azzuro' against its Italian origins. Research identified the target audience as confident, socially mobile, 25–34-year-old status seekers, who were optimistic about the future and their ability to control it. They were referred to as 'Modern Sophisticates'. Using conventional media, the brand was associated with 'the Golden Age of Italy'. Television advertising uses stereotypical images of Italy, 1960s nostalgia, and premium brand cues, such as flying boats, a carefree lifestyle, and powerboats.

Leffe's repositioning strategy focused on presenting the product as the perfect aperitif.

Source: © Shutterstock / mandritoiu.

1 **Identify two other ways in which Leffe and Peroni could be positioned.**

2 **What problems might arise when positioning museums and other cultural attractions?**

3 **Choose a market (such as fashion, haircare, air travel) and determine how any three brands in that market are positioned. Is that positioning successful?**

Sources: Hollis (2014a, 2014b); http://www.brandunion.com.

are based on attributes relating to the type of fruit used and the taste. It can be seen that leading brands Lanson, Bollinger, and Moët et Chandon occupy distinct positions in their 'own' quadrants. (See Case Insight 5.1 for more information about Lanson International, a leading champagne house.)

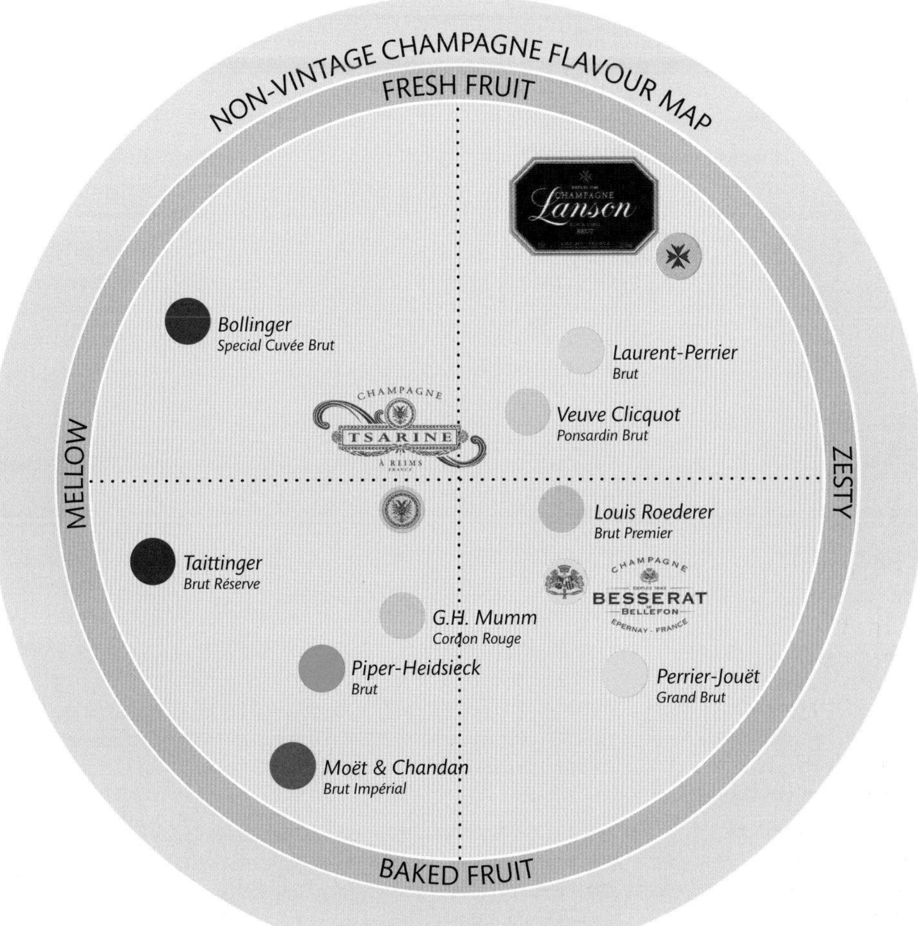

Figure 5.8 Perceptual map for non-vintage champagne flavour

Source: Reproduced with kind permission of Lanson International UK Ltd.

Perceptual mapping data reveal strengths and weaknesses that can inform strategic decisions about how to differentiate in terms of the attributes that matter to customers the most.

Positioning and Repositioning

Marketing communications try to adjust customers' brand perceptions and can be used to position brands either functionally or expressively (symbolically) (see Table 5.6). *Functionally* positioned brands emphasize features and benefits, whereas *expressive* brands emphasize the ego, social, and hedonic satisfactions a brand brings. Different positioning approaches are likely to be more successful than others, with particular offerings. For example, in the compact car market, Fuchs and Diamantopoulos (2010) found that direct benefit positioning (based on functional aspects) is likely to be more effective than indirect benefit positioning (based on experiential or symbolic dimensions) and that expressive positioning is more

Table 5.6 Proposition positioning strategies

Position	Strategy	Explanation
Functional	Product features	Brand positioned on the basis of attributes, features, or benefits relative to the competition, e.g. Volvos are safe; Red Bull provides energy.
	Price quality	Price can be a strong communicator of quality. John Lewis Partnership (the UK department store) uses the tagline 'never knowingly undersold' to indicate how it will match competitors' prices on the same items to ensure its customers always get good value.
	Use	By informing when or how an offering can be used, we create a mental position in buyers' minds, e.g. Kellogg's repositions its offerings (e.g. Special K) to be consumed throughout the day, not only at breakfast.
Expressive	User	By identifying the target user, messages can be communicated clearly to the right audience. Flora margarine was initially for men, then it became 'for all of the family'. Some hotels position themselves as places for weekend breaks, as leisure centres, or as conference centres, or as all three.
	Benefit	Positions can be established by proclaiming the benefits that usage confers on consumers. The benefit of using Sensodyne toothpaste is that it alleviates the pain associated with sensitive teeth.
	Heritage	Heritage and tradition are sometimes used to symbolize quality, experience, and knowledge. Kronenbourg 1664, 'Established since 1803', and the use of coats of arms by many universities are designed to convey heritage to build long-term trust.

effective than functional approaches. User positioning can also provide a sound alternative to benefit positioning.

Technology, customer tastes, and competitors' new offerings are reasons why markets might change. Disney acquired Lucasfilm in 2012 with a plan to launch the seventh Star Wars film in 2015 and others beyond; to be successful, however, Disney needed to reposition and target the new films at the generation who grew up with the *Clone Wars* cartoon and Lego *Star Wars* characters rather than those who watched the original trilogy in the late 1970s and 1980s (Garrahan, 2012). Thus if the brand positioning adopted is strong and the position is continually reinforced with clear messages, there may be little need to alter the position originally adopted. Sometimes, marketers need to reposition their offering relative to those of competitors. Repositioning is often difficult to accomplish because of the entrenched perceptions and attitudes held by customers towards brands and the cost of the vast (media) resources required to make these changes.

There are four approaches to repositioning, depending on the individual situation facing a brand.

Research Insight 5.2

To take your learning further, you might wish to read this influential book.

Ries, A., and Trout, J. (2006) ***Positioning: The Battle for your Mind*****, London: McGraw-Hill Professional.**

Al Ries and Jack Trout's book, originally published in 1981, remains the bible of advertising strategy. They define 'positioning' not as what you do to an offering to make it acceptable to potential customers, but as what you do to the mind of the prospect. Positioning requires an outside-in rather than an inside-out thinking approach.

 Visit the **online resources** to read more about the book.

1. Change the tangible attributes and then communicate the new proposition to the same market. UBS, the financial services firm whose reputation was shattered following an estimated US$2 billion loss owing to insider trading, spent four years transforming itself internally before relaunching and repositioning as a wealth management company (Rooney, 2015).
2. Change the way *in which* a proposition is communicated to the original market. Norwegian oil and gas company Statoil Hydro was repositioned globally as Statoil by communications agency Hill & Knowlton Strategies, raising its profile in key markets across Europe, including in the UK.
3. Change the target market and deliver the same proposition. On some occasions, repositioning can be achieved through marketing communications alone, but targeted at a new market. For example, soft drink Orangina was repositioned as a premium adult drink, targeting those who remember it from childhood French holidays.
4. Change both the proposition (attributes) and the target market. For example, Xerox has repositioned itself from a document company to a diversified business services company, running call centres, and processing insurance claims and even toll payments (Carone, 2013).

Chapter Summary

To consolidate your learning, the key points from this chapter are summarized below.

- **Describe the principles of market segmentation and the segmentation, targeting, and positioning (STP) process.**

  Whole markets are subdivided into different segments through the STP process. 'STP' refers to the three activities that should be undertaken, sequentially, if segmentation is to be successful: segmentation, targeting, and positioning. Market segmentation is the division of a market into different groups of customers with distinctly similar needs and offering requirements. The second part of the STP process determines which segments should be targeted with a comprehensive marketing mix programme. The third part of the STP process involves positioning a brand within the target market(s).

- **List the characteristics and differences between market segmentation and product differentiation.**

  Market segmentation is related to product differentiation. Given an increasing proliferation of tastes, marketers have sought to design offerings around consumer demand (market segmentation) more than around their own production needs (product differentiation).

- **Explain consumer and business-to-business (B2B) market segmentation.**

  Data, based on differing consumer, user, organizational, and market characteristics, are used to segment a market. These characteristics differ for business-to-consumer (B2C) and B2B contexts. To segment consumer goods and service markets, market information based on certain key customer-, product-, or situation-related criteria (variables) is used. These are classified as segmentation bases, and include profile, behavioural and psychological criteria. To segment business markets, two main groups of interrelated variables are used: organizational characteristics and buyer characteristics.

- **Describe different targeting strategies.**

  Once identified, the organization selects its target marketing approach. Four differing approaches exist: undifferentiated; differentiated; concentrated, or niche marketing; and customized target marketing.

- **Discuss the concept of 'positioning'.**

  Positioning provides the means by which offerings can be differentiated from one another and gives customers reasons to buy. It encompasses physical attributes, the way in which a brand is communicated, and how customers perceive the brand relative to competing brands.

- **Consider how the use of perceptual maps can assist in the positioning process.**

  Perceptual maps are used in the positioning process to illustrate the differing attributes of a selection of brands. They also illustrate: existing levels of differentiation between brands; how a brand and competing brands are perceived in the marketplace; how a market operates; and strengths and weaknesses that can assist with making strategic decisions about how to differentiate the attributes that matter to customers to compete more effectively in the market.

Review Questions

1. **Define 'market segmentation' and explain the STP process.**
2. **What is the difference between market segmentation and product differentiation?**
3. **Identify four different ways in which markets can be segmented.**
4. **How do market segmentation bases differ in B2B and consumer markets?**
5. **How can market segmentation bases be evaluated when target marketing?**
6. **What are the different approaches to selecting target markets?**
7. **Describe the principle of positioning and why it should be undertaken.**
8. **What are perceptual maps and what can they reveal?**
9. **Explain three ways in which brands can be positioned.**
10. **Make a list of four reasons why organizations need to reposition brands.**

Worksheet Summary

To apply the knowledge you have gained from this chapter, and to test your learning about the STP process used to develop who to market to, in what way, and while differentiating from the competition, visit the **online resources** and complete Worksheet 5.1.

Discussion Questions

1 Having read Case Insight 5.1, how would you recommend that Lanson position itself in the UK market?

2 In a group, with other colleagues from your seminar or tutor group, discuss answers to the following questions.

- **A** Using the information in Table 5.7 on the champagne market and a suitable calculator, determine which segments have the greatest potential profit.
- **B** What other data do we need to determine the size of the market (market potential)?

Table 5.7 Champagne and sparkling wine market by segment

Social class	Enthusiasts (%) AP = £20 F = 5/yr	Sparkling sceptics (%) AP = £10, F = 3/yr	Price driven (%) AP = £8.50, F = 3/yr	Uneducated (%) AP = £15 F = 2/yr
AB (*n* = 8m)	25	31	30	14
C1 (*n* = 14m)	23	23	32	21
C2 (*n* = 8m)	27	26	33	14
DE (*n* = 10m)	20	26	40	14

Notes: AP = average price, F = no. of bottles purchased per year, *n* = population size (all data hypothetical).
Source: Percentage segment sizes per socio-economic group and segment descriptions only from Mintel (2012).

3 Discuss which market segmentation bases might be most applicable to the following.

- **A** A fashion retailer segmenting the market for womenswear
- **B** A commercial radio station specializing in dance music and celebrity news/gossip
- **C** A Belgian chocolate manufacturer supplying multiple retail grocers and confectionery shops across Europe, for example Godiva
- **D** The Absolut Company, headquartered in Sweden, supplying high-quality vodka around the world
- **E** RAKBANK in Dubai, United Arab Emirates, when segmenting the market for its credit card

4 Write a one-sentence description of the attributes and benefits that are attractive to target consumers for an offering with which you are particularly familiar (for example Apple, in the computer category, or Samsung, in the mobile phones category), using the statement provided. Explain how these attributes and benefits are different from those of competitors. Your positioning statement might be as follows:

[Product A] provides [target consumers] with [one or two salient product attributes]. This distinguishes it from [one or two groups of competing product offerings] that offer [attributes/benefits of the competing products].

A Briefly describe the target market segment. This should summarize the defining characteristics of the segment (for example demographic, psychographic, geographic, or behavioural).

B Briefly explain your reasons for believing that the attributes or benefits of your positioning statement are important for your target segment. Draw a perceptual map that summarizes your understanding of the market and shows the relative positions of the most important competing products.

Visit the **online resources** and complete the multiple-choice questions to assess your knowledge of the chapter.

Glossary

benefits sought by understanding the benefits that customers derive from their purchases, it is possible to have an insight into the motivations behind product use.

breakdown method an approach to segmentation based on the view that the market consists of customers who are essentially the same, so the task is to identify groups that share particular differences.

build-up method an approach to segmentation based on the view that a market consists of customers that are all different, so the task is to find similarities.

business markets markets characterized by organizations that consume products and services for use within the manufacture of other products or for use in their daily operations.

business-to-business (B2B) activities undertaken by one company that are directed at another.

choice criteria the principal dimensions on the basis of which we select a particular product or service, for example, or a hairdresser, price, location, range of services, level of expertise, friendliness, and so on.

communication the sharing of meaning created through the transmission of information.

concentrated, or niche, marketing strategy a marketing strategy that recognizes that there are segments in the market; implemented by focusing on only one or two, or a few, of those market segments.

customer relationship marketing (CRM) a strategy whereby all marketing activities aim to retain customers, achieved by providing customers with relationship-enhancing products and/or services that are perceived to be of value to the individual customer and superior to those offered by a competitor.

customized targeting strategy a marketing strategy that is developed for each customer as opposed to each market segment.

decision-making unit (DMU) a structure on which segmentation can focus whereby organizations' attitudes, policies, and purchasing strategies can be clustered.

demographics key variables concerning age, sex, occupation, level of education, religion, and social class, many of which determine a potential buyer's ability to purchase a product or service.

differentiated targeting approach an approach that recognizes several market segments to target, each being attractive to the marketing organization, whereby a distinct marketing strategy is developed for each.

firmographics criteria such as company size, geography, standard industrial classification (SIC) codes, and other company-oriented classification data used to inform an approach to segmentation of B2B markets.

geo-demographics criteria informing an approach to segmentation that presumes that there is a relationship between the type of housing and location in which people live and their purchasing behaviours.

lifestage analysis analysis based on the principle that people need different products and services at different stages in their lives (for example childhood, adulthood, young couples, retired, etc.).

market segmentation the division of customer markets into groups of customers with distinctly similar needs.

organizational size a criterion by means of which organizations can be grouped—for example multinational corporations (MNCs, international corporations, large companies, small and medium-sized enterprises (SMEs))—which enables the identification of common design, delivery, usage rates, or order size and other purchasing characteristics.

perceptual mapping a diagram, typically two-dimensional, of 'image space' derived from attitudinal market research data, which displays the differences in perceptions that customers, consumers, or the general public have of different products or services specifically, or brands in general.

positioning the way in which an audience of consumers or buyers perceives a product or service, particularly as a result of the marketing communications process aimed at a target audience.

product differentiation a strategy that involves companies seeking to produce offerings that are different from those of competing firms.

product usage a criterion whereby segments derive from analysing markets on the basis of their usage of the product offering, brand, or product category, in terms of frequency, timing, and circumstances of use.

psychographics criteria relating to consumers' activities, interests, and opinions that allows us to understand individual lifestyles and patterns of behaviour, which in turn affect their buying behaviour and decision-making processes, on which basis we can also identify similar product and/or media usage patterns.

purchase situation an approach to segmentation that clusters organizational buyers in terms of the way in which a buying company structures its purchasing procedures, the type of buying situation, and whether buyers are at an early or late stage in the purchase decision process.

standard industrial classification (SIC) codes codes used to identify and categorize all types of industry and business.

STP process the method by which whole markets are subdivided by means of Segmentation, for subsequent Targeting and Positioning of products, services, and brands.

undifferentiated approach an approach to segmentation in which there is no delineation between market segments, with the market viewed instead as a single mass market and only one marketing strategy applied to the whole.

References

Anon. (2013) 'Berger to reposition Sherwin Williams brand', *Chemical Business*, 27(10): 60.

Beane, T. P., and Ennis, D. M. (1987) 'Market segmentation: A review', *European Journal of Marketing*, 32(5): 20–42.

Belk, R. W., Bahn, K. D., and Mayer, R. N. (1982) 'Developmental recognition of consumption symbolism', *Journal of Consumer Research*, 9(1): 4–17.

Carone, C. (2013) 'Xerox's brand repositioning challenge', *Ad Age*, 12 March. Available online at http://adage.com/article/cmo-strategy/xerox-s-brand-repositioning-challenge/240285/ [accessed 4 May 2013].

French, S., and Rogers, G. (2010) 'Understanding the LOHAS consumer: The rise of ethical consumerism'. Available online at http://www.lohas.com/Lohas-Consumer [accessed 18 April 2016].

Freytag, P. V., and Clarke, A. H. (2001) 'Business-to-business segmentation', *Industrial Marketing Management*, 30(6): 473–86.

Fuchs, C., and Diamantopoulos, A. (2010) 'Evaluating the effectiveness of brand-positioning strategies from a consumer perspective', *European Journal of Marketing*, 44(11–12): 1763–86.

Garrahan, M. (2012) 'Disney grabs a galaxy of opportunity', *Financial Times*, 1 November, 19.

Griffith, R. L., and Pol, L. A. (1994) 'Segmenting industrial market', *Industrial Marketing Management*, 23: 39–46.

Haley, R. I. (1968) 'Benefit segmentation: A decision-oriented research tool', *Journal of Marketing*, 32(3): 30–5.

Holbrook, M. B., and Hirschman, E. C. (1982) 'The experiential aspects of consumer behaviour: Consumer fantasies, feelings and fun', *Journal of Consumer Research*, 9(2): 132–40.

Hollis, N. (2014a) 'How Peroni uses images of Italy's "Golden Age" to justify a price premium', *Millward Brown Blog*, 7 July. Available online at http://www.millwardbrown.com/global-navigation/blogs/post/mb-blog/2014/07/07/how-peroni-uses-images-of-italy-s-golden-age-to-justify-a-price-premium [accessed 11 November 2015].

Hollis, N. (2014b) 'Beer brand Leffe taps into contemporary food trends to grow', *Millward Brown Blog*, 5 November. Available online at http://www.millwardbrown.com/global-navigation/blogs/post/mb-blog/2014/11/05/beer-brand-leffe-taps-into-contemporary-food-trends-to-grow#sthash.eR1mDL3G.dpuf [accessed 11 November 2015].

Hunt, S. D., and Arnett, D. B. (2004) 'Market segmentation strategy, competitive advantage and public policy: Grounding segmentation strategy in resource-advantage theory', *Australasian Marketing Journal*, 12(1): 7–25.

Keaveney, S. M. (1995) 'Customer switching behaviour in service industries: An exploratory study', *Journal of Marketing*, 59(2): 71–82.

Kotler, P. (1984) *Marketing Management* (Int'l edn), Upper Saddle River, NJ: Prentice Hall.

Liu, A., Leach, M., and Chugh, R. (2015) 'A sales process framework to regain B2B customers', *Journal of Business & Industrial Marketing*, 30(8): 906–14.

Lopes, L., Alves, H., and Brito, C. (2001) 'Lost customers: Determinants and process of relationship dissolution', Paper presented at the 40th EMAC Conference, 24–27 May, Lyubliana, Slovenia. Available online at https://bibliotecadigital.ipb.pt/bitstream/10198/6257/4/Lost%20customers_EMAC2011.pdf [accessed 1 November 2015].

McAlister, L., and Pessemier, E. (1982) 'Variety seeking behaviour: An interdisciplinary review', *Journal of Consumer Research*, 9(3): 311–22.

McDonald, M., and Dunbar, I. (2004) *Market Segmentation: How to Do It; How to Profit from It*, Oxford: Elsevier.

McKenna, P. J. (2013) 'Four key questions to achieve meaningful differentiation', *Of Counsel*, 32(5): 11–16.

Mintel (2016) *Wine and Sparkling Wine in the UK (2016)—Market Sizes*. Available online at http://store.mintel.com/wine-sparkling-wines-in-uk-2016-market-sizes [accessed 24 February 2017].

Naudé, P., and Cheng, L. (2003) 'Choosing between potential friends: Market segmentation in a small company', Paper presented at the 19th IMP Conference, 4–6 September, Lugano, Switzerland. Available online at http://www.impgroup.org/conferences.php [accessed 1 January 2017].

Ottman, J. (2011) *The New Rules of Green Marketing: Strategies, Tools, and Inspiration for Sustainable Branding*, Sheffield: Greenleaf.

Ries, A., and Trout, J. (1972) 'The positioning era cometh', *Advertising Age*, 24 April, 35–8.

Rooney, L. (2015) 'UBS unveils major brand overhaul', *Forbes.com*, 1 September. Available online at http://web.b.ebscohost.com/ehost/detail/detail?vid=6&sid=49c728c8-b54f-4b4e-8e1e-30afe33a7cdb%40sessionmgr115&hid=123&bdata=JnNpdGU9ZWhvc3QtbGl2ZQ%3d%3d#AN=109219931&db=bch [accessed 9 November 2015].

Sinclair, S. A., and Stalling, E. C. (1990) 'Perceptual mapping: A tool for industrial marketing—A case study', *Journal of Business and Industrial Marketing*, 5(1): 55–65.

Smith, W. R. (1956) 'Product differentiation and market segmentation as alternative marketing strategies', *Journal of Marketing*, 21(1): 3–8.

Solomon, M. R. (1983) 'The role of products as social stimuli: A symbolic interactionism perspective', *Journal of Consumer Research Conference*, 10 (Dec): 319–29.

Srivastava, R. K., Shocker, A. D., and Day, G. S. (1978) 'An exploratory study of the influences of usage situations on perceptions of product markets', *Advances in Consumer Research*, 5: 32–8.

Wind, Y. (1978) 'Issues and advances in segmentation research', *Journal of Marketing Research*, 15(3): 317–37.

Wind, Y., and Cardozo, R. N. (1974) 'Industrial market segmentation', *Industrial Marketing Management*, 3(3): 155–66.

Implementing the Marketing Mix

Part 1 Understanding Customers

Part 2 Designing and Delivering the Market Strategy

Part 3 Implementing the Marketing Mix

Part 4 Managing Marketing Relationships

Chapter 6
Proposition and Branding Decisions

Learning Outcomes

After studying this chapter, you will be able to:

- explain the different levels of a proposition and the product life cycle;
- explore the processes associated with innovating new propositions and how propositions are adopted;
- explain the characteristics and principal types of brand and branding; and
- explain how brands can be built.

Case Insight 6.1
Aston Martin

Market Insight 6.1
Co-creating the Perfect Pizza

Market Insight 6.2
Kopparberg: The Unconventional Brand

Market Insight 6.3
Musicians Dying for Success

Market Insight 6.4
Building a Responsible Brand: Nestlé's Case

Case Insight 6.1 **Aston Martin**

The Aston Martin brand, founded in 1913, is synonymous with hand-crafted luxury, peerless beauty, incredible performance, and international motorsport glory. We speak to Simon Sproule (pictured), director of global marketing and communications, to find out how the brand is promoted in China.

'Aston Martin's brand projects: Power. Beauty. Soul. We see this as more than a tagline. It's about the mission for the company. Naturally, these words describe the attributes of our cars, but we bring more than a beautiful car to our customers. As with all **products** in the luxury market, they are a discretionary purchase and bought for a variety of reasons. The common denominator, however, is the emotional connection our cars have with customers and the physical product and the values of the company/brand. With an Aston Martin, you join an exclusive club with only 80,000 members (the total number of cars produced in our 103-year history). By contrast, our large mainstream competitors will produce that many cars in three days!

'The Aston Martin brand also stands for beautiful hand-crafted cars—evident in every aspect of the product and, for our customers, when they visit the factory in Gaydon, Warwickshire, and see the cars being made. Iconic Hollywood British spy character James Bond has become a brand attribute for Aston Martin through the 50-year association that started with the DB5 in *Goldfinger*. However, for our customers in new and emerging markets such as China, James Bond may not have the same cultural resonance as it does in the UK. For those customers new to Aston Martin, we stand for the best of British style and elegance, combined with the power of our V8 and V12 engines. In essence, we are the quintessential British GT car and more. We describe our branding approach as the 'Goldilocks strategy': getting the balance between exclusivity and accessibility *just right*. Although we are selling a luxury product to 1 per cent of the world's population, we have a massive popular following: 6.5 million Facebook fans and more than 1 million fans on Instagram. We need to be constantly mindful that the respect granted to our brand from our fans is an important motivator for our customers buying an Aston Martin. The simplest way to describe this is to be stuck in heavy traffic at a busy intersection. Our customers tell us that they always get let out of a junction . . . which, in the most basic way, speaks to the respect and affection people have for our cars. So our brand strategy is to balance the aspirational nature of the company and its products, but at the same time be friendly and accessible to all.

'To implement our branding strategy, we combine high technology—we are in the process of implementing Salesforce to run our customer engagement—and a very personal touch. Buying an Aston Martin is about not only the cars, but also becoming part of a family in which you feel welcomed and valued. Like the majority of auto makers, we operate a franchise business, with dealers handling the majority of the sales and service interface. That said, our customers also seek a direct relationship with the 'factory', and we encourage and embrace those relationships. I spend time with customers every week! To convey the brand values to target customers, we are moving towards story-telling driven by content and experiences. We invest relatively little in conventional advertising, preferring to engage our customer and fans with interesting

Case Insight 6.1 (continued)

and cool content. We want to encourage customers to spend time with us, visit the factory, and attend events and motor races. The most convincing way to sell an Aston Martin is a test drive.'

The question for Aston Martin was: how should it go about raising brand awareness and brand familiarity in China—an important emerging market?

Introduction

After studying how companies define their marketing strategies (see Chapters 4 and 5), we focus now on how they can implement these strategies. The first step is the study of **propositions** and **brands**.

A Samsung smartphone, a train journey from Calgary to Vancouver on the Rocky Mountaineer Train, a cappuccino at Costa in Stockholm, and the Singapore *Straits Times* newspaper are all commercial propositions or offerings. The term 'proposition' includes the tangible and intangible attributes related not only to physical goods, but also to services, ideas, people, places, experiences, and even a mix of these various elements. Anything that can be offered for use and consumption, in exchange for money or some other form of value, is referred to as a proposition, or offering. In this chapter, we consider the nature of propositions, before exploring issues associated with their innovation and development.

The second part of the chapter examines how brands can be developed to help customers to identify specific propositions and appreciate their value. Our world is full of brands—from soap powders and soft drinks, to airlines, and financial services. So what exactly is a 'brand'? How are they developed? Who really creates them? These are key questions also explored in this chapter.

Product Levels

The taste of coffee granules is an important benefit arising from the purchase of a jar of instant coffee. However, in addition to this core benefit, people are also attracted to the packaging, the price, the strength of the coffee, and also some of the psychosocial associations that we have learnt about a brand. The Cafédirect brand, for instance, seeks to help people to understand its ties with the Fairtrade movement and so to provide some customers with a level of psychosocial satisfaction through their contribution to that movement.

To understand these different elements and benefits, we refer to three different proposition forms: the core, the embodied, and the augmented forms (see Figure 6.1).

- The *core* proposition consists of the real core benefit or service. This may be a functional benefit, in terms of what the offering will enable you to do, or it may be an emotional benefit, in terms of how the product or service will make you feel.

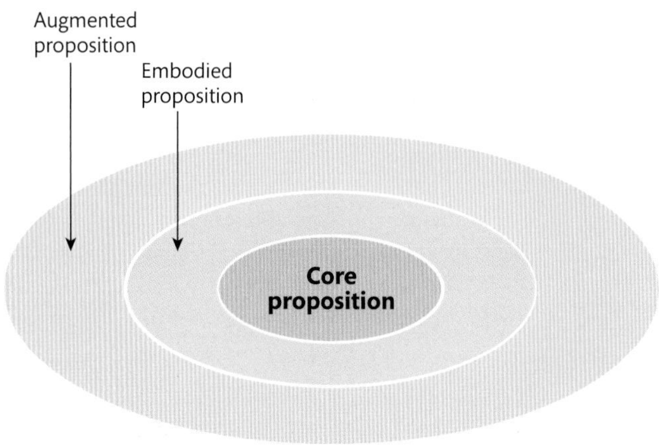

Figure 6.1 The three proposition forms

- The *embodied* proposition consists of the physical good or delivered service that provides the expected benefit. For example, cars are supplied in different styles, with different engines, seats, colours, and boot space.
- The *augmented* proposition consists of the embodied offering plus all of those other factors that are necessary to support the purchase and any post-purchase activities, such as credit and finance, training, delivery, installation, guarantees, and the overall perception of customer service.

Each individual combination, or 'bundle', of benefits constitutes added value and serves to differentiate, for example, one sports car from another sports car and one disposable camera from another.

Consumer Products

The first way of classifying consumer products is to consider them in terms of their durability. **Durable goods**, such as bicycles, music players, and refrigerators, can be used repeatedly and provide benefits each time they are used. **Non-durable goods**, such as yoghurt and newspapers, have a limited duration and are often used only once.

Durable goods often require the purchaser to have high levels of involvement in the purchase decision. There is a high perceived risk in these decisions, and so consumers can spend time, care, and energy searching, formulating, and making the 'right' decision.

Non-durable goods—typically, food and grocery items—reflect low levels of involvement and buyers are seldom concerned with which particular product they buy. Risk is seen to be low and so there is little or no need to shop around for the best possible price. Buyers may base their choice on availability, price, habit, or brand experience.

A deeper and more meaningful way of classifying consumer products is to consider how and where consumers buy them. In Chapter 2, we considered how consumers make purchases. In particular, we looked at **extensive problem-solving**, **limited problem-solving**, and **routinized response behaviour**. Classifying products according to the behaviours that consumers demonstrate when buying them enables marketing managers to develop more suitable and appropriate marketing strategies. Four main behavioural categories have been established: **convenience products**; **shopping products**; **speciality products**; and unsought products.

Convenience products are non-durable and are bought because the consumer does not want to put very much, if any, effort into the buying decision. Routinized response behaviour corresponds most closely to convenience products, because they are bought frequently and are inexpensive. Most decisions in this category are made habitually, and if a usual brand is unavailable, an alternative brand is selected, or none at all if it is seen to be too inconvenient to visit another store.

Shopping products are not bought as frequently as convenience products and, as a result, consumers do not always have sufficient up-to-date information to make a buying decision. The purchase of shopping products such as furniture, electrical appliances, jewellery, and mobile phones requires some search for information, if only to find out about the latest features. Consumers dedicate time and effort to planning these purchases, if only because the level of risk is more substantial than that associated with convenience products. They will visit several stores, and use the Internet and word-of-mouth, to make price comparisons, to find out product information, and to learn from the experiences of other customers.

Product Life Cycles

Underpinning the concept of the **product life cycle** is the belief that offerings move through a sequential, predetermined pattern of development similar to the biological path that lifeforms follow. This pathway, known as the 'product life cycle', consists of five distinct stages—namely, development, introduction, growth, maturity, and decline. Sales and profits rise and fall across the various life stages of the product, as shown in Figure 6.2.

Products move through an overall cycle that consists of different stages. Speed of movement through the stages will vary, but each product has a limited lifespan. Although the life of a product can be extended in many ways, such as introducing new ways of using the product, finding new users, and developing new attributes, the majority of products have a finite period during which management needs to maximize its returns on the investment made.

Different marketing strategies, relating to the offering and its distribution, pricing, and promotion, need to be deployed at particular times in the product life cycle so as to maximize financial returns. Moreover, the concept does not apply to all offerings in the same way. For example, some offerings reach the end of the introduction stage and then die as it becomes clear that there is no market to sustain them. Other products follow the path into decline, but then linger, sustained by heavy advertising and sales promotions, or are recycled back into the growth stage by repositioning activities. Yet other products grow really quickly and then fade away rapidly. Fashion products are pertinent examples of this latter instance, with Zara changing its product range on average every three weeks (Saren, 2006).

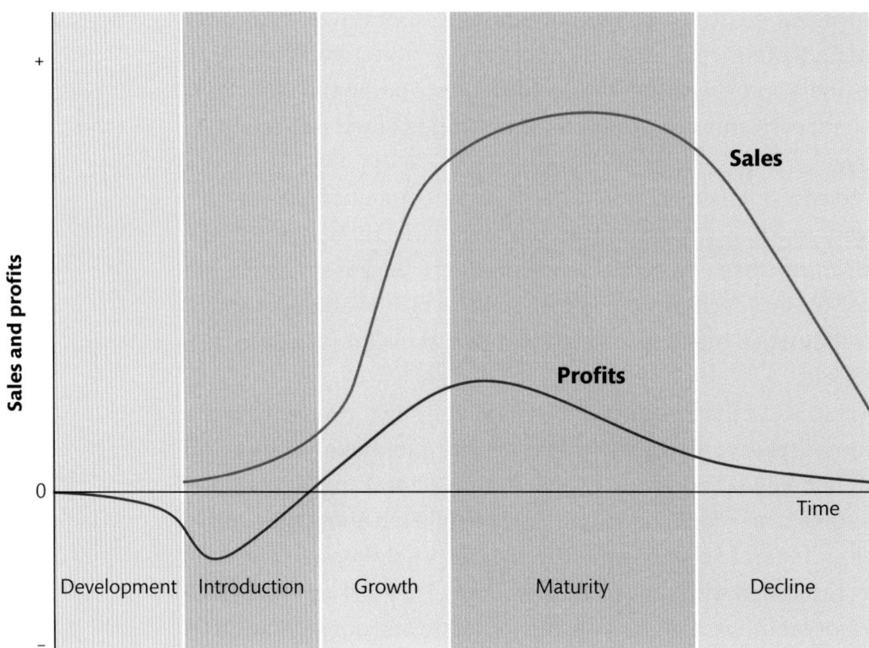

Figure 6.2 The product life cycle

The concept of the product life cycle can apply to a product class (such as computers), a product form (such as a laptop), or a brand (such as Sony). The shape of the lifecycle curve varies, with product classes having the longest cycle as the mature stage is often extended.

Despite its usefulness, the concept has several limitations. One problem is identifying which stage an offering has reached in the cycle. Some brands do not follow the classical S-shaped curve (see Figure 6.3), but rise steeply and then fall away immediately after sales reach a crest. Other possible shapes are generated when demand for a brand is rejuvenated, such as when Swiss watchmakers (Rolex and Omega, for example) redefined their products as status goods rather than timepieces (Anon., 2014), and when a product becomes rapidly out-of-date (e.g. when a new format is released for a track like streaming versus CDs). The model works reasonably well when the environment is relatively stable and not subject to dynamic swings or short-lived customer preferences.

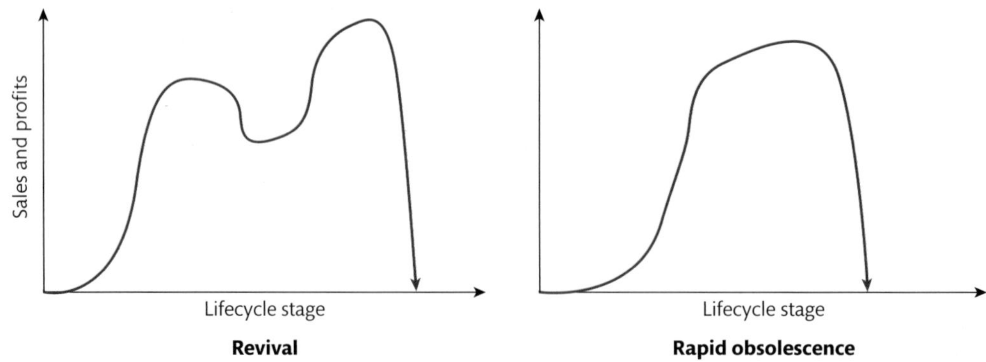

Figure 6.3 Types of product life cycle

Developing New Product Propositions

An organization needs continually to offer superior value to its customers. A key management task is therefore to control the organization's range, or portfolio, of products and to anticipate when one product will become tired, and when new ones will be necessary to sustain the organization and to help it to grow.

The term 'new products' can be misleading. This is because there is a range of newness, relevant to both the organization and to customers: some new products might be totally new to both the organization and the market, whereas others might be only minor product adaptations that have no real impact on a market other than to introduce an interesting new feature, for example features such as new colours, flavours, and pack sizes.

To ensure a stream of new propositions, organizations have the following three main options:

- to buy in finished products from other suppliers, perhaps from other parts of the world, or to license the use of other products for specific periods of time, as does Samsung with its processor technology;
- to develop products through collaboration with suppliers or even competitors, as Sony tried, but failed, to do with Ericsson in the mobile phone business (Parnell, 2012); or
- to develop new products internally, often by means of research and development (R&D) departments or by adapting current products through minor design and engineering changes, as Dyson did with its vacuum cleaner.

The success rate of new products is consistently poor. No more than one in ten new consumer products succeed and, according to Drucker (1985), there are three main reasons for this:

1. that no market exists for the product—as was the case with the Sinclair C5, an infamous electric car launched in 1985 in the UK and swiftly withdrawn nine months later when the company folded (Roberts, 2015);
2. that there is a market need, but the product fails to meet customer requirements—for example Frito-Lay's WOW! fat-free crisps, made with olestra, launched in the United States in 1998, but caused consumers gastrointestinal problems and were quietly withdrawn in 2004 (Glass, 2012); or
3. the product's ability to meet the market need, although satisfactory, is not adequately communicated to the target market—as was the case for Buckler, a very low-alcohol beer in the Dutch market in the 1980s (Institute of Brilliant Failures, n.d.).

The development of new propositions is a complex and high-risk task, so organizations usually adopt a procedural approach. The procedure consists of several phases (stages and gates) that enable progress to be monitored, test trials to be conducted, and the results analysed before there is any commitment to the market. The most common new product development process (NPDP) is set out in Figure 6.4.

The NPDP is generally (but not necessarily) perceived to be linear in that new proposition development occurs only after managers are satisfied with progress of the development project at each stage. There is a therefore a 'go–no go' decision at each stage (that is, a gate) and hence this process is often referred to as a 'stage–gate model'.

Visit the **online resources** and follow the web link to the Product Development and Management Association (PDMA) to learn more about the professional development, information, collaboration, and promotion of new product development and management.

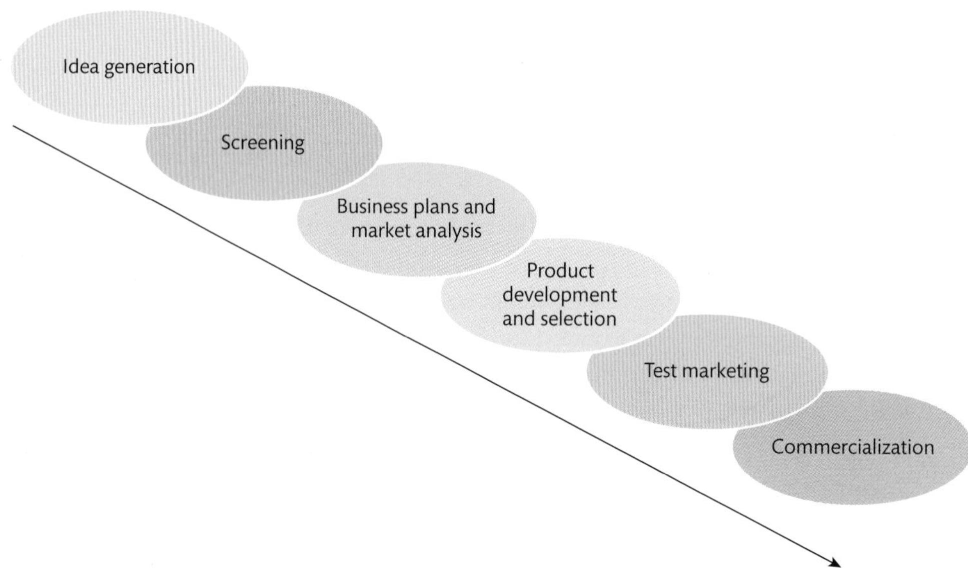

Figure 6.4 Stages in the new product development process

Idea Generation

Ideas can be generated through customers, competitors (through websites and sales literature analysis), market research data (such as reports), social media analyses, R&D, customer service employees, the sales force, project development teams, and secondary data sources such as sales records. What this means is that organizations should foster a corporate culture that encourages creativity, supporting people when they propose new ideas for product enhancements and other improvements. 3M famously allows its engineers and scientists to spend 15 per cent of their time pursuing projects of their own choice and 30 per cent of a division's revenue must come from products developed in the last four years. Over the years, the company has introduced such pioneering products as the Post-It note, Scotch tape, and the first electronic stethoscope with Bluetooth technology (Govindarajan and Srinivas, 2013).

Screening

All ideas need to be assessed so that only those that meet predetermined criteria are advanced. Key criteria include the fit between the proposed new idea and the overall corporate strategy and objectives. Another consideration involves the views of customers, determined using concept testing. Other approaches consider how the market will react to the idea and what effort the organization will need to make if the offering is to be brought to market successfully. Whatever approaches are used, screening must be a separate activity to the idea generation stage; if it is not, creativity might be impaired.

Business Planning and Market Analysis

The development of a business plan is crucial, simply because it will indicate the potential and relative profitability of the product. To prepare the plan, important information about the size, shape, and dynamics of the market should be determined. The resultant profitability forecasts will be significant in determining how and when the product will be developed, if at all.

Product Development and Selection

In many organizations, several product ideas are considered simultaneously. It is management's task to select those that have commercial potential and are in the best interests of the organization, in terms of its longer-term strategy, goals, and use of resources. There is a trade-off between the need to test and reduce risk and the need to go to market and drive income to get a return on the investment committed to the new proposition. This phase is expensive, so only a limited number of projects are allowed to proceed into development. Prototypes and test versions are developed for those projects that are selected for further development. These are then subjected to functional performance tests, design revisions, manufacturing requirements analysis, distribution analysis, and a multitude of other testing procedures.

Test Marketing

Before committing a new product to a market, most organizations decide to test market the finished product. By piloting and testing the product under controlled real-market conditions, many of the genuine issues that only customers may perceive can be raised and resolved, while minimizing any damage or risk to the organization and the brand. **Test marketing** can be undertaken using a particular geographical region or specific number of customer locations. The intention is to evaluate the product and the whole marketing programme under real-world working conditions. Test marketing, or field trials, enables the product and marketing plan to be refined or adapted in the light of market reaction, before its release to the whole market. British supermarket group Sainsbury's, for example, has built a central London lab and hired 500 specialists to test new ways of shopping, especially on mobile apps, given that customers' lives have changed and they have become more 'promiscuous shoppers' (Ghosh, 2015).

It is vital for organizations to set up systems with which to measure the success or failure of new product development. Criteria for measuring success and failure include (but are not limited to) measures based on customer acceptance, financial performance, and product- and firm-level considerations (Griffin and Page, 1993), including the following.

- Customer acceptance measures:
  - Customer acceptance
  - Customer satisfaction
  - Net revenue goals
  - Net market share goals
  - Net unit sales goals
- Financial performance measures:
  - Break-even period
  - Margin goals
  - Profitability goals
  - Internal rate of return (IRR)/return on investment (ROI)
- Product level measures:
  - Development cost
  - Launched on time

  - Product performance level
  - Net quality guidelines
  - Speed to market
- Firm level measurements:
  - Percentage of sales attained as a proportion of new products/services

Commercialization

To commercialize a new product, a launch plan is required. This considers the needs of **distributors**, end-user customers, marketing communication agencies, and other relevant stakeholders. The objective is to schedule all of those activities that are required to make the launch successful. These include communications (to inform audiences of the product's capabilities, and to position and persuade potential customers), training, and product support for all customer-facing employees.

Any perceived rigidity in this formal process should be disregarded. Many new offerings come to market via different routes, at different speeds and different levels of preparation.

Market Insight 6.1 **Co-creating the Perfect Pizza**

With the objective of creating private-label products that would help to make Coop Sweden a destination store, the Coop brand was ready to offer more than only 'me too' products competing on price. At the same time, the category manager for frozen foods identified a downward trend in sales of frozen pizza. The solution? Co-creating the perfect private-label pizza, specifically tailored to Coop's customers.

First, an online survey consisting of open-response questions was used to identify insights into what makes a great frozen pizza. The study was carried out in Coop's proprietary online consumer panel (consisting of more than 20,000 customers at the time).

Second, point-of-sales (POS) data were used to identify 1,300 frozen pizza consumers from among the consumer panel. These customers had experience of Coop's frozen pizza assortment. The sample included both private-label buyers and private-label non-buyers, providing Coop with high-quality insights. Moreover, these consumers were highly motivated to contribute, as indicated by response rates as high as 75 per cent (far above the panel average).

Coop Sweden co-created a successful private-label pizza for its customer base.

Source: © Shutterstock / pilipphoto.

The study contributed many consumer insights that were directly applicable to the new product specification. To the category manager's surprise, there was no need to complicate things; consumers of frozen pizza asked for traditional Swedish pizza

Market Insight 6.1 (continued)

tastes, with ham and cheese said to be the most important ingredients. Pizza consumers also wanted 'more'—more topping, more cheese, and more taste. They commonly said that the pizza on the picture of the package looked very good, but that it led to disappointment on seeing the actual product inside: the picture and the product did not correspond. One final insight was the fact that a large majority of buyers wanted a high-quality pizza and, at the same time, agreed to a higher price, rather than a cheap one with lower quality. Those insights gave the strategic purchaser the power, and courage, to go for a pizza that was not only a 'me too' product.

The whole co-creation process took only five weeks from starting the project to finalizing the conclusions and making recommendations to Coop's strategic purchaser. The recommendations gave her a clear objective in terms of the kind of frozen pizzas for which she should be looking. In fact, the findings from the study were directly transferred into a product specification.

Five new products that met both consumer wishes and Coop's quality standards were launched at the end of May 2014. In all cases, there was more topping, the quality of the ingredients was better, and the package design was an accurate reflection of the product inside.

The new Coop pizzas were instantly appreciated by the consumers and sales started to increase only one month after they were launched. By April 2015, sales were up 66 per cent on sales of the previous Coop pizzas. Moreover, the total category sales had increased by 20 per cent, demonstrating that the new pizzas did not simply cannibalize other products in the category.

This project showed other category managers and strategic purchasers at Coop that excellent products can be developed when being proactive, and the value of starting a consumer insight process at an early stage of the product development process, in a short time frame and at a low cost.

1 **What would you say were the key success factors in the development of Coop's new pizza?**

2 **What benefits and drawbacks can you see of using existing customers when developing new products?**

3 **What other uses do you see for Coop's proprietary web panel?**

Sources: Allen et al. (2016); Liljedal (2016); http://www.coop.se.

This Market Insight was kindly contributed by Fredrik Törn, PhD, Head of Insight, Analytics, and Intelligence, Coop Sweden.

The Process of Adoption

The process by which individuals accept and use new propositions is referred to as 'adoption' (Rogers, 1983). The different stages in the **process of adoption** are sequential and are characterized by the different factors that are involved at each stage (for example the media used by each individual). The process starts with people gaining awareness of a proposition, then moves through various stages of adoption, before a purchase is eventually made. Figure 6.5 sets out the various stages in the process of adoption.

1 In the *knowledge* stage, consumers become aware of the new proposition. They have little information and have yet to develop any particular attitudes towards the product. Indeed, at this stage, consumers are not interested in finding out any more information.

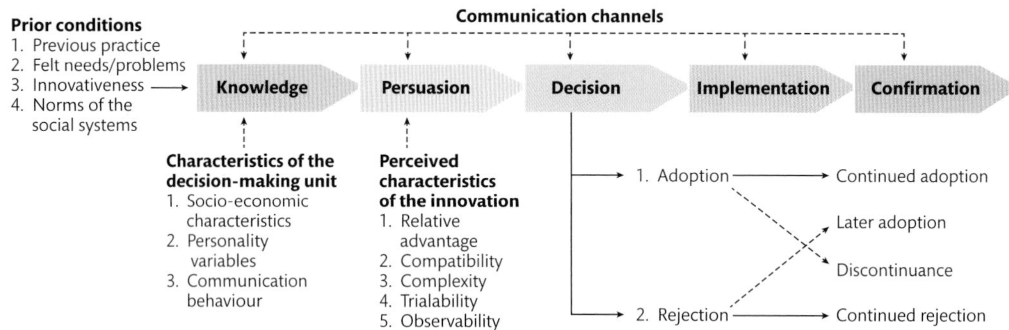

Figure 6.5 Stages in the innovation decision process of adoption

Source: Reprinted with the permission of Free Press, a Division of Simon & Schuster, Inc., from DIFFUSION OF INNOVATIONS, FIFTH EDITION by Everett M. Rogers. Copyright © 1995, 2003 by Everett M. Rogers. Copyright © 1962, 1971, 1983, by Free Press, a Division of Simon & Schuster, Inc. All rights reserved.

2 The *persuasion* stage is characterized by consumers becoming aware that the innovation may be of use in solving a potential problem. Consumers become sufficiently motivated to find out more about the proposition's characteristics, including its features, price, and availability.

3 In the *decision* stage, individuals develop an attitude toward the proposition and they reach a decision about whether the innovation will meet their needs. If this is positive, they will experiment with the innovation.

4 During the *implementation* stage, the innovation is tried for the first time. Sales promotions are often used as samples to allow individuals to test the product without any undue risk. Individuals accept or reject an innovation on the basis of their experience of the trial. Consider, for example, the way in which supermarkets or duty-free airport retailers use sampling to encourage people to try new food and drink products.

5 The final *confirmation* stage is signalled when an individual successfully purchases the proposition on a regular basis without the help of the sales promotion or other incentives.

The adoption stages do not always occur in sequence. Rejection of the innovation can occur at any point—even during implementation and the very early phases of the confirmation stage. Generally, mass communications are more effective in the earlier phases of the adoption process

Product sampling in supermarkets is used as a tactic to facilitate the adoption of new products.

Source: © Tyler Olson/Shutterstock.

for propositions in which buyers are actively interested and more interpersonal forms are more appropriate in later stages—especially implementation and confirmation.

Diffusion Theory

Consumers may have both functional and emotional motives when purchasing, but customers adopt new propositions differently. Their different attitudes to risk, and their levels of education, experience, and needs, mean that different groups of customers adopt new propositions at varying speeds. The rate at which a market adopts an innovation is referred to as the **process of diffusion** (Rogers, 1962). According to Rogers, there are five categories of adopter, as shown in Figure 6.6.

- **Innovators**—This group, which constitutes 2.5 per cent of the buying population, is important because it has to kick-start the adoption process. These people like new ideas, and are often well educated, young, confident, and financially strong. They are more likely to take risks associated with new propositions. Innovative attitudes and behaviour can be specific to only one or two areas of interest.
- **Early adopters**—This group, which comprises 13.5 per cent of the market, is characterized by a high percentage of opinion leaders. These people are very important for speeding up the adoption process. Consequently, marketing communications need to be targeted at these people, who in turn will stimulate word-of-mouth communications to spread information. Although early adopters prefer to let innovators take all of the risks, they enjoy being at the leading edge of innovation, tend to be younger than any other group, and have above-average levels of education. Other than innovators, this group reads more publications and consults more salespeople than all others.
- **Early majority**—This group, which forms 34 per cent of the market, is more risk-averse than the previous two groups. Individuals requires reassurance that the offering works and has been proven in the market. They are above average in terms of age, education, social status, and income.

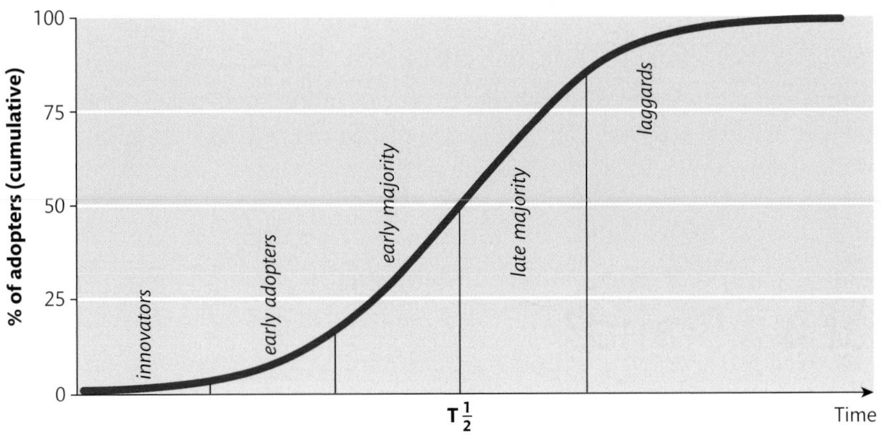

Figure 6.6 The process of diffusion

Source: Reprinted with the permission of Free Press, a Division of Simon & Schuster, Inc., from DIFFUSION OF INNOVATIONS, FIFTH EDITION by Everett M. Rogers.

Research Insight 6.1

To take your learning further, you might wish to read this influential paper.

Peres, R., Muller, E., and Mahajan, V. (2010) 'Innovation diffusion and new product growth models: A critical review and research directions', *International Journal of Research in Marketing*, 27(2): 91–106.

This paper usefully explains that diffusion of new propositions is far more complex and multifaceted than it was assumed to be in the past, because consumers are now exposed to a greater range of influences, including word-of-mouth communications, network externalities, and social signalling. The authors discuss how social networking sites are altering the diffusion process (because of online **influentials** and the presence of online social hubs) and how network effects impact upon diffusion (with slow initial growth in diffusion followed by a surge in demand, especially with high-technology products, as consumers wait and see if a particular technology standard takes off). Importantly, they also discuss turning points in diffusion, such as 'take-offs' (that is, when adoption increases exponentially, often as prices are reduced and consumer uncertainty is reduced) and 'saddles' (that is, when demand dips temporarily and increases again, for example as a result of technological changes or macroeconomic events). Technological generations (that is, when an upgraded proposition is introduced) also impact on diffusion, not least because they encourage existing users to shift to the new proposition, but also because they may encourage non-users to leapfrog to the new technological standard without having bought the previous incarnation.

 **Visit the online resources to read the abstract and access the full paper.**

Unlike the early adopters, they tend to wait for prices to fall and prefer more informal sources of information, and they are often prompted into purchase by other people who have already purchased.

- **Late majority**—Of a similar size to the previous group (34 per cent), the late majority are sceptical of new ideas and adopt new offerings only because of social or economic factors. They read few publications and are below average in terms of education, social status, and income.
- **Laggards**—This group of people, comprising 16 per cent of the buying population, are suspicious of all new ideas and their opinions are very hard to change. Laggards have the lowest income, social status, and education of all of the groups, and take a long time to adopt an innovation, if they adopt it at all.

What is a Brand?

A 'brand' can be distinguished from its proposition or unbranded commodity counterparts by means of the perceptions and feelings consumers' have about its attributes and its performance. Bottled water, for example, is essentially a commodity, but brands such as Highland Spring, Aqua Falls, and Crystal Clear have all developed their offerings with imagery that serves to enhance customer

Even basic commodities like water can be successfully branded.

Source: Courtesy of Highland Spring.

feelings and emotions about the actual water in the packaging. Ultimately, a brand resides in the minds of the consumer (Achenbaum, 1993).

Brand positioning is a strategic activity used to differentiate and distinguish a brand so that a consumer understands the brand, not only remembers it. As Tudor and Negricea (2012) rightly assert, branding and positioning are interrelated: a credible position cannot be sustained without a strong brand, and a brand cannot be developed or preserved without the audience perceiving a justifiable position.

Successful brands capture three core brand elements: promises, positioning, and performance—that is, the 'three brand Ps' (3BPs) (see Figure 6.7). At the core of this concept is communication, which enables a promise to be known (known as 'brand awareness'), positions the

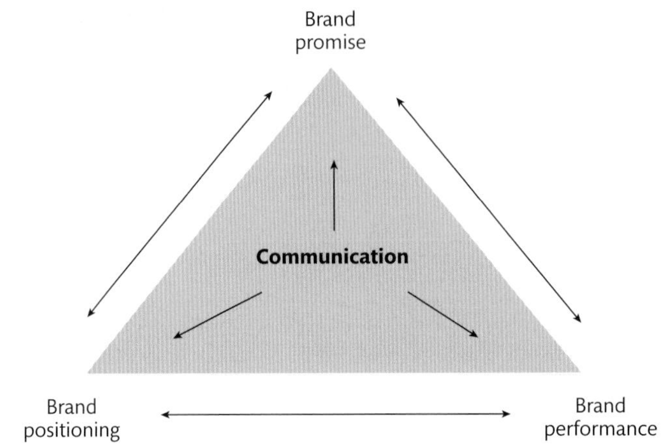

Figure 6.7 The triangulation of the 3BPs

Source: Marketing Communications: Discovery, Creation, and Conversations (7th edn.) Fill, C. and Turnbull, S. (2016). Pearson Education Limited.

brand correctly (known as 'brand attitude'), and delivers brand performance (known as 'brand response').

Commonly, a brand is represented by a name, symbol, words, or mark that identifies and distinguishes a proposition or company from its competitors. However, brands consist of much more than these various elements. As Aaker (2014: 1) remarks, 'far more than a name or a logo it is an organization's promise to a customer to deliver what a brand stands for . . . in terms of functional benefits but also emotional, self-expressive and social benefits'.

Why Brand?

Brands represent opportunities for both consumers and organizations (manufacturers and retailers) to buy and to sell products and services easily, more efficiently, and relatively quickly. The benefits can be considered from each perspective.

Consumers like brands because they:

- help people to identify their preferred offerings;
- reduce levels of perceived risk and, in doing so, improve the quality of the shopping experience;
- help people to gauge the level of quality of a product/service or experience;
- reduce the amount of time that a customer must spend making proposition-based decisions and, in turn, decrease the time spent shopping;
- provide psychological reassurance or reward, especially for offerings bought on an occasional basis; and
- inform consumers about the source of an offering (in terms of country or company).

Many brands are deliberately imbued with human characteristics, to the point at which they are identified as having particular personalities. These **brand personalities** might be based around being seen as 'friendly', 'approachable', 'distant', 'aloof', 'calculating', 'honest', 'fun', or even 'robust' or 'caring'. For example, Timberland is 'rugged', Victoria's Secret, 'glamorous', Virgin is associated with youthfulness and rebelliousness, and management consultancies such as PricewaterhouseCoopers (PwC) seek to be seen as successful, accomplished, and influential. Marketing communications play an important role in communicating the essence of a brand's personality. By developing positive emotional links with a brand, a company can reassure consumers about their brand purchases.

Manufacturers and retailers use brands because they:

- can increase the company's financial valuation;
- enable premium pricing;
- help to differentiate the proposition from competitive offerings;
- can deter competitors from entering the market;
- encourage cross-selling of other brands owned by the manufacturer;
- help the company to develop customer trust, customer loyalty and retention, and repeat-purchase buyer behaviour;
- help in the development and use of integrated marketing communications;
- contribute to corporate identity programmes; and
- provide some legal protection.

Visit the **online resources** and complete Internet Activity 6.1 to learn more about how major organizations perceive the importance of branding and their brands.

How Brands Work: Associations and Personalities

The development of successful brands requires customers to be able to make appropriate brand-related associations. Normally, these should be based on utilitarian, functional issues, as well as emotions and feelings towards a brand.

Clayton and Heo (2011) refer to brand image, perceived quality, and brand attitude as the main dimensions of **brand associations**, citing work by Aaker (1991), Keller (1993), and Low and Lamb (2000) in this area.

Keller (1993) believes that brand associations themselves are made up of the physical and non-physical attributes and benefits aligned with attitudes to create a brand image in the mind of the consumer. Belk (1988), meanwhile, suggested that brands offer a means of self-expression, whether this is in terms of who they want to be (the 'desired self'), who they strive to be (the 'ideal self'), or who they think they should be (the 'ought self'). Brands therefore provide a means for individuals to indicate to others their preferred personality.

This emotional and symbolic approach is intended to provide consumers with additional reasons to engage with a brand, beyond the normal functional characteristics that a brand offers (Keller, 1998), which are so easily copied by competitors. Aaker (1997) developed the **brand personality scale**,

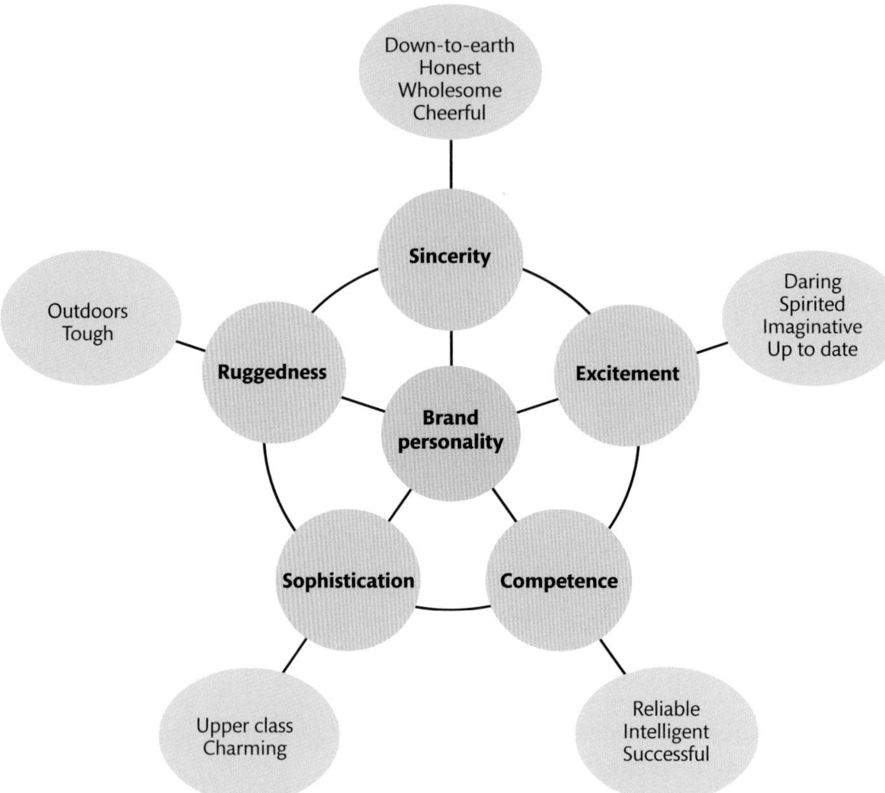

Figure 6.8 Five dimensions of psychosocial meaning

Source: Reprinted with permission from J. Aaker (1997) 'Dimensions of brand personality', ***Journal of Marketing Research*** 34 (August), 347–56, published by the American Marketing Association.

which consists of five main dimensions of psychosocial meaning, subdivided into 42 personality traits (see Figure 6.8):

- sincerity ('wholesome', 'honest', 'down-to-earth');
- excitement ('exciting', 'imaginative', 'daring');
- competence ('intelligent', 'confident');
- sophistication ('charming', 'glamorous', 'smooth'); and
- ruggedness ('strong', 'masculine').

Aaker's initial research was conducted in the mid-1990s and revealed that, in the United States, MTV was perceived to be best at excitement, CNN best on competence, Levi's best on ruggedness, Revlon best on sophistication, and Campbell's best on sincerity.

These psychosocial dimensions have subsequently become enshrined as dimensions of brand personality. Aaker developed a five-point framework around these dimensions to provide a consistent means of measurement. Various studies have found that consumers choose brands that reflect their own personality (Linville and Carlston, 1994; Phau and Lau, 2001)—that is, they prefer brands that project a personality that is consistent with their self-concepts. As Arora and Stoner (2009: 273) indicate, 'brand personality provides a form of identity for consumers that expresses symbolic meaning for themselves and for others'. Brand personality can therefore be construed as a means of creating and maintaining consumer loyalty, if only because this aspect is difficult for competitors to copy.

Brand Names

Choosing a name for a brand is a critical foundation stone because, ideally, it should enable the brand to be:

- easily recalled, spelled, and spoken;
- strategically consistent with the organization's branding policies;
- indicative of the offering's major benefits and characteristics;
- distinctive;
- meaningful to the customer; and
- capable of registration and protection.

Sometimes, social pressure, or even a crisis, can stimulate a change of name. For example, Philip Morris changed the overall company name to the Altria Group following sustained attacks about its cigarette and tobacco products. Brand names need to transfer easily across markets, and if they are to do so successfully, it helps if customers can not only pronounce the name, but also recall the name unaided.

Cadbury—the company prefix to a range of different brand names.

Source: © Ekaterina_Minaeva/Shutterstock.

Brand names should have some internal strategic consistency and be compatible with the organization's overall positioning. Ford Transit, Virgin Atlantic, and Cadbury Dairy Milk are names that reflect the parent company's policies because the company name prefixes the product brand names.

Increasingly, brands are being developed through the use of social media. This is essentially about people talking—either spontaneously to one another, through blogs, or within formal or informal communities—about brands that they have experienced in some way. The role of brand managers has transitioned from one of guardian to that of a brand host (Christodoulides, 2009), who now listens to these conversations and then adapts the brands accordingly. What this suggests is that the control and identity of a brand has moved from the company to the consumer.

Visit the **online resources** and complete Internet Activity 6.2 to learn more about generating brand names.

Branding Strategies

An overall branding strategy can provide direction, consistency, and brand integrity within an organization's portfolio of brands. This provides the basis of the brand architecture. There are three core brand strategies: individual, family, and corporate.

Individual Branding

Once referred to as a 'multibrand policy', individual branding requires that each product offered by an organization is branded independently of all of the others. Grocery brands offered by Unilever (such as Knorr, Cif, and Dove) and Procter & Gamble (such as Fairy, Crest, and Head & Shoulders) typify this approach.

One of the advantages of this approach is that it is easy to target specific segments and to enter new markets with separate names. If a brand fails or becomes subject to negative media attention, the other brands are not likely to be damaged. However, there is a heavy financial cost, because each brand needs to have its own promotional programme and associated support.

Family Branding

A family of cereals: Kellogg's image reinforces the image of the individual brands in its product lines.

Source: © Everything/Shutterstock.

Once referred to as a 'multiproduct brand policy', family branding requires that all of the products use the organization's name, either entirely or in part. Microsoft, Heinz, and Kellogg's all incorporate the company name, because it is hoped that customer trust will develop across all brands and that therefore promotional investment need not be as high. The idea is that there will always be a halo effect across all of the brands when one is communicated and that brand experience will stimulate word-of-mouth following usage. A prime example of this is Google, which has pursued a family brand strategy across Google Adwords, Google Maps, and Google Scholar, to name only a few. What is more impressive is that Google's shattering achievements have been accomplished in only ten years and with minimal advertising spend.

Corporate Brands

Many retail brands adopt a single umbrella brand, based on the name of the organization. This name is then used at all locations, and is a way of identifying the brand and providing a form of consistent differentiation, and of recognition, whether on the high street or online. Major supermarkets such as Tesco in the UK, Carrefour in France, and Asda Wal-Mart use this branding strategy to attract, and to help to retain, customers.

Corporate branding strategies are also used extensively in business markets, such as IBM, Cisco, and Caterpillar, and in consumer markets in which there is technical complexity, such as financial services. Companies such as HSBC and Prudential adopt a single name strategy. One of the advantages of this approach is that promotional investments are limited to one brand. However, the risk is similar to that of family branding, whereby damage to one offering or operational area can cause problems across the organization. The British Broadcasting Corporation (BBC), for example, experienced editorial problems with its *Newsnight* programme that resulted in extensive and persistent negative media coverage. In this instance, not only did the director-general decide to resign, but also questions surfaced about declining trust and reputation concerning the whole of the BBC.

Visit the **online resources** and follow the web link to learn more about IBM's corporate brand.

How to Build Brands

The development of successful brands is critical to an organization's success. Keller (2009) believes that this is best accomplished by considering the brand-building process in terms of steps. The first step is to enable customers to identify with the brand and help them to make associations with a specific product class or customer need. The second is to establish what the brand means, by linking various tangible and intangible brand associations. The third step is concerned with encouraging customer responses based around brand-related judgments and feelings. The final step is about fostering an active relationship between customers and the brand.

Figure 6.9 depicts these rational steps on the left-hand side, with the emotional counterpart shown on the right-hand side. In the centre are six blocks that make up a pyramid, echoing these

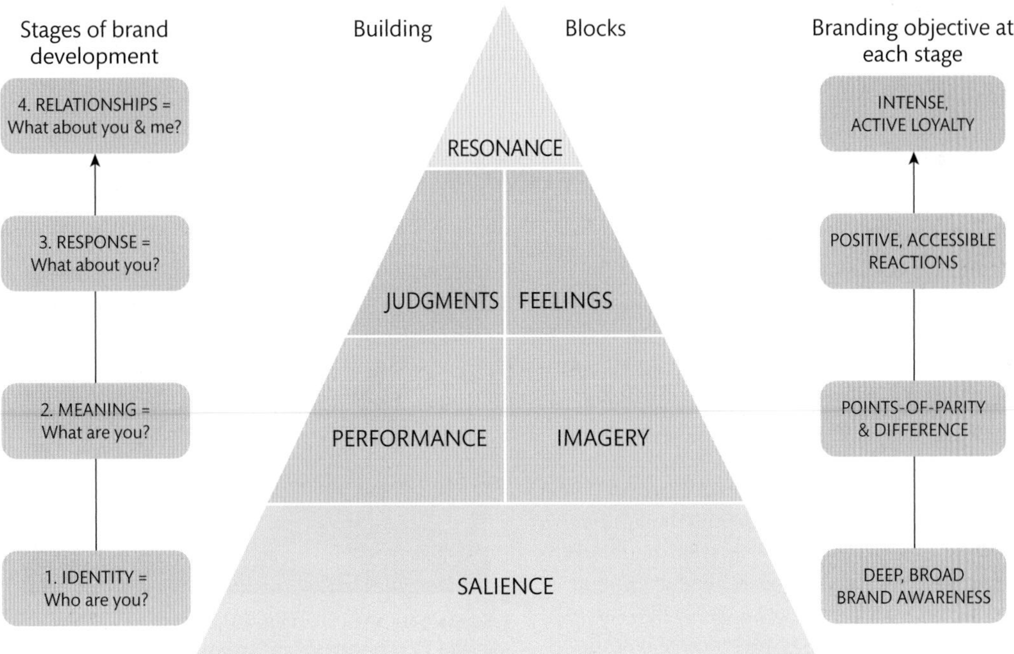

Figure 6.9 Brand pyramid: Building blocks

Source: 'Building strong brands in a modern marketing communications environment', Keller, K.L., ***Journal of Marketing Communications***, July 2009, Taylor & Francis. Reprinted by permission of the publisher (Taylor & Francis Ltd, http://www.tandf.co.uk/journals).

rational and emotional steps. To achieve a successful brand, or 'brand resonance', Keller argues that a foundation is necessary and that these building blocks need to be developed systematically.

Let us apply the brand pyramid to a shampoo brand to understand the terminology further.

- *Brand salience*—How easily and often do customers think of the shampoo brand when thinking about haircare brands or when shopping?
- *Brand performance*—How well do customers believe the shampoo brand cleans and conditions their hair?
- *Brand imagery*—What are the extrinsic properties of the shampoo (the colour, the packaging, the product consistency, associations) and to what level do these satisfy customers' psychological or social needs?
- *Brand judgments*—What are customers' own personal opinions and evaluations about the shampoo?
- *Brand feelings*—What are customers' emotional responses and reactions to the shampoo brand when prompted by communications, friends, or when washing their own hair?
- *Brand resonance*—What is the nature of the relationship that customers have with the shampoo brand and to what extent do they feel loyal to the brand?

Brand resonance is most likely to result when marketers create proper salience and breadth and depth of awareness. From this position, 'points of parity' and 'points of difference' need to be established, so that positive judgments and feelings can be made that appeal to both the head and the heart, respectively.

Visit the **online resources** and follow the web link to learn more about Keller's **brand equity** model.

Market Insight 6.2 **Kopparberg: The Unconventional Brand**

In 1882, local brewers in the Swedish town of Kopparberg joined up to form Kopparberg's Bryggeri AB. Today, the company is led by brothers Peter and Dan-Anders Bronsman. Peter bought a disused mineral water bottling plant, and began making lager and cider. Kopparberg capitalizes on natural soft water in the area, which has low mineral content and enables natural tastes to come through unchanged. Even though cider is claimed to be a way of life in Sweden, traditional apple cider was seen as too dull and unexciting for the younger generation. A gap in the market existed for a fruitier and sweeter cider aimed at young people. Kopparberg therefore decided to innovate with non-traditional flavours for ciders,

Kopparberg often uses innovative events to build its image. TV presenters Lilah Parsons and A.J. Odudu were two of the opinion formers who participated in the latest Kopparberg Urban Forest in London.

Source: Getty / David M. Benett / Contributor.

Market Insight 6.2 (continued)

such as 'naked apple', 'toffee apple', 'kiwi fruit', 'blackcurrant and raspberry', 'strawberry and lime', 'elderflower and lime', and 'cranberry and cinnamon'.

However, a difficulty arose when launching and marketing the new ranges of cider in Sweden owing to a government ban on alcohol advertising. Kopparberg found a way around the problem by focusing its advertising in Ibiza, Greece, and Majorca, where young people from Sweden and other European countries go to party every summer. The idea was that, while partying, they would be drinking Kopparberg's fruitier and sweeter ciders. When they returned home from their summer holidays, they would bring back with them awareness and knowledge about the taste and the brand. This was how Kopparberg launched its products and brand to a young Swedish market without advertising in Sweden.

When Kopparberg expanded its market to the UK in 2007, it found itself a small fish swimming in a big cider pond! It faced strong competition from players such as Magners, Bulmers, and Strongbow. Since then, Kopparberg's fruity ciders have grown to become the most popular amongst UK cider drinkers. In 2014, it was the UK's second best-selling cider, with sales totalling £112 million, beating its major competitors in spite of smaller marketing budgets.

Differentiation and innovation has been the key to Kopparberg's success. Instead of investing in traditional advertising, it identified opinion formers—that is, people who were more adventurous and willing to try new fruity ciders. These people could also influence and spread popularity of these cool, innovative products through word-of-mouth. Cool pubs and bars where young hipsters hang out were targeted in the main UK cities, such as London, Manchester, and Glasgow; free ciders were also supplied to events organized in art galleries and bars in east London: these activities acted as an advert for the brand. Based on product differentiation and its unconventional marketing approach, Kopparberg is now sold in more than 40 countries. In 2015, 75 million litres were sold worldwide, with £225 million in revenue.

1 **What do you think was the most important factor in Kopparberg's success in Sweden: the unconventional advertising, or the new product development?**

2 **Why do you think Kopparberg has been successful in the UK market, given the strong competition?**

3 **How might Kopparberg innovate further to keep ahead of the competition?**

Sources: Torrance (2014); Eads (2015); Trott (2016).

This case was kindly contributed by Dr Ning Baines, Birkbeck, University of London.

Brand Relationships

Although branding has its roots in identification and differentiation, a 'brand-mark is a relational asset whose value to the firm is contingent on past, present and future interactions with various firm stakeholders' (Ballantyne and Aitken, 2007: 366).

Fournier (1998) was one of the first researchers to introduce and utilize relationship theory to understand the roles that brands play in the lives of consumers. She explored ideas about consumers who think about brands as if they were human characters—that is, the personification of brands. She also found that consumers accept attempts by marketers to personalize brands, for example through advertising, which suggests interaction and relationship potential. She identified six facets that characterize brand relationship quality: love and passion; a connection between the brand and self; a high degree of interdependence; a high level of commitment; intimacy; and a positive evaluation of brand quality.

Fournier (1998) believes that it is important to understand consumer–brand relationships and that, by understanding how consumers interact with brands and the meaning that brands represent to people through consumption, marketing theory and practice can be advanced. She argues that it is necessary to consider the broad context of consumers' lives to understand the role and relationship that brands play in them. In addition, meaningful consumer–brand relationships can be observed when the brand represents the key dimension, 'perceived ego significance' (Fournier, 1998: 366). Fournier stresses the importance of understanding what consumers do with brands that adds meaning to their lives (see Market Insight 6.3).

Market Insight 6.3 **Musicians Dying for Success**

Michael Jackson, Bob Marley, Kurt Cobain, and Ian Curtis are all highly regarded music icons whose lucrative businesses have thrived since their death.

Although their reputations might not have been extended if fans were not so emotionally impacted by news of their death, it is the post-death branding activities that have contributed to their brand longevity. The bombardment of new memorabilia merchandise and the release of previously unknown material by marketers and estate holders keen to squeeze every drop of profit appears to have become a regular branding exercise for deceased musicians.

The grief felt by Amy Winehouse's fans following her death was accompanied by a surge of interest in her music.
Source: © Dutourdumonde Photography/Shutterstock.

The importance of emotional impact on consumers is commonly recognized and we can see how such exploitation of our intrinsic functions can impact on buying decisions in the wake of the death of a music artist. News about Michael Jackson's death in June 2009, for example, spread like wildfire. This was followed by a huge surge in sales of his back catalogue, as well as driving his *Greatest Hits* album to the top of the charts that month.

Once they are gone, the value of musicians' portfolios rise, because generally the artist can release no more new material and copyright ownership passes to the next of kin who, if they act quickly, can turn the late artist into an iconic brand. Bob Marley's family was quick to exploit his musical stature, in the form of T-shirts, mugs, and lighters—even naming a cannabis strain after the Rastafarian icon.

Media coverage of Ian Curtis's suicide in 1980 led people to become curious to explore more of Joy Division. As a consequence, the band's album *Unknown Pleasures*, which had initially struggled to sell, entered the music charts in the top ten, and generated huge new admiration of and interest in Joy Division in the months following Curtis's death.

Market Insight 6.3 (continued)

Years later, Joy Division is still a strong influence in the music world, with new generations discovering the band's music even today. The album cover for *Unknown Pleasures* is widely reproduced on T-shirts, and numerous books have been written on Curtis's life and death, by former band mates and by his former wife. These constant reminders have led consumers to associate Ian's sad story with the band's music, so creating a strong emotional connection—all of which gives the estate owners a rationale to perpetuate the brand through remasters, re-releases, and memorial-related merchandise.

In a similar vein, during the year after her death, Amy Winehouse's download sales rose to 1.15 million in the United States, compared to 170,000 downloads earlier that year. Four years later, a documentary commemorating her life had been released as well as a book by her father, making US$1.5 million for the Amy Winehouse Charity Foundation.

And in 2000 alone, the estate of Elvis Presley—arguably the most iconic of them all, who died in 1977—earned US$32 billion from record sales, merchandise, and licensing deals.

1 **How might the more recent passing of David Bowie and Prince be reflected not only in sales of their music, but also in other areas of culture and society?**

2 **Using the Internet find out more about social influence theory and apply the core concept to this scenario.**

3 **Make a list of other brand-related situations in which the termination of the brand has led to increased or delayed sales.**

Source: Anon. (2009); Caulfield (2012); Adebayo (2014); Elvis.net (n.d.).

This market insight was kindly contributed by Naomi Ramage, then an undergraduate student in music business management, branding, and public relations (PR) at Buckinghamshire New University.

Research Insight 6.2

To take your learning further, you might wish to read this influential paper.

Fournier, S. (1998) 'Consumers and their brands: Developing relationship theory in consumer research', ***Journal of Consumer Research*****, 24(4): 343–73**

The article has already been characterized as a modem classic by Bengtsson (2003), such is its significance and contribution to our understanding about marketing and consumer research. The paper discusses the need to incorporate relationship marketing theory with branding and explores the types of relationship that people form with brands.

 **Visit the online resources to read the abstract and access the full paper.**

Brand Co-creation

The managerial perspective assumes that manufacturers or service providers develop and manage brands, while individual consumers are passive and can influence only brand meaning or perception of a brand. This requires marketers to perform three essential branding activities, which Pennington and Ball (2009) suggest are to enable identification and differentiation, to maintain consistency, and to communicate the existence and attributes to customer and marketing channel audiences.

In recent years, this perspective and process has been challenged by increasing evidence that customers can create brands. In **customer branding**, customers attach a name, term, or other feature that enables them to identify one seller's goods or service as distinct from those of other sellers (AMA, 2012). This is commonly referred to as 'co-creation' and although many indicate that this is not a recent phenomenon, France and colleagues (2015: 6) point out that there is no exact understanding of the co-creation construct and that there is 'some confusion in the literature, especially in the area of brand co-creation and brand engagement'.

Pennington and Ball (2009: 455) define 'customer branding' as 'a process in which a customer, or customers, define, label and seek to purchase a subset of an otherwise undifferentiated or unbranded product. The customer can be anywhere along the value chain, including intermediate and end-user customers.'

In conventional branding processes, a business is able to influence external stakeholders and customers, through promises of value creation, and internal stakeholders as a means of employee branding and organizational identity. Where there is customer branding, however, the organization surrenders control of the brand's ability to convey these and other clear messages to customers and employees (Pennington and Ball, 2009).

Pennington and Ball (2009) identify three key conditions that need to be met if customer branding is to occur: first, there must be a variety of offerings in the market; second, the delivery and quality of offerings must be unacceptable; and third, customers must be able to obtain a reliable and satisfactory alternative from within the marketing channel. As they phrase it, 'for the customer to expend the effort to take over branding activities that the marketer is not performing, the customer must show certain needs, perceptions and abilities' (Pennington and Ball, 2009: 459).

In addition to customer branding, customers can co-create in different ways, most of which are rooted in brand value. France and colleagues (2015) refer to co-creation in the context of exchanges with and experiences of a brand, influencing customer perception of a brand, customer-generated advertising, new product development, social media, and word-of-mouth.

Ideas about brand co-creation are not confined to product or service offerings. For example, Juntunen (2012) found that a range of stakeholders, not only customers, are involved in corporate brand co-creation. These include employees, relatives, friends, university researchers, students, employees and managers of other companies, advertising agencies, financiers, lawyers, graphic designers, and customers. She revealed that stakeholders engage in various sub-processes of corporate brand co-creation, even before a company is formed (Kollmann and Suckow, 2007). These sub-processes include inventing the corporate name before a company is established, developing a new corporate name, updating the logo and communications material, and developing the proposition and the business after establishment of the company.

Global Branding

Brands can be considered in terms of the markets in which they operate, sometimes referred to as 'scope'. **Brand scope** can vary, spanning operating in local and domestic markets, operating in selected foreign markets, and operating across a range of international markets. Townsend and colleagues (2010) provide a useful typology of brands (see Table 6.1).

The scope, or reach, of a brand is a result of decisions to enter different geographic regions to achieve particular goals. As organizations extend their scope, so their branding and marketing strategies must adapt to influence local cultures and customer needs. However, global branding is characterized by a consistency of marketing strategies—a transfer of the same strategy across all markets, as practised by IBM, AT&T, and China Mobile.

Table 6.1 A hierarchy of brand scope

Brand scope	Criteria and characteristics	Examples
Domestic brand	A brand with a presence only in the home market and managed locally.	Thornton's Timothy Taylor White Stuff William Hill
International brand	Sold across a few country markets and managed largely by the home market, often using local agents in international markets. Positioning, identity, image, distinguishing characteristics including attributes, associations, and identifiers of the brand virtually identical to the home market.	Eddie Stobart Ideal Standard
Multi-domestic Brand	Sold across multiple country markets and managed through decentralized management, with local control. Positioning, identity, image, distinguishing characteristics including attributes, associations, and identifiers of the brand varying across markets.	Caterpillar Diageo Ferrero GM Philips Samsung
Global brand	Sold across multiple country markets, with distribution located in three major developed continents. Centralized brand management coordinates local execution, but core essence of the brand remains unchanged. Positioning, identity, image, distinguishing characteristics including attributes, associations, and identifiers maintain a high degree of consistency across worldwide markets.	Apple Coca-Cola Google IBM McDonald's

Source: Adapted from Townsend et al. (2010).

Research Insight 6.3

To take your learning further, you might wish to read this influential paper.

Holt, D. B., Quelch, J. A., and Taylor, E. L. (2004) 'How global brands compete', *Harvard Business Review*, 82(9): 68–81.

This is an important paper that all those interested in global marketing and global brands should read. The authors review the ways in which global brands compete and reflect on the need for companies to manage their national identities, as well as their 'globalness'.

Visit the online resources to read the abstract and access the full paper.

Whatever the merits, the purity of the global brand concept has not been entirely realized, because issues of adaptation to local market needs, including social and cultural issues, has led to a need to achieve a balance between these two extremes. Coca-Cola, for example, adapts the taste of its products to meet the needs of local markets, even across Europe. So, because the consumption of different offerings naturally varies across countries (such as chocolate, milk, coffee, cars), it is unsurprising that we find manufacturers and producers varying their marketing strategies. What this means is that marketers need to determine which elements can be standardized (for example products, name, packaging, service) and which need to be adapted (typically, language, communications, and voiceovers) to meet local needs.

Brand Equity

Brand equity is a measure of the value and strength of a brand. It is an assessment of a brand's wealth, sometimes referred to as 'goodwill'. Financially, brands consist of their physical assets plus a sum that represents their reputation, or goodwill, with the latter far exceeding the former. So when Premier Foods, which owns Branston sauces and Ambrosia Creamed Rice, paid £1.2 billion to buy Rank Hovis McDougall (RHM), which owns Oxo, Hovis, and Mr Kipling cakes, it bought the physical assets and the reputation of RHM brands, the sales of which amount to £1.6 billion annually (OFT, 2007).

Brand equity is considered important because of the increasing interest in measuring the return on promotional investments and pressure by various stakeholders to value brands for balance-sheet purposes. A brand with a strong equity is more likely to be able to preserve its customer loyalty and to fend off competitor attacks.

There are two main views about how brand equity should be valued, one from a financial and the other from a marketing perspective (Lasser et al., 1995). The financial view is founded on a consideration of a brand's asset value that is based on the net value of all of the cash the brand is expected to generate over its lifetime. The marketing perspective is grounded in the images, beliefs, and core associations that consumers have of and with particular brands, and the degree of loyalty or retention that a brand is able to sustain. Measures of market awareness, penetration, involvement, attitudes, and purchase intervals (frequency) are typical. Feldwick (1996), however, suggests that there are three parts associated with brand equity:

- brand value, based on a financial and accounting base;
- brand strength, measuring the strength of a consumer's attachment to a brand; and
- brand description, represented by the specific attitudes customers have towards a brand.

Market Insight 6.4 **Building a Responsible Brand: Nestlé's Case**

Nestlé is the largest multinational corporation (MNC) in the world in the food and beverage sector. Nestlé also has equally ambitious targets on sustainability and human rights. In particular, the multinational giant has an impressive policy on responsible sourcing, with commitments to working conditions of suppliers of an array of resources, including:

- fish and seafood, in relation to which Nestlé promises 'continuous improvement' on its traceability;
- coffee, in relation to which its Nescafé Plan has the concrete goal to 'source 100% of the coffee for Nespresso's permanent range through its AAA Sustainable Quality Program on coffee sourcing, and improve farmer social welfare'; and
- cocoa, in relation to which Nestlé aims to eliminate all forms of child labour from its supply chain.

To implement these polices and to meet its goals, Nestlé works with different non-governmental organizations (NGOs) and supplier auditor firms. However, during 2015 and 2016, Nestlé was accused by different human rights activist NGOs for sourcing cocoa from suppliers using child labour in the Ivory Coast, shrimp from suppliers using slaves in Thailand, and coffee from Brazilian plantations with forced labour.

In an innovative and bold manner, Nestlé responded to these claims by admitting that it did indeed have these issues in their supply chains, because these

Retaining ethical standards across the supply chain can be very difficult as demonstrated by the challenges faced by Nestlé.

Source: Courtesy of Nespresso.

are systemic problems associated with political governance in many developing countries. Nestlé has claimed that it is impossible for any large company to eliminate these human rights abuses from its supply chain when sourcing cocoa from Ivory Coast, fish or seafood from Thailand, and coffee from Brazil.

With regards to Brazil, but equally applicable to the difficulties involved in upholding human rights globally in a supply chain, Nestlé has said: 'Unfortunately, forced labour is an endemic problem in Brazil and no company sourcing coffee and other ingredients from the country can fully guarantee that it has completely removed forced labour practices or human rights abuses from its supply chain.'

Market Insight 6.4 (continued)

1 **What do you think are the implications of Nestlé's statement for its branding strategy? What are the strengths and weaknesses of Nestlé's reaction?**

2 **Discuss how Nestlé can work with its local partners to try to live up fully to its ethical sourcing commitments.**

3 **What more can global corporations do to ensure that their marketing commitments on responsible sourcing are consistent with their practices?**

Sources: Perego and Kolk (2012); Rodríguez-Garavito (2015); Hodal (2016); Nespresso (n.d.).

The case has been kindly contributed by Dr Rajiv Maher, post-doctoral researcher at the Pontifical Catholic University of Chile.

Chapter Summary

To consolidate your learning, the key points from this chapter are summarized below.

- **Explain the different levels of a proposition and the product life cycle.**

  Propositions encompass three levels, including: the *core* proposition, consisting of the real core benefit or service (for example bottled water is thirst-quenching); the *embodied* proposition, consisting of the physical good or delivered service that provides the expected benefit (for example the packaging); and the *augmented* proposition, consisting of the embodied offering plus all those other factors that are necessary to support the purchase and any post-purchase activities. Propositions are thought to move through a sequential pattern of development, referred to as the 'product life cycle'. It consists of five distinct stages—namely, development, birth, growth, maturity, and decline. Each stage of the cycle represents a different set of market circumstances and customer expectations that need to be met with different strategies.

- **Explore the processes associated with innovating new propositions and how propositions are adopted.**

  The development of new propositions is complex and high risk, so organizations usually adopt a procedural approach. The procedure consists of several phases. The process by which individuals accept and use new propositions is referred to as 'adoption' (Rogers, 1983). The different stages in the adoption process are sequential and are characterized by the different factors that are involved at each stage. The rate at which a market adopts an innovation differs according to an individual's propensity for risk and is referred to as the 'process of diffusion' (Rogers, 1962).

- **Explain the characteristics and principal types of brand and branding.**

  Brands are products and services that have added value. Brands help customers to differentiate between the various offerings and to associate certain attributes or feelings with a particular brand. Brands are capable of triggering associations in the minds of consumers. These associations may sometimes enable consumers to construe a psychosocial meaning associated with a particular brand. This psychosocial element can be measured in terms of the associations consumers make along five key dimensions: sincerity, excitement, competence, sophistication, and ruggedness. Brand personality provides a form of identity for consumers that expresses symbolic meaning for themselves and for others.

- **Explain how brands can be built.**

  Keller's (2009) brand pyramid consists of several building blocks and posits that brands are built through a series of steps. The first aims to enable customers to identify with the brand and help them to make associations with a specific product class or customer need. The second aims to establish what the brand means by linking various tangible and intangible brand associations. The third step encourages customer responses based around brand-related judgments and feelings. Th e final step is about fostering an active relationship between customers and the brand.

Review Questions

1. **Identify the three levels that make up a proposition.**
2. **Describe the four types of good by behavioural category and find examples to illustrate each one.**
3. **What is the product life cycle and what key characteristics make up each of its stages?**
4. **What are the main stages associated with the development of new product propositions?**
5. **Why is a knowledge about the process of adoption useful to marketers?**
6. **Why is branding important to consumers and to organizations?**
7. **Why is it necessary to consider the broad context of consumers' lives to understand the role and relationship that brands play in them?**
8. **What are Aaker's (1997) five dimensions of psychosocial meaning?**
9. **Draw Keller's (2009) brand pyramid and label the individual building blocks.**
10. **Write brief notes explaining the two main views about brand equity.**

Worksheet Summary

To apply the knowledge you have gained from this chapter, and to test your understanding of branding insight, visit the **online resources** and complete Worksheet 6.1.

Discussion Questions

1. Prepare a brief report in which you explain the nature of the product life cycle for a grocery brand of your choice. Consider how it might be used to improve your chosen brand's marketing activities and, from this, highlight any difficulties that might arise when using the product life cycle to develop strategies.

2. Discuss the view that it is not worth the huge investment necessary to develop new propositions when it is just as easy to copy those of the market leader.

3 If brands are capable of having a personality, are they consequently susceptible to personality disorders? Justify your answer.

4 When Ingrid Stevenson was appointed brand manager for a range of well-established fruit juices, one of her first tasks was to understand the market and how consumers related to the brand. How might an understanding of Aaker's (1997) brand personality scale help her in this task?

Visit the **online resources** and complete the multiple-choice questions to assess your knowledge of the chapter.

Glossary

brand multidimensional and emotional construct that people use to embrace an abstract object or a set of associations.

brand associations the physical and non-physical product attributes and benefits aligned with attitudes that consumers use to create an image of a brand.

brand equity a measure of the value and strength of a brand. It is an assessment of a brand's wealth, sometimes referred to as 'goodwill'.

brand personalities the associations and images that enable consumers to construe a psychosocial meaning associated with a particular brand.

brand personality scale a framework of dimensions used to measure brand personality, developed by Aaker (1997).

brand positioning a strategic activity used to differentiate and distinguish a brand.

brand scope the range of international markets in which a brand operates.

convenience products non-durable goods or services, often bought with little pre-purchase thought or consideration.

customer branding the name, term, or other feature devised by customers that enables them to identify otherwise undifferentiated or unbranded products.

distributors organizations that buy goods and services, often from a limited range of manufacturers, and normally sell them to retailers or resellers.

durable goods goods bought infrequently, which are used repeatedly and which involve a reasonably high level of consumer risk.

early adopters a group of people in the process of diffusion who enjoy being at the leading edge of innovation and buy into new products at an early stage.

early majority a group of people in the process of diffusion who require reassurance that a product works and has been proven in the market before they are prepared to buy it.

extensive problem-solving occurs when consumers give a great deal of attention and care to a purchase decision, in circumstances in which there is no previous or similar product purchase experience.

influentials People who have the ability to persuade others to think, believe, or behave in a certain way.

innovators a group of people in the process of diffusion who like new ideas and who are most likely to take risks associated with new products.

laggards a group of people in the process of diffusion who are suspicious of all new ideas and whose opinions are very hard to change.

late majority a group of people in the process of diffusion who are sceptical of new ideas and adopt new products only because of social or economic factors.

limited problem-solving occurs when consumers have some product and purchase familiarity.

non-durable goods low-priced products that are bought frequently, used only once, and incur low levels of purchase risk.

process of adoption the process through which individuals accept and use new products. The different stages in the adoption process are sequential and each is characterized by different factors.

process of diffusion the rate at which a market adopts an innovation.

product anything that is capable of satisfying customer needs.

product life cycle the pathway that a product assumes over its lifetime, in which there are said to be five main stages: development, introduction, growth, maturity, and decline.

proposition a product or service that represents a promise made to customers and stakeholders.

routinized response behaviour a form of purchase behaviour that occurs when consumers have suitable product and purchase experience and they perceive low risk.

shopping product a type of consumer product that is bought relatively infrequently and requires consumers to update their knowledge prior to purchase.

speciality product a type of consumer product that is bought very infrequently, is very expensive, and represents very high risk.

test marketing a stage in the new product development process, undertaken when a new product is tested with a sample of customers or is launched in a specified geographical area, to judge customers' reactions prior to a national launch.

References

Aaker, D. A. (1991) *Managing Brand Equity*, New York: The Free Press.

Aaker, D. A. (2014) *Aaker on Branding*, New York: Morgan James.

Aaker, J. (1997) 'Dimensions of brand personality', *Journal of Marketing Research*, 34(3): 347–56.

Achenbaum, A. A. (1993) 'The mismanagement of brand equity', Paper presented at the Fifth ARF Annual Advertising and Promotion Workshop, 1 February, New York.

Adebayo, D. (2014) 'Bob Marley's legacy is going up in cannabis smoke', *The Guardian*, 20 November. Available online at http://www.theguardian.com/commentisfree/2014/nov/20/bob-marley-legacy-cannabis-smoke-reggae-dopeheads [accessed 5 March 2015].

Allen, B. J., Dholakia, U. M., and Basuroy, S. (2016) 'The economic benefits to retailers from customer participation in proprietary web panels', *Journal of Retailing*, 92(2): 147–61.

American Marketing Association (AMA) (2012) 'Brand', *Dictionary*. Available online at http://www.marketingpower.com/_layouts/Dictionary.aspx?dLetter=B [accessed 1 January 2017].

Anon. (2009) 'Michael Jackson set to be number one in charts following his death', *The Telegraph*, 27 June. Available online at http://www.telegraph.co.uk/news/worldnews/5662997/Michael-Jackson-set-to-be-number-one-in-charts-following-his-death.html [accessed 1 May 2015].

Anon. (2014) 'Schumpeter: Second wind', *The Economist*, 14 June, 76.

Arora, R., and Stoner, C. (2009) 'A mixed method approach to understanding brand personality', *Journal of Product & Brand Management*, 18(4): 272–83.

Ballantyne, D., and Aitken, R. (2007) 'Branding in B2B markets: The service-dominant logic', *Journal of Business & Industrial Marketing*, 22(6): 363–71.

Belk, R. (1988) 'Possessions and the extended self', *Journal of Consumer Research*, 15(2): 139–68.

Bengtsson, A. (2003) 'Towards a critique of brand relationships', *Advances in Consumer Research*, 30(1): 154–8.

Caulfield, K. (2012) 'Amy Winehouse's death led to surge in sales, chart moves', *Billboard*, 23 July. Available online at http://www.billboard.com/articles/news/480976/amy-winehouses-death-led-to-surge-in-sales-chart-moves [accessed 27 September 2015].

Christodoulides, G. (2009) 'Branding in the post-Internet era', *Marketing Theory*, 9(1): 141–4.

Clayton, M., and Heo, J. (2011) 'Effects of promotional-based advertising on brand associations', *Journal of Product & Brand Management*, 20(4): 309–15.

Drucker, P. F. (1985) 'The discipline of innovation', *Harvard Business Review*, 63(3): 67–72.

Eads, L. (2015) 'UK cider market suffers £35m loss', *The Drink Business*, 2 October. Available online at https://www.thedrinksbusiness.com/2015/10/uk-off-trade-cider-market-suffers-35m-loss/ [accessed 12 June 2016].

Elvis.net (n.d) 'Elvis in the *Guinness World Record Book*'. Available online at http://www.elvis.net/guinness/guinnessframe.html [accessed 3 November 2015].

Feldwick, P. (1996) 'What is brand equity anyway, and how do you measure it?', *Journal of Marketing Research*, 38(2): 85–104.

Fournier, S. (1998) 'Consumers and their brands: Developing relationship theory in consumer research', *Journal of Consumer Research*, 24(4): 343–73.

France, C., Merrilees, B., and Miller, D. (2015) 'Customer brand co-creation: A conceptual model', *Marketing Intelligence & Planning*, 33(6): 848–64.

Ghosh, S. (2015) 'Sainsbury's trials connected kitchens to understand "promiscuous" shoppers', *Campaign*, 11 May. Available online at http://www.campaignlive.co.uk/article/1346564/sainsburys-trials-connected-kitchens-understand-promiscuous-shoppers [accessed 17 November 2016].

Glass, S. (2012) 'What were they thinking? The chips that sent us to the loo', *Fast Company*, 17 January. Available online at http://www.fastcompany.com/1809002/what-were-they-thinking-chips-sent-us-running-loo [accessed 23 December 2015].

Govindarajan, V., and Srinivas, S. (2013) 'The innovation mindset in action: 3M Corporation', *Harvard Business Review*, 6 August. Available online at https://hbr.org/2013/08/the-innovation-mindset-in-acti-3 [accessed 22 December 2015].

Griffin, A., and Page, A. L. (1993) 'An interim report on measuring product development success and failure', *Journal of Product Innovation Management*, 10(4): 291–308.

Hodal, K. (2016) 'Nestlé admits slave labour risk on Brazil coffee plantations', *The Guardian*, 2 March. Available online at http://www.theguardian.com/global-development/2016/mar/02/nestle-admits-slave-labour-risk-on-brazil-coffee-plantations [accessed 3 August 2016].

Holt, D. B., Quelch, J. A., and Taylor, E. L. (2004) 'How global brands compete', *Harvard Business Review*, 82(9): 68–81.

Institute of Brilliant Failures (n.d.) 'Buckler beer on the Dutch market'. Available online at http://www.briljantemislukkingen.nl/EN/failures/submit-reaction/buckler-beer-on-the-dutch-market/ [accessed 23 December 2015].

Juntunen, M. (2012) 'Co-creating corporate brands in start-ups', *Marketing Intelligence & Planning*, 30(2): 230–49.

Keller, K. L. (1993) 'Conceptualizing, measuring, and managing customer-based brand equity', *Journal of Marketing*, 57(1): 1–22.

Keller, K. L. (1998) *Strategic Brand Management: Building, Measuring, and Managing Brand Equity*, Upper Saddle River, NJ: Prentice-Hall.

Keller, K. L. (2009) 'Building strong brands in a modern marketing communications environment', *Journal of Marketing Communications*, 15(2–3): 139–55.

Kollmann, T., and Suckow, C. (2007) 'The corporate brand naming process in the net economy', *Qualitative Market Research: An International Journal*, 10(4): 349–61.

Lasser, W., Mittal, B., and Sharma, A. (1995) 'Measuring customer based brand equity', *Journal of Consumer Marketing*, 12(4): 11–19.

Liljedal, K. T. (2016) 'Communicated consumer co-creation: Consumer response to consumer co-creation in new product and service development', Unpublished PhD dissertation, Stockholm School of Economics.

Linville, P., and Carlston, D. E. (1994) 'Social cognition of the self', in P. G. Devine, D. L. Hamilton, and T. M. Ostrom (eds) *Social Cognition: Impact on Social Psychology*, San Diego, CA: Academic Press, 143–93.

Low, G. S., and Lamb, C. W. (2000) 'The measurement and dimensionality of brand associations', *Journal of Product and Brand Management*, 9(6): 350–68.

Office for Fair Trading (OFT) (2007) 'Anticipated acquisition by Premier Foods plc of RHM plc', 14 February. Available online at https://assets.publishing.service.gov.uk/media/555de3a940f0b666a20000a8/Premier.pdf [accessed 1 January 2017].

Nespresso (n.d.) 'Coffee'. Available online at https://www.nestle-nespresso.com/sustainability/the-positive-cup/coffee [accessed 16 November 2016].

Parnell, B.-A. (2012) 'Official: Sony and Ericsson are divorced', *The Register*, 16 February. Available online at http://www.theregister.co.uk/2012/02/16/sony_ericsson_divorce_final/ [accessed 23 December 2015].

Pennington, J. R., and Ball, D. A. (2009) 'Customer branding of commodity products: The customer-developed brand', *Brand Management*, 16(7): 455–67.

Perego, P., and Kolk, A. (2012) 'Multinationals' accountability on sustainability: The evolution of third-party assurance of sustainability reports', *Journal of Business Ethics*, 110(2): 173–90.

Peres, R., Muller, E., and Mahajan, V. (2010) 'Innovation diffusion and new product growth models: A critical review and research directions', *International Journal of Research in Marketing*, 27(2): 91–106.

Phau, I., and Lau, K. C. (2001) 'Brand personality and consumer self-expression: Single or dual carriageway?', *Journal of Brand Management*, 8(6): 428–44.

Roberts, G. (2015) 'Sinclair C5: Sir Clive Sinclair's one seat wonder celebrates 30 years since its launch', *The Mirror*, 5 January. Available online at http://www.mirror.co.uk/news/uk-news/sinclair-c5-sir-clive-sinclairs-4920067 [accessed 23 December 2015].

Rodríguez-Garavito, C. A. (2005) 'Global governance and labor rights: Codes of conduct and anti-sweatshop struggles in global apparel factories in Mexico and Guatemala', *Politics & Society*, 33(2): 203–333.

Rogers, E. M. (1962) *Diffusion of Innovations*, New York: Free Press.

Rogers, E. M. (1983) *Diffusion of Innovations* (3rd edn), New York: Free Press.

Saren, M. (2006) *Marketing Graffiti: The View from the Street*, Oxford: Butterworth-Heinemann.

Torrence, J. (2014) 'How Kopparberg use hipsters to take the UK market by stealth', *Real Business*, 10 February. Available online at http://realbusiness.co.uk/article/25481-how-kopparberg-used-hipsters-to-take-the-uk-market-by-stealth [accessed 12 June 2016].

Townsend, J. D., Cavusgil, S. T., and Baba, M. L. (2010) 'Global integration of brands and new product development at General Motors', *Journal of Product Innovation Management*, 27(1): 49–65.

Trott, D. (2016) 'Fear-free marketing', *Campaign*, 3 June. Available online at http://www.campaignlive.co.uk/article/view-dave-trott-fear-free-marketing/1396946 [accessed 18 June 2016].

Tudor, E., and Negricea, I. C. (2012) 'Brand positioning: A marketing resource and an effective tool for small and medium enterprises', *Journal of Knowledge Management, Economics and Information Technology*, 11(1): 182–90.

Chapter 7
Pricing and Value Creation

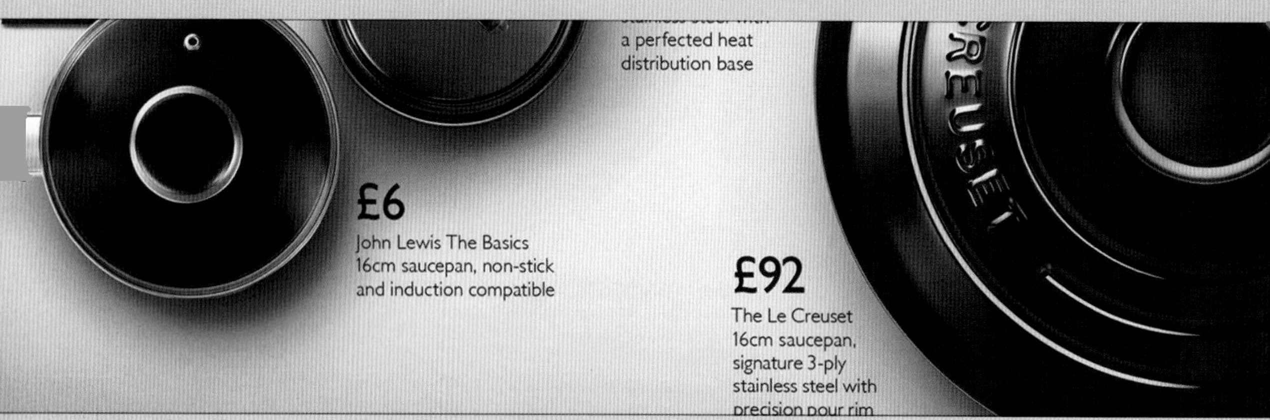

Learning Outcomes

After studying this chapter, you will be able to:

- explain the concept of price elasticity of demand;
- describe how customers perceive price;
- understand pricing strategies and how to price new offerings;
- explain cost-, competitor-, demand-, and value-oriented approaches to pricing; and
- explain how pricing operates in the business-to-business (B2B) setting.

Case Insight 7.1
Simply Business

Market Insight 7.1
Sugar Tax: Paying Sweetly?

Market Insight 7.2
Is the Price Right?

Market Insight 7.3
John Lewis: Still Never Knowingly Undersold?

Market Insight 7.4
Everlane: Pricing for Ethics

Case Insight 7.1 **Simply Business**

Founded in 2005, Simply Business is an online insurance broker. We speak to its director of strategy and pricing, Philip Williams (pictured), to find out more about how the company has developed its pricing strategy.

'Simply Business has grown from a team of six in a room near Tower Bridge in London to become one of the UK's largest small-to-medium-sized enterprise (SME) insurance providers. It provides cover for some 360,000 small businesses in the UK for liability insurance lines (employers' liability, professional indemnity, and public or product liability) in addition to speciality landlord insurance. Its simple and fast online quote process allows customers to receive quotes and buy from a range of different insurance companies simultaneously, providing an instantly comparable, and ordered, panel of **prices**.

'We are proud of our technological capability, seeing ourselves as a tech business first and foremost, which happens to operate as an insurance brokerage. Our main competition in the online SME insurance market includes Hiscox, Direct Line for Business, AXA, and Towergate, but our market is constantly developing. The online market has grown around 20 per cent year on year. Of the 5.8 million businesses in the UK, 5.1 million are classified as SMEs, but businesses usually buy their insurance through local high-street brokers. This is changing, especially at the microbusiness end, as customers get used to comparing and buying their personal insurance online. Four large price comparison websites have grown in the UK to dominate personal insurance (Compare the Market, Money Supermarket, GoCompare, and Confused.com). Whilst price comparison for home and motor insurance is now well established, the comparison sites have not ventured into the less homogeneous and smaller SME insurance market. Simply Business moved into this vacuum and formed strategic partnerships with two of the large aggregators (Money Supermarket and GoCompare) to develop a **white-labelled product** price comparison portal.

'Since a management buyout in 2013, we have continued to grow revenues by around 25 per cent year on year. We have won numerous awards, including, in 2015 and 2016, the number one spot in the "*Sunday Times* Best Company to Work for" awards. To develop our unique proposition, we felt we needed to extend our control over the **value** chain. Therefore, we not only provide a platform for customers to compare business insurance rates, but we also have obtained delegated authority from our panel of around 20 insurance providers to bind policies on their behalf. So we handle all customer interactions, including payment, and have agreement to handle all but the largest claims without the need for the insurers' involvement.

'To set prices in the business insurance market, the traditional approach has been to use the cost-plus method. Insurers set a risk rate for each customer based on the details provided by a customer within a proposal form (for example postcode, turnover, number of staff). With these details, a base cost is determined, before adding additional loads for expenses, reinsurance, and broker commission. Broker commission is typically negotiated between each broker and insurer on a broker-by-broker basis. Those brokers able to provide higher volumes of business, or those that can provide superior quality clients (through unique selection processes or route

Case Insight 7.1 (continued)

to market), are most able to negotiate higher levels of commission.

'Whilst this strategy and business model is straightforward, for us at Simply Business it was based on two negatives as far as customer value was concerned. First, a price comparison using the standard methodology would show customers an unfair picture, with business insurance prices with lower costs before commission appearing below prices with higher costs (as a result of a higher negotiated commission level). From a customer viewpoint, we knew it would be difficult to justify to our customers why our commission received from different insurers should be different. Second, control of customer volumes is difficult to manage, because any commission change must be negotiated with a supplier. This is easily manageable in an offline environment, but more difficult in an online world, with significantly increased volumes and increased customer price sensitivity driven by ease and access to competition. So we used our scale to negotiate a flexible commission structure with our insurance providers. This has allowed Simply Business to move to a demand-orientated pricing approach and to standardize commissions on quotes, presenting a fair comparison to customers with no incentive for Simply Business to sell one product over another. This transparent approach reflects our brand, which focuses on honesty and simplicity.

'One extra difficulty is that all prices quoted for customers are generated specifically for that individual or business and tailored to their requirements, and different customers have different price sensitivities. We wanted to respond to some customers' requirements for price discounts, but it would be too onerous to negotiate with each of our suppliers for each quotation. We also knew we could not afford to discount all of our customers' policies across the board.'

The question that therefore arose for Simply Business was: how could it develop a system that offered tailored policies, including discounts, to those customers who were more price sensitive?

Introduction

How do companies set prices? What procedures do they use? How do customers perceive prices for different products and services? How do companies determine their prices? These are some of the questions we set out to consider in this chapter.

Our understanding of pricing and costing has developed from accounting practice. Economics has also contributed to our understanding of pricing through models of supply and demand, operating at an aggregate level (that is, across all customers in an industry). Psychology contributes greatly to our understanding of customers' perceptions of prices. Marketing, as a field, integrates all of these components to provide a better understanding of how the firm sets price to achieve higher profits and maintain satisfied customers. Pricing is the most difficult aspect of the marketing mix to comprehend, because an offering's price is linked to the cost of the many different components that make up a particular proposition. The marketing manager rarely controls costs and prices of a particular offering, and usually refers to the accounting and finance department, or the marketing/financial controller, to set prices.

In this chapter, we provide insight into how customers respond to price changes. We define price, quality, costs, and value, and outline the relationship between them. We provide insights into how customers perceive and learn about prices—a necessary step prior to evaluating them and their fairness, which impacts on customers' willingness to pay. We describe the four main approaches to pricing, based on evaluating costs and adding a margin, copying competitors' prices, basing prices on demand, and pricing according to perceived customer value. We also consider the two principal means by which to price a new proposition—that is, skim and market penetration pricing. Finally, we consider what pricing tactics are used in the business-to-business (B2B) setting.

Price Elasticity of Demand

The concept of '**price elasticity** of demand' was first developed in the field of economics. It grants us an insight into how demand shifts with changes in price. Such information is useful, but the data needed to determine price elasticities require detailed research of price and quantity changes over time. Price elasticity is affected by both brand and category characteristics, as well as general economic conditions, including such factors as time, product category, brand (manufacturer versus own-label), stage of product life cycle, country, household disposable income, and inflation rates (Bijmolt et al., 2005).

In some categories, for example cigarettes but not for example washing powder, changes in price (whether positive or negative) lead to smaller changes in demand. For instance, a 10 per cent increase in cigarette prices might lead to only a 2 per cent decrease in quantity sold, while a 10 per cent increase in washing powder prices might lead to a 20 per cent decrease in sales. In this case, we say the washing powder is the more 'price elastic' offering. We define 'price elasticity' as the percentage change in quantity demanded as a proportion of the percentage change in price. Mathematically, this is displayed as:

$$\textit{Price elasticity of demand} = \eta \text{ (pronounced } \textit{eta}\text{)} = \frac{\text{Percentage change in quantity demanded}}{\text{Percentage change in price}} \qquad (1)$$

When the price of an offering rises or falls, the quantity demanded falls or rises. When the percentage change in price is positive (negative), the percentage change in quantity demanded is negative (positive). Consequently, the price elasticity of demand is always negative. The price elasticity of demand for most marketed goods is somewhere between –9 and –1. In a meta-analysis of a set of 1,851 price elasticities, based on 81 studies, the average price elasticity was found to be –2.62 (Bijmolt et al., 2005). In other words, for these goods (including **consumer durables** and other types of product), a 10 per cent increase in price would produce an average 26.2 per cent decrease in quantity demanded. This, however, is an average across offerings. Individual products and services can vary greatly from this average.

Generally, we can refer to three main extremes of price elasticity, as follows.

1 ***Unit price elasticity of demand*** ($\eta = 1$)—In this case, a 10 per cent increase (decrease) in price produces a 10 per cent decrease (increase) in quantity demanded.

2 ***Zero price elasticity of demand*** ($\eta = 0$)—In this situation, any change in price, either positive or negative, has absolutely no, or only an infinitesimal, impact on quantity sold. Such a situation is highly unlikely ever to occur.

3 ***Infinite price elasticity of demand*** ($\eta = \infty$)—In this case, changes in quantity sold have no, or an infinitesimal, impact on price. This situation is also highly unlikely to occur.

Governments use price elasticity data to determine which offerings to tax (see Market 7.1). For example, petrol and tobacco have tended to be taxed because increases in prices resulting from tax increases have a lesser impact on quantity supplied compared to other offerings. Marketing managers should seek to understand whether or not their offerings are price elastic or inelastic, because this allows them to predict how price changes will affect the total quantity supplied in the market.

Market Insight 7.1 **Sugar Tax: Paying Sweetly?**

In the March 2016 budget in the UK, then Chancellor of the Exchequer George Osborne introduced a sugar tax on fizzy drinks. The idea was to introduce the tax to reduce the consumption of sugar, which is thought to be a leading cause of obesity and related diseases (for example heart disease, diabetes), costing the National Health Service (NHS) up to £27 billion per year. The government believed that the tax would raise £520 million in its first year of introduction in 2018, much of which is ring-fenced for spending on sport in schools.

The government plans two tax rates: drinks with high sugar content, for example the 330 ml Coke, with a price of around 68 pence in supermarkets in 2016, will attract 8 pence extra tax in 2018; and drinks with lower sugar content, for example the 330 ml Coca-Cola Life, also around 68 pence in supermarkets in 2016, will be taxed at 6 pence in 2018. The government's intention, taking account of inflation, appears to be to add about 10 per cent to the price of high-sugar drinks and about 7.5 per cent to the low-sugar versions.

A previous study of the price elasticity of demand in the United States between 1938 and 2007 indicated that a 10 per cent increase in soft drinks prices should reduce consumption by 8–10 per cent. A study in the UK in the early 1990s indicated that soft drinks had a price elasticity of demand of −0.935 and an associated **advertising elasticity** of 0.015. This indicates that had there been a 10 per cent increase in price in the UK in the 1990s, there would have been a 9.4 per cent decrease in demand, and that had there been a 10 per cent increase in advertising expenditures, there would have been a 0.2 per cent increase in demand. The government, however, is far more worried about end-of-aisle display and the impact of price discounting than broadcast advertising on the consumption of sugary drinks, since these have a higher influence than the imposition of a tax, increasing consumption by up to 50 per cent and 22 per cent, respectively.

A sweet tax? Governments are introducing new taxes on sugary drinks to influence consumer behaviour.

Source: © Marcos Mesa Sam Wordley/Shutterstock.

When Mexico, the country with the highest obesity rate in the world, introduced a sugar tax in 2014, the 10 per cent tax reduced sales of fizzy drinks by

Market Insight 7.1 (continued)

12 per cent (a price elasticity of demand of −1.2). Norway, Finland, Hungary, and France have all also imposed sugar taxes and seen declines in sugar consumption as a result. However, in 2013, Denmark abandoned its plan for a tax on sugar after a similar tax on fat was unsuccessful. The drinks industry has also fought back, impeding sugar taxes in some US states and in Slovenia. In France, when the country imposed the sugar tax in 2012, the evidence indicated that retailers passed on nearly all of the tax to consumers. In the UK, this approach is not a foregone conclusion. Manufacturers might decide to swallow the tax and maintain their prices at existing levels. If they do, they would lower their profit margins, but consumption is unlikely to be affected. If they could also reduce their cost structures at the same time, they might even be able to completely mitigate the effects of the tax.

An alternative strategy would to develop new lower sugar offerings that attract less tax, but which do not compromise taste. Either way, given the difficult market for soft drink manufacturers in the UK, neither option hits a sweet spot.

1 **What decision would you make if you were the chief executive officer (CEO) of Coca-Cola in the UK?**

2 **What other data might help you to make a decision? Why?**

3 **To offset the likely drop in demand when the tax is imposed, do you think it would make sense to increase advertising? Why, or why not?**

Sources: Duffy (1999); Andreyeva et al. (2010); Lavin and Timpson (2013); Anon. (2015, 2016a); Colchero et al. (2015); PHE (2015); Donnelly (2016).

The Concept of Pricing and Cost

Pricing

The term 'price' has come to encompass:

> . . . the amount of money expected, required, or given in payment for something; an unwelcome experience or action undergone or done as a condition of achieving an objective; decide the amount required as payment for something offered for sale; and discover or establish the price of something for sale.
>
> (Oxford Dictionaries, 2016)

In marketing terms, we consider price to be the amount the customer has to pay or exchange to receive an offering. For example, when purchasing a Burger King cheeseburger meal for children (incorporating the burger, small apple fries, a Tropicana drink, and a toy), the price exchanged for the meal might be, say, $3.59 in the United States or £3.99 in the UK. The £3.99 element is the price—that is, the assigned numerical monetary worth of the kid's cheeseburger meal in the UK. However, the notion of pricing an offering is often confused with a number of other key marketing concepts—particularly cost and value.

Visit the **online resources** and follow the web link to the Professional Pricing Society (PPS) to learn more about pricing and the pricing profession.

Proposition Costs

To price properly, we need to know what the offering costs us to make, produce, or buy. Cost represents the total money, time, and resources sacrificed to produce or acquire an offering. For example, the costs incurred to produce the Burger King cheeseburger meal for children includes the cost of heat and light in the restaurant, advertising and sales promotion costs, costs of rent or of the mortgage interest accrued from owning the restaurant, management and staffing costs, and the franchise fees paid to Burger King's central headquarters to cover training, management, and marketing. There are additionally costs associated with the distribution of the product **components** to and from farms and other catering suppliers to the restaurants. There are also the costs to acquire and maintain computer and purchasing systems, and the costs of the packaging, bags, and any extras such as the BK® crown and other gifts and toys.

Typically, a firm determines what its fixed costs are and what its variable costs are for each proposition. These items vary for individual industries. Fixed costs do not vary according to the number of units of goods made or services sold and are independent of sales volume. In a Burger King restaurant, fixed costs are the costs of heating and lighting, rent, and staffing. In contrast, variable costs vary according to the number of units of goods made or services sold. For example, with the production of Burger King cheeseburger meals, when sales and demand decrease, fewer raw goods, such as cheeseburger ingredients, product packaging, and novelty items such as toys, are required, so less spending on raw materials is necessary. Conversely, when sales increase, more raw materials are used and spending rises.

The Relationship Between Pricing and Proposition Costs

The relationship between price and costs is important, because costs should be substantially less than the price assigned to a proposition; otherwise, the firm will not sell sufficient units to obtain sufficient revenues to cover costs and make long-term profits (see Equations (2) and (3)):

$$\textit{Total revenue} = \text{Volume sold} \times \text{Unit price} \tag{2}$$

$$\textit{Profit} = \text{Total revenue} - \text{Total costs} \tag{3}$$

The price at which a proposition is set is important, because increases in price have a disproportionately positive effect on profits and decreases in price have a disproportionately negative effect on profits. For example, in one study (Baker et al., 2010: 5), it was identified that:

- a 1 per cent improvement in price achieves an 8.7 per cent improvement in operating profit;
- a 1 per cent improvement in variable costs achieves only a 5.9 per cent improvement in operating profit;
- a 1 per cent improvement in volume sales achieves a 2.8 per cent improvement in operating profit; and
- a 1 per cent improvement in fixed costs achieves only a 1.8 per cent improvement in operating profits.

Until recently, organizations have had fairly rudimentary methods of assessing the effectiveness of their pricing decisions, but changes in computing power and the availability of data now allow companies to simulate thousands of 'what if?' pricing scenarios to predict likely demand and profit levels (Michard, 2016). Whenever possible, we should therefore aim to increase prices.

Customer Perceptions of Price, Quality, and Value

Marketers are concerned with how individuals react to the way in which offerings are priced, questioning how consumers perceive prices and why they perceive them as they do. Here, we consider individual perceptions of proposition quality and value, and their relationship to customer response to prices.

Proposition Quality

Quality is important in setting proposition pricing levels. 'Quality' is defined as 'the standard of something as measured against other things of a similar kind; the degree of excellence of something; a distinctive attribute or characteristic possessed by someone or something' (Oxford Dictionaries, 2016). In this context, the quality of goods and services relates to standards to which that offering performs as a need satisfier. For example, a very high-quality car (such as the Aston Martin DB11 or the Porsche Panamera) will satisfy both our aesthetic needs for aerodynamic beauty and our ego, and functional needs for high-performance road-handling, speed, and power.

Expensive cars are not necessarily of better quality. Quality, much like beauty, is in the eye of the beholder.

Source: © Lokuttara/Shutterstock.

Quality is multifaceted (that is, comprising different functional and non-functional needs) and multilayered (that is, comprising degrees of satisfaction). Because people all have their own definitions of quality, we prefer to talk of **perceived quality**: one person might be very dissatisfied and another highly satisfied with the same offering.

The Relationship Between Quality and Pricing Levels

There is an assumption that as price increases, so does quality and that, in general, price reflects quality. However, research has demonstrated that there is only a weak relationship between price and perceived quality, although this is category-dependent (Gerstner, 1985). The idea that price indicates quality (perceived quality) assumes that prices are objectively determined by market forces. In truth, people within firms set prices, often dispassionately, to try to obtain the maximum profit possible. A general price–perceived quality relationship does not exist (Gerstner, 1985; Zeithaml, 1988), except in the case of wine and perfume (Zeithaml, 1988).

The Relationship Between Perceived Value, Product Quality, and Pricing Levels

'Value' is defined as:

> ... the regard that something is held to deserve; importance, worth, or usefulness of something; principles or standards of behaviour; one's judgment of what is important in life; the numerical amount denoted by an algebraic term; a magnitude, quantity, or number.
>
> (Oxford Dictionaries, 2016)

In marketing terms, value refers to the quality of what we get for what we pay. Leszinski and Marn (1997), consultants at McKinsey, suggest Equation (4) to calculate the value to the customer:

$$\textit{Value} = \text{Perceived benefits} - \text{Perceived price} \quad (4)$$

In this equation, the customer perceives positive value if the perceived benefits (a proxy for quality) outweigh the price paid for those benefits. Usefully, if the price paid is zero (that is, if an item is given away), the value to the customer is the value of the perceived benefits (which makes sense), and if there are no benefits, the value is the negative value of the price paid. When the benefits of an offering are reduced, the value is also seen to be reduced if customers notice the difference in offerings. An example of this occurred when Cadbury reduced the number of chocolate fingers in its traditional pack from 24, weighing 125 g, to 22, weighing 114 g, with an increase in price from around £1.19 in 2014 to around £1.43 in 2015 (Hayward, 2015), changing the cost of each chocolate finger from 4.96 pence to 6.5 pence (for a marginally lighter chocolate finger at 5.18 g compared to 5.21 g).

Influences on Customer Price Perceptions

A Framework for Price Perception Formation

How we perceive prices as customers can be summarized in a theoretical framework (see Figure 7.1). Here, price perceptions are based on a variety of antecedents. Once we see a price, we make a judgment. This judgment is a newly formed price perception, which affects our willingness to pay, in turn affecting our purchase behaviour. Price perceptions are affected by prior beliefs, prior knowledge of **reference prices**, prior experiences with the offering or brand under consideration, price consciousness (that is, how aware we are of prices), our own price sensitivities (how much extra we are prepared to pay for something), customer characteristics, and cultural factors. We compare the price we see with internal reference prices (price knowledge gained from experience) and external reference prices (what others tell us prices should be, perhaps in the form of price

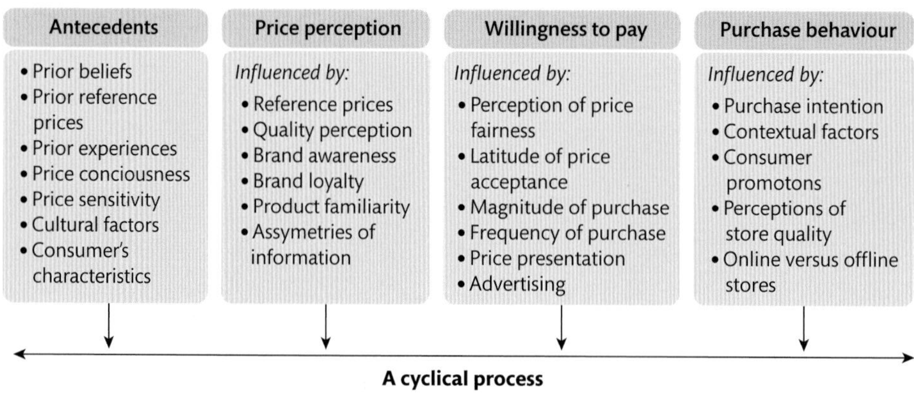

Figure 7.1 A framework for price perception formation

Source: Mendoza and Baines (2012).

comparison websites). Reference prices are price bands against which customers judge the purchase price of offerings. Reference prices can be viewed as predictive price expectations based on prior experience with those offerings or gained through word-of-mouth.

Price perception formation is influenced by exposure to reference prices (internal and external), quality perceptions, brand awareness, brand loyalty, product familiarity, memory of prices (paid previously and seen previously), and asymmetries of information (the extent to which customers do not know various factors about those offerings). Price perceptions affect customers' willingness to pay. Willingness to pay is influenced by perceptions of the fairness of prices set, latitude of price acceptance (customers appear willing to accept a price within a range of prices, suggesting a 'price zone of tolerance'), magnitude (absolute price) and frequency of purchase, price presentation (how prices are presented might produce different levels of willingness to pay), and advertising.

Actual purchase behaviour is influenced by purchase intention, contextual factors (such as store format, location, timing, and out-of-stock situations), promotions (such as in-store and external promotions), perceptions of store quality, and whether or not the customer is online or in-store, partly because it is much easier to comparison shop online than it is in-store. However, price perception formation is a dynamic process. In other words, the framework indicates that once the purchase behaviour occurs, there is a recalibration of the customer's price perception, because new purchase experiences and new information provide the stimulus for that recalibration. Therefore the process is cyclical.

Next, we consider key elements within the price perception process: willingness to pay, price consciousness, and **pricing cues**.

Willingness to Pay

We memorize certain prices for some items; when companies deviate from those prices, we perceive them as unfair. A key question is: why do some consumers see one proposition's price as fair and others do not? If we are to price an offering according to customer needs, we should understand

Research Insight 7.1

To take your learning further, you might wish to read this influential paper.

Völckner, F., and Hofmann, J. (2007) 'The price–perceived quality relationship: A meta-analytic review and assessment of its determinants', *Marketing Letters*, 18(3): 181–96.

This article uses a meta-analytic approach to evaluate various studies performed between 1989 and 2006, aiming to provide evidence that there is an increasingly weakening relationship between price and perceived quality.

 Visit the **online resources** to read the abstract and access the full paper.

What determines price fairness? Superdrug was accused of 'sexist' price discrimination.

Source: © mubus7/Shutterstock.

which customers think a particular price is a fair price to pay, or what they expect to pay, or what they think others would pay. For example, in the UK Superdrug was forced to review its 'sexist' pricing after an investigation by *The Times* revealed that women were being charged more than men on certain offerings, such as razors. In some retailers, the gender price surplus that women were expected to pay for similar products was 37 per cent (Hipwell and Ellson, 2016).

Price Consciousness

In addition to deciding whether or not a price is fair, or what customers expect to pay, we also need to know whether or not customers are conscious of prices in a particular category. Most people do not have a good knowledge of prices. Think of your parents or of friends significantly older than you: do they know the monthly subscription price for streaming music tracks? Do you know the price of a quality dining table or £200,000 worth of life insurance cover? These examples indicate that our price experience contributes to what we know about reference prices. Our experience is limited to previous actual or considered purchases. So if people do not know the reference prices of particular offerings, how can they determine their fairness? In the UK, supermarkets are under increasing pressure to pay farmers more for their produce, since many supermarket chains have been selling it at less than the price they were paying the farmers and the public has increasingly seen this as unfair (Neville, 2015).

Pricing Cues

When customers assess prices, they estimate value using pricing cues, because they do not always know the true cost and price of the item that they are purchasing. These pricing cues include sale signs, odd-number pricing, the purchase context, and **price bundling** and rebates.

- *Sale signs*—Sale signs act as cues, indicating the availability of a bargain. This seduces the customer to buy, suggesting to the buyer that an item is desirable and may not be available if it is not bought quickly enough. The sale sign uses scarcity as a persuasive device, because the scarcer we perceive an offering to be, the more we want it (Cialdini, 1993)—sometimes regardless of whether or not we need it.
- *Odd-number pricing*—Another pricing cue is the use of odd-number endings, such as prices that end in the figure 9. Have you ever wondered why the Nintendo Wii U that you bought was, say, US$299, or £229, or SEK2,999? According to Anderson and Simester (2003), raising the price of a woman's dress in a national mail order catalogue from US$34 to US$39 increased demand by 33 per cent, but demand remained unchanged when the price was raised to US$44! The question is: why did the increase in demand take place when there was a higher price? It is unlikely that demand would have increased if the item were priced at $38. The reason is that we perceive the first price as relative to a reference price of £30 (which is £34 rounded down to the nearest unit of ten) and more expensive, whereas the second price of $39 we perceive as cheaper than a reference price of $40 (which we rounded up to the nearest ten).
- *Purchase context*—Our perception of risk is greater if we are continually reminded of it than if we consider it only at the point of purchase. For example, gyms use the technique of charging a monthly fee, even though they often demand a yearly membership agreement, for precisely this reason. In fact, a monthly price (instead of an annual, semi-annual, or quarterly charge) drives a higher level of gym attendance, because customers are more regularly reminded of their purchase. So the way you set your price not only influences demand, but also drives consumption (Gourville and Soman, 2002).

Visit the **online resources** and complete Internet Activity 7.1 to learn more about the impact that the purchase context (for example time of day, week, online versus telephone booking, etc.) has on the pricing of budget airline services.

Pricing Strategies

Companies establish their pricing strategy based on what their pricing objectives are. The four main pricing strategies include the following.

- *Premium pricing*—This focuses on pricing an offering to indicate its distinctiveness in the marketplace. For example, Aston Martin prices its DB11 in this way, at around £150,000.
- *Penetration pricing*—This occurs when the price is set low relative to the competition to gain market share. Amazon has adopted this approach to build its now substantial customer base.
- *Economy pricing*—This strategy sees prices set at the bare minimum to attract price-sensitive customers. Supermarkets often use this approach with their everyday low-pricing approach (for example Walmart in the United States, Aldi all over Europe, and Jumbo in the Netherlands).

Market Insight 7.2 **Is the Price Right?**

ICA is Sweden's largest grocery retailer, with a market share in 2015 of 36 per cent, more than 1,300 stores in four different formats, and total store sales of €11.7 billion. The company was founded in 1917 as a purchasing federation of independent retailers, which remains its basic operating structure to this day.

Lidl is the largest discounter in Europe – lower prices is a key differentiator for this supermarket chain

Source: © Getty/Francis Dean.

Two critical components of any offer in retailing are price and quality. Price can determine store choice, patronage behaviour, basket size, and overall customer satisfaction. Retail managers have to consider two dimensions of their chain's positioning: the actual prices to use ('on shelf'); and how customers perceive them ('in mind'). These two sometimes diverge.

When comparing prices between the chains, baskets of everyday groceries are typically used to create an index of actual prices, in which 100 denotes a market average price for the basket. In a perfect world, the 'in mind' position closely tracks the 'on shelf' prices indicated by this index.

In the Swedish market, the in-mind discount price position is occupied by the largest European discount chain Lidl, with the price-fighting local supermarket chain Willy's as runner-up. ICA and some other local Swedish actors, such as Hemköp and City Gross, are perceived as quality players, with a good value-for-money offer.

In ICA's case, however, many consumers perceive the prices to be somewhat higher than they actually are. This is reflected in a misalignment between consumer rankings of grocery chains as 'low price' or giving 'good value for money' and ICA's performance on price index comparisons. In the United States, Whole Foods Market suffers from a similar misalignment. Paradoxically, this phenomenon can then affect discount actors positively, meaning that they are sometimes perceived as somewhat less expensive than they actually are.

In conclusion, price perception is an important concept for any manager to understand. A poor price perception can lead to lost sales and a pressure on prices and profits. The manager has to learn how to work with both sides of the value equation: actual price levels and added value. This can help the manager to balance the perceptions of the firm's customer offer.

1. **Under what circumstances is misalignment between actual prices ('on shelf') and customers' price perceptions ('in mind') beneficial for a retailer?**
2. **Under what circumstances is misalignment between actual prices ('on shelf') and customers' price perceptions ('in mind') troublesome for a retailer?**
3. **Why do you think price perceptions are sometimes misaligned for premium retailers (for example ICA, Whole Food Markets)?**
4. **Why do you think price perceptions are sometimes misaligned for discount retailers (for example Lidl)?**

Sources: Hamilton and Chernev (2013); Mägi et al. (2016); http://www.ica.se.

This market insight was kindly contributed by Dr Jonas Gunnarsson, market and consumer research manager at ICA AB, Sweden.

Research Insight 7.2

To take your learning further, you might wish to read this influential paper.

Gourville, J., and Soman, D. (2002) 'Pricing and the psychology of consumption', *Harvard Business Review*, 80(9): 90–6.

This is a useful article summarizing how marketing managers should consider not only the price at which customers are likely to purchase an offering, but also how the way in which price is set also affects consumption. This article suggests that marketers might counter-intuitively want to draw customers' attention to the price paid, so that they can achieve greater value in using the offering and generate a longer-term impact on customer retention. The article has strong implications for organizations selling subscriptions and memberships.

Visit the online resources to read the abstract and access the full paper.

- *Price skimming*—In this model, the price is initially set high, then lowered in sequential steps. Apple iPhone adopted this strategy, for example. This strategy is frequently used for the launch of new offerings (at which we look next).

Launch Pricing

When launching new offerings, organizations tend to adopt one of two classic pricing strategies. With the first approach, price skimming, they charge an initially high price and then reduce the price over time, recouping the cost of the research and development (R&D) investment from sales to the group of customers that is prepared to pay the higher price (hence 'skimming' the market). In the second approach, they charge a lower price in the hope of generating a large volume of sales and recouping R&D investment that way (hence 'penetration pricing'). Figure 7.2 shows both market penetration and market-skimming price strategies, along with their hypothetical impact on quantity demanded (Q1 and Q2, respectively).

The price-skimming approach is a fairly standard approach for high-technology offerings or those offerings that require substantial R&D investment initially (such as games consoles and prescription pharmaceuticals). For example, Microsoft dropped the price for its Xbox One machine, bringing the official base price to US$299 in 2016, having opened with a launch price of US$500 (Thier, 2016). The price-skimming approach is also particularly appropriate when demand is likely to be inelastic and there are few economies of scale in the product or category (Dean, 1950; Doyle, 2000).

The market penetration pricing approach is used for fast-moving consumer goods and consumer durables, when the new offering introduced is not demonstrably different from existing formulations. Items aimed at capturing price-sensitive customers might use this approach. The penetration approach is more effective when there is a strong threat from competition and demand is very elastic (Dean, 1950; Doyle, 2000).

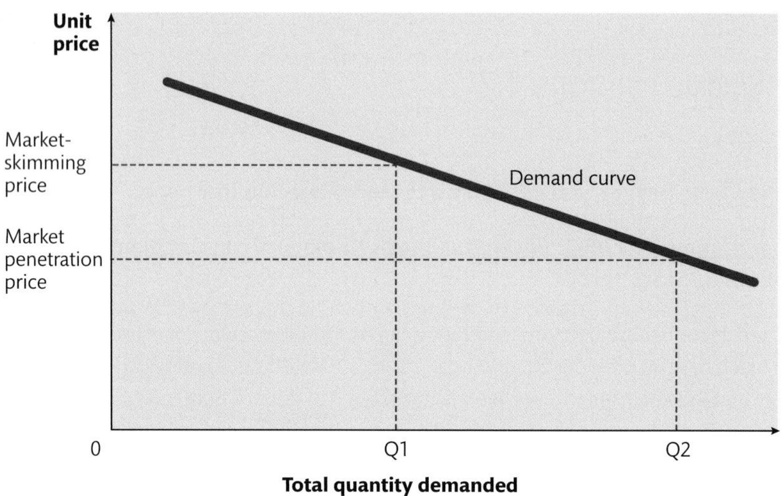

Figure 7.2 Launch pricing strategies

Source: Adapted from Burnett (2002). Reproduced with the kind permission of the author, John Burnett.

Pricing Approaches

Price setting depends on various factors, including how price affects demand, how sales revenue is linked to price, how cost is linked to price, and how investment costs are linked to price (Doyle, 2000). Broadly, there are four types of underlying pricing approach:

- the *cost-oriented* approach (that is, prices set based on costs);
- the *demand-oriented* approach (that is, prices set based on price sensitivity and demand);
- the *competitor-oriented* approach (that is, prices set based on competitors' prices); and
- the *value-oriented* approach (that is, prices based on what customers believe to offer value).

The Cost-Oriented Approach

The cost-oriented approach advances the idea that the most important element of pricing is the cost of the component resources that constitute the offering. Therefore the marketer sells output at the highest price possible, regardless of the buyer's preferences or costs. If that price is sufficiently high compared with the seller's costs, the firm earns a profit and survives; if not, the seller must find a way of either increasing the price or lowering costs, or both, or it will not survive (Lockley, 1949). The cost-oriented approach considers the total costs of a proposition in the pricing equation, but does not take into account non-cost factors, such as brand image, degree of prestige in ownership, or effort expended.

One approach to determining price is using mark-up pricing, often found in the retail sector. This method operates on the basis of a set percentage mark-up. When used, the cost-oriented method leads to the use of list prices, with single prices set for all customers. We simply add a mark-up to the cost of X per cent and this constitutes the price. In supermarket retailing in the US, the mark-up on produce is around 50–75 per cent. Mark-ups on wine served in restaurants are typically between 200 per cent and 300 per cent. The cost-oriented approach requires us first to determine the price we set that just covers our costs. This is known as 'breakeven pricing'. It represents the point at which our total costs and our total revenues are exactly equal.

The cost-oriented approach does not mean that we have to use a mark-up pricing approach. In some industries, prices are instead based on fixed formulae, set with a supplier's costs in mind. For example, in the ethical prescription pharmaceutical industry in France, Italy, and Spain, government-fixed formulae have tended to dictate prices, with limited scope for pharmaceutical manufacturers to negotiate, whereas in the UK and Germany, the tradition has been for the country's national health authorities not to fix individual product prices, but to set an overall level of profitability with which the pharmaceutical manufacturer must agree, based on a submission of its costs (Attridge, 2003).

The Demand-Oriented Approach

With the demand-oriented approach to pricing, the firm sets prices according to how much customers will pay. This approach is prevalent in marketing services, but again could be used in B2B or consumer marketing contexts. Airline companies frequently operate this approach, with customers paying different amounts for seats with varying levels of service attached, as illustrated in Figure 7.3. Most airline companies operate three types of cabin service. Emirates, for instance, offers first class, business class, and economy, with varying benefits according to the price paid based on the seat pitch (and availability as a bed), the entertainment package, the quality of the meal

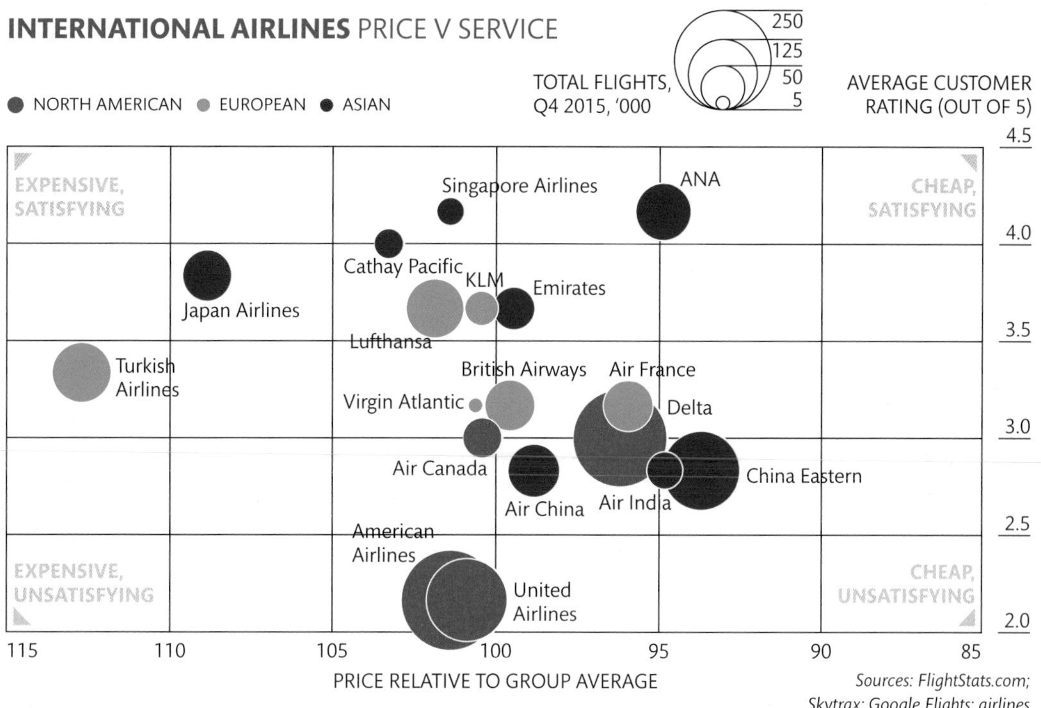

Figure 7.3 International airlines: Price vs service

options, the availability and quality of airport lounges, transportation to and from the airport, the in-flight service offered, and the experience through immigration and security.

The Competitor-Oriented Approach

Companies can also set prices based on competitors' prices—that is, the so-called going rate—sometimes known as 'me too' pricing. This approach is used in B2B, services, and consumer marketing contexts. The advantage here is that when your prices are lower than those of the competition, customers are more likely to purchase from you—provided that they know your prices are lower.

Price guarantee schemes like that outlined in Market Insight 7.3 seek to provide customers with the peace of mind of knowing that the price paid is a competitive one. In reality, such schemes are expensive to operate, requiring continuous monitoring of the full range of competitors' prices and a strong focus on cost control. It is also worth considering that adopting a competitor-oriented pricing strategy can lead to price wars.

Visit the **online resources** and complete Internet Activity 7.2 to learn more about how John Lewis brings the 'Never Knowingly Undersold' promise to life in its advertising.

Price wars occur when competitors' pricing policies are almost exclusively focused on competitors rather than customers, when price is pushed downwards, and when pricing results in interactions between competitors that lead to unsustainable prices. For example, in 2003, when Dutch supermarket retailer Albert Hejn slashed its prices in response to competition from Aldi and Lidl, the resulting battle saw an 8.2 per cent reduction in food prices, costing Dutch supermarkets €900 million (£700 million) and 30,000 jobs in only one year (van Heerde et al., 2008; Blackhurst, 2014)—although by 2005, after the price war had ended, Albert Hejn had managed to regain lost market share to regain market leadership (Reinemoeller, 2014).

Calculating and anticipating competitor response is important when setting prices and responding to competitors' price cuts. We should analyse consumer responses when a competitor starts to cut prices, but if purchase behaviour changes only modestly or temporarily, other marketing mix elements (such as promotion, place or distribution, or product differentiation) may be more likely to win back customers (van Heerde et al., 2008). We do not always have to respond to a price war with a price cut; instead, we might promote increased service quality (Rust et al., 2000) or customer value improvements more generally.

The Value-Oriented Approach

Even in the consumer durables category (for example furniture, **white goods**, carpets), in which we might expect customers to be less price sensitive, firms practise pricing approaches with customers' considerations in mind (Foxall, 1972). We term this the value-oriented approach to pricing, because prices are set based on buyers' perceptions of specific product or service attribute values rather than on costs or competitors' prices. This approach can be used in B2B, services, and consumer contexts. With value-based pricing, the pricing process begins with customers, determining what value they derive from the offering and then determining price, rather than the opposite approach used in cost-oriented pricing, whereby costs are determined first and then the price is set.

In value-based pricing, deciding what is of value to the customer is based on customer research. The result may be that the company does not necessarily offer a cheaper price. In fact, it could mean a higher-priced offering. If that offering were to represent true value to customers, they must

Market Insight 7.3 **John Lewis: Still Never Knowingly Undersold?**

The leading department store in the UK, John Lewis Partnership, owns 32 department stores, 12 John Lewis at Home stores, 346 Waitrose supermarkets, a production unit, shops at St Pancras train station and at London Heathrow Airport Terminal 2, and a farm, and operates the e-commerce site Johnlewis.com. In 2014, it celebrated its 150th birthday. With around 91,500 staff, John Lewis saw gross sales of just over £11 billion in 2016. What is unique about John Lewis is that it operates through a constitution whereby the company is owned by its employees and has as its mission the 'happiness of its members'. Despite the economic doldrums, the company's Christmas trading statement for 2016 indicated great success at the tills, with like-for-like sales up 5.1 per cent on the previous year and a 21.4 per cent rise in online revenues.

But John Lewis Partnership also differs in another unique way from its competitors: it offers a policy of price matching and refunds customers if they can find the same product cheaper at another retailer—a policy made possible by its social enterprise nature and the fact that it does not seek to purely maximize short-term profits. Its policy, named 'Never Knowingly Undersold', has been available since 1925—perhaps the longest-running price promotion in British retailing. Things changed in 2011, when it changed the policy to match prices offered by other physical store retailers who were also online. John Lewis does occasionally come under flack with some customers looking for a refund when they have identified something sold cheaper elsewhere, but have not been refunded because, according to John Lewis, the product is not exactly the same. Often, this has been the result of the fact that John Lewis offers different warranty terms. The question now for most customers is: will they continue to perceive this price promotion as fair, or will they not care about the price difference because the quality of the offering is so good?

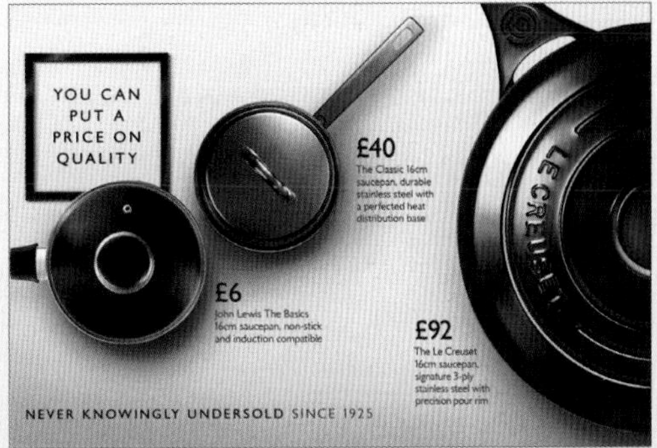

John Lewis's famous price promotion.

Source: Courtesy of John Lewis. © David Gill Photography.

1. **Do you think that the cost of collecting the competitor pricing data is justified for this promotion commercially? Why, or why not?**
2. **What other data does John Lewis need to determine how customers perceive competing prices from different retailers?**
3. **Do you think that is it ethical to offer a price guarantee scheme with strict conditions before paying out a claim? Why, or why not?**

Sources: Brignall (2011); Benady (2015); Anon. (2016b); http://www.johnlewispartnership.co.uk/about.html.

feel that it has more benefits than equivalent offerings. A recent study of 1,812 pricing professionals demonstrated that a value-based pricing strategy is positively linked to firm performance, whereas a cost-based approach is not (Liozu and Hinterhuber, 2013). A good example of a brand using this approach is L'Oréal, which has, for a long time, advertised its products using spokesmodels, such as South Korean model Soo-Joo Park, British pop sensation and television personality Cheryl Fernandez-Versini, Chinese model Xiao Wen Ju, Dutch model Lara Stone, and Hollywood

Research Insight 7.3

To take your learning further, you might wish to read this influential paper.

Reinemoeller, P. (2014) 'How to win a price war', *Sloan Management Review*, 55(3): 15–17.

This article, based on a study of Albert Hejn in The Netherlands, explains that companies can win price wars by leveraging five strategic capabilities, including:

- the ability to affirm the need for a price war;
- the ability to carefully select an appropriate battlefield using advanced analytics capabilities;
- the ability to pick a single target competitor;
- staying under the radar (by targeting former customers rather than explicitly poaching new customers); and
- the ability to align revenues with reformed cost structures.

Visit the online resources to read the abstract and access the full paper.

actress Naomi Watts, among many others, on the basis that we should use its products 'because we're worth it'.

When setting value-based prices, it is important to consider the following questions (Anderson et al., 2010).

1. What is the market strategy for the segment? What does the supplier want to accomplish?
2. What is the differential value that customers are likely to perceive (that is, the value between this offering and the next-best alternative, assuming that the differential value can be verified with the customer's own data)?
3. What is the price of the next-best alternative?
4. What is the cost of the supplier's offering?
5. What pricing tactics will be used initially (for example price discounting)?
6. What is the customer's expectation of a 'fair' price?

Pricing Management

In the information era, marketing information systems (MkIS), database technologies, and Internet-enabled technologies have changed how companies make pricing decisions. Pricing strategies such as 'real-time' or 'dynamic' pricing have increasingly developed in both consumer and B2B markets, sometimes through online price comparison sites, online auctions, and companies' own websites, because prices can be changed easily. For example, Amazon updates its price list every

10 minutes based on constant data analysis (Anon., 2016c). Dynamic pricing even allows changes at the customer level (Grewal et al., 2011).

Visit the **online resources** and follow the web links to Kelkoo.co.uk, PriceRunner.se, touslesprix.com, beslist.nl, and preissuchmaschine.de, all of which are examples of online price comparison sites in different European countries.

Comparison sites have developed large customer databases covering all types of offering, including complex services such as gas and electricity supply, insurance, mobile phone packages, and travel, as well as standard offerings such as cars and breakdown cover. Marketers are working in an increasingly price-transparent environment and they should recognize that pricing is a capability at which some companies are better than others. Those companies that are excellent at pricing manage their costs and price complexity well, and offer sustainability and innovation in pricing approaches (Hinterhuber and Liozu, 2012). Online retailers are increasingly recognizing that it is not only the price that matters, but also how easy it is to pay online, because a more efficient payment process can lead to more time shopping.

Market Insight 7.4 **Everlane: Pricing for Ethics**

Pricing in the fashion industry is probably one of the biggest mysteries in marketing. One can find products that are incredibly cheap, while other consumers are willing to pay an exorbitant price for brands, the value of which is determined by intangible traits such as prestige and design.

Everlane, a US-based apparel start-up, challenges this status quo by offering consumers a new solution under its 'Radical Transparency' policy.

The company identified factories that produce for high-end fashion brands around the world. By establishing direct and close relationships with these factories, and selling exclusively online, Everlane can deliver high-quality products at a reasonable price. More importantly, it outlines the cost breakdown of all of the products it sells at each stage of the value chain on its website, from material, labour, duties, and transport, to the mark-up it takes.

Against a backdrop of recent scandals about some fashion brands whose products are manufactured by suppliers in factories in which workers' rights are not respected and conditions are often very poor, Everlane's transparent pricing strategy has a meaningful implication for business ethics. All of the factories that work with Everlane are well documented on its website, with clear information

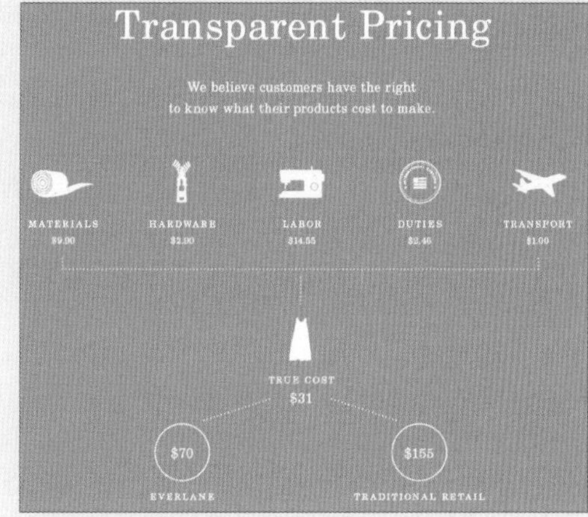

This infographic offers an example of the type of information Everlane provides to its customers.

Source: Courtesy of Everlane

on and photos of the working environment, products manufactured, and the reasons why Everlane chose the factory. This not only shows customers where and how the products they purchase are made, but also serves as a 'reason to believe' to justify the pricing structure presented by the company. Additonally, this approach also educates customers on the hidden costs behind cheap clothing, because it shows a clear breakdown of costs across the supply chain.

Market Insight 7.4 (continued)

In 2016, five years after it was founded, Everlane recorded US$51 million in sales and was reported to have a valuation of US$250 million.

1 **What are the implications of this type of pricing transparency for price perception in the clothing industry?**

2 **What are the barriers to consumers' understanding and learning of this pricing approach? (Think about what you learned in Chapter 2 on customer behaviour.)**

3 **In what way might Everlane's pricing strategy help in the promotion of business ethics?**

Source: O'Toole (2016).

This market insight was kindly contributed by Jenny Li, senior retail analyst, IGD UK.

Pricing Tactics

In reality, when setting prices, an organization trades off the different approaches against each other by considering all of the following factors.

- *Competition*—How much are competitors charging for similar offerings?
- *Cost*—How much do the individual components that make up our offering cost?
- *Demand*—How much of this product or service will we sell at what price?
- *Value*—What components of the offering do customers value and how much are they prepared to pay for them?

Business-to-Business (B2B) Pricing

In B2B markets, buyers are professionally trained procurement executives, often with qualifications from professional institutes (for example the Chartered Institute of Purchasing and Supply in the UK, the Australian Association of Procurement and Contract Management in Australia, or the Swedish National Association of Purchasing and Logistics). Their function is often highly technical, even for apparently simple offerings. For example, to produce a pen, a manufacturer might buy the pens in Italy, packaging and printing in China, refills in Germany, and the final product assembly in Bulgaria.

In the B2B context, the discussion of price takes place between the buyer and the seller in an atmosphere in which both are trying to make the best commercial decision for their organizations. The seller wants to maximize profit (buy getting a high price), and the buyer wants to procure at a low price to lower costs and maximize their profits. Their task is to resolve their mutual needs in a win–win situation. From the seller's perspective, there are numerous pricing tactics that can be adopted, including the following.

- *Geographical pricing*—Prices may be based on customer location. For example, pharmaceutical companies (sometimes controversially) sell their prescription drugs at different prices in different countries.

- *Negotiated pricing*—Prices may be set according to specific agreements between a company and its clients or customers (for example professional services, such as architectural or structural engineering). This approach occurs where a sale is complex and consultative, although sales representatives should not concede on price too quickly before properly understanding a client's needs (Rackham, 2001).
- *Discount pricing*—Companies may reduce the price on the basis that a customer commits to buying a large volume of that offering now or in the future, or is prepared to pay for it quickly. Large retailers work on the discount principle when buying for their stores.
- *Value-in-use pricing*—This approach focuses attention on customer perceptions of the attributes of offerings and away from cost-oriented approaches. It prices offerings based on what the customer is prepared to pay for individual benefits received from that proposition, so the company must first ascertain what benefit components the customer perceives to be important, quantify those benefit values, determine the price equivalence of value, rate competitive and alternative products to provide a benchmark for price determination, and quantify the value in use (that is, the value in using the product vis-à-vis those of competitors), and only then is the price actually fixed. (See Christopher, 1982, for a detailed discussion.) This approach is particularly used for industrial propositions.
- *Relationship pricing*—This approach seeks to understand customers' needs before pricing the offering around those needs to generate a long-term relationship. This means offering excellent financial terms, credit or more lenient time periods for payment, or discounts based on future sales revenue or the risk involved in the purchase.
- *'Pay what you want' pricing*—This approach allows customers to pay whatever they want for an offering. For example, legal services firm CMS Cameron McKenna has offered this pricing approach to its corporate clients (Hollander, 2010).
- **Transfer pricing**—This occurs in large organizations in which considerable internal dealing between different company divisions occurs, often across national boundaries. Prices may be set at commercial rates, on the basis of negotiated prices between divisions, or using a cost-based approach, depending on whether the division is a cost or profit centre. Internal dealings can sometimes mean that the final offering is overpriced for a given customer. Airbus Industries, the European aircraft manufacturer owned by parent European Aeronautic Defence and Space Company (EADS), adopts this approach when constructing its planes built from components made in different countries.
- *Economic value to the customer (EVC) pricing*—With this approach, a company prices an offering according to its perceived value by the purchasing organization (that is, total profit generated less the costs paid), typically by means of a comparison with a reference or market-leading offering, taking into consideration not only the actual purchase price of the offering, but also the start-up and post-purchase costs, to give an overall indication of how much better its pricing structure is compared with that of a competitor. The final price is then set based on a negotiation between the buyer and seller over the difference in value and how likely this value is to be achieved. This kind of pricing approach might be used by a large consultancy solutions company such as IBM, when it sells its system solutions.
- *Tendering and bid pricing*—With this approach, organizations invite other organizations to bid for the right to deliver a particular job or task (a tender) and to name their own price. This approach is used heavily by public-sector organizations. The difficulty arises in that organizations do not always

provide a budgetary range to allow bidders an idea of what price would be accepted. The manager should know the profitability of a bid when determining the price, and aim to discover the winning bidder's name and price on lost jobs, where possible (Walker, 1967). Ross (1984) argues that it is often better not to ask 'What price will it take to win this order?', but 'Do we want this order, given the price our competitors are likely to quote?' Where the winning bidder obtains an unprofitable contract that it is duty-bound to deliver, because its bid price was set so low, this is known as the 'winner's curse'.

Chapter Summary

To consolidate your learning, the key points from this chapter are summarized below.

- **Explain the concept of price elasticity of demand.**

  Price elasticity of demand allows us to determine how the quantity of an offering relates to the price at which it is offered. Inelastic propositions are defined as such because increases or decreases in price produce relatively smaller decreases or increases in sales volumes, whereas elastic offerings have larger similar effects. Understanding price elasticity helps us to devise demand-oriented pricing mechanisms.

- **Describe how customers perceive price.**

  Understanding how customers and consumers perceive pricing helps in the setting of prices. Customers have an idea of reference prices based on what they ought to pay for an offering, what others would pay, or what they would like to pay. Their knowledge of actual prices is limited to well-known and frequently bought and advertised offerings. Consequently, customers tend to rely on price cues, such as odd-number pricing, sale signs, the purchase context, and price bundles, when deciding whether or not value exists in a particular proposition.

- **Understand pricing strategies and how to price new offerings.**

  There are four main pricing strategies, including premium pricing (pricing an offering to indicate its distinctiveness in the marketplace), penetration pricing (pricing low relative to the competition to gain market share), economy pricing (pricing at the bare minimum to attract price-sensitive customers), and price skimming (setting the price high initially, then lowering in sequential steps).

- **Explain cost-, competitor-, demand-, and value-oriented approaches to pricing.**

  There are a variety of different pricing policies that can be used depending on whether we are pricing a consumer, service, or industrial offering. These are cost-oriented (based on what we paid for it and what mark-up we intend to add), competitor-oriented (based on the so-called going rate or on at what price competitors sell an offering), demand-oriented (based on how much of an offering can be sold at what price), or value-oriented (what attributes of the offering are of benefit to our customer and what will they pay for them) approaches.

- **Explain how pricing operates in the business-to-business (B2B) setting.**

  A variety of pricing tactics are used in the B2B setting, including geographical, negotiated, discount, value-in-use, relationship, 'pay what you want', transfer, economic value to the customer, and bid pricing. Business-to-business pricing differs in that buyers are frequently expert in purchasing for their organizations. They are likely to pay particular attention to the value that they derive from the offering.

Review Questions

1. Define 'price', 'cost', 'quality', and 'value', and how they relate to each other.
2. Explain the concept of 'price elasticity of demand', giving examples of offerings that are both price elastic and price inelastic.
3. What are pricing cues?
4. How does odd-number pricing work?
5. What are the four main pricing strategies?
6. When might you use price skimming as a pricing approach?
7. When might you use penetration pricing?
8. Name four B2B pricing tactics.
9. Under what circumstances does the 'pay what you want' pricing approach work best?
10. How does pricing operate in tender and bidding exercises?

Worksheet Summary

To apply the knowledge you have gained from this chapter and to test your understanding of price decisions, visit the **online resources** and complete Worksheet 7.1.

Discussion Questions

1. Having read Case Insight 7.1, how would you advise Simply Business to develop a pricing system that offers tailored policies, including discounts, to those customers who are more price sensitive?

2. A range of scenarios are presented in which you are given some information on the price context. What pricing policy would you use when setting the price in each of the following situations? (State the assumptions under which you are working when you decide on each one.)
   - **A** The owner of a newly refurbished themed Irish pub in a central city location (for example Amsterdam or Oslo) wants to set the prices for his range of beers, with the objective of attracting a new customer base.
   - **B** The product manager at American car manufacturer Ford wants to set the price range for the Ford Mustang in the UK launched in Summer 2016 (http://www.ford.co.uk/Cars/newmustang).
   - **C** You are the manager at a large, well-known legal services firm (such as Bird & Bird) in Denmark, and your client, from a €20 million turnover medium-sized import/export company, commissions work in relation to a recent company acquisition. What further information would you require to price such work and what pricing approaches could you offer?

3 How would you go about determining the price sensitivity of your customers if you were a cinema marketing manager and you were to want your cinemas to operate at full capacity throughout the week, including for matinée and late (after 10 pm) seats, and not only at weekends and in the evenings?

4 Research and examine the prices of five different items in two different supermarkets (where possible, selling similar or identical products and pack sizes in each to allow comparison). What are the average prices for each of the items and how does each supermarket compare with the other?

Visit the **online resources** and complete the multiple-choice questions to assess your knowledge of the chapter.

Glossary

advertising elasticity a measure of how responsive the demand for offerings is to changes in advertising expenditure (that is, how effective an advertising campaign is in generating new sales).

components a part of something larger, for example an engine as part of a car, or the casing, ink, and packaging as parts of a pen.

consumer durables manufactured consumer products that are relatively long-lasting (for example cars or computers) as opposed to non-durables (for example foodstuffs).

perceived quality a relative subjective measure of quality. We talk of 'perceived' quality because there is no truly objective absolute measure of product or service quality.

price the amount that the customer has to pay to receive a good or service.

price bundling when a product or service is offered together with another typically complementary product or service, which is not available separately, to make the original product or service seem more attractive (for example a CD with a music magazine).

price elasticity the percentage change in volume demanded as a proportion of the percentage change in price, usually expressed as a negative number. A score close to zero indicates that a product or service price change has little impact on quantity demanded, whereas a score of −1 indicates that a product or service price change effects an equal percentage quantity change. A value above −1 indicates a disproportionately higher change in quantity demanded as a result of a percentage price change.

pricing cues proxy measures used by customers to estimate a product or service's reference price, such as quality, styling, packaging, sale signs, and odd-number endings.

reference price the price band against which customers judge the purchase price of goods and services.

transfer pricing typically occurs in large organizations and represents the pricing approach used when one unit of a company sells to another unit within the same company.

value the regard that something is held to be worth, typically, although not always, expressed in financial terms.

white goods large electrical goods used in residences, typically, but not necessarily, white in colour, such as refrigerators or washing machines.

white-labelled product an offering developed by one organization that other organizations rebrand and market as if it were their own.

References

Anderson, E., and Simester, D. (2003) 'Mind your pricing cues', *Harvard Business Review*, 81(9): 96–103.

Anderson, J. C., Wouters, M., and Van Rossum, W. (2010) 'Why the highest price isn't the best price', *Sloan Management Review*, 51(2): 69–76.

Andreyeva, T., Long, M. W., and Brownell, K. D. (2010) 'The impact of food prices on consumption: A systematic review of research on the price elasticity of demand for food', *American Journal of Public Health*, 100(2): 216–22.

Anon. (2015) 'Stopping slurping: Tax on fizzy drinks seem to work as intended', *The Economist*, 28 November. Available online at http://www.economist.com/news/finance-and-economics/21679259-taxes-fizzy-drinks-seem-work-intended-stopping-slurping [accessed 21 March 2016].

Anon. (2016a) 'A tax on sugar: Pricier pop', *The Economist*, 19 March. Available online at http://www.economist.com/news/britain/21694993-levy-drinks-may-change-recipes-not-waistlines-britain-gets-new-tax-sugary-drinks [accessed 1 January 2017].

Anon. (2016b) 'John Lewis hails strong Christmas trading', *Sky News*, 6 January. Available online at http://news.sky.com/story/1617537/john-lewis-hails-strong-christmas-trading [accessed 19 March 2016].

Anon. (2016c) 'Schumpeter: Flexible figures', *The Economist*, 30 January. Available online at http://www.economist.com/news/business/21689541-growing-number-companies-are-using-dynamic-pricing-flexible-figures [accessed 19 March 2016].

Attridge, J. (2003) 'A single European market for pharmaceuticals: Could less regulation and more negotiation be the answer?', *European Business Journal*, 15(3): 122–43.

Baker, W. L., Marn, M. V., and Zawada, C. C. (2010) *The Price Advantage* (2nd edn), Hoboken, NJ: John Wiley.

Benady, A. (2015) 'Peter Cross: Never knowingly undersold', *PR Week*, 19 April. Available online at http://www.prweek.com/article/1341269/peter-cross-knowingly-oversold [accessed 19 March 2016].

Bijmolt, T. H. A., van Heerde, H. J., and Pieters, R. G. M. (2005) 'New empirical generalisations on the determinants of price elasticity', *Journal of Marketing Research*, 42(2): 141–56.

Blackhurst, C. (2014) 'Check out the Dutch for supermarket price wars', *Evening Standard*, 2 October, 47.

Brignall, M. (2011) 'John Lewis Partnership: Never knowingly undersold?', *The Guardian*, 5 February. Available online at http://www.guardian.co.uk/money/2011/feb/05/john-lewis-never-knowingly-undersold [accessed 18 March 2016].

Burnett, J. (2002) *Core Concepts in Marketing*, Chichester: John Wiley.

Christopher, M. (1982) 'Value-in-use pricing', *European Journal of Marketing*, 16(5): 35–46.

Colchero, M. A., Salgado, J. C., Unar-Munguía, M., Hernández-Ávila, M., and Rivera-Dommarco, J. A. (2015) 'Price elasticity of the demand for sugar-sweetened beverages and soft drinks in Mexico', *Economics & Human Biology*, 19: 129–37.

Cialdini, R. B. (1993) *Influence: The Psychology of Persuasion*, New York: Quill William Morrow.

Dean, J. (1950) 'Pricing policies for new products', *Harvard Business Review*, 54(6): 45–53.

Donnelly, L. (2016) 'Sugar tax in Mexico cuts sales of sugary drinks by 12%', *The Telegraph*, 6 January. Available online at http://www.telegraph.co.uk/news/health/news/12085408/Children-aged-five-eating-own-weight-in-sugar-every-year.html [accessed 21 March 2016].

Doyle, P. (2000) *Value-Based Marketing: Marketing Strategies for Corporate Growth and Shareholder Value*, Chichester: John Wiley.

Duffy, M. (1999) 'The influence of advertising on the pattern of food consumption in the UK', *International Journal of Advertising*, 18(2): 131–68.

Foxall, G. (1972) 'A descriptive theory of pricing for marketing', *European Journal of Marketing*, 6(3): 190–4.

Gerstner, E. (1985) 'Do higher prices signal higher quality?', *Journal of Marketing Research*, 22(2): 209–15.

Gourville, J., and Soman, D. (2002) 'Pricing and the psychology of consumption', *Harvard Business Review*, 80(9): 90–6.

Grewal, D., Ailawadi, K. L., Gauri, D., Hall, K., Kopalle, P., and Robertson, J. R. (2011) 'Innovations in retail pricing and promotions', *Journal of Retailing*, 87(S1): S43–S52.

Hamilton, R., and Chernev, A. (2013) 'Low prices are just the beginning: Price image in retail management', *Journal of Marketing*, 77(6): 1–20.

Hayward, S. (2015) 'So this is what Cadbury thinks of biscuit lovers', *Sunday Mirror*, 12 April, 24.

Hinterhuber, A., and Liozu, S. (2012) 'Is it time to rethink your pricing strategy?', *Sloan Management Review*, 53(4): 69–77.

Hipwell, D., and Ellson, A. (2016) 'Superdrug takes razor to sexist pricing', *The Times*, 5 February. Available online at http://www.thetimes.co.uk/tto/money/consumeraffairs/article4683212.ece [accessed 19 March 2016].

Lavin, R., and Timpson, H. (2013) *Exploring the Acceptability of a Tax on Sugar-Sweetened Beverages: Brief Evidence Review*, Paper for the Centre for Public Health, Liverpool John Moores University, April. Available online at http://www.cph.org.uk/wp-content/uploads/2013/11/SSB-Evidence-Review_Apr-2013-2.pdf [accessed 21 March 2016].

Leszinski, R., and Marn, M. V. (1997) 'Setting value, not price', *McKinsey Quarterly*, February. Available online at http://www.mckinsey.com/business-functions/marketing-and-sales/our-insights/setting-value-not-price [accessed 14 March 2016].

Liozu, S. M., and Hinterhuber, A. (2013) 'Pricing orientation, pricing capabilities, and firm performance', *Management Decision*, 51(3): 594–614.

Lockley, L. C. (1949) 'Theories of pricing in marketing', *Journal of Marketing*, 13(3): 364–7.

Mägi, A., Gunnarsson, J., and Rosengren, S. (2016) 'Consumer updating of store price perceptions', Paper presented at the 2016 Academy of Marketing Science (AMS) Annual Meeting, 18–21 May, Lake Buena Vista, FL.

Mendoza, J., and Baines, P. (2012) 'Towards a consumer price perception formation framework: A systematic review'. Available online at http://pandora.nla.gov.au/pan/25410/20140311-1105/anzmac.org/conference/2012/papers/173ANZMACFINAL.pdf [accessed 19 March 2016].

Michard, Q. (2016) 'Why brands should be using data analytics to inform pricing strategy', *Impact*, 8: 68–9.

Neville, S. (2015) 'Supermarkets surrender to farmers after milk price protest', *The Independent*, 15 August. Available online at http://www.independent.co.uk/news/business/news/supermarkets-surrender-to-farmers-after-milk-price-protest-10456920.html [accessed 7 July 2016].

O'Toole, M. (2016) 'At Everlane, transparent is the new black', *Forbes*, 5 January. Available online at http://www.forbes.com/sites/mikeotoole/2016/01/05/at-everlane-transparent-is-the-new-black/#168f9a143127 [accessed 7 July 2016].

Oxford Dictionaries (2016) 'Price', 'Quality', 'Value'. Available online at http://oxforddictionaries.com/definition/english/price?q=price; http://oxforddictionaries.com/definition/english/quality?q=quality; http://oxforddictionaries.com/definition/english/value?q=value [accessed 23 November 2016].

Public Health England (PHE) (2015) *Sugar Reduction: The Evidence for Action*, October. Available online at https://www.gov.uk/government/uploads/system/uploads/attachment_data/file/470179/Sugar_reduction_The_evidence_for_action.pdf [accessed 21 March 2016].

Rackham, N. (2001) 'Winning the price war', *Sales and Marketing Management*, 253(11): 26.

Reinemoeller, P. (2014) 'How to win a price war', *Sloan Management Review*, 55(3): 15–17.

Ross, E. B. (1984) 'Making money with proactive pricing', *Harvard Business Review*, 62(6): 145–55.

Rust, R. T., Danaher, P. J., and Varki, S. (2000) 'Using service quality data for competitive marketing decisions', *International Journal of Service Industry Management*, 11(5): 438–69.

Taylor, M. (2010) 'Cameron invites legal clients to pay what they want for legal work', *The Lawyer*, 5 August. Available online at: http://www.thelawyer.com/cameron-invites-clients-to-pay-what-they-want-for-legal-work/1005236.article [accessed 1 January 2017].

Thier, D. (2016) 'Microsoft just dropped the Xbox One price again', *Forbes/Tech*, 18 March. Available online at http://www.forbes.com/sites/davidthier/2016/03/18/microsoft-just-dropped-the-xbox-one-price-again/#3527d83920f1 [accessed 20 March 2016].

van Heerde, H. J., Gijsbrechts, E., and Pauwels, K. (2008) 'Winners and losers in a major price war', *Journal of Marketing Research*, 45(5): 499–518.

Völckner, F., and Hofmann, J. (2007) 'The price–perceived quality relationship: A meta-analytic review and assessment of its determinants', *Marketing Letters*, 18(3): 181–96.

Walker, A. W. (1967) 'How to price industrial products', *Harvard Business Review*, Sept–Oct: 125–32.

Zeithaml, V. A. (1988) 'Consumer perceptions of price, quality and value: A means–end model and synthesis of evidence', *Journal of Marketing*, 52(3): 2–22.

Chapter 8
Marketing Communications Principles

Learning Outcomes

After studying this chapter, you will be able to:

- describe the nature, purpose, and scope of marketing communications;
- explain the three models of communication;
- understand the models used to explain how marketing communications and advertising work;
- understand the role of marketing communications in marketing; and
- describe the different steps in the strategic marketing communications planning process.

Case Insight 8.1
The Guardian

Market Insight 8.1
The Biggest Influencer on YouTube

Market Insight 8.2
Carambar Pulls a Prank on an Entire Nation

Market Insight 8.3
Motivating Energy Saving Behaviour Change in Hospitals

Market Insight 8.4
Reinventing Advertising for the Digital Age

Case Insight 8.1 *The Guardian*

How could an organization realize its objective not only to shift audience perceptions, but also to also change behaviours? We speak to Agathe Guerrier (pictured), strategy director at advertising agency Bartle Bogle Hegarty (BBH), to find out more about the work it undertook for its client *The Guardian*.

The Guardian is a truly impartial media organization that is rooted in the principles of independent journalism. The Scott Trust was set up to protect this independence and, to this day, *The Guardian*'s sole purpose remains the pursuit of the truth. This philosophy shapes the way it communicates: 'Facts are sacred, but comment is free.'

The Guardian is made by progressives, for progressives. A progressive is a curious and connected individual who welcomes change as a positive force. Progressives are not defined by income, age, or any other demographic data.

Today's *The Guardian* is defined by its open operating system (OOS). By encouraging participation and debate, by welcoming contributions and challenges, it seeks to provide the broadest, most comprehensive view of the world. Openness means that it does not put its content behind a pay wall—a radical stance in today's media landscape. It also means that it does not believe journalists to be the only voices of authority or to be able to complete the entire editorial process on their own; instead, what they do is initiate the creation of content, and then invite bloggers, contributors, readers, and commentators to enrich and evolve it.

The Guardian uses marketing communications to support the key drivers of its commercial strategy. The first of these is to drive newspaper sales, which, although in structural decline, still represent nearly half of *The Guardian*'s revenues. Therefore it is strategically crucial that it defends them in a competitive marketplace.

A second driver concerns the digital reach of the brand via desktop and mobile products. As a media brand, its reach is a key driver of digital advertising revenue. Marketing and communications aim to grow its UK and international reach.

The third driver is digital engagement. Known, active, engaged users of digital products are more valuable to *The Guardian* than anonymous and disengaged visitors. To this end, a strand of the marketing and communications strategy is dedicated to increasing digital engagement—registrations, participation, time spent, and frequency.

However, *The Guardian* has had to face certain problems. The first concerns its potential audience of progressives. It was known from brand health tracking that they were not aware of how much *The Guardian* had changed (mainly the OOS philosophy), and they scored low on image items such as 'modern', 'innovative', and 'dynamic'.

Second, from its trade audience (advertisers and media agencies), it knew that it was struggling with being perceived as a worthy, left-wing, pedantic, and niche newspaper brand.

In terms of direct competition, most of the traditional newspaper sector was actually suffering from a similar fate. The real threat was from the new entrants in the knowledge sector, those of the digital age—Twitter, TED, YouTube—that are really redefining people's attitudes and behaviours when it comes to seeking, consuming, and understanding news content.

Case Insight 8.1 (continued)

For a long time, there had been little investment in the brand, with marketing spend focused on tactical campaigns, such as promoting a certain supplement or feature. The challenge now was to find a way of changing perceptions of *The Guardian* (as a dusty left-wing newspaper brand) among a large potential audience of digitally connected, inquisitive news readers. *The Guardian* wanted this audience to realize that it had evolved and was now a radically innovative leader of the digital age.

The problem was therefore not only how *The Guardian* could go about shifting perceptions, but also how it could change behaviours by driving a larger online audience to the desktop product?

Introduction

Have you ever wondered how organizations such as *The Guardian* manage to communicate effectively with so many different people and organizations? Just how do companies go about planning communication campaigns? This is the first of two chapters that explain how this can be accomplished through the use of marketing communications. This chapter introduces and explains what 'marketing communications' is, and how it can be planned. Chapter 9 considers the configuration of the marketing communications mix.

Marketing communications is about developing messages that can be understood and acted on by target audiences. The chapter commences with a definition of 'marketing communications'. It then goes on to discuss the scope and functions of marketing communications, and to consider communications theory. This is important because it provides a basis on which to appreciate the different ways in which marketing communications are used. Communication theory specifies the scope of the subject and provides a framework within which to appreciate the various communication activities undertaken by organizations. We then present communication principles based on which marketing messages are communicated and consider how marketing communications might work.

Defining 'Marketing Communications'

'Marketing communications' can be defined as a management process through which an organization attempts to engage with its various audiences. By conveying messages that are of significant value, audiences are encouraged to offer attitudinal and behavioural responses (Fill, 2013).

There are three main aspects associated with this definition, as follows.

- *Engagement*—What are the audiences' communications needs and is it possible to engage with them on their terms using one-way, two-way, or dialogic communications?
- *Audiences*—Which specific audience(s) do we need to communicate with, and what are their various behaviour and information-processing needs?

- *Responses*—What are the desired outcomes of the communication process? Are they based on changes in perception, values, and beliefs, or are changes in behaviour required?

Engagement deals with the way in which communication influences its audiences (see the section after next 'How marketing communication works'). What to expect in terms of engagement is largely dependent on the decisions made with regards to the target audience and target responses for different marketing communication activities (see 'Planning marketing communication').

The Scope of Marketing Communications

As was discussed in Chapter 1, promotion is one of the 'P's of the marketing mix and encompasses the communication of the proposition to the target market. 'Marketing communications' is a more contemporary term for promotion. It is used to refer to the communication of elements of an organization's offerings to target audiences.

Marketing communications should be regarded as an audience-centred activity comprising three elements: a set of tools; the media; and messages. The five common *tools* are advertising, sales promotion, **personal selling**, direct marketing, and public relations (PR). In addition, a range of *media*, such as television, radio, press, and the Internet, are used to convey *messages* to target audiences (covered in more detail in Chapter 9).

These tools, media, and messages are not, however, the only sources of information for consumers. There is also implicit and important communication through the other elements of the marketing mix (such as a high price being symbolic of high quality), as well as unplanned or unintended experiences (such as empty stock shelves or accidents) in relation to the offer.

Figure 8.1 highlights the breadth and the complexity of managing marketing communications. Our focus in this chapter will be on planned marketing communications (Duncan and Moriarty, 1998). This component is really important because it has the potential not only to present offers in

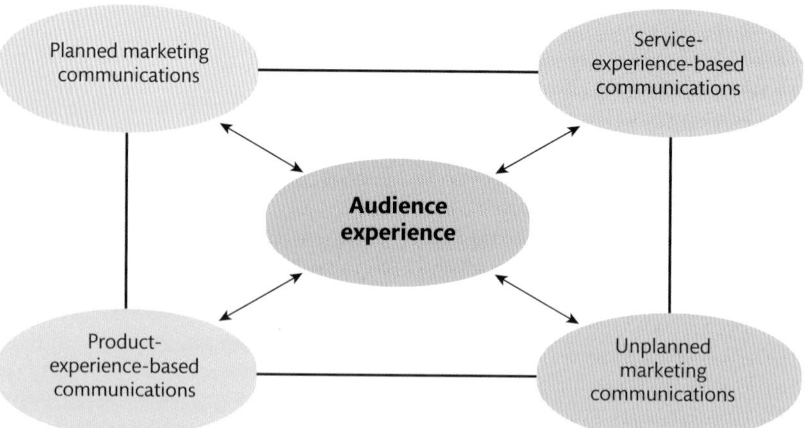

Figure 8.1 The scope of marketing communications

Source: Hughes and Fill (2007). Adapted with the kind permission of Emerald Group Publishing Ltd and Westburn Publishers.

the best possible way, but also to influence people's expectations about both product and service experiences.

Visit the **online resources** and follow the web link to the European Association of Communication Agencies (EACA) to learn more about advertising, media, and sales promotion activities across Europe.

How Marketing Communications Works

Ideas about how marketing communications works have been a constant source of investigation. Although no firm conclusion has been reached, some ideas have played a very influential role in shaping our thinking about this fascinating topic.

Communication Theory

Communication theory explains how and why certain marketing communication activities take place. Communication is the process by which individuals share meaning. Therefore it is necessary for participants to be able to interpret the meanings embedded in the messages they receive and then, as far as the sender is concerned, be able to respond coherently. The act of responding is important because it completes an episode in the communication process. Communication that travels only from the sender to the **receiver** is essentially a one-way process and the full communication process remains incomplete. This type of communication is depicted in Figure 8.2.

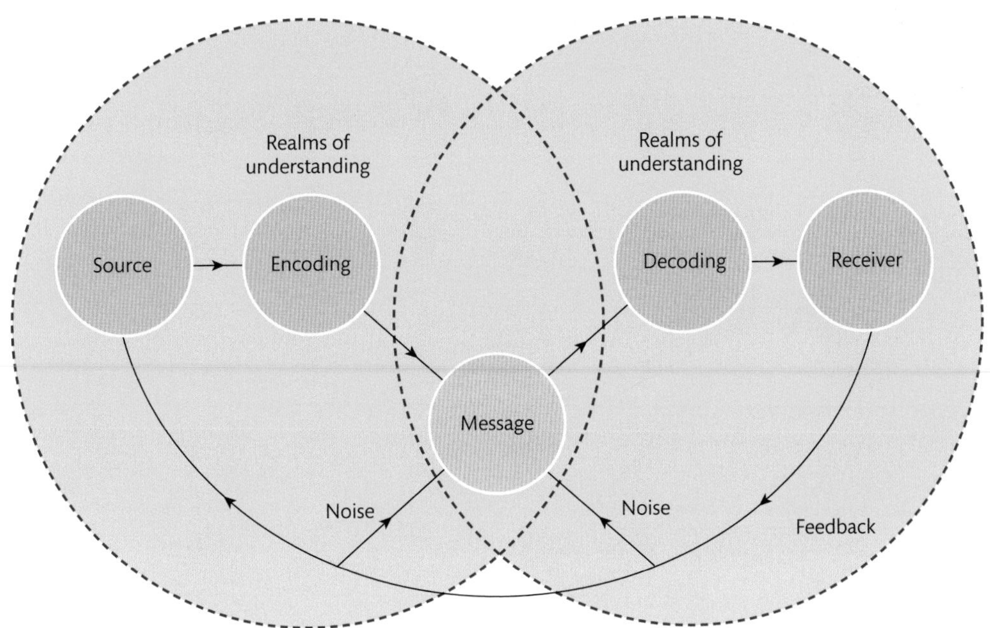

Figure 8.2 A linear model of communications

Sources: Based on Schramm (1955) and Shannon and Weaver (1962).

When Marabou displays its chocolate bars on a poster in the Stockholm metro, the person standing on the platform can read the poster, understand it, and may even be entertained by it. However, the person does not have any immediate opportunity to respond to the poster in such a way that Marabou can hear, understand, and act on the person's comments and feelings. When that same advert is presented on a website or a sales promotion representative offers that same person a chunk of Marabou milk chocolate when they are shopping in a supermarket, there are opportunities to hear, record, and even respond to the comments that the person makes. This form of communication travels from a sender (Marabou) to a receiver (the person in the supermarket) and back again to Marabou. It is referred to as a two-way communication and represents a complete communication episode. This type of communication is depicted in Figure 8.3.

Visit the **online resources** and follow the web link to the International Association of Business Communicators (IABC), a business network that aims to improve marketing communications effectiveness among communication professionals.

These basic models form the basis of this introduction to communication theory. Understanding the way in which communication works provides a foundation for better understanding not only the way in which marketing communications work, but also how organizations can use them effectively.

Three main models or interpretations of how communication works are considered here: the linear model, the two-way model, and the interactive model of communication.

The Linear Model of Communication

The linear model of communication, first developed by Wilbur Schramm (1955), is regarded as the basic model of mass communications. The key components of this model of are set out in Figure 8.2.

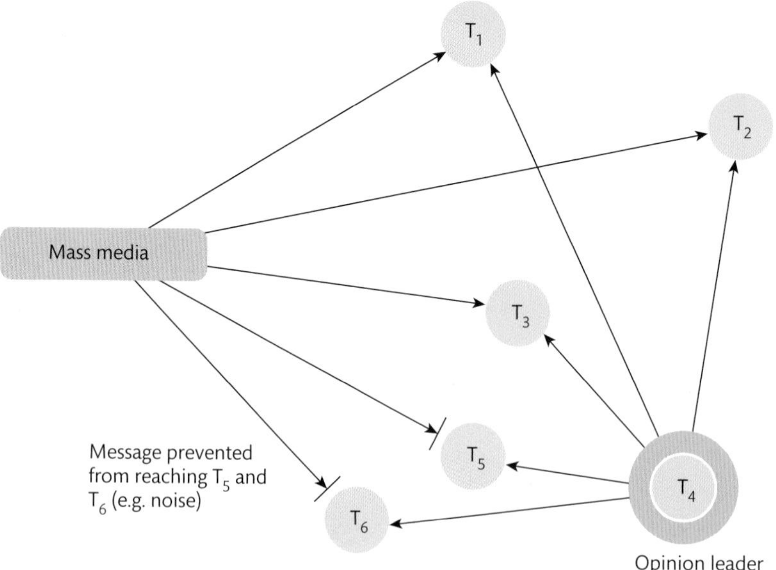

Figure 8.3 The two-step model of communications

Source: Fill (2013). Reproduced with the kind permission of Pearson Education Limited.

The model can be broken down into a number of phases, each of which has distinct characteristics. The linear model emphasizes that each phase occurs in a particular sequence—a linear progression—which, according to Theodorson and Theodorson (1969: 13–14), enables the 'transmission of information, ideas, attitudes, or emotion from one person or group to another (or others), primarily through symbols'. The model and its components are straightforward, but it is the quality of the linkages between the various elements in the process that determines whether the communication will be successful.

The source is an individual or organization, which identifies a problem requiring transmission of a message. The source of a message is an important factor in the communication process: not only must the source identify the right problem, but also a receiver who perceives a source to lack conviction, authority, trust, or expertise is not likely to believe the messages sent by that source.

Encoding is the process by which the source selects a combination of appropriate words, pictures, symbols, and music to represent the message to be transmitted. The various bits are 'packed' in such a way that they can be unpacked and understood. The goal is to create a message that is capable of being easily comprehended by the receiver.

Once encoded, the message must be put into a form that is capable of transmission. It may be oral or written, verbal or non-verbal, in a symbolic form or in a sign. The channel is the means by which the message is transmitted from the source to the receiver. These channels may be personal or non-personal. Personal channels involve face-to-face contact and **word-of-mouth** communications, which can be extremely influential. Non-personal channels are characterized by mass media advertising, which can reach large audiences. Adverts placed in newspapers such as *The Guardian* are typical of this latter approach. Whatever the format chosen, the source must be sure that what is being put into the message is what it wants the receiver to decode.

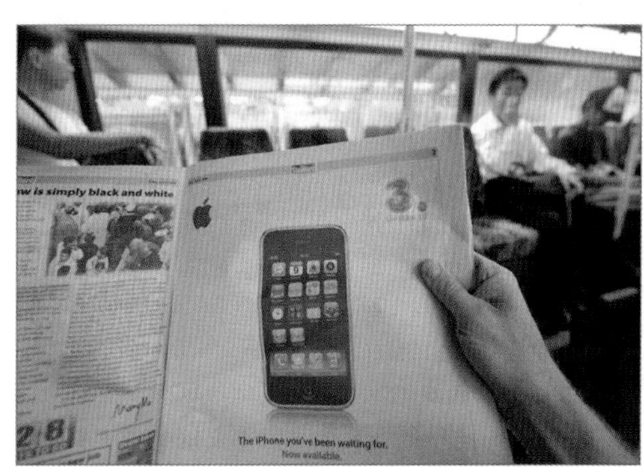

A newspaper ad represents a classical attempt at persuasion through a linear communication process.

Source: © Getty / AFP / Stringer.

Once the receiver, an individual or organization, has seen, heard, smelt, or read the message, they decode it. In effect, they are 'unpacking' the various components of the message, starting to make sense of it and give it meaning. The more clearly the message is encoded, the easier it is to 'unpack' and comprehend what the source intended to convey when it constructed the message. Therefore **decoding** is that part of the communication process in which receivers give meaning to a message.

Once the message is understood, receivers provide a set of reactions referred to as a 'response'. These reactions may vary from an emotional response based on a set of feelings and thoughts about the message to a behavioural or action response.

Feedback is another part of the response process. It is important to know not only that the message has been received, but also that it has been correctly decoded and the right meaning attributed. However, although feedback is an essential aspect of a successful communication event, feedback through mass media channels is generally difficult to obtain, mainly because of the inherent time delay involved in the feedback process. Feedback through personal selling, meanwhile, can be instantaneous, through explicit means such as questioning, raising objections, or signing an order form. For the mass media advertiser, the process can be vague and prone to misinterpretation. If a suitable feedback system is not in place, the source will be unaware that the communication has been unsuccessful and is liable to continue wasting resources. This represents inefficient and ineffective marketing communications.

Noise is concerned with influences that distort information and, in turn, make it difficult for the receiver to correctly decode and interpret the message as intended by the source. So if a telephone rings or is someone rustles sweet papers during a sensitive part of a film screened in a cinema, the receiver is distracted from the message.

The final component in the linear model concerns the 'realm of understanding'. This is an important element in the communication process because it recognizes that successful communications are more likely to be achieved if the source and the receiver understand each other. This understanding concerns attitudes, perceptions, behaviour, and experience—the values of both parties to the communication process. Effective communication is more likely when there is some common ground—that is, a 'realm of understanding' between the source and receiver.

One of the problems associated with the linear model of communication is that it ignores the impact that other people can have on the communication process. People are not passive; they actively use information, and the views and actions of other people can impact on the way in which information is sent, received, processed, and given meaning. One of the other difficulties with the linear model is that it is based on communication through mass media.

Today, people engage with interactive-based communications and, in some circumstances such as online gaming, organizations and individuals can be involved in real **dialogue**. The linear model is consequently no longer sufficient to explain how consumers react to communications in all circumstances. It is, however, still useful for our purposes because it analyses specifically the process of message encoding and decoding, and remains crucial for understanding popular forms of marketing communication (such as print and television advertising).

The Two-Step Model of Communication

One interpretation of the linear model is that it is a one-step explanation: information is directed and shot at prospective audiences, rather like a bullet being propelled from a gun. However, we know that people can have a significant impact on the communication process and the **two-step model**, sometimes referred to as the 'influencer model', goes some way towards reflecting their influence.

The two-step model recognizes the importance of personal influences when informing and persuading audiences to think or behave in particular ways. This model depicts information flowing via various media channels to particular types of person, to whom other members of the audience refer for information and guidance. There are two main types of influencer: one is referred to as an 'opinion leader'; the other, as an 'opinion former'.

Opinion leaders are simply ordinary people who have a heightened interest in a particular topic. For example, *Vogue* magazine has an 'Influencer Network', a panel of 1,000 women who, as opinion leaders, provide feedback on a range of issues, including new offerings, upcoming fashion collections, and advert creatives. They are encouraged to talk about particular offerings on their social networks, raising awareness of them and of *Vogue* itself (Moses, 2011).

Opinion formers are instead involved professionally in the topic of interest. Their defining characteristic is that they exert personal influence because their profession, authority, education, or status is associated with the object of the communication process. For example, shop assistants in music equipment shops are often experienced musicians in their own right. Aspiring musicians seeking to buy their first proper guitar will often consult these perceived 'experts' about guitar brands, styles, models, and associated equipment, such as amplifiers.

Both leaders and formers have enormous potential to influence audiences. This may be because messages from personal influencers provide reinforcement and message credibility, or it may be because this is the only way of reaching the end-user audience (see Market Insight 8.1).

Market Insight 8.1 **The Biggest Influencer on YouTube**

In April 2010, Felix Kjellberg, then a 21-year-old Swedish engineering student, created a new account on YouTube. For some time, he had been posting videos of himself playing video games on YouTube, but, having forgotten the password to the initial account, he was forced to set up a new one: PewDiePie. Little did he know that this account was going to change his life.

Kjellberg's videos turned out to be very popular. In fact, Kjellberg's foul-mouthed videos have dominated YouTube over the past years. Many attribute his success to the attention he pays to his fans. Kjellberg spends lots of time talking about them, answering their questions in the YouTube comments section, and forming a community of 'bros'.

In 2011, he dropped out of university to be able to devote more time to his YouTube channel and, in 2012, the channel had more than 1 million subscribers. Since then, Kjellberg has broken numerous records on YouTube. For example, his PewDiePie channel grew from 12 million subscribers in August 2013 to more than 20 million in January 2014. In September 2015, PewDiePie was the world's largest independent YouTube channel, with 10.1 billion total views and 39.3 million total subscribers. By January 2016, the channel had grown to more than 11 billion views and close to 42 million subscribers.

In 2015, media reported that Kjellberg had made approximately US$7.4 million (SEK36.7 million) via his YouTube channel in 2014. Although the figure is

Felix Kjelberg, better known by his online alias 'PewDiePie', is an online sensation and influencer.

Source: Wikimedia Commons.

staggering in itself, relating it to his popularity clearly highlights why many YouTubers turn to sponsorships for funding. In fact, given the size of his channel at that time, this means that he made only about 20.6 cents per subscriber that year.

1. **At what stage would you say that Kjellberg moved from being an opinion leader to becoming an opinion former? Is it possible to say?**
2. **Visit the PewDiePie YouTube channel. To what extent is Kjellberg's communication with his followers based on interaction and dialogue?**
3. **Visit the PewDiePie YouTube channel. What opportunities does it offer to marketers?**

Sources: Rosengren (2012); Tamburro (2014); Kosoff and Jacobs (2015).

The Interaction Model of Communications

In the **interaction model** of communications, the parties are seen to interact among themselves and communication flows among all of the members in what is regarded as a communication network (see Figure 8.4). Mass media are not the only source of the communication.

The interaction model recognizes that messages can flow through various channels, and that people can influence the direction and impact of a message. It is not necessarily one-way, but interactive communication that typifies much of contemporary communications. In Case Insight 8.1, we saw how the desire of *The Guardian* to be 'open' required the use of social media to encourage audience participation. The interaction among different people, sometimes referring to *The Guardian* only indirectly, is a good demonstration of the interaction model in practice. See Market Insight 8.2 for an interesting case of how interactive processes can be used to enhance the effectiveness of a campaign.

Interaction is an integral part of communication. Think of a conversation with a friend: the face-to-face, oral-, and visual-based communication enables both of you to consider what the other is saying and to react in whatever way is appropriate. Mass communication does not facilitate this interactional element and hence the linear model might be regarded as an incomplete form of the pure communication process. However, care needs to be taken because the content associated with an interactional event might be based on an argument, a statement of opinion, or a mere casual social encounter. What is important here is interaction that leads to mutual understanding. This type of interaction concerns 'relationship-specific knowledge' (Ballantyne, 2004)—that is, interaction that is about information that is relevant to both parties. Once this is established,

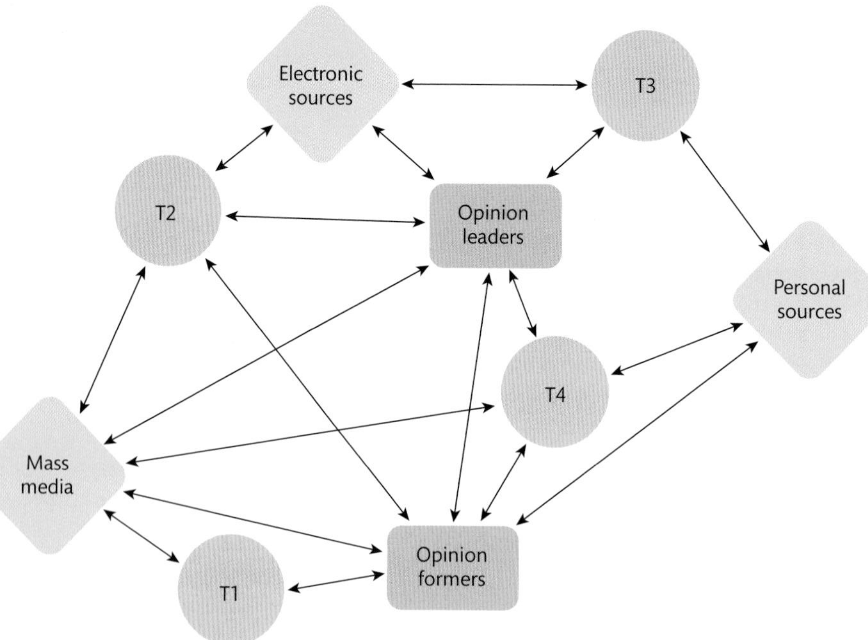

Figure 8.4 An interaction model

Market Insight 8.2 **Carambar Pulls a Prank on an Entire Nation**

Carambar is a French brand of caramel candies. It has been popular in France for more than 40 years for its association with 'Carambar jokes'. Each candy stick is wrapped in paper on which is printed one joke. Over the years, these jokes have become strongly linked with the brand and one of the distinctive features of consuming a Carambar.

To revitalize the brand with its key audiences, agency Fred & Farid developed an astute campaign aimed at leveraging the popularity of the jokes and the power of interactions in social media. On 21 March 2013, the agency sent a press kit to key influencers, announcing that the company would replace its traditional jokes with maths exercises and other similar quizzes for school children. In less than 48 hours, all major media outlets in France were covering the story and the brand's decision generated intense debate in social media. Seventeen petitions were created to ask the brand to revert to its original jokes and abandon its new policy.

One of Carambar's famous jokes.

Source: © Getty / THOMAS COEX / Staff.

On 25 March, the company revealed, by means of a video on social media, that the story itself was a joke! Of course, the announcement generated additional publicity for the company, and reminded all consumers of the importance of the association between the company and its jokes. The campaign, run with virtually no financial costs, generated significant impacts in terms of brand awareness and brand preference. In only five days the brand had been mentioned 950 times on different media and generated 55,000 tweets. In spring 2013, the brand regained popularity, with significant sales increases compared to its key competitors.

1. **What are they key strengths of the campaign used by Carambar?**
2. **Consider to what extent components of the linear communication model are still relevant in this context. How would you say processes of information encoding and decoding work in this context? What would constitute feedback and noise in this campaign?**
3. **The campaign started with a press release distributed to key influencers. If you were a manager running this campaign, how would you choose these influencers?**

Sources: Anon. (2014); https://www.youtube.com/watch?v=RaNfoclPIRo.

increased levels of trust develop between the participants so that, eventually, a dialogue emerges between communication partners. Therefore interactivity is a prelude to dialogue, the highest or purest form of communication.

Dialogue occurs through reasoning, which requires both listening and adaptation skills. Dialogue is concerned with the development of knowledge that is specific to the parties involved and is referred to as 'learning together' (Ballantyne, 2004: 119). The development of digital technologies has been instrumental in enabling organizations to provide increased interaction opportunities with their customers and other audiences: think, for example, of the number of times, when watching television, that you are prompted to press the red button to get more information.

Marketing Communication Theory

The first important idea about how advertising works was based on how the personal selling process works. Developed by Strong (1925), the **AIDA** model has become extremely well known and is used by many practitioners. The acronym 'AIDA' refers to the need to, first, create Awareness, then generate Interest and drive Desire, from which Action (a sale) emerges. As a broad interpretation of the sales process, this is generally correct, but it fails to provide insight into the depths of how advertising works. Thirty-six years later, Lavidge and Steiner (1961) presented a model based on what is referred to as the **hierarchy of effects (HoE)** approach. Similar in nature to AIDA, it assumes that a prospect must pass through a series of steps for a purchase to be made. It is assumed—correctly—that advertising cannot generate an immediate sale because there are a series of thought processes that need to be fulfilled prior to action. These steps are represented in Figure 8.5.

These models have become known as 'hierarchy of effects' (HoE) models, simply because the effects (on audiences) are thought to occur in a top-down sequence. Hierarchy of effects models and frameworks are straightforward, simple, easy to understand, and (if used when creating advertising materials) provide a helpful broad template on which to base and evaluate campaigns.

Although attractive, however, this sequential approach has several drawbacks. People do not always process information nor do they always purchase offerings following a series of sequential steps. This logical progression is not reflected in reality when, for example, an impulse purchase is followed by an emotional feeling towards a brand. There are also questions about what actually constitutes adequate levels of awareness, comprehension, and conviction. How can it be known

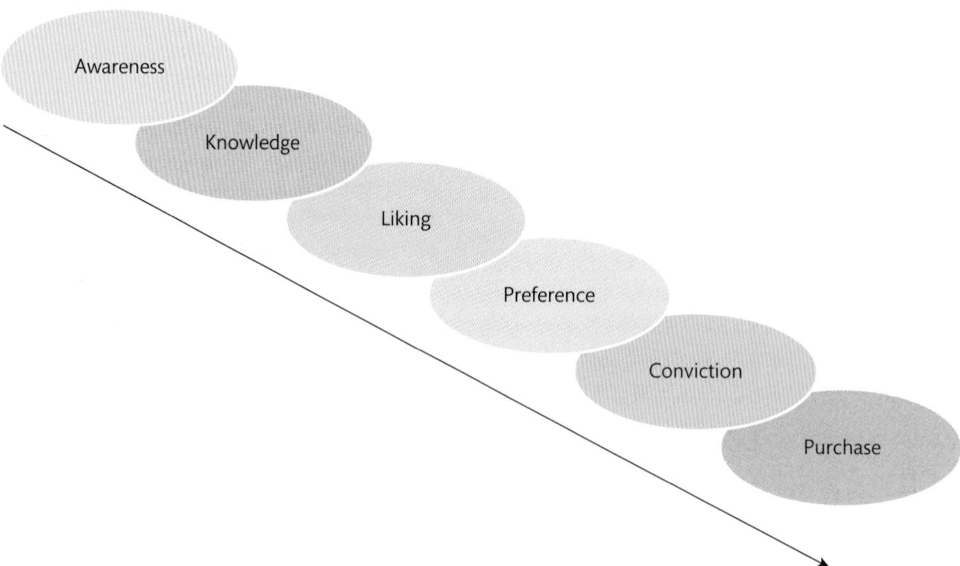

Figure 8.5 Stages in the hierarchy of effects model

Research Insight 8.1

To take your learning further, you might wish to read this influential paper.

Duncan, T., and Moriarty, S. (1998) 'A communication-based marketing model for managing relationships', *Journal of Marketing*, 62(2): 1–13.

This is one of the most important academic papers in the field of marketing communications. It is important because it led the move from a functional perspective of integrated marketing communications to one that emphasized its role within relationship marketing.

 **Visit the online resources to read the abstract and access the full paper.**

which stage the majority of the target audience has reached at any one point in time and whether this purchase sequence is applicable to all consumers for all purchases?

The Strong and Weak Theories of Advertising

According to Jones (1991), advertising has a *strong* effect, because it can persuade people to buy an offering that they have not previously purchased. Advertising can also generate long-run purchase behaviour. Under the **strong theory**, advertising is believed to be capable of increasing sales for a brand and for the **product class**. These upward shifts are achieved through the use of manipulative and psychological techniques, which are deployed against largely passive consumers who, possibly because of apathy, are either generally incapable of processing information intelligently, or have little or no motivation to become involved.

This interpretation is a persuasion view and corresponds very well to the HoE models referred to earlier. Persuasion occurs by moving buyers towards a purchase by easing them through a series of steps, prompted by timely and suitable promotional messages. It seems that this approach correlates closely with new offerings for which new buying behaviours are required.

Contrary to the strong perspective is the view that a consumer's brand choices are driven by purchasing habit rather than by exposure to promotional messages. One of the more prominent researchers in this area was Ehrenberg (1974), who believed that advertising represents a *weak* force. He believed that advertising has little impact on persuading consumers to buy offerings, mainly because consumers are active, not passive, information processors.

Ehrenberg proposed that an awareness–trial–reinforcement (**ATR**) framework would be a more appropriate interpretation of how advertising works. Both Jones and Ehrenberg agree, however, that *awareness* is required before any purchase can be made, although the elapsed time between awareness and action may be very short or very long. Of the mass of people exposed to a message, a few will be sufficiently intrigued to want to try an offering (*trial*)—the next phase. *Reinforcement* follows, to maintain awareness and provide reassurance, encouraging customers to repeat the pattern of thinking and behaviour. Advertising's role is to breed brand familiarity and identification (Ehrenberg, 1997).

According to the **weak theory**, advertising is employed as a defence, to retain customers and to increase brand usage. Advertising is used to reinforce existing attitudes, not necessarily to drastically change them. This means that when people say that they 'are not influenced by advertising', they are, in the main, correct.

Both the strong and the weak theories of advertising are important because they are equally right and equally wrong. The answer to the question 'how does advertising work?' lies somewhere between the two and is dependent on the context. For advertising to work, involvement is likely to be high, and so here the strong theory is the most applicable. However, the vast majority of product purchase decisions generate low involvement and so decision-making is likely to be driven by habit. Here, advertising's role is to maintain a brand's awareness with the purchase cycle, so the weak theory is most applicable.

Visit the **online resources** and complete Internet Activity 8.1 to learn more about the strong and the weak theories of advertising.

A Composite Approach

Most of the frameworks presented so far have their roots in advertising. If we are to establish a model that explains how marketing communications works, a different perspective is required—one that draws on the key parts of all of the models. This is possible because the three key components of the attitude construct lie within these different models. Attitudes have been regarded as an important aspect of marketing communications activities and advertising is thought to be capable of influencing the development of positive attitudes towards brands (see also Chapter 2).

The three stages of attitude formation are that we learn something (that is, a cognitive or learning component), feel something (that is, an affective or emotional component), and then act on our attitudes (that is, a behavioural or conative component). So, in many situations, we learn something, feel something towards a brand, and then proceed to buy or not to buy. These stages are set out in Figure 8.6.

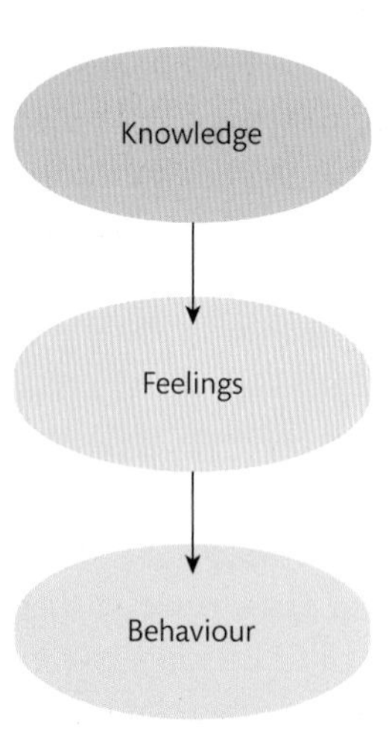

Figure 8.6 Attitude construct: Linear

The HoE models and the strong theory contain this sequential approach of learn–feel–do. However, we do not always pass through this particular sequence, and the weak theory puts greater emphasis on familiarity and reminding (awareness) than the other components.

If we look at Figure 8.7, we can see that these components have been worked into a circular format. This means that, when using marketing communications, it is not necessary to follow each component sequentially. The focus can be on what the audience requires and this might be on the learning, feeling, or doing components, as the audience determines. In other words, for marketing communications to be audience-centred, we should develop campaigns based on the overriding need of the audience at any one time—that is, based on their need to learn, feel, or behave in particular ways.

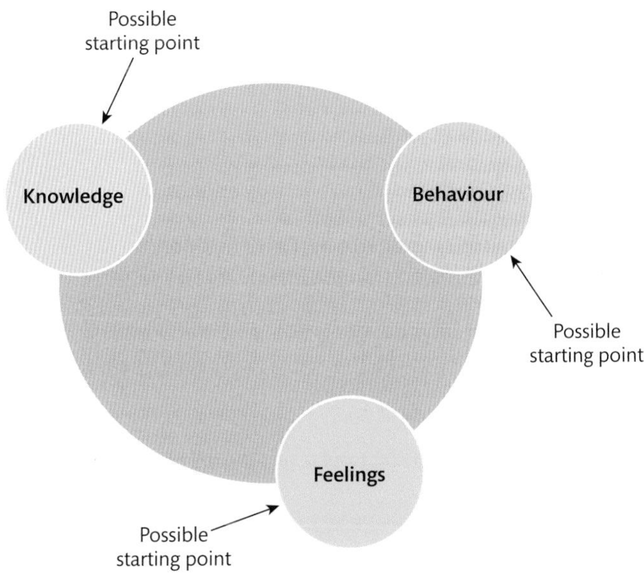

Figure 8.7 Attitude construct: Circular

Learn

Where learning is the priority, the overall goal should be to inform or educate the target audience. If the offering is new, it will be important to make the target audience aware of the offering's existence, and to inform them of the brand's key attributes and benefits. This is a common use for advertising, because it has the capacity to reach both large and targeted audiences.

Feel

Once the audience is aware of a brand and knows something about how it might be useful to them, it is important that they develop a positive attitude towards the brand. This can be achieved by presenting the brand with a set of emotional values that it is thought will appeal, and be of interest, to the audience. These values need to be repeated in subsequent communications to reinforce the brand attitudes. *The Guardian* knew that it had to use marketing communications to change the perception that some people had of the newspaper.

Do

Most organizations find that, to be successful, they need to use a much broader set of tools and that the goal is to change the behaviour of the target audience. This behavioural change may be about getting people to buy the brand, but it may often be about motivating them to visit a website, call for a brochure, fill in an application form, or simply encouraging them to visit a shop and sample the brand free of payment and any other risk. This behavioural change is also referred to as a 'call to action'. *The Guardian* had to use marketing communications to increase the number and frequency of visitors to its website—in other words, to effect a change of behaviour. Market Insight 8.3 offers an example of communications campaign aimed at driving behaviour change.

Research Insight 8.2

To take your learning further, you might wish to read this influential paper.

Gilliland, D. I., and Johnston, W. J. (1997) 'Toward a model of business-to-business marketing communications effects', *Industrial Marketing Management*, 26(1): 15–29.

This is an interesting paper that is based around a model designed to address how marketing communications work in a business-to-business (B2B) environment. The authors introduce a number of important concepts and issues that relate to the subject in different ways.

 **Visit the online resources to read the abstract and access the full paper.**

Market Insight 8.3 Motivating Energy Saving Behaviour Change in Hospitals

Global Action Plan (GAP) is a leading environmental charity in London, which seeks to help people to live more sustainably. In 2014, GAP designed an innovative energy-saving behavioural intervention for two NHS hospitals, called 'Operation TLC', which focused on encouraging three energy-saving behaviours among hospital employees (nurses, doctors, administrators, etc.):

- **T**urn off machines;
- **L**ights out when not needed; and
- **C**lose doors when possible.

The behavioural intervention was delivered via multiple communication platforms. Face-to-face discussions were carried out with employees using electronic tablets as props to help hospital employees to become familiar with the energy-saving actions. Posters and stickers were placed on doors throughout the hospital, and pens were distributed, as reminders of energy-saving actions. The first phase, in two hospitals, resulted in reducing lights left on and doors left unnecessarily open, leading to energy savings of 765 MWh across the two hospitals (equating to a saving of over £100,000).

The intervention highlighted benefits to employees (working more efficiently during quieter times) and a positive effect of employee pro-environmental behaviours on patients (a positive change in quality of sleep after the intervention, which in turn would be likely to increase patient satisfaction, as was evident by this data collection, and in the future potentially to speed up recovery from illness). The benefits of Operation TLC are thus not only for the environment in terms of reducing CO_2 emissions and for the hospitals themselves in terms of monetary savings, but also of benefit to the hospital employees and also to hospital patients.

This is an example of how organizations can reduce costs, increase operational efficiency, build a competitive advantage, and increase reputation and favourable consumer responses, among others, as well as benefit society and the environment at large, through innovative sustainability interventions. It is also an example of a communication campaign that is aimed primarily at activating behavioural change. One assumption of these initiatives is that, through changes in behaviour, the environmental attitudes of the audiences engaged can be also leveraged in the long term.

Market Insight 8.3 (continued)

A summary of TLC's achievements.

Source: Courtesy of GlobalActionPlan.org.

Positive reinforcement: Operation TLC celebrates the achievements of the participating hospitals in promoting virtuous behaviour.

Source: Courtesy of GlobalActionPlan.org.

An example of the reminders used to influence behaviour directly.

Source: Courtesy of GlobalActionPlan.org.

Market Insight 8.3 (continued)

1 **What might be the advantages and disadvantages of face-to-face discussions with hospital employees to motivate them to take energy-saving actions?**

2 **Which method would you use to educate and motivate employees to take energy-saving actions?**

3 **Using the models reviewed so far in this chapter, how would you describe the effects of this communication campaign? Which model fits the nature of this intervention best?**

Sources: Manika et al. (2016); http://www.globalactionplan.org.uk/operationtlc.

*This market insight was kindly contributed by Dr Danae Manika, Queen Mary University of London. Appreciation is extended to Global Action Plan (*http://www.globalactionplan.org.uk*) and the Real World Sustainability Research Team (*http://www.globalactionplan.org.uk/News/the-real-world-sustainability-research-team*) for providing information for this case study.*

Word-of-Mouth

The development of technologies such as social media, which facilitates interaction between customers, has intensified the importance of word-of-mouth for marketers. This type of communication does not involve any payment for media because communication is freely given through conversation. Word-of-mouth communication is 'interpersonal communication regarding products or services where the receiver regards the communicator as impartial' (Stokes and Lomax, 2002: 350).

Customers perceive word-of-mouth recommendations as objective and unbiased. In comparison with advertising messages, word-of-mouth communications are more robust (Berkman and Gilson, 1986). Word-of-mouth messages are used either as information inputs prior to purchase, or as a support and reinforcement of their own purchasing decisions.

For every positive comment, however, there are ten negative comments. For this reason, word-of-mouth communication was once seen as negative, unplanned, and having a corrosive effect on a brand's overall communications. Today, organizations actively manage word-of-mouth communications to generate positive comments and as a way of differentiating themselves in the market. Viral marketing, or 'word-of-mouse', communication is an electronic version of the spoken endorsement of an offering. Both online and offline word-of-mouth is becoming increasingly important if marketing communications are to have their desired impact (Keller and Fay, 2012).

Visit the **online resources** and complete Internet Activity 8.2 to learn more about the importance of word-of-mouth in contemporary advertising.

Marketing Communications Tasks

Fundamentally, marketing communications can be used to engage audiences by undertaking one of four main tasks, referred to by Fill (2002) as the '**DRIP** model'. The acronym refers to the ways in which communications can be used to Differentiate brands and organizations, to Reinforce brand memories and expectations, to Inform audiences (that is, to make them aware or to educate them), and to Persuade them to do things or to behave in particular ways (see Table 8.1).

Visit the **online resources** and complete Internet Activity 8.3 to learn more about the way in which fashion house Burberry uses marketing communications.

These tasks are not mutually exclusive; indeed, campaigns might be designed to target two or three of them. For example, the launch of a new brand will require that audiences be informed—that is, made aware of its existence—and enabled to understand how it is different from competitor brands. A brand that is well established might try to reach lapsed customers by reminding them of the key features and benefits, and offering them an incentive (persuasion) to buy again.

Table 8.1 DRIP tasks for marketing communications

Marketing communication tasks	Explanation
To differentiate	In many markets, there is little to separate brands (e.g. of mineral water, coffee, printers). In these cases, it is the images created by marketing communications that help to *differentiate* one brand from another and position them, so that consumers develop positive attitudes and make purchasing decisions.
To reinforce	Communications may be used to *remind* people of a need they might have or of the benefits of past transactions, with a view to convincing them that they should enter into a similar exchange. In addition, it is possible to provide *reassurance* or comfort either immediately prior to an exchange or, more commonly, post-purchase. This is important, because it helps to retain current customers and improve profitability. This approach to business is much more cost-effective than constantly striving to lure new customers.
To inform	One of the most common uses of marketing communications is to *inform* and make potential customers aware of the features and benefits of an organization's offering. In addition, marketing communications can be used to educate audiences, i.e. to show them how to use an offering or what to do in particular situations.
To persuade	Communication may attempt to *persuade* current and potential customers of the desirability of entering into an exchange relationship.

Market Insight 8.4 **Reinventing Advertising for the Digital Age**

The digital age hit advertising like a wrecking ball. It smashed existing power structures and empowered ordinary people to create their own mass communication. It also broke the consumer decision journey into pieces, leaving advertisers to figure out how the new reality fits together. The following are three important changes shaping the future of advertising.

1 *The zero moment of truth*—The first effect of the digital age was the end of control. Brands can no longer control what is being said about their brand and in what order or form their communications reach the masses. People have the power to universally share and access actual experiences of a brand, influencing the choices of people only starting their own decision journey. The experience of initial users moves 'upstream' to affect future users. Google dubbed this the 'zero moment of truth' (ZMOT). This phenomenon is most clearly illustrated by Yelp reviews, whereby real customer experiences trumps restaurant reviews and own promotions. A quick smartphone search is now the starting point for many brand experiences, and the bridge between initial need and final decision.

2 *The attention economy*—The second effect of the digital age was to make it increasingly difficult to buy attention. The media landscape grew more user-centric, putting pressure on brands to earn attention—that is, to engage rather than interrupt. A successful campaign now goes beyond bought media, straight into the news and our personal newsfeeds. Increasingly, this means that the new aim of advertising is to create either fame or friendship: to make the brand a celebrity that creates a big splash; or to make the brand a 'friend', providing relevant updates in social media (H&M on Instagram being a good example). The brand needs to have a social role that makes it earn attention—again and again—and builds salience and preference over time.

3 *The brand purpose*—The third effect is a shift from communication to action—from message to mission, and from talk to walk. It is no longer enough for a brand to claim a benefit; it also needs to prove and believably act on it. This creates a need to find a clear purpose—that is, a brand mission, ideal, or theme that it can put into practice in all contact points, and which serves as a platform for innovation and relationship building. This is a property shared by many great brands, but well exemplified by Red Bull's mission to uplift mind and body—'to give you wings'—put into

Real customer experiences are important to consider in marketing communications.

Source: © Gil C/Shutterstock.

Red Bull sponsorships tend to reinforce its brand proposition focused on the 'Red Bull gives you wings' tagline.

Source: © Shutterstock/David Acosta Allely.

Market Insight 8.4 (continued)

practice through numerous sponsorships, bold stunts, and, of course, the product itself.

These key changes mark the end of the age of interruption and the beginning of an age of disruption—for the people, by the people—in which smartphones act as decision guides, entertainment centres, and voting booths, all rolled into one. The new advertising model is being built right now, with advertisers looking for new ways in which to create experiences that are emotional, relevant, and shareable, and which will launch brands to fame, familiarity, and (hopefully) fortune.

This insight was kindly contributed by Karl Wikström, planner, TBWA Stockholm, Sweden.

1 **Do you agree with the changes described in the insight?**

2 **How might each of the three changes impact on marketing communications?**

3 **What examples have you seen of marketing communications that seem to have been developed with each of the three changes in mind?**

Source: Based on the author's own experience.

Marketing Communications Planning

Management's task is to formulate and implement a communication strategy that blends the right mix of tools and media to deliver the right messages in the right place, at the right time, for the right audience. Strategically, the main decisions have to do with defining the appropriate target audience and setting the right objectives.

To understand what a marketing communications plan should achieve, it is helpful to appreciate the principal tasks facing marketing communications managers. These are to decide the following.

- Who should receive the messages?
- What should the messages say?
- What image of the organization or brand are receivers expected to retain?
- How much is to be spent establishing this new image?
- How are the messages to be delivered?
- What actions should the receivers take?
- How do we control the whole process once implemented?
- What was achieved?

For many reasons, planning is an essential management activity, and if planned marketing communications are to be developed in an orderly and efficient way, the use of a suitable framework is necessary. A framework for integrated marketing communications plans is presented in Figure 8.8.

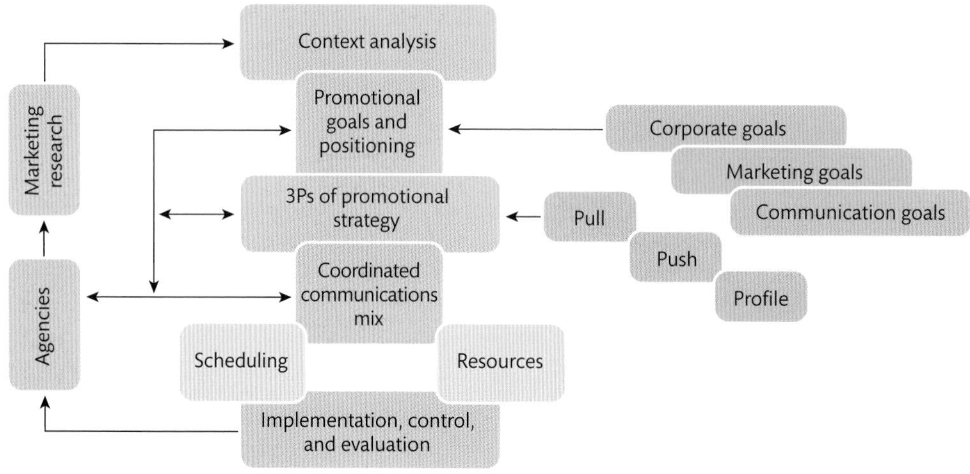

Figure 8.8 The marketing communications planning framework

Source: Marketing Communications (6th edn) Fill, C. (2013). Reproduced with the kind permission of Pearson Education Limited. © Pearson Education Limited 2013.

The marketing communications planning framework (MCPF) provides a visual guide to what needs to be achieved and brings together the various elements in a logical sequence of activities. As with all hierarchical planning models, each level of decision-making is built on information generated at a previous level in the model. Another advantage of using the MCPF is that it provides a suitable checklist of activities that need to be considered. The MCPF represents a sequence of decisions that marketing managers undertake when preparing, implementing, and evaluating communication strategies and plans. This framework reflects a deliberate or planned approach to strategic marketing communications.

However, in practice, marketing communications planning is not always developed as a linear process, as depicted in this framework. Indeed, many marketing communications decisions are made outside any recognizable framework, because some organizations approach the process as an integrative and sometimes spontaneous activity. The MCPF approach presented here is, however, intended to highlight the tasks to be achieved, the way in which they relate to one another, and the order in which they should be accomplished.

Elements of the MCPF

A marketing communications plan should be developed for each level of communications activity, from strategy to individual tactical aspects of a campaign. The difference between them is the level of detail that is included.

Context Analysis

The marketing plan is the bedrock of the context analysis. This will already have been prepared, and contains important information about the target segments, the business and marketing goals, the competitors, and the time frames within which the goals are to be achieved. The context analysis needs to elaborate and build on this information to provide the detail, so that the plan can be developed and justified.

The first and vital step is to analyse the context in which marketing communications activities are to occur. Unlike a situation analysis used in general planning models, the context analysis should be communications-oriented and should use the marketing plan as a foundation. There are four main components to the communications context analysis: the customer, and the business, internal, and external environmental contexts.

Understanding the *customer* context requires information and market research data about the target audiences specified in the marketing plan. Here, detailed information about their needs, perceptions, motivation, attitudes, and decision-making characteristics relative to the proposition category (or issue) is necessary. In addition, information about the media and the people they use for information about the category needs to be determined.

Understanding the *business, or marketing*, context in general, and the marketing communications environment in particular, is also important, because these influence what has to be achieved. If the marketing strategy specifies growth through market penetration, then not only will messages need to reflect this goal, but it will also be important to understand how competitors are communicating with the target audience and which media they are using to do this.

Analysis of the *internal* context is undertaken to determine the resource capability with respect to supporting marketing communications. Three principal areas need to be reviewed:

- people resources—that is, whether people, including agencies, with suitable marketing communications skills are available;
- financial resources—that is, how much is available to invest in marketing communications; and
- technological resources—that is, whether the right systems and processes are available to support marketing communications.

The final area to be reviewed is the wider external context. Similar to the areas considered during the strategic analysis, emphasis is placed on the political, economic, societal, ecological, and technological conditions. However, stress needs to be given to the impact on marketing communications. For example, if economic conditions get tough, people have lower levels of disposable income. Sales promotions, promotional offers, and extended credit terms become more attractive in this context.

The context analysis provides the rationale for the rest of the plan. It is from the context analysis that the marketing objectives (from the marketing plan) and the marketing communications objectives are derived. The type, form, and style of the message are rooted in the characteristics of the target audience, and the media selected to convey messages should be based on the nature of the tasks, the media preferences and habits of the audience, and the resources available.

Marketing Communications Objectives

Having performed a context analysis, the next step is to define marketing communication objectives. Ideally, marketing communications objectives should consist of three main elements: corporate, marketing, and communications objectives:

- *Corporate* objectives are derived from the business or marketing plan. They refer to the mission and the business area that the organization believes it should be in.

- *Marketing* objectives are derived from the marketing plan and are sales-oriented. These might be market share, sales revenues, volumes, return on investment (ROI), and other profitability indicators.
- *Communications* objectives are derived from the context analysis, and refer to levels of awareness, perception, comprehension/knowledge, attitudes, and overall degree of preference for a brand. The choice of communications goal depends on the tasks that need to be accomplished.

These three elements constitute the overall set of marketing communications objectives. They should be set out in **SMART** terminology—that is, each should be Specific, Measurable, Achievable, Realistic, and Timed.

Marketing Communications Strategy

The marketing communications strategy is derived from the objectives and context analysis. There are three types of strategy: pull, for the end-user markets; push, for the trade and channel intermediaries; and profile, designed to reach all significant stakeholders.

A traditional *pull* strategy in the grocery sector used to be based on delivering mass media advertising supported by below-the-line communications—most notably, sales promotions delivered in-store and through direct mail and email to registered customers (such as Tesco Clubcard customers). The decision to use a pull strategy should be supported by a core message that will try to differentiate (position), remind or reassure, inform, or persuade the audience to think, feel, or behave in a particular way.

A *push* strategy, targeting trade buyers, should be treated in a similar way. Profile strategies are aimed at stakeholders (e.g. government employees). The need to consider the core message is paramount because it conveys information about the essence of the strategy.

Although these three strategies are represented here as individual entities, they are often used as a 'cluster'. For example, the launch of a new toothpaste brand will involve a push strategy to get the product on the shelves of the key supermarkets and independent retailers. The strategy would focus on gaining retailer acceptance of the new brand and positioning it for them as a profitable new brand. To achieve this, personal selling supported by trade sales promotions will be the main marketing communications tools. But a push strategy alone would be insufficient to persuade a retailer to stock a new brand; rather, the promise of a pull strategy aimed at creating brand awareness and customer excitement also needs to be created, accompanied by appropriate PR activities and any initial sales promotions necessary to motivate consumers to change their brand of toothpaste. The next step is therefore to create particular brand associations and thereby position the brand in the minds of the target consumer audience. Messages may be primarily informational or emotional, but will endeavour to convey a brand promise. This may be accompanied or followed by the use of incentives to encourage consumers to trial the product. To support the brand, carelines and a website, as well as a buyer reference point, will need to be put in place to provide credibility.

Communications Method

The communications method part of the plan is relatively complex and a number of activities need to be accomplished. For each specified target audience in the strategy, a creative or message needs to be developed. This should be based on the positioning requirements and will often be developed by an outside communications agency. Simultaneously, it is necessary to formulate the right

The market for toothpaste is crowded and competitive: a push strategy is necessary to grab customers' attention.
Source: © defotoberg/Shutterstock.

mix of communication tools to reach each particular audience. In addition, the right media mix needs to be determined, for both online and other delivery routes. Again, media experts will most probably undertake this task. Here, integration is regarded as an important feature of the communication mix. This is covered more in detail in the next chapter.

The Schedule

The next step is to schedule the way in which the campaign is to be delivered. Events and activities should be scheduled according to the goals and the strategic thrust. So, if it is necessary to communicate with the trade prior to a public launch, those activities tied into the push strategy should be scheduled prior to those calculated to support the pull strategy. Similarly, if awareness is a goal, then, funds permitting, it may be best first to use television and poster advertising offline plus banners and search engine advertising online, before using sales promotions (unless sampling is used), direct marketing, point-of-purchase, and personal selling.

Resources

The resources necessary to support the plan need to be determined. These refer not only to the financial issues, but also to the quality of available marketing expertise. This means that, internally, the right sort of marketing knowledge may not be present and may have to be recruited. For example, if a customer relationship management (CRM) system initiative is being launched, it will be important to have people with knowledge and skills related to running CRM programmes.

Control and Evaluation

Once launched, campaigns should be monitored. This is to ensure that, should there be any major deviance from the plan, opportunities exist to get back on track as soon as possible. In addition, all marketing communications plans should be evaluated. There are numerous methods of evaluating the individual performance of the tools and the media used, but perhaps the most important measures concern the achievement of the communication objectives.

Feedback

The marketing communications planning process is completed when feedback is provided. Not only should information regarding the overall outcome of a campaign be considered, but so too should individual aspects of the activity. For example, the performance of the individual tools used within the campaign, whether sufficient resources were invested, the appropriateness of the strategy in the first place, whether any problems had been encountered during implementation, and the relative ease with which the objectives were accomplished are aspects that need to be fed back to all internal and external parties associated with the planning process.

Chapter Summary

To consolidate your learning, the key points from this chapter are summarized below.

- **Describe the nature, purpose, and scope of marketing communications.**

  Marketing communications is a management process through which an organization attempts to engage with its various audiences. Marketing communications, or 'promotion' as it was originally called, is one of the 'P's of the marketing mix. It is used to communicate an organization's offer relating to products, services, or the overall organization. In broad terms, this management activity consists of several components. There are the communications experienced by audiences relating to both their use of products and their consumption of services. There are also communications arising from unplanned or unintended experiences, and there are planned marketing communications.

- **Explain the three models of communication.**

  The linear, or one-way, model of communication is the traditional mass media interpretation of how communication works. The two-way model incorporates the influence of other people in the communication process, whereas the interactional model explains how communication flows not only between sender and receiver, but also throughout a network of people. Interaction is about actions that lead to a response and—most importantly, in an age of interactive communication—interactivity is a prelude to dialogue, the highest or purest form of communication.

- **Understand the models used to explain how marketing communications and advertising work.**
  These models have evolved from sequential approaches such as AIDA (Awareness, Interest, Desire, and Action) and the hierarchy of effects (HoE) models. A circular model of the attitude construct helps us to understand the tasks of marketing communication—namely, to inform audiences, to create feelings and a value associated with offerings, and to drive behaviour.
- **Understand the role of marketing communications in marketing.**
  The role of marketing communications is to engage audiences and there are four main tasks that it can be used to complete. These tasks are summarized as 'DRIP', that is, to Differentiate, Reinforce, Inform, or Persuade audiences to behave in particular ways. Several of these tasks can be undertaken simultaneously within a campaign.
- **Describe the different steps in the strategic marketing communications planning process.**
  Management's task is to formulate and implement a communication strategy that blends the right mix of tools and media to deliver the right messages in the right place, at the right time, for the right audience. The marketing communications planning framework (MCPF) identifies the following key steps in this process: context analysis; marketing communications objectives; marketing communications strategy; communications method; scheduling; resources; control and evaluation; and feedback.

Review Questions

1. What role does marketing communication ('promotion') play in the marketing mix?
2. What is the linear model of communication? Describe each of its main elements.
3. Make brief notes outlining the meaning of interaction and how dialogue can develop.
4. What is a hierarchy of effects (HoE) model?
5. What are the strong and weak theories of advertising?
6. Why is the circular interpretation of the attitude construct better than the linear form?
7. Explain the key role of marketing communications and find examples to illustrate the meaning of each element in the DRIP framework.
8. What is the relation between corporate objectives, marketing objectives, and communications objectives?
9. Define a marketing communications plan and describe its main components.

Worksheet Summary

To apply the knowledge you have gained from this chapter and test your understanding of marketing communications, visit the **online resources** and complete Worksheet 8.1.

Discussion Questions

1 Having read Case Insight 8.1, how would you advise the marketing team at *The Guardian* to use marketing communications to change perceptions and behaviour of progressive newspaper readers?

2 Consider the key market exchange characteristics that will favour the use of linear or one-way communication and then repeat the exercise with respect to interactional communication. Discuss the differences and find examples to illustrate these conditions.

3 Day Birger et Mikkelsen is a leading Danish fashion retailer, providing a range of fashion clothing for young people aged 18–35. As a marketing assistant, you have just returned from a conference at which the role of personal influencers was highlighted. You now wish to convey your new knowledge to your manager. Prepare a brief report in which you explain the nature of opinion leaders and opinion formers, as well as consumer word-of-mouth in general, and discuss how Day Birger et Mikkelsen might use them to improve its marketing communications. Using at least three examples, make it clear who you think would make good opinion formers for Day Birger et Mikkelsen.

4 Discuss the extent to which organizations should use marketing communications to persuade audiences to buy their offerings.

Visit the **online resources** and complete the multiple-choice questions to assess your knowledge of the chapter.

Glossary

AIDA a hierarchy of effects, or sequential, model used to explain how advertising works, as an acronym of Awareness, Interest, Desire, and Action (to create a sale).

ATR a framework developed by Ehrenberg (1974) to explain how advertising works, as an acronym of Awareness–Trial–Reinforcement.

decoding that part of the communication process during which receivers unpack the various components of the message and begin to make sense of and give the message meaning.

dialogue the development of knowledge that occurs when all parties to a communication event listen, adapt, and reason with one another about a specific topic.

DRIP an acronym of the four primary tasks marketing communications can be expected to accomplish—that is, Differentiate, Reinforce, Inform, and Persuade.

encoding a part of the communication process during which the sender selects a combination of appropriate words, pictures, symbols, and music to represent a message to be transmitted.

feedback a part of the communication process referring to the responses offered by receivers.

hierarchy of effects (HoE) a type of general sequential model used to explain how advertising works. Popular in the 1960s–1980s, these models provided a template that encouraged the development and use of communication objectives.

interaction model the flow of communication messages that leads to mutual understanding about a specific topic.

noise influences that distort information in the communication process, which, in turn, make it difficult for the receiver to decode and interpret a message correctly.

opinion formers people who exert personal influence because of their profession, authority, education, or status associated with the object of the communication process. They are not part of the same peer group as the people whom they influence.

opinion leaders people who are predisposed to receiving information and then reprocessing it to influence others. They belong to the same peer group as the people whom they influence; they are not distant or removed.

personal selling the use of interpersonal communications with the aim of encouraging people to purchase particular products and services, for personal gain and reward.

product class a broad category referring to various types of related product, for example cat food, shampoo, or cars.

receiver an individual or organization who has seen, heard, smelt, or read a message.

SMART an approach used to write effective objectives, as an acronym of Specific, Measurable, Achievable, Realistic, and Timed.

strong theory a persuasion-based theory designed to explain how advertising works.

two-step model a communication model that reflects a receiver's response to a message.

weak theory a view that suggests advertising works only by reminding people of preferred brands.

word-of-mouth a form of communication founded on interpersonal messages regarding products or services sought or consumed. Receivers regard word-of-mouth communicators as impartial and credible, because they are not attempting to sell products or services.

References

Anon. (2014) 'Carambar: The countrywide joke', *Creative Review*, 34(5): 44.

Ballantyne, D. (2004) 'Dialogue and its role in the development of relationship-specific knowledge', *Journal of Business and Industrial Marketing*, 19(2): 114–23.

Berkman, H., and Gilson, C. (1986) *Consumer Behavior: Concepts and Strategies*, Boston, MA: Kent.

Duncan, T., and Moriarty, S. (1998) 'A communication-based marketing model for managing relationships', *Journal of Marketing*, 62(2): 1–13.

Ehrenberg, A. S. C. (1974) 'Repetitive advertising and the consumer', *Journal of Advertising Research*, 14(3): 25–34.

Ehrenberg, A. S. C. (1997) 'How do consumers come to buy a new brand?' *Admap*, March, 20–4.

Fill, C. (2002) *Marketing Communications: Contexts, Strategies and Applications* (3rd edn), Harlow: FT/Prentice Hall.

Fill, C. (2013) *Marketing Communications: Brands, Experiences and Participation* (6th edn), Harlow: FT/Prentice Hall.

Gilliland, D. I., and Johnston, W. J. (1997) 'Toward a model of business-to-business marketing communications effects', *Industrial Marketing Management*, 26(1): 15–29.

Hughes, G., and Fill, C. (2007) 'Redefining the nature and format of the marketing communications mix', *Marketing Review*, 7(1): 45–57.

Jones, J. P. (1991) 'Over-promise and under-delivery', *Marketing and Research Today*, 19(40): 195–203.

Keller, E., and Fay, B. (2012) 'Word-of-mouth advocacy: A new key to advertising effectiveness', *Journal of Advertising Research*, 52(4): 459–64.

Kosoff, M., and Jacobs. H. (2015) 'The 15 most popular YouTubers in the world', *Business Insider*, 18 September. Available online at http://uk.businessinsider.com/the-most-popular-youtuber-stars-in-the-world?r=US&IR=T [accessed 24 January 2016].

Lavidge, R. J., and Steiner, G. A. (1961) 'A model for predictive measurements of advertising effectiveness', *Journal of Marketing*, 25(6): 59–62.

Manika, D., Gregory-Smith D., Wells, V., Comerford, L., and Aldrich-Smith, L. (2016) 'Linking environmental sustainability and healthcare: Exploring the effects of an energy saving intervention in two hospitals', Working paper on file with the author.

Moses, L. (2011) 'Vogue casts 1,000 "influencers" for network', *Adweek*, 11 July. Available online at http://www.adweek.com/news/advertising-branding/vogue-casts-1000-influencers-network-133299 [accessed 1 January 2017].

Rosengren, L. (2012) 'Han hoppade av Chalmers: blev heltidskändis på Youtube', IDG.se, 19 November. Available online at http://cio.idg.se/2.1782/1.477094/han-hoppade-av-chalmers---blev-heltidskandis-pa-youtube [accessed 24 January 2016].

Schramm, W. (1955) 'How communication works', in W. Schramm (ed.) *The Process and Effects of Mass Communications*, Urbana, IL: University of Illinois Press, 3–26.

Shannon, C., and Weaver, W. (1962) *The Mathematical Theory of Communication*, Urbana, IL: University of Illinois Press.

Stokes, D., and Lomax, W. (2002) 'Taking control of word-of-mouth marketing: The case of an entrepreneurial hotelier', *Journal of Small Business and Enterprise Development*, 9(4): 349–57.

Strong, E. K. (1925) *The Psychology of Selling*, New York: McGraw-Hill.

Tamburro, P. (2014) 'PewDiePie's $7.4 million salary actually highlights YouTube's low wages', *Crave Online*, 8 July. Available online at http://www.craveonline.com/site/875679-pewdiepies-7-4-million-salary-actually-highlights-youtubes-low-wages#aMwrUeZ4WY2Cv86K.99 [accessed 24 January 2016].

Theodorson, S. A., and Theodorson, G. R. (1969) *A Modern Dictionary of Sociology*, New York: Cromwell.

Chapter 9
Managing Marketing Communications

Learning Outcomes

After studying this chapter, you will be able to:

- describe the role and configuration of the marketing communications mix;
- explain the characteristics of each of the primary tools, media, and messages;
- set out the criteria that should be used to select the right communication mix; and
- consider the principles and issues associated with integrated marketing communications.

Case Insight 9.1
Budweiser Budvar

Market Insight 9.1
Variable Mixes

Market Insight 9.2
Sustainability Communications and 'Greenwashing'

Market Insight 9.3
Damart Modernizes Its Welcome Programme

Market Insight 9.4
Do it for Denmark!

Market Insight 9.5
A New Integrated Mix for Soberana

Case Insight 9.1 **Budweiser Budvar**

How should a heritage brand in the Czech Republic design a campaign to reposition itself against competing foreign brands? We speak to Lubos Jahoda (pictured), account director of Budweiser Budvar's advertising agency, to find out more.

Budweiser Budvar has a 750-year tradition of brewing beer in the Czech Republic. Although there has been a long-running dispute with other brewers who use the same Budweiser name, one of the current issues facing the Budvar brand concerns the decline in the overall size of the Czech beer market. Since 2009, there has been a shift towards small, authentic local breweries. This is because Czechs believe the multinationals (SAB Miller, Heineken, Molson Coors) have destroyed the essence of Czech beer by using inferior ingredients and making what is called 'EuroBeer', a universal beer that has no clear distinguishing taste or character. The big breweries have been trying to resolve the situation through innovation, from which we now see loads of radler beer-flavoured drinks on the market.

Surprisingly, many customers saw Budvar as a 'big brewery team' and similar to the big breweries. We have also seen consumers move from away from Budvar towards small, local breweries. But, as everyone who has ever visited the brewery knows, Budvar is more authentic than the smallest of breweries, using the same ingredients and production processes as used 118 years ago. Another problem concerns the way in which the brand was perceived. Budvar is seen as a very rational beer, a quality beer, or 'Czech beer', but there is little emotional connection with the brand.

It was clear that we needed to reposition the Budvar brand, to differentiate it and enable Czech consumers to make an emotional connection with the brand. The question was how best to achieve this.

Research has shown that Czech people are generally more inclined to adopt a line of least resistance to avoid problems and that means agreeing, or saying 'yes'. However, many Czech people deeply resent such concessions and do not identify themselves with these types of compromise. This issue of dissent provided us with a pertinent platform on which to reposition the brand. This is because Budvar has repeatedly rejected various pressures. For example, we have refused to dumb down or use substitute ingredients. Budvar has also rejected the idea that we should reduce the maturing time during the brewing process. We have also refused outright to sell our brand name to our competitors and have also said no to licensing production away from České Budějovice (Budweis).

From this insight, we developed the 'No' campaign—one that is rooted in the Czech psyche, Budvar's foundations, and one that can be seen in everything Budvar does, from just 'making beer', to fighting for its name and reputation across the world. The campaign had two main aims: first, at a product level, it aimed to build the image of Budvar as a quality beer and one not associated with the multinational brewers; and second, at a brand level, it aimed to build a strong emotional link towards consumers.

The question was: how should Budwar develop this 'No' campaign? How should it interpret and communicate the 'No' message without being negative? Obviously, advertising was going to play a central role, but which other disciplines should Budwar use? Which mix of media would be best at delivering the 'No' campaign to realize the greatest impact?

Introduction

Organizations use a variety of tools, media, and messages to engage their audiences. Collectively, these are referred to as the **marketing communications mix**: a set of tools, a variety of media, and messages that can be used in various combinations, and with different degrees of intensity, to communicate successfully with target audiences.

The five principal marketing communications tools are **advertising**, **sales promotion**, **public relations (PR)**, **direct marketing**, and **personal selling**. In addition, the media are used primarily, but not exclusively, to deliver advertising messages to target audiences. Although 'media' refers to any mechanism or device that can carry a message, we refer to paid-for media, processes, and systems that are owned by third parties, such as the News Corporation, which owns *The Sun* and *Sunday Times* newspapers plus the BSkyB television platform, Condé Nast, which owns *Tatler*, *Vanity Fair*, and *Vogue* magazines, among others, Singapore Press Holdings, which owns the *Business Times* in Singapore, and Time Warner Inc., which is a leading media and entertainment company, whose businesses include interactive services, cable systems, filmed entertainment, TV networks and publishing. These organizations rent out time and space to client organizations, so that they can deliver their messages to, and make content available to engage, various audiences. The list of available paid-for media is expanding, but it is possible to identify six key classes of media: broadcast, print, outdoor, in-store, digital, and other (which includes both cinema and ambient media). All of these are explored in this chapter.

On completing this chapter, you should understand the main characteristics associated with the principal tools, messages, and media that make up the mix. You should also appreciate that, by reconfiguring the mix, it is possible to achieve different goals. Finally, the chapter should make it clear that an integrated approach to marketing communications can deliver a more efficient and effective outcome.

The Role of the Marketing Communications Mix

The marketing communication mix consists of five main tools, four forms of message or content, and three types of medium. These are depicted in Figure 9.1 and each is explored later in this chapter.

Traditionally, organizations have been able to use a fairly predictable and stable range of tools and media. Advertising was used to build awareness and brand values, sales promotions were used to stimulate demand, PR conveyed goodwill messages about organizations, and personal selling was seen as a means of getting orders, particularly in the business-to-business (B2B) market. There have, however, been some major changes in the environment and in the way in which organizations communicate with their target audiences. Digital technology has given rise to a raft of different media and opportunities for advertisers to reach their audiences. We now have access to hundreds of commercial television and radio channels. Cinemas show multiple films at multiplex sites, and the Internet has transformed the way in which we communicate, educate, inform, and entertain ourselves.

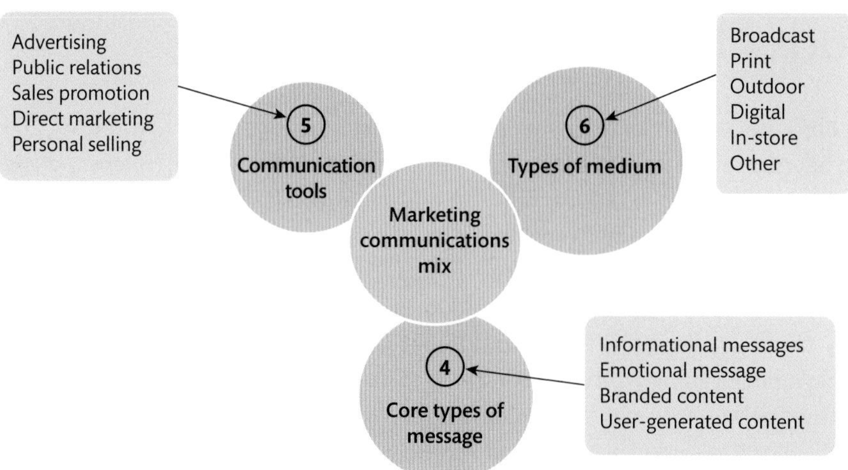

Figure 9.1 The elements of the marketing communications mix

This expansion of the media is referred to as **media fragmentation**. At the same time, people have developed a whole host of new ways in which to spend their leisure time; they are no longer restricted to a few media. This expansion of an audience's choice of media is referred to as **audience fragmentation**. So, although the range and type of media have expanded, the size of audiences that each medium commands has generally shrunk.

The development of the Internet has created new opportunities to engage consumers at different points in their day and at different stages in their purchase decision-making journeys. Many organizations have found that the principles through which particular tools work offline do not necessarily apply in an interactive environment.

For organizations, one of the key challenges is to find the right mix of tools, messages, and media that will enable them to reach and engage with their target audiences effectively and economically. To do this, they have had to revise and redevelop their marketing communications mixes. For example, in the 1990s, there was a dramatic rise in the use of **direct-response media** when direct marketing emerged as a new and powerful tool. Now, the Internet and digital technologies have enabled new interactive forms of communication in which receivers have far greater responsibility for their part in the communication process and are encouraged to interact with the sender. As a result of these changes, many organizations are reducing their investment in traditional media and investing instead in digital media (see Chapter 11).

Visit the **online resources** and complete Internet Activity 9.1 to learn more about how Toyota uses an interactive website to inform its target audience about a complex proposition, the Hybrid Synergy Drive.

This has shifted the role of the media. Previously, the emphasis of a mix was to enable and persuade customers to buy products and services, in the short term. Today, although a short-term focus still prevails for many firms, goals such as developing understanding and preference, reminding and reassuring customers, and building brand value have now come to be accepted as

Market Insight 9.1 **Variable Mixes**

Benadryl

Hay fever suffers can be affected by different types of grass and tree pollen, at virtually any time of the year. The unpredictability of pollen counts led market-leading brand Benadryl to raise its brand profile within the allergy market, by means of The BENADRYL® Social Pollen Count.

The tool involved the use of Benadryl's own interactive map and the **sponsorship** of part of the Met Office site. The goal was to help sufferers to fight hay fever. Using daily updates of official Met Office data and encouraging hay fever sufferers to report local pollen levels, Benadryl was able to show other sufferers across the UK what the pollen count was in different areas. It was also able to direct people to nearby stockists of the BENADRYL® product range.

Benadryl engaged in a communications campaign aimed at building a map of the levels of pollen: very valuable information for its customers.

Source: Courtesy of Johnson and Johnson.

The LEGO Movie

To celebrate the release of *The LEGO Movie*, an entire television advert break made of LEGO® was broadcast in February 2014, during *Dancing on Ice*. Four recent UK television adverts—for British Heart Foundation, Confused.com, BT, and Premier Inn—were all recreated, frame by frame and brick by brick, using LEGO®.

People were helped to connect to *The LEGO Movie* (not only LEGO®) because the adverts were separated by five different 2-second 'stings'. These featured characters from the movie and *The LEGO Movie* logo. The break ended with a 40-second trailer for *The LEGO Movie*. The entire break was also simultaneously released in full on YouTube to ensure that those who missed the advert could see it and catch up with the social media conversation. The advert was never screened again on television, but was used in cinemas before screenings of *The Lego Movie*.

Volvo Trucks

To drive perceptions and awareness of the launch of a new range of heavy-duty Volvo trucks, a **viral marketing** campaign featuring a series of live test videos was produced. Each showcased different new technical aspects, such as their stability (with a tightrope walker), and reliability and strength of the front towing hooks (hoisting a truck 20 metres above the water in Gothenburg harbour, with the president of Volvo Trucks standing on its front panel). Others included a video demonstrating the ground clearance (by driving 'over' one of Volvo's technicians, buried up to his neck in sand), and a truck manoeuvring through tight streets in Pamplona in Spain, chased by furious bulls, to demonstrate agility and speed.

The final video featured actor Jean-Claude Van Damme performing a spectacular splits, balanced on the wing mirrors of two reversing Volvo FM trucks. This showcased the precision of the dynamic steering, enabling the truck drivers to maintain the exact same distance apart and speed while travelling in reverse.

The videos were posted on YouTube and Facebook channels, whilst the use of PR and tailored press information made sure that they were distributed online to the news media and bloggers to amplify the story.

1. **Describe the key elements of the message in each of these campaigns.**
2. **How do the media used for these campaigns enable messages to reach target audiences?**
3. **Which of these three campaigns impresses you most? Why?**

Source: Carter (2014); Ridley (2014); Anon. (2015a); http://www.benadryl.co.uk/social-pollen-count; http://www.metoffice.gov.uk/health/public/pollen-forecast.

important aspects of marketing communications. This longer-term brand-building perspective has been shown by Binet and Field (2013) to be a more profitable approach than a short-term direct-response focus on sales.

Selecting the Right Tools

The principal or primary tools referred to above subsume other tools such as **brand placement**, sponsorship, and **exhibitions**. Although the tools can be seen as independent entities, each with its own skills and attributes, a truly effective mix works when the tools complement each other and work as an interacting unit.

Advertising

Richards and Curran (2002: 74) advanced a definition of 'advertising' as 'a paid, mediated form of communication from an identifiable source, designed to persuade the receiver to take some action, now or in the future'.

Dahlen and Rosengren (2016) have identified three particular dynamics that they believe need to be incorporated within any contemporary definition of advertising: (new) media and formats; (new) 'consumer' behaviours related to advertising; and the extended effects of advertising.

Sales Promotion

Sales promotions offer a direct inducement or an incentive to encourage customers to buy an offering. These inducements can be targeted at consumers, distributors, agents, and members of the sales force. Sales promotions are concerned with offering customers additional value, to induce an immediate sale. These sales might well have taken place without the presence of an incentive, but the inducement brings the time of the sale forward. The key forms of sales promotion are

Research Insight 9.1

To take your learning further, you might wish to read this influential paper.

Dahlen, M., and Rosengren, S. (2016) 'If advertising won't die, what will it be? Towards a new definition of advertising', *Journal of Advertising*, 45(3): 334–45.

This paper provides a timely and interesting consideration of the way in which advertising has been, and should be, defined within an academic context. Taking into account a range of issues and developments, the authors propose a new definition that they believe is a better fit for purpose.

 **Visit the online resources to read the abstract and access the full paper.**

sampling, coupons, deals, premiums, contests and sweepstakes, and (in the trade) various forms of allowance.

Public Relations

Public relations is used to influence the way in which an organization is perceived by various groups of stakeholders, such as employees, the public, supplier organizations, and the media. Public relations does not require the purchase of airtime or space in media vehicles, such as television magazines or online. These types of message are low cost and are perceived to be extremely credible. It attempts to integrate its own policies with the interests of stakeholders, and formulates and executes a programme of action to develop mutual goodwill and understanding.

Different types of PR can be identified, but the main approach is referred to as 'media relations', and consists of press releases, conferences, and events. Other forms of PR include lobbying, investor relations, and corporate advertising. Two further activities, sponsorship and **crisis communications**, are discussed in brief later in this chapter. Through the use of PR, relationships can be developed that, in the long run, are considered to be in the interests of all parties.

Direct Marketing

The primary role of direct marketing is to drive a response and shape the behaviour of the target audience with regard to a brand. This is achieved by sending personalized and customized messages, often requesting a 'call to action', designed to provoke a change in the audience's behaviour.

Direct marketing is used to create and sustain a personal and intermediary-free communication with customers, potential customers, and other significant stakeholders. In most cases, this is a media-based activity, and offers great scope for the collection and utilization of pertinent and measurable data. Some of the principal techniques are direct mail, telemarketing, email, and, increasingly, Internet-based communications, such as searches. One of the key benefits of direct marketing is that there is limited communication wastage. The precision associated with target marketing means that messages are sent to, received by, processed by, and responded to by members of the target audience and no others. This is unlike advertising, whereby messages often reach some people who are not targets and are unlikely to be involved with the brand.

Visit the **online resources** and follow the web links to the Federation of European Direct and Interactive Marketing Association (FEDMA) and the Institute of Promotional Marketing (IPM) to learn more about the communication tools of direct marketing and sales promotions.

Personal Selling

Personal selling involves interpersonal communication through which information is provided, positive feelings developed, and behaviour stimulated. Personal selling is an activity undertaken by an individual representing an organization, or collectively in the form of a sales force. It is a highly potent form of communication simply because messages can be adapted to meet the requirements of both parties. Objections can be overcome, information can be provided in the context of

Table 9.1 The relative strength of the tools of the marketing communication mix

Level of	Advertising	Sales promotion	Public relations	Direct marketing	Personal selling
Control	Medium	High	Low	High	Medium
Cost	High	Medium	Low	Medium	High
Credibility	Low	Medium	High	Medium	Medium
Dispersion					
Consumer audiences	Low	Medium	High	High	Medium
B2B audiences	Medium	High	High	Medium	High
Primary DRIP tasks	Differentiating Informing	Persuading	Differentiating Informing	Persuading Reinforcing	Persuading

Source: Adapted from Fill (2013). Used with permission.

the buyer's environment, and the conviction and power of demonstration can be brought to the buyer when requested.

Table 9.1 provides a summary of the relative strengths of each of the tools in terms of a number of important criteria. It also considers how each tool delivers on each of the DRIP tasks (see Chapter 8). Although depicted individually, the elements of the mix should be regarded as a set of complementary instruments.

Marketing Communications Messages

Our consideration of communication theory at which we looked in Chapter 8 confirms the importance of sending the right message—that is, one that can be understood and responded to in context. We can identify four main forms of message content that are not independent entities: informational, emotional, user-generated, and **branded content**.

Informational Messages

Messages can be categorized as either proposition-oriented and rational or customer-oriented and based on feelings and emotions. As a general, but not universal, guideline, when audiences experience high involvement (see Chapter 2), the emphasis of a message should be on the information content, emphasizing the key attributes and the associated benefits. For example, advertising campaigns for charities (such as Greenpeace or Oxfam), financial services (such as Allianz, Banco do Brasil, Aviva), or weight loss and supplements (such as Weightwatchers and Holland & Barrett), and government campaigns for health, tax, and other state services normally make a statement about the product ingredients, then deliver a rational reason why the receiver should behave in a particular way.

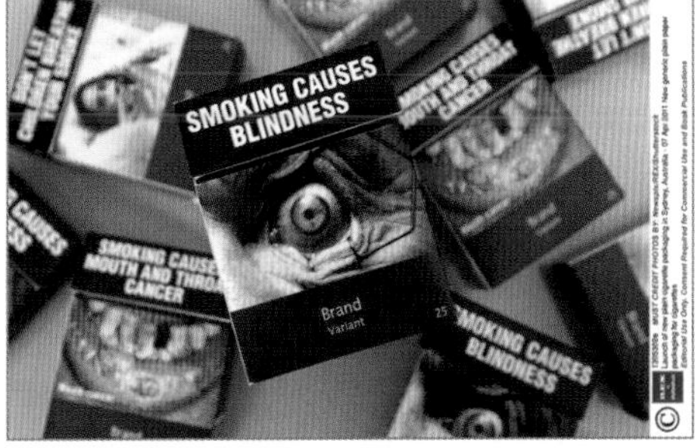

Tobacco packaging using informational, shock-based images to deter users.

Source: © Newspix/REX/Shutterstock.

Emotional Messages

When audiences experience low involvement, then messages should attempt to gain an emotional response. For example, adverts for fashion, cosmetics, fast food, and soft drinks often engage audiences through the use of fear, humour, animation, and storytelling. The use of celebrity endorsers and peer-to-peer word-of-mouth can also amplify these messages.

There are of course, many products and services in relation to which both rational and emotional messages are needed by buyers to make purchasing decisions. These include cars, smartphones, dentistry, energy suppliers, and apps, to name only a few.

Visit the **online resources** and complete Internet Activity 9.2 to learn more about how Bacardi uses product demonstration and a digital media format (.mp3) to inform target audiences how to make a Bacardi mojito.

A common strategy for advertisers is to generate an emotional response that can have a positive influence on brand perception.

Source: © Getty / Richard Levine / Contributor.

User-Generated Content

The development of social media has enabled individuals to communicate with organizations, communities, friends and family. The content of the message can be about brands, experiences, or events, and is developed and shared by individuals. This is referred to as **user-generated content (UGC)** and can be seen in action, for example, at YouTube, Snapchat, Flickr, and Twitter. Kaplan and Haenlein (2010) consider UGC to comprise all of the ways in which people make use of social media, and to refer to the various forms of media content that are publicly available and created by end-users.

There are three main elements that can be used to identify the presence of UGC. The first is that the content needs to be freely accessible to the public. This means that it should be published either on an open website or on a social networking site accessible to a selected group of people. Second, the material needs to demonstrate creativity and, third, it should be amateur in nature, in the sense that it has not been created by an agency or professional organization.

Although there have been instances of commercial involvement in UGC, the very nature of this type of content takes the communication initiative away from organizations. As a result, marketers are listening to and observing consumers through UGC. Through this approach, many are finding out the different meanings that consumers attribute to brands, helping in brand development and helping organizations to reposition brands.

However, UGC can work against an organization's best interests. Following a dramatic fall in the value of an Australian taxi licence, after the arrival of peer-to-peer models such as Uber, the Victorian Taxi Association launched a social media campaign aiming to rally customers to support their local cab drivers and to share their positive experiences of riding in a taxi—only for the #yourtaxis hashtag to motivate thousands of seething users to unleash their feelings about poor service and dubious driving. Customers swamped Twitter with stories of overcharging, sexual perversion, and personal sanitary issues, as well as drivers' inability to get from A to B (Ritson, 2015).

Market Insight 9.2 **Sustainability Communications and 'Greenwashing'**

'Greenwashing' is a form of deceptive communication that occurs when an organization purports to have green or environmentally friendly products or policies even when this is not the case. Researchers have found a tenfold increase over the last ten years in new products and services that make environmental, ecological, or 'green' claims. At the same time, however, independent assessments suggest that 95 per cent of these claims are either false or dubious. The tip of the iceberg is the massive emissions scandal that engulfed Volkswagen (VW), one of the largest car manufacturers in the world, in 2015 when it was found that the company had installed devices that would cheat emissions control tests for diesel engines. The ultimate costs of ongoing prosecutions in different jurisdictions arising from the scandal is likely to cost the German company tens of billions of dollars in penalties.

While VW has admitted breaching specific emissions regulations, in many cases greenwashing claims are difficult to challenge, because they are vague. Consumers, however, are increasingly sceptical of unsubstantiated claims and non-governmental organizations (NGOs) work constantly to hold

Market Insight 9.2 (continued)

corporations accountable. Kimberly-Clark, maker of disposable nappies brand Huggies, faced a lawsuit in the United States at the hands of disgruntled customers who claimed to have been misled by the product line called 'Pure and Natural'. The customers argued that the nappies (in the United States, 'diapers') were neither pure nor natural, containing harmful chemicals that contradicted the stated product promise.

Ultimately, greenwashing can be costly for both companies and society. Corporations are at risk of consumer backlash if they are exposed when communicating incorrect information. At the same time, consumer trust is eroded by thousands of unsubstantiated or vague claims made by companies in different industries. Experts suggest that stricter regulation is required to ensure that the claims made by companies are closer to the truth. However, policing is only part of the answer and companies need to take responsibility for more transparent internal processes that ultimately lead to a reduction in false claims delivered to the public. The good news is that a recent content analysis of green advertising claims has found a marked improvement on the results of earlier similar investigations into the quality of the messages delivered: around 60 per cent of the claims were considered trustworthy and reliable.

After installing 'cheat devices' in their diesel cars, the VW brand is no longer squeaky clean.

Source: © villorejo/Shutterstock.

1. **Why do companies engage in greenwashing?**
2. **How can consumers check whether environmental claims are truthful?**
3. **How can companies ensure they do not commit greenwashing?**

Sources: Gelles (2015); Kleinman (2016); Segev et al. (2016).

Research Insight 9.2

To take your learning further, you might wish to read this influential paper.

Dahl, D. W., Frankenberger, K. D., and Manchanda, R. V. (2003) 'Does it pay to shock? Reactions to shocking and non-shocking advertising content among university students', *Journal of Advertising Research*, 43(3): 268–81.

This classic paper examines the effectiveness of shock advertising in comparison to fear and information appeals. The authors find that shocking content in an advertisement significantly increases attention, benefits memory, and positively influences behaviour. The literature review and consideration of different types of appeal is helpful.

 Visit the **online resources** to read the abstract and access the full paper.

Branded Content

Branded content is the use of entertainment material delivered through paid or owned media, featuring a single company or brand. The recent growth in branded content rests with a drive to realize the potential that 'owned' media offers. Branded content enables conversations, particularly in social media, serving to raise a brand's profile and its credibility. One of the earlier forms of branded content is customer publishing. Under this model, organizations develop magazines with articles and content considered to be of interest to their customers. The magazine includes references to, and even articles and stories about, the sponsoring brand. The development and distribution of these magazines to the brand's customer base is a paid media operation. Today consumers use a variety of platforms and so organizations, or rather their content agencies, need to develop content for use across a wide variety of digital media including social media. This provides an opportunity to integrate material and allow customers to form a coherent or interconnected experience of the brand. The entertainment material is still distributed to customers, but non-customers are also included. Distribution is entirely through media owned by the brand.

The Media

Once a client has decided to use a particular message, decisions need to be made about how and when the message is to be conveyed to engage target audiences. Table 9.2 lists media by classification, type, and vehicle. Some media are owned by a client organization, for example its website or the signage outside a building. These media, however, do not enable messages to reach a very large or targeted audience nor do they allow for specific proposition-oriented messages to be conveyed to particular target audiences. In most circumstances, therefore, client organizations need to use the media owned by others, paying a fee for renting the space and time to convey their messages. The next section considers the terminology and then the role of the media, before we examine digital media and, finally, the principles of direct response media.

The development of digital media has had a profound impact on the way in which client organizations communicate with their audiences. Generally, the trend has been to reduce the amount of traditional media used, and to increase the amount of digital online and mobile media.

Visit the **online resources** and complete Internet Activity 9.3 to learn more about the differing media that was used for Ray-Ban's 'Never Hide' campaign.

An Overview of Each Class of Media

Using the classification presented in Table 9.2, the following section provides a brief description of each class of media.

Broadcast

Advertisers use broadcast media (television and radio) because they can reach mass audiences with their messages at a relatively low cost per target reached. Broadcast media allow advertisers to add visual and/or sound dimensions to their messages. This helps them to demonstrate the benefits of using a particular offering, and can bring life and energy to an advertiser's message.

Table 9.2	Summary classification of the main forms of media	
Class	**Type**	**Vehicles**
Broadcast	Television	*Coronation Street*, *The X Factor*
	Radio	Classic FM, Capital Radio
Print	Newspapers	*The Sunday Times*, *The Mirror*, *The Telegraph*
	Magazines: consumer	*Cosmopolitan*, *Woman*
	Magazines: business	*The Grocer*, *Plumbing News*
Out-of-home (OOH)	Billboards	96-, 48- and 6-sheet
	Street furniture	Adshel
	Transit	Underground stations, airport buildings, taxis, hot-air balloons
Digital media	Internet	Websites, email
	Social media	Facebook, Instragram, Twitter
	Auctions	eBay
	Billboards	Clear Channel
	Apps	Google Play
In-store	Point-of-purchase	Bins, signs, and displays
	Packaging	Coca-Cola's contoured bottle
Other	Cinema	Pearl & Dean, Orange Wednesdays
	Exhibitions and events	Ideal Home, The Motor Show
	Product placement	Films, television, books
	Ambient	Litter bins, golf tees, petrol pumps, washrooms
	Guerrilla	Flyposting

Source: Fill (2013). Used with permission.

Print

Newspapers and magazines are the two main media in the print media class; others include custom magazines and directories. Print is very effective at delivering messages to target audiences because it allows for explanation in a way that most other media cannot. This may be in the form of either a picture or a photograph demonstrating how an offering should be used.

Out-of-Home (OOH)

Out-of-home (OOH), or outdoor, media consist of three main formats: street furniture (such as bus shelters); billboards (which consist primarily of 96-, 48-, and 6-sheet poster sites); and transit (which includes buses, taxis, and the London Underground). The key characteristic associated with OOH media is that they are observed by their target audiences at locations away from home and they are normally used to support messages that are transmitted through primary media—namely, broadcast and print.

Digital

Generally, most traditional media provide one-way communications, in which information passes from a source to a receiver, but there is little opportunity for feedback, let alone interaction. Digital media enables two-way, interactive communication, with information flowing back to the source and again to the receiver, as each participant adapts its message to meet the requirements of its audience. For example, banner ads can provoke a click method by which the receiver is taken to a new website, where the source presents new information and the receiver makes choices, responds to questions (for example registers at the site), and the source again provides fresh information. Indeed, the identity of the source and receiver in this type of communication becomes blurred.

In-Store

There are two main forms of in-store media: point-of-purchase (POP) displays and packaging. Retailers control the former and manufacturers, the latter. The primary objective of using in-store media is to get the attention of shoppers and to stimulate them to make purchases. The content of messages can be controlled easily by both retailers and manufacturers. In addition, the timing and the exact placement of in-store messages can be equally well controlled. There are a number of POP techniques, but the most used are window displays, floor and wall racks in which merchandise can be displayed, and posters and information cards, plus counter and checkout displays. Packaging has to protect and preserve products, but it also has a significant communication role and is a means of influencing brand choice decisions.

Other

Two main media can be identified: cinema and ambient. *Cinema* advertising has all of the advantages of television-based messages, such as high-quality audio and visual dimensions, which combine to provide high impact. However, the vast majority of cinema visitors are people aged 18–35, so if an advertiser wishes to reach different age groups or perhaps a national audience, not only will cinema be inappropriate, but also the costs will be much higher than those for television. *Ambient* media are regarded as OOH media that fail to fit any of the established outdoor categories. Ambient media can be classified according to a variety of factors. These include posters (typically found in washrooms), distribution (for example adverts on tickets and carrier bags), digital media (in the form of video and LCD screens), sponsorships (as in golf holes and petrol pump nozzles), and aerials (in the form of balloons, blimps, or towed banners).

Using Media for Brand Building or Direct Response

For a long time, commercial media have been used to convey messages designed to develop consumers' attitudes and feelings towards brands. This is referred to as an 'attitudinal response' and concerns building a brand over the longer term. Today, many of the messages are designed to provoke audiences into responding, either physically, cognitively, or emotionally. This is referred to as a 'behavioural (direct) response', which concerns activation and is essentially a short-term activity. It therefore follows that attitude and behaviourally oriented communications require different media.

Direct-response media are characterized by the provision of a contact mechanism, such as a telephone number or web address, and increasingly through search activities on the Internet. These mechanisms enable receivers to respond to messages. Direct mail, searches, telemarketing, and door-to-door activities are the main direct-response media, because they allow more personal, direct, and evaluative means of reaching precisely targeted customers. However, in reality, any type

Table 9.3	Direct-response (DR) media formats
Types of DR medium	**Explanation**
Direct mail	Refers to personally addressed advertising delivered through the postal system. Can be personalized and targeted with great accuracy, and results are capable of precise measurement. Can be expensive: between £250 and £500 per 1,000 items dispatched. Should therefore be used selectively and for purposes other than creating awareness.
Telemarketing	Provides interaction, flexibility, immediate feedback, and opportunity to overcome objections, all within the same communication event. Also allows organizations to undertake separate marketing research that is both highly measurable and accountable, in that effectiveness can be verified continuously and call rates, contacts reached, and number and quality of positive and negative responses easily recorded and monitored.
Carelines and contact centres	Enable customers to complain about product performance and related experiences, and to seek product-related advice, make suggestions regarding product or packaging development, and comment about an action or development concerning the brand as a whole.
Inserts	Media materials placed inside magazines or direct mail letters. Provide factual information about product or service and enable recipients to respond to the direct marketer's request to place an order, visit a website, or post back a card for more information, such as a brochure. Popular because they are good at generating leads, even though cost is substantially higher than a four-colour advertisement in magazine in which the insert is carried.
Print	Comprises two main forms: catalogues; and magazines/newspapers. Consumer direct print ads sometimes offer an incentive and are designed explicitly to drive customers to a website, where transactions can be completed without reference to retailers, dealers, or other intermediaries.
Door-to-door	Although content and quality can be controlled in the same way as direct mail, response rates are lower because of lack of a personal address mechanism. Can be much cheaper than direct mail because there are no postage charges.
Radio and television	Television has a much greater potential than radio as a DR mechanism because it can provide a visual dimension. Originally, pricing restrictions limited use of elevision in this context, but now, following deregulation, nearly half of all television ads carry a response mechanism.
Digital media	Digital television, Internet, email, viral marketing, blogging, and social networking sites represent major new forms of interactive and direct marketing opportunities. In particular, Internet searches enable brands to be reached by audiences, who can then be converted into customers.

of media can be used, simply by attaching a telephone number, website address, mailing address, or response card. Table 9.3 sets out the main media used within direct-response marketing.

Direct-response media also allow clients the opportunity to measure the volume, frequency, and value of audience responses. This enables them to determine which direct-response media work best and so helps them become more efficient, as well as effective.

Market Insight 9.3 **Damart Modernizes Its Welcome Programme**

Damart, a French clothing company, operates in the UK, Belgium, Luxembourg, Switzerland, and the United States, and also through partnerships in Australia, Cyprus, and Spain, distributing its products to over 10 million customers worldwide.

Damart UK started to update its direct-response campaigns targeted at new customers owing to a desire to modernize its welcome programme to reflect the changes in recruited customers' preferences. Previously, customers ordering for the first time were entered into an intensive welcome campaign. This involved sending them a catalogue every two weeks for a 26-week period. After this, they would then enter a more traditionally modelled customer mailing plan.

This approach had generated a high level of second orders from customers. Unfortunately, it also brought a high level of customer attrition, with newly recruited customers requesting to be removed from the company's marketing programmes.

It was clear that this method was not appropriate and a new communications approach was needed. So, rather than focus its direct-response campaigns based solely on transactions, Damart developed a new mix to build relationships over the longer term and so realize higher lifetime customer value.

Any fresh approach required a more informed understanding of new customers, which could then be used to reconfigure the communications mix to influence their subsequent orders. For example, if a customer's first order were placed on the web, Damart wanted to know the source of the order: was it prompted by an online advert, a media insert, or an off-the-page magazine advert? Where a new customer could be identified as 'pure web and email', subsequent customer communications would now be channelled through the web via improved personalization in marketing emails.

If a new customer had responded to a heavily discounted offer, analysis could reveal whether a full-price order might be obtained from a main catalogue or if this customer would be likely to have an overall lower lifetime value. If the latter were the case, then Damart could reduce its initial investment in marketing communications.

By driving new customers to order online, Darmart was able to reduce the operational costs associated with processing off-line orders and expose forms of cross-selling not available via mail order. It also meant that it could invest more in web-based activities, including searches.

1 **To what extent does the shift in the balance of the mix represent a brand nearing maturity rather than any other factor? What role might social media play in developing this brand?**

2 **Should organizations such as Damart be concerned about upsetting or irritating a few customers when a campaign successfully drives sales?**

3 **Visit the site of another fashion retailer and consider whether its mix is configured to drive brand response or build brand associations. What is the reasoning behind your judgment?**

Source: Based on the author's own experience.

This market insight was kindly contributed by Leon Savidis, business analyst at Damart.

Other Promotional Methods and Approaches

There are numerous other instruments used by organizations to reach their audiences. These can be regarded as secondary tools that are used to support the primary mix. Some of these other instruments are briefly considered here.

Sponsorship is normally associated with PR, but it has strong associations with advertising. Now considered as an important discipline in its own right, sponsorship can be regarded as 'a commercial activity, whereby one party permits another an opportunity to exploit an association with a target audience in return for funds, services, or resources' (Fill, 2009: 599). Sports, arts, and programme sponsorship are the principal types, designed to generate awareness and brand associations, and to cut through the clutter of commercial messages. Some sponsorship arrangements are being used actively to demonstrate a firm's business credentials. For example, logistics company DHL sponsors the Red Bull Air Race. In addition to the normal exposure and associations, DHL also provides transportation services. So, by moving planes, fuel, and broadcast equipment, the brand is able to demonstrate its functional expertise and tell stories about these activities (Anon., 2015b).

Brand placement is also a form of sponsorship, and represents a relationship between film/television producers and managers of brands. Through this arrangement, brand managers are able, for a fee, to present their brands 'naturally' within a film or entertainment event. Such placement is designed to increase brand awareness, to develop positive brand attitudes, and to potentially lead to purchase activity.

Field marketing is about providing support for the sales force and merchandising personnel. One of the tasks is concerned with getting free samples of a product into the hands of potential customers; another task is to create an interaction between the brand and a new customer; yet another is to create a personal and memorable brand experience for potential customers.

Exhibitions are held for both consumers and business markets. Organizations benefit from meeting their current and potential customers, developing relationships, demonstrating products, building industry-wide credibility, placing and taking orders, generating leads, and gathering market information. For customers, exhibitions enable them to meet new or potential suppliers, find out about new offerings and leading-edge brands, and bring themselves up to date with market developments. In business markets, exhibitions and trade shows can be an integral element of the marketing communications mix.

Viral marketing is a fairly recent development based on the credibility and reach associated with word-of-mouth communications. Porter and Golan (2006: 33) refer to viral marketing in terms of how information is communicated and suggest that it commonly involves the 'unpaid peer-to-peer communication of provocative content originating from an identified sponsor using the Internet to persuade or influence an audience to pass along the content to others'.

Numerous definitions have been proposed, but, according to van der Lans and colleagues (2010), 'viral marketing' concerns the mutual sharing and spread of marketing-relevant information, initially distributed deliberately by marketers to stimulate and capitalize on word-of-mouth behaviours.

Crisis communications have become increasingly necessary as the incidence of crises has increased. This appears to be the result of an increasing number of simple managerial mistakes, incorrect decision-making, technology failures, and uncontrollable events in the external environment. For example, both Talk Talk, a telecoms provider, and AshleyMadison.com, a clandestine dating website, have had to communicate with their stakeholders and try to restore customer and media confidence following the loss of customer data to computer hackers.

Organizations are encouraged to plan for crisis events so that they can respond quickly using planned communications. Using websites, social media, and mobile technologies, managers of an afflicted organization can post up-to-date information quickly; through video and news media, they can attempt to reassure communities by explaining events honestly, by demonstrating concern and sympathizing with any affected groups, before explaining what is being done to rectify the situation.

Market Insight 9.4 **Do it for Denmark!**

Companies can sometimes rely on humorous campaigns to attract consumers' interest. This is the case of Spies Rejser, a Danish travel agency, which, in 2014, launched a bold advertising campaign to promote European city breaks as a way in which to address Denmark's declining birth rate. The country has an average of 1.7 children for each couple, which is below replacement levels. The advert uses scientific data to claim that people are more likely to conceive when on holiday and offers tips to improve young couples' ability to become pregnant in the name of patriotism.

The advertisement is also linked with a direct-marketing response component. Customers are invited to register online for a tongue-in-cheek campaign whereby couples will be sent a pregnancy kit to use after the holiday. If the result is positive, Spies Rejser will offer three years' free baby supplies.

The advert received a lot of publicity in national and international media (the advert has more than 9 million views on YouTube), leading the company to use the same theme in a more recent campaign. This time, Spies is inviting Danish couples to 'Do it for Mom!' Concerned parents are invited to participate through a direct-response element. In exchange for a discount on the holiday, parents can contribute to their children's vacation to show how much they want to become grandparents. Once again, the campaign has received significant media attention (the advert has more than 7 million views on YouTube) and has creatively linked a humorous appeal with an interactive dimension.

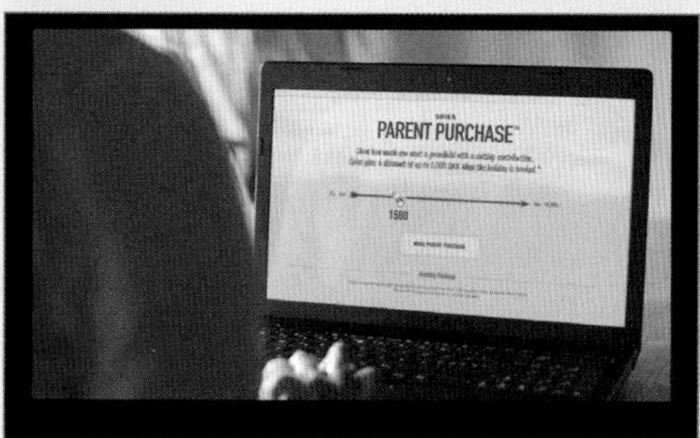

A humorous communications campaign that went viral: Do it for Denmark!

Source: Courtesy of Robert/Boisen & Like-minded.

1. **What tasks is the campaign performing according to the DRIP taxonomy (see Chapter 8)?**
2. **What are the potential strengths and weaknesses of this campaign?**
3. **Which tools and media were used for this campaign? Can you think of ways in which Spies might extend the campaigns to include additional tools and media?**

Sources: Saul (2014); Basu (2015).

Integrated Marketing Communications

So far in this chapter, we have looked briefly at the five main tools, ideas about how messages should be developed, and how the media landscape is evolving. For these to work most effectively and most efficiently, however, it makes sense to integrate them, so that they work as a unit. In this way, they will have a greater overall impact. This bringing together is referred to as **integrated marketing communications (IMC)**.

Integrated marketing communications has become a popular approach with both clients and communications agencies. Ideas about IMC originated in the early 1990s. At first, IMC was regarded as a means of orchestrating the tools of the marketing communications mix, so that audiences perceive a single, consistent, unified message whenever they have contact with a brand. Duncan and Everett (1993) referred to this new, largely media-oriented approach as 'orchestration', 'whole egg', and 'seamless' communication.

At a strategic level, Luxton and colleagues (2015) consider IMC to be part of a firm's overall capability that contributes to brand performance. This is achieved by enabling the development and implementation of IMC campaigns that results in positive brand-related market performance and improved financial outcomes. Kerr and Patti (2015) developed a measure of strategic integration, one that evaluates organizational proficiency and diagnoses the integration of IMC campaigns—but this has yet to be operationalized.

For a period soon after IMC was first considered, numerous definitions emerged as the concept was explored. Since then, Duncan (2002), Grönroos (2004), Kitchen and colleagues (2004), and Kliatchko (2008) have provided the most useful definitions and valuable insights into IMC. Although there have been fewer definitions advanced in recent years, there is still little conformity about what constitutes and defines IMC (Reinold and Tropp, 2012). In the light of this vagueness, the following definition can be supplied:

> IMC can represent both a strategic and tactical approach to the planned management of an organisation's communications. IMC requires that organisations coordinate their various strategies, resources and messages in order that they enable meaningful engagement with audiences. The main purposes are to develop a clear positioning and encourage stakeholder relationships that are of mutual value.
>
> (Fill and Turnbull, 2016: 000)

Embedded within this definition are links with both business-level and marketing strategies, along with confirmation of the importance of the coherent use of resources and messages. What should also be evident is that IMC can be used to support the development and maintenance of effective relationships—a point made first by Duncan and Moriarty (1998), and then by both Ballantyne (2004) and Grönroos (2004).

One quite common use of an integrated approach can be seen in the use of the tools. For example, rather than use advertising, PR, sales promotions, personal selling, and direct marketing separately, why not use them in a coordinated manner? Hence organizations often use advertising or sales promotion to create awareness, then involve PR to provoke media comment, and then reinforce these messages through direct marketing or personal selling. The Internet can also be incorporated to encourage comment, interest, and involvement in a brand, yet still convey the same message in a consistent way. Mobile communications are used to reach audiences to reinforce messages and to persuade audiences to behave in particular ways, wherever they are. The evolution of digital media poses problems for IMC and for planning marketing communications activities, however, some of which relate to campaign metrics and measurement, budgeting, brand control, and content development (Winer, 2009).

Another important aspect of integration concerns the question: what else should be integrated? One element might be the planning and campaign development process. Using an integrated approach during the planning phase can serve to integrate clients, agencies, suppliers, and employees, as well as other resources.

Market Insight 9.5 **A New Integrated Mix for Soberana**

Soberana is a mainstream beer brand in Panama, owned by Cervecerias Baru Panama (part of the Heineken group). The brand was relaunched in 2012 and, since then, it has experienced incredible growth: it has tripled its volume and size of market in just three years.

Soberana needed to be repositioned from a value brand consumed by people over the age 40 years to an aspirational brand appealing to young consumers aged 18–25, and thereby assure the brand's continued growth.

The creative territory 'Live a Sovereign life' (*Vive una vida Soberana*) was developed to give the brand a clear role (*Soberana* means 'Sovereign' in English). A 'sovereign life' suggests a life full of rights and no obligations. Soberana developed six different rights, including the 'the right to be yourself', 'the right to defeat your fears', and 'the right to go out on Mondays'. This creative territory is strongly associated with Soberana's functional benefit: the brand is considered a soft beer, with low bitterness and alcohol, which allows consumers to extend their drinking time.

The 'Megaphone Man' character was developed to announce the rights of the 'sovereign life'. He is a personification of the brand: a cool young man who remains unknown—that is, we never see his face. Megaphone Man was launched at the end of 2015 with a fully integrated campaign plan, including a strong media plan, with a teaser phase to introduce the central character.

To create awareness about Megaphone Man, he first appeared unbranded in more than 15 nationwide television afternoon and night-time shows, and asserted a different 'right' related to each television presenter. He appeared in a variety of news, entertainment, sports, and celebrity shows. The campaign consisted of three television commercials, cinema, radio, and print adverts, as well as OOH materials and digital content, which leveraged relevant rights for consumers. Each communication event in the integrated campaign conveyed different rights, customized per media. Having many rights was extremely important, because the new creative territory was about living a life *full* of rights, not a life with only one or two. Research identified the most important and these were amplified through different media.

Besides traditional digital formats, the brand also exploited two of the fastest growing platforms, Instagram and Spotify. With the aim of generating relevant social media content, Megaphone Man declared rights and took selfies with more than 40 celebrities, reaching more than 600,000 users. Moreover, by communicating the right to listen 'to music without interruptions,' Soberana gave away more than 150 Spotify Premium accounts through different online promotions.

In addition, the brand started using experiential consumer platforms. Surfing is a relevant and aspirational sport for young consumers, so Soberana became the main sponsor of the Panamanian surf tournament. This has helped to associate the brand with a 'cool' lifestyle.

Soberana had previously updated its packaging, which served to reinforce the new positioning. Out went the returnable bottle with a serigraphy logo and in came a new, sleek, modern design. This change had an incredibly positive impact on consumers' perceptions of Soberana.

Market Insight 9.5 (continued)

Soberana's OOH communications in 2015.

Source: Courtesy of Soberana.

Soberana's old (left) and new (right) packaging.

Source: Courtesy of Soberana.

1. **Identify the key elements of the communication mix used by Soberana. What else might have been included?**
2. **Describe the objectives of the different elements identified in Soberana's promotional mix.**
3. **What are the key integrating elements in this campaign?**

Source: Based on the author's own experience.

This market insight was kindly contributed by Fermin Paus, brand franchise manager for Soberana in Panama.

Research Insight 9.3

To take your learning further, you might wish to read this influential paper.

Ots, M., and Nyilasy, G. (2015) 'Integrated marketing communications (IMC): Why does it fail?', *Journal of Advertising Research*, 55(2): 132–45.

This paper provides an interesting view of IMC implementation as a reason for its failure. The researchers identify four aspects of IMC implementation dysfunction: miscommunication, compartmentalization, loss of trust, and decontextualization.

 **Visit the online resources to read the abstract and access the full paper.**

Integrated marketing communications has emerged for many reasons, but two main ones concern customers and costs. First, organizations began to realize that their customers are more likely to understand a single message, delivered through various sources, rather than to try to appreciate a series of different messages transmitted through different tools and a variety of media. Integrated marketing communications is therefore concerned with harmonizing the messages conveyed, so that audiences perceive a consistent set of meanings within the messages they receive, through all touchpoints. The second reason concerns costs. As organizations seek to lower their costs, it is becoming clear that it is far more cost-effective to send a single message, using a limited number of agencies and other resources, rather than to develop several messages through a number of different agencies.

At first glance, IMC might appear to be a practical and logical development that should benefit all concerned with an organization's marketing communications. There are issues however, concerning the concept, including what should be integrated, over and above the tools, media, and messages. For example, what about the impact of employees on a brand, and other elements of the marketing mix, as well as the structure, systems, processes, and procedures necessary to deliver IMC consistently through time? There is also some debate about the nature of IMC and the contribution that it can make to an organization, if only because there is a no main theory to underpin the topic (Cornelissen, 2003).

Promotion and Ethics

There are many issues relating to marketing communications that prompt ethical consideration.

Advertisers often use emotional appeals to capture attention. We are persuaded by them because we are less likely to consider objections about why we might not agree with the message. For Baudrillard (2005), all advertising has an erotic element to it, because it seduces us to buy something. But the ethical question arises where sexual themes are used explicitly (for example naked or semi-naked models) and depending on the circumstances. Italian fashion brand Diesel has famously used sexual appeals, advertising on dating apps Tinder and Grindr, and adult website Pornhub (Allwood, 2016). Pornhub became its top referral website following the advertising deal (Maytom, 2016).

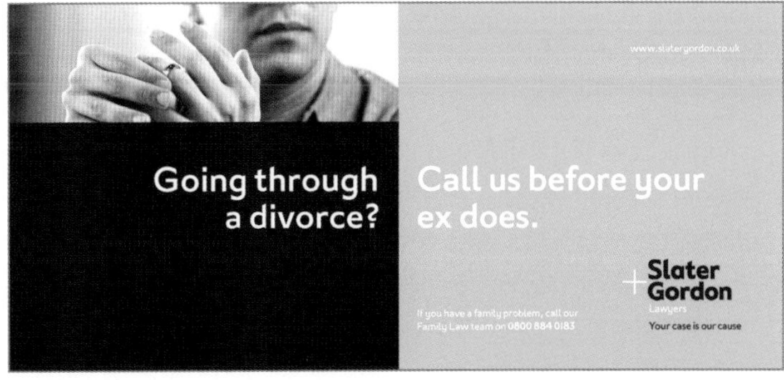

This shockingly humorous advert from a British law firm created a firestorm on social media, raising awareness of legal services in an area not renowned for advertising: family law.

Source: Courtesy of Slater and Gordon (http://www.slatergordon.co.uk).

Critics argue that sex appeals exploit women, and sometimes men, as sex objects. The fashion industry has decided not to use models aged 16 years or under, but it does use—and encourage them to become—painfully thin models. Israel was the world's first country to ban the use of female models whose body mass index (BMI) was less than 18.5 in 2013 (Bannerman, 2015). Others argue that sexual advertising appeals can be appropriate, depending on the offering, for example perfume.

Shock advertising appeals can also create controversy. Charities often use hard-hitting guilt appeal messages to raise funds for sick children in Africa, for example. Slater and Gordon, a British law firm, used a shock appeal with the tagline 'Going through a divorce? Call us, before your ex does', causing upset on social media. But the firm argued that such an approach was necessary to raise awareness of the firm's services in a sector in which clients generally have a weak understanding of what solicitors actually offer, including mediation for couples (McAlister, 2015).

Product labelling can also raise ethical issues when it is perceived as potentially misleading the public. Proper labelling is important in the food, pharmaceutical, and cosmetic industries, because we consume and absorb these offerings into our bodies. Food products—and particularly meat products in Europe and elsewhere—are required to demonstrate their country of origin. For Europe's Muslims, whether or not food products are labelled halal is important, because Muslims believe that animals should be slaughtered according to the custom of cutting the animal's throat while it is alive and then draining its blood. Some animal rights groups condemn the practice, and Sweden, Norway, Iceland, Switzerland, and Poland have all banned 'ritual slaughter' despite the fact that it is allowed under European Union law (Hasan, 2012).

Another contentious area of marketing communications is political advertising. In many countries, political advertising is exempt from the rules and regulations associated with traditional advertising. As a consequence, it can be highly negative, making vitriolic statements to damage the credibility of other candidates and parties. In the UK, political advertising on billboards, in cinemas, and in magazines is exempt from the advertising rules set by the Advertising Standards Authority (ASA). Political parties are not expected to be truthful—that is, to validate their claims—unlike their commercial counterparts. For example, the 'No' campaign during the Scottish independence referendum was criticized for an overly negative message, labelled 'Project Fear' by some (Pike, 2015), but others argue that the political context often justifies a negative campaign stance when the risks posed to society are great (Morris, 2008). The ethical question therefore is: should politicians be exempt from the rules and regulations associated with traditional marketing activity, when many of the adverts used can be so negative?

Scholars frequently comment on whether or not children should be targeted for advertising, given their immature views of time, money, and identity. Researchers have found evidence that children are explicitly targeted in promotional campaigns and that parents are concerned by this, with the following points particularly pertinent (Daniels and Holmes, 2005).

- Children are more exposed to marketing than before and parents increasingly feel that they are losing control of the marketing directed at their children.
- Parents are particularly concerned about the marketing channels used (for example Internet, mobile phone, social media, and advergames) that target children directly.
- Inappropriate marketing to children damages the brand, making it less likely that marketers will get past the parent as gatekeeper.
- More appropriate marketing methods are informative and help parents to feel more in control.
- Consumers are willing to support companies that communicate with children in a responsible way.
- Marketers—especially advertisers—should use the means of communication appropriately, and educate parents and children alike on newer and less traditional communication media.

An example of a company under pressure for its promotion to children is McDonald's, whose offerings appeal particularly to children via the use of licensed characters and celebrity endorsement. Child obesity is regarded as a major problem in many countries (for example Australia, the United States, and the UK, along with the European Union generally). The problem is partly caused by advertising food to children, although inactive lifestyles and lack of exercise also play a part. Fast-food retailers are consequently coming under increasing pressure to make their menus healthier.

All of these issues lead us back to the discussion of the moral principles that should guide marketers' behaviour presented in Chapter 1. In the configuration of their marketing communications mix, therefore, marketers should consider the potential harm that might be caused by their campaigns and they should strive to act responsibly to foster trust in the marketing system.

Chapter Summary

To consolidate your learning, the key points from this chapter are summarized below.

- **Describe the role and configuration of the marketing communications mix.**

  Organizations use the marketing communications mix to convey messages and to engage their various audiences. The mix consists of five tools, four main forms of messages or content, and three forms of media. These elements are mixed and adapted to meet the needs of the target audience and the context in which marketing communications operate. Tools and media are not the same, the former being methods or techniques and the latter, the means by which messages are conveyed to the target audience.

- **Explain the characteristics of each of the primary tools, media, and messages.**

  Each of the tools—advertising, sales promotion, public relations (PR), direct marketing, and personal selling—communicates messages in different ways and achieves different outcomes. Messages are a balance of informational and emotional content. Some content can be branded and some can be generated by users. Each medium has a set of characteristics that enable it to convey messages in particular ways to and with target audiences.

- **Set out the criteria that should be used to select the right communication mix.**

  Using a set of criteria can help to simplify the complex and difficult process of selecting the right marketing communications mix. There are five key criteria—namely, the degree of control over a message, the credibility of the message conveyed, the costs of using a tool, the degree to which a target audience is dispersed, and the task that marketing communications is required to accomplish.

- **Consider the principles and issues associated with integrated marketing communications.**

  Rather than use advertising, PR, sales promotions, personal selling, and direct marketing separately, integrated marketing communications (IMC) is concerned with working with these tools (and media) as a coordinated whole. Hence organizations often use advertising to create awareness, then involve PR to provoke media comment, and sales promotion to create, trial, and then reinforce these messages through direct marketing or personal selling to persuade audiences. The Internet can also be incorporated to encourage comment, interest, and involvement in a brand, yet still convey the same message. Mobile communications are used to reach audiences to reinforce messages and persuade audiences to behave in particular ways, wherever they are.

Review Questions

1. **Make brief notes about the nature and role of the marketing communications mix and explain how its configuration has changed.**
2. **Write a definition for advertising, PR, and one other tool from the mix. Identify the key differences.**
3. **Why do organizations like to use direct-response media?**
4. **How does media fragmentation impact on audiences?**
5. **What five criteria can be used to select the right mix of communication tools?**
6. **Make a list of the four main message formats and find an example to illustrate each.**
7. **Write brief notes explaining the differences between informational and emotional messages.**
8. **Write a list that categorizes the media. Find a media vehicle to represent each type of medium.**
9. **To what extent are online, mobile, and digital media likely to replace the use of traditional media?**
10. **What are the principles of integrated marketing communications?**

Worksheet Summary

To apply the knowledge you have gained from this chapter and test your understanding of the marketing communications mix, visit the **online resources** and complete Worksheet 9.1.

Discussion Questions

1 Having read Case Insight 9.1, how would you advise Budweiser Budvar on how to develop its 'No' campaign? How should it communicate the 'No' message without being negative? What promotional tools should it use for the campaign? What mix of media would be best at delivering the 'No' campaign to realize the greatest impact?

2 Select an organization with which you are familiar or for which you would like to work. Visit its website and try to determine its use of the marketing communications tools, messages, and media. How might its mix be improved?

3 Select an organization in the consumer technology industry or one for which you would like to work. Visit its website, view its advertising archive, and read its press releases. Determine the organization's approach to marketing communications. Now visit the website for its main competitor and determine its marketing communications. Discuss the similarities and differences.

4 Zylog is based in Denmark, and manufactures and distributes a range of consumer electronic equipment. Ennike Christensen, Zylog's new marketing manager, has indicated that she wants to introduce an integrated approach to the firm's marketing communications. However, Zylog does not have any experience of IMC and Red Spider, its current communications agency, has started to become concerned that it may lose the Zylog account. Discuss the situation facing Zylog and suggest ways in which it might acquire the expertise it needs. Discuss ways in which Red Spider might acquire an IMC capability.

Visit the **online resources** and complete the multiple-choice questions to assess your knowledge of this chapter.

Glossary

advertising a form of non-personal communication, by an identified sponsor, that is transmitted through the use of paid-for media.

audience fragmentation the disintegration of large media audiences into many smaller audiences caused by the development of alternative forms of entertainment that people can experience. This means that, to reach large numbers of people in a target market, companies need to use a variety of media, not only rely on a few mass-media channels.

brand placement the planned and deliberate use of brands within films, television, and other entertainment vehicles, with a view to developing awareness and brand values.

branded content use of entertainment material delivered through paid-for or owned media and which features a single company or product/service brand.

crisis communications a part of public relations that is used to protect and defend a brand (individual or organization) when its reputation is damaged or threatened.

direct marketing a marketing communications tool that uses non-personal media to create and sustain a personal and intermediary-free communication with customers, potential customers, and other significant stakeholders. In most cases, this is a media-based activity.

direct-response media media that carry advertising messages enabling audiences to respond immediately. Most commonly used in print, banner adverts, and on television (known as DRTV).

exhibitions events at which groups of sellers meet collectively with the key purpose of attracting buyers.

field marketing a marketing communications activity concerned with providing support for the sales force and merchandising personnel.

integrated marketing communications (IMC) an approach associated with the coordinated development and delivery of a consistent marketing communication message(s) with a target audience.

marketing communications mix a set of five tools, a variety of media, and messages that can be used in various combinations, and with different degrees of intensity, to communicate with specific audiences.

media fragmentation the splintering of a few mainstream media channels into a multitude of media and channel formats.

packaging protects contents, and communicates key rational and emotional information about a brand.

personal selling the use of interpersonal communications aiming to encourage people to make a purchase, for personal gain and reward.

public relations (PR) a non-personal form of communication used by companies to build trust, goodwill, interest, and ultimately relationships with a range of stakeholders.

sales promotion a communication tool that adds value to a product or service, with the intention of encouraging people to buy now rather than at some point in the future.

sponsorship a marketing communications activity whereby one party permits another an opportunity to exploit an association with a target audience in return for funds, services, or resources.

user-generated content (UGC) content made publicly available over the Internet that reflects a certain amount of creative effort and is created by users, not professionals.

viral marketing the unpaid peer-to-peer communication of often provocative content originating from an identified sponsor, aiming to use the Internet to persuade or influence an audience to pass along the content to others.

References

Allwood, E. H. (2016) 'Why diesel is about to start advertising on Pornhub', *Dazed*, January. Available online at http://www.dazeddigital.com/fashion/article/29089/1/why-diesel-is-about-to-start-advertising-on-pornhub [accessed 30 April 2016].

Anon. (2015a) 'Case study: Volvo Trucks Live Test Series', *The Best of Global Digital Marketing*. Available online at http://www.best-marketing.eu/case-study-volvo-trucks-live-test-series/ [accessed 17 December 2015].

Anon. (2015b) 'DHL turns sponsorship into "active ads" ', *Warc*, 10 November. Available online at http://www.warc.com/LatestNews/News/DHL_turns_sponsorship_into_active_ads.news?ID=35692 [accessed 14 November 2015].

Ballantyne, D. (2004) 'Dialogue and its role in the development of relationship-specific knowledge', *Journal of Business & Industrial Marketing*, 19(2): 114–23.

Bannerman, L. (2015) 'I won't lose weight, says angry model', *The Times*, 16 October. Available online at http://www.thetimes.co.uk/tto/life/fashion/article4587534.ece [accessed 13 May 2016].

Basu, T. (2015) 'Denmark encourages couples to "do it for Mom" ', *Time*, 1 October Available online at http://time.com/4057865/do-it-for-mom-denmark/ [accessed 13 May 2016].

Baudrillard, J. (2005) *The System of Objects* (trans. J. Benedict), London: Verso Books.

Binet, L., and Field, P. (2013) *The Long and Short of It*, London: IPA.

Carter, M. (2014) 'How Volvo trucks pulled off an epic split and a game-changing campaign', *Fast Company*, 18 June. Available online at http://www.fastcocreate.com/3031654/cannes/how-volvo-trucks-pulled-off-an-epic-split-and-a-game-changing-campaign [accessed 17 December 2015].

Cornelissen, J. P. (2003) 'Change, continuity and progress: The concept of integrated marketing communications and marketing communications practice', *Journal of Strategic Marketing*, 11(4): 217–34.

Dahlen, M., and Rosengren, S. (2016) 'If advertising won't die, what will it be? Towards a new definition of advertising', *Journal of Advertising*, 45(3): 334–45.

Daniels, J., and Holmes, C. (2005) *Responsible Marketing to Children: Exploring the Impact on Adults' Attitudes and Behaviour*, London: Business in the Community.

Duncan, T. (2002) *IMC: Using Advertising and Promotion to Build Brand* (Int'l edn), New York: McGraw Hill.

Duncan, T., and Everett, S. (1993) 'Client perceptions of integrated marketing communications', *Journal of Advertising Research*, 3(3): 30–9.

Duncan, T., and Moriarty, S. (1998) 'A communication-based marketing model for managing relationships', *Journal of Marketing*, 62(2): 1–13.

Fill, C. (2009) *Marketing Communications: Interactivity, Communities and Content* (5th edn), Harlow: FT/Prentice Hall.

Fill, C. (2013) *Marketing Communications: Brands, Experience and Participation* (6th edn), Harlow: FT/Prentice Hall.

Fill, C., and Turnbull, S. (2016) *Marketing Communications: Discovery, Creation andConversations* (7th edn), Harlow: Pearson Education.

Gelles, D. (2015) 'Social responsibility that rubs right off', *The New York Times*, 18 October. Available online at http://www.nytimes.com/2015/10/18/business/energy-environment/social-responsibility-that-rubs-right-off.html [accessed 13 May 2016].

Grönroos, C. (2004) 'The relationship marketing process: Communication, interaction, dialogue, value', *Journal of Business and Industrial Marketing*, 19(2): 99–113.

Hasan, M. (2012) 'Mehdi Hasan on the not-so-hidden fear behind halal hysteria', *New Statesman*, 9 May. Available online at http://www.newstatesman.com/politics/politics/2012/05/halal-hysteria [accessed 5 April 2016].

Kaplan, A. M., and Haenlein, M. (2010) 'Users of the world, unite! The challenges and opportunities of social media', *Business Horizons*, 53(1): 59–68.

Kerr, G., and Patti, C. (2015) 'Strategic IMC: From abstract concept to marketing management tool', *Journal of Marketing Communications*, 21(5): 317–39.

Kitchen, P., Brignell, J., Li, T., and Spickett Jones, G. (2004) 'The emergence of IMC: A theoretical perspective', *Journal of Advertising Research*, 44(1): 19–30.

Kleinman, D. (2016) 'Will Volkswagen's possible $18 billion emissions penalty drive transparency in manufacturing?', *Forbes*, 25 January. Available online at http://www.forbes.com/sites/danielkleinman/2016/01/25/will-volkswagens-possible-18-billion-emissions-penalty-drive-transparency-in-manufacturing/#36c40286a971 [accessed 13 May 2016].

Kliatchko, J. (2008) 'Revisiting the IMC construct: A revised definition and four pillars', *International Journal of Advertising*, 27(1): 133–60.

Luxton S., Reid, M., and Mavondo, F. (2015) 'Integrated marketing communication capability and brand performance', *Journal of Advertising*, 44(1): 37–46.

Maytom, T. (2016) 'Pornhub becomes Diesel's top referral website following ad deal', *Mobile Marketing*, 21 March. Available online at http://mobilemarketingmagazine.com/pornhub-becomes-diesels-top-referral-site-following-ad-deal/ [accessed 30 April 2016].

McAlister, A. (2015) 'Call us before your ex does . . .', *Slater & Gordon*, 19 November. Available online at http://www.slatergordon.co.uk/media-centre/blog/2015/11/call-us-before-your-ex-does-/ [accessed 29 March 2016].

Morris, D. (2008) 'Negative campaigning is good for America', *US News & World Report*, 6 October. Available online at http://www.usnews.com/opinion/articles/2008/10/06/dick-morris-negative-campaigning-is-good-for-america [accessed 1 April 2016].

Pike, J. (2015) *Project Fear: How an Unlikely Alliance Left a Kingdom United but a Country Divided*, London: Biteback.

Porter, L., and Golan, G. J. (2006) 'From subservient chickens to brawny men: A comparison of viral advertising to television advertising', *Journal of Interactive Advertising*, 6(2): 30–8.

Reinold, T., and Tropp, J. (2012) 'Integrated marketing communications: How can we measure its effectiveness?', *Journal of Marketing Communications*, 18(2): 113–32.

Richards, J. I., and Curran, C. M. (2002) 'Oracles on "advertising": Searching for a definition', *Journal of Advertising*, 31(2): 63–77.

Ridley, L. (2014) 'Watch "groundbreaking" Lego ad break by PHD', *campaign*, 10 February. Available online at http://www.campaignlive.co.uk/article/watch-groundbreaking-lego-ad-break-phd/1230530#k3XwhqoVTjhwSBkB.99 [accessed 17 December 2015].

Ritson, M. (2015) 'Postcards from the digitally disrupted', *Marketing Week*, 1 December. Available online at http://www.marketingweek.com/2015/12/01/mark-ritson-postcards-from-the-digitally-disrupted/ [accessed 7 December 2015].

Saul, H. (2014) 'Do it for Denmark: Competition calls for Danes to have more sex to tackle declining birth rates', *The Independent*, 28 March. Available online at http://www.independent.co.uk/news/world/europe/do-it-for-denmark-competition-calls-for-danes-to-have-more-sex-to-tackle-declining-birth-rates-9218490.html [accessed 13 May 2016].

Segev, S., Fernandes, J., and Hong, C. (2016) 'Is your product really green? A content analysis to reassess green advertising', *Journal of Advertising*, 45(1): 85–93.

van der Lans, R., van Bruggen, G., Eliashberg, J., and Wierenga, B. (2010) 'A viral branching model for predicting the spread of electronic word-of-mouth', *Marketing Science*, 29(2): 348–65.

Winer, R. S. (2009) 'New communications approaches in marketing: Issues and research directions', *Journal of Interactive Marketing*, 23(2): 108–17.

Chapter 10
Managing Channels and Distribution

Learning Outcomes

After studying this chapter, you will be able to:

- describe the nature and characteristics of a marketing channel;
- explain the different types of intermediary and their roles in the marketing channel;
- understand the different marketing channel structures and their core characteristics;
- explain the factors that influence the design and structure of marketing channels;
- describe the main elements that constitute supply chain management; and
- consider the role and function of retailers in the marketing channel.

Case Insight 10.1
Åhléns

Market Insight 10.1
Channelling Motorbikes

Market Insight 10.2
Troubling Power in the Channel

Market Insight 10.3
Getting it There, on Time . . . : Medicine, IT, and Fashion

Market Insight 10.4
Enhancing Channel Experiences

Market Insight 10.5
Programmatic Commerce

Case Insight 10.1 **Åhléns**

As shopper behaviour turns increasingly digital, established retailers are having to adapt their channel strategies. We talk to Lotta Bjurhult (pictured), business developer, retail operations, at Sweden's largest department store chain Åhléns, to find out what it takes to add an online channel to an existing network of department stores.

Åhléns is Sweden's leading department store chain. You could say that we hold a position similar to that of John Lewis in the UK or Karstadt in Germany. In 2015, we had a turnover of about SEK5 billion, employed 3,000 people, and served a total of 65 million visitors in our 70 department stores located throughout Sweden. Our customer base is very loyal, with more than 2.2 million club members who shop, on average, 8.5 times a year at our stores.

Our mission is to offer carefully selected, priceworthy, and sustainable solutions that we believe can satisfy people's requirements in a simple, inspiring, and accessible way. As with most department stores, we offer a broad assortment of products and provide a wide array of customer service facilities for store customers. In our department stores, customers are offered a carefully considered collection of selected brands and proprietary labels all under one roof. Our customers are able to browse among an inspiring assortment of value-for-money products within home styling and interior design, fashion, beauty, foodstuffs, and entertainment.

Adding an online channel to an existing department store operation is complex. The challenge is to keep the overall experience of Åhléns, which is very much centred on the in-store shopping experience, while simultaneously adapting it to an online setting. Customers consider Åhléns as one department store—they don't care if they buy something offline or online. In developing our online offer, we have looked at a range of issues.

In terms of assortment, we have used statistics on what customers are already buying online as a starting point. We have also considered what products are currently not available in all of our local department stores. At the end of 2016, our online channel will hold around 50,000 different products, which means that it will offer a larger assortment than most of our physical department stores, but of equal size to our larger department stores in Uppsala and Malmö. Over time, we are aiming to provide the same assortment online as we do in our flagship store Åhléns City Stockholm.

We have also developed a tailor-made information technology (IT) system to support the online channel. In creating our online store, we have gone through and developed all of our internal processes—starting with how to relate to suppliers

A key challenge for Åhléns is translating the in-store shopping experience online.

Source: Courtesy of Åhléns.

Case Insight 10.1 (continued)

and vendors, through where to stock and how to deliver products, to the role of physical store employees. Going online exposes any weaknesses you might have in your business operations. If something is not really working in a physical store, you have store employees that can fix it. Things such as payments and returns, which are quite easily managed in a physical department store, become a lot trickier online.

Another key consideration for us has been how to engage store employees and make them embrace the online channel as part of the overall value proposition of Åhléns. The online channel has profound and long-lasting effects on the role they play in creating a high-quality customer experience.

One of my key tasks has been to ensure that in-store employees and customer service embrace the online channel, and make it a part of the experience offered to our customers every day. This is a must if we are to offer our customers a seamless experience.

Key questions for Åhléns have been: what roles should store employees play in integrating the offline and online channels? And what activities are needed to ensure their support for a new online channel?

Introduction

Have you ever considered the journey that a bottle of water, a computer, or a bag of potatoes might take from its source (its manufacturer or producer) to be available for you to purchase at the point you prefer? In many cases, this journey can be complex, involving transactions between many organizations, countries, and people.

The organizations involved with any one journey are collectively termed a **distribution channel**, or a **marketing channel**. These are chains of organizations that are concerned with the management of the processes and activities involved in creating and moving products from producers and manufacturers to end-user customers. Each organization adds something of value before passing it to the next, and it is this interaction that provides mutual advantage (Kotler and Keller, 2009) and which underpins the concept of 'channel marketing'.

In this chapter, we consider three main elements. The first concerns the management of the intangible aspects or issues of ownership—that is, the control and flows of communication between the parties responsible for making an offering accessible for target customers, commonly referred to as 'marketing channel management'.

The second element concerns the management of the tangible or physical aspects of moving a product from the producer to the end user. This must be undertaken so that a customer can freely access an offering, and so that the final act of the buying process is as convenient and easy as possible. This is part of **supply chain management (SCM)**, which includes the logistics associated with moving products closer to end users.

The third and final element is about **retailing**, a critical element of the way in which consumers access the products they desire.

Channel Management

Europe's largest clothing maker and retailer Inditex has seen its clothing sales rise consistently in recent years, because it adds new stock to its fashion stores (for example Zara, Pull&Bear, and Massimo) twice a week, keeping the stock fresh and up to date with the latest fashion trends. It achieves this by manufacturing over 50 per cent of its stock in Spain or Portugal; although more costly in production, Inditex can get new designs into European and American stores twice as quickly than if it were to have to wait for delivery for stock manufactured in Asia. This shows that, by managing its marketing channels, Inditex has improved its overall business performance.

If we consider the skills that Inditex needs to design and assemble a range of garments, to source the materials, and to manufacture, package, and then distribute the final fashion garments to its stores and other customers, globally, we can see that a major set of complex operations are required. For many organizations, trying to undertake all of these operations is beyond their skill-set or core activities. For all organizations, there is a substantial risk associated with producing too many or too few, too soon or too late, for the target market. There are risks associated with changing buyer behaviours, and with storage, finance, and competitors' actions, to name but a few of the critical variables.

By collaborating with other organizations that have the necessary skills and expertise, organizations can reduce these uncertainties. Working with organizations that can create customer demand or access and manage specialist financial issues, storage, or **transportation**, adds value and develops competitive advantage. For example, to reach the 600,000 rural villages in India, Samsung partnered with the Indian Farmers Fertiliser Cooperative Ltd to sell its handsets. With this new marketing channel, Samsung can now reach over 90 per cent of the villages in India.

Collectively, organizations that combine to enable offerings to reach end users quickly and efficiently constitute a 'marketing channel', sometimes referred to as a 'distribution channel'. Organizations that combine to reduce risk and uncertainty do so by exchanging offerings that are of value to each other. Marketing channels therefore enable organizations to share or reduce uncertainty. When the uncertainty experienced by all members in a channel is reduced, each is in a better position to concentrate on other tasks.

How Channels Help to Reduce Uncertainty

Marketing channels enable different types of uncertainty to be lowered in several ways (Fill and McKee, 2012). These include reducing the complexity, increasing value and competitive advantage, routinization, and providing specialization.

Reducing Complexity

The number of transactions and the frequency of contact a producer might have with each individual end-user customer would be so high that the process would be unprofitable. This volume of activity can be seen in Figure 10.1.

Now, if an intermediary is introduced into the process, the number of transactions falls drastically, as demonstrated in Figure 10.2.

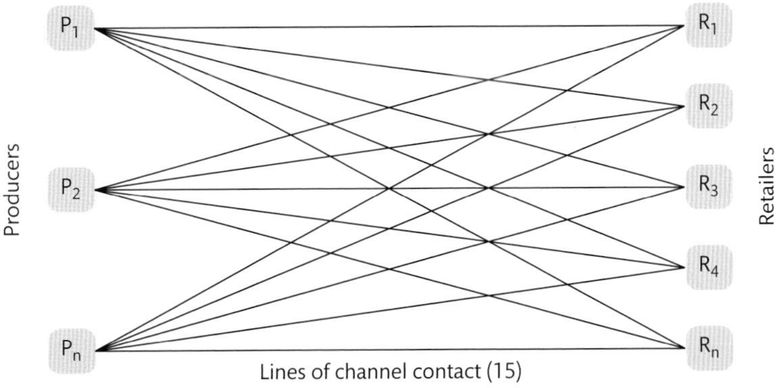

Figure 10.1 The complexity of channel exchanges without intermediaries

The fall in the number of transactions indicates not only that are costs reduced, but also that producers are better placed to redirect their attention to the needs of intermediaries. This allows them to focus on their core activities: production or manufacturing. In much the same way, end-user customers can get much improved individual support from channel intermediaries than they would be likely to get from a producer.

Increasing Value and Competitive Advantage

By using intermediaries, producers can reduce purchase risk—that is, the uncertainty that customers might reject the offering. Intermediaries, rather than producers, have the skills and core competences necessary to meet end-user requirements, for example retailing. By improving the overall value that customers perceive in an offering, relative to competing products and customer experience, it is possible to develop competitive advantage.

Routinization

Performance risk can be reduced by improving transaction efficiency. By standardizing, or 'routinizing' the transaction process, perhaps by regulating order sizes, automating operations, or managing delivery cycles and payment frequencies, distribution costs can be reduced.

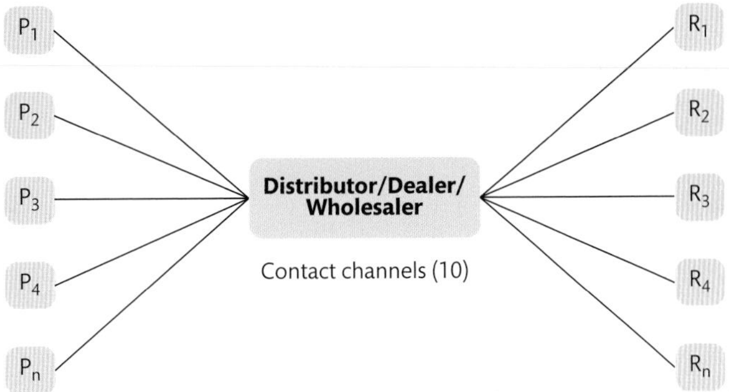

Figure 10.2 The impact of intermediaries on channel exchanges

Specialization

By providing specialist training services, maintenance, installation, bespoke deliveries, or credit facilities, intermediaries can develop a service that has real value to other channel members or end-user customers. Value can also be improved for customers by helping them to locate offerings they want. Intermediaries can provide these specialist resources, whereas producers are not normally interested in doing or able to do so. This is because they prefer to produce large quantities of a small range of goods. Unfortunately, end-user customers want only a limited quantity of a wide variety of goods.

Intermediaries provide a solution by bringing together and sorting out all of the goods produced by different manufacturers in the category. They then represent these goods in quantities and formats that enable end-user customers to buy the quantities they wish, as frequently as they prefer.

Intermediaries provide other utility-based benefits. For example, they assist end users by bringing a product produced a long way away to a more convenient location for purchase and consumption—that is, they offer **place utility**. The product might be manufactured during the day, but purchased and consumed at the weekend. Here, manufacturing, purchase, and consumption occur at differing points in time, and intermediaries provide **time utility**.

Immediate product availability through retailers enables ownership to pass to the consumer within a short amount of time—that is, **ownership utility**. Finally, intermediaries can also provide information about the product to aid sales and usage. The Internet has led to the development of a new type of intermediary, an information intermediary (for example Expedia, Google). Here, the key role is to manage information to improve the efficiency and effectiveness of the distribution channel—that is, **information utility**.

Visit the **online resources** and complete Internet Activity 10.1 to learn more about the role of intermediaries within the film and television industry.

Types of Intermediary

Having seen that intermediaries play a significant role in marketing channels, we now need to consider the different types that are available. Some of the more common ones are as follows.

- *Agents or brokers*—These act as a principal intermediary between the seller of an offering and buyers, bringing them together without taking ownership of the offering. These intermediaries have the legal authority to act on behalf of the manufacturer. For example, universities often use agents to recruit students in overseas markets (such as China, India).
- *Merchants*—A merchant undertakes the same actions as an agent, but takes ownership of a product.
- *Distributors or dealers*—These distribute the product. They offer value through services associated with selling inventory, credit, and aftersales service. Often used in business-to-business (B2B) markets, they can also be found dealing directly with consumers, for example automobile distributors. (See Market Insight 10.1 for a view of Honda's dealers and distributors.)
- *Franchises*—A franchisee holds a contract to supply and market an offering to the requirements or blueprint of the franchisor, the owner of the original offering. The contract might cover many aspects of the design of the offering, such as marketing, product assortment, or service delivery.

The uniformity of differing branches of McDonald's and KFC is an indication of franchisee contracts; however, franchise agreements are not used only in the fast-food or product sectors.

Visit the **online resources** and follow the web link to the European Franchise Association (EFA) to learn more about business franchise collaboration activities across Europe.

- *Wholesalers*—A wholesaler stocks goods before the next level of distribution, and takes both legal title and physical possession of the goods. In consumer markets, wholesalers do not usually deal with the end consumer, but with other intermediaries (for example retailers). In B2B markets, sales are made direct to end-user customers. Examples include Costco Wholesalers in the United States and Makro in Europe.
- *Retailers*—These intermediaries sell directly to end consumers and may purchase direct from manufacturers or deal with wholesalers. This is dependent on their purchasing power and the volume purchased. Leading retailers include Walmart, Marks and Spencer, Carrefour, and electronics retailers such as Media-Saturn.
- *Infomediaries*—These Internet-based organizations are intermediaries aiming to provide information to channel members, including end-users.

Managing Marketing Channels

There are two main issues associated with the management of marketing channels. These are the design of the channel—that is, its structure and activities—and the relationships between channel members. These are considered in turn.

Channel Design

The design of an appropriate channel—that is, its structure, length, membership, and the roles of those members—varies according to context. For example, the channels necessary to support a new start-up product or organization are different from those needed when an existing structure must adapt to changing market conditions. The channel design decision process requires consideration of three main factors.

1. the level of purchase convenience required by the different end-user customer segments to be served, known as the 'distribution intensity decision';
2. the number and types of intermediary necessary to deliver products to the optimum number of sales outlets, known as the 'channel configuration decision'; and
3. the number of different types of channel to be used, known as the 'multichannel decision'.

This helps us to determine what is the most effective and efficient way of getting the offering to the customer.

Visit the **online resources** and follow the web links to the Institute of Supply Chain Management (ISM) and the Chartered Institute of Purchasing and Supply (CIPS) to learn more about the profession and activities of managing the distribution and supply chain.

Market Insight 10.1 **Channelling Motorbikes**

Honda sells more than 12 million motorcycles each year in the Asia Oceania region alone, and the management of its distribution networks is a vital element in maintaining customer access and satisfaction. Honda produces a wide range of motorcycles, ranging from the 50cc class to the 1,800cc class, and is the largest manufacturer of motorcycles in the world in terms of annual units of production. In the region, Honda's motorcycles are produced at sites in Japan, Indonesia, Philippines, Pakistan, and India.

In Japan, sales of Honda motorcycles (and automobiles and power products) are made through different distribution networks. Honda's products are sold to consumers primarily through independent retail dealers and motorcycles are distributed through more than 11,500 outlets, including approximately 1,400 authorized dealerships. These authorized dealerships sell all of Honda's Japanese motorcycle models, not only selected models.

Most of Honda's overseas sales are made through its main sales subsidiaries, which distribute Honda's products to local wholesalers and retail dealers. In Indonesia, Honda has recently developed its dealer network of 4,000 dealers and service shops to support sales and to provide excellent aftersales service. In the United States, Honda's wholly owned subsidiary markets Honda's motorcycle products through a sales network of approximately 1,260 independent local dealers. Many of these motorcycle dealers also sell other Honda products.

In Europe, subsidiaries of the company in the UK, Germany, France, Belgium, the Netherlands, Spain, Switzerland, Austria, Italy, and other European countries distribute Honda's motorcycles through approximately 1,600 independent local dealers.

One core element of Honda's dealer strategy, worldwide, is its comprehensive '4S' support system, which covers Sales, Service, Spare parts, and Safety. For example, Honda provided its dealers in Thailand, Indonesia, Vietnam, and India with an easy-to-use riding simulator, called 'Riding Trainer', which offers riders risk awareness training and riding practice and, of course, engagement with the Honda brand.

Honda uses simulators, enabling riders to practise riding, receive risk awareness training, and experience the brand.

Source: © Getty / Bloomberg / Contributor.

Recently, a fifth 'S' has been added: Second-hand (or used) business. In Thailand, for example, the second-hand motorcycle business has been deliberately strengthened as a means of developing business. The strategy encourages potential motorcycle owners and those ready for an upgrade to purchase pre-owned Honda models, drawing this segment into the brand.

1 **Why does Honda set up subsidiary organizations in each overseas region or country?**

2 **What do you think are the benefits of the (now) '5S' support system?**

3 **What might affect Honda's dealer network (marketing channel) in the future?**

Sources: http://sec.edgar-online.com; http://www.findarticles.com/p/articles/; http://www.world.honda.com/

Distribution Channel Strategy

When devising a distribution channel strategy, several key decisions need to be made to serve customers and to establish and maintain appropriate buyer–seller relationships. These are summarized in Figure 10.3. These choices are important because they can affect the benefits provided to customers.

Channel Structure

Distribution channels can be structured in a number of ways. There are three main configurations involving producers, intermediaries, and customers: a **direct channel structure** involves selling directly to end-user customers with little involvement from other organizations; an **indirect channel structure** uses intermediaries; and a **multichannel structure** combines both (see Figure 10.4). We now consider the advantages and disadvantages of each of type of channel structure.

Direct Channel Structure

In direct channels, the producer uses strategies to reach end users directly rather than dealing through an intermediary, such as an agent, broker, retailer, or wholesaler (see Figure 10.4). Have you ever been to a farmers' market and purchased produce directly from a farmer, or downloaded music directly from the website of a local band? These are examples of direct distribution. The advantages of this structure include the producer or manufacturer maintaining control over its product and profitability, and building strong customer relationships. This structure, however, is not suitable for all products. It is ideally suited to those products that require significant customization, technical expertise, or commitment on behalf of the producer to complete a sale (Parker et al., 2006).

Electronic technologies such as the Internet have enabled a greater number of product manufacturers to reach customers directly and can allow efficiency within the direct channel structure to be improved. Orders can be processed directly with customers and the communication of supporting information is also more efficient. For example, Dell Computer Corp. sells computer equipment

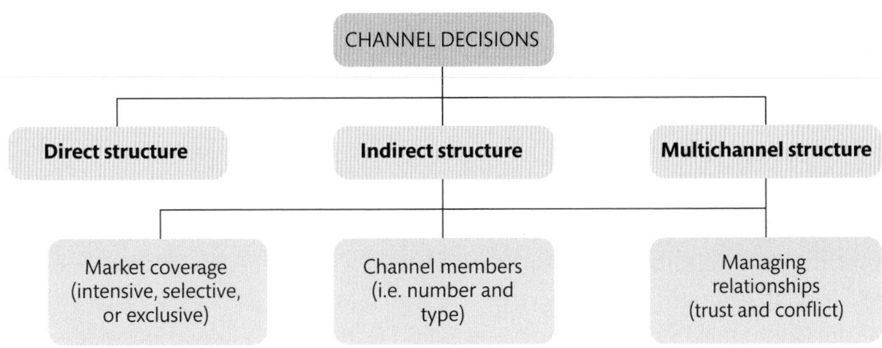

Figure 10.3 Distribution channel strategy decisions

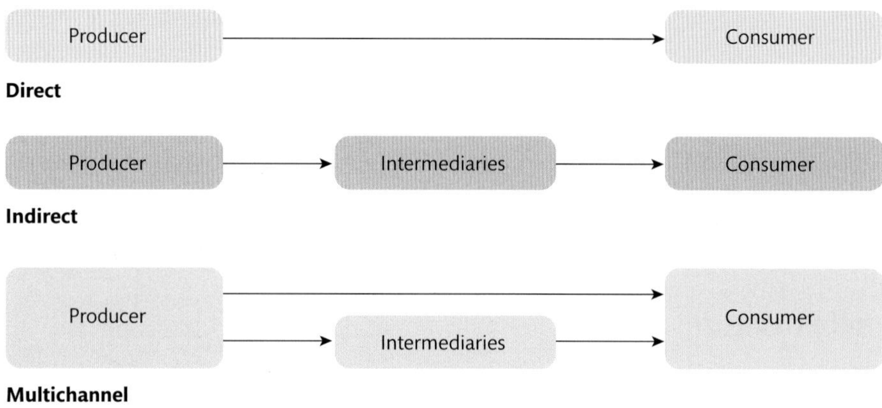

Figure 10.4 Distribution channel structure

through its website, using telesales for product ordering, database technology for order processing, tracking, and inventory, and delivery management.

The disadvantages of a direct channel structure typically include the large amount of capital and resources required to reach customers. This means that there are virtually no economies of scale. Manufacturers might also suffer from offering a low variety of offerings, which may not meet the needs of buyers. This is especially apparent in consumer markets, such as fast-moving consumer goods (FMCGs). Imagine having to shop for bread, milk, and a soft drink at three differing retail outlets owned by each product manufacturer. Few consumers today would purchase their offerings from individual manufacturers owing to the inconvenience and time costs involved. Thus retailers fulfil the needs of end consumers for variety—something that a direct channel of distribution cannot necessarily do.

Indirect Channel Structure

Indirect channel structures enable producers to concentrate on the skills and processes necessary to make offerings, and use one or more intermediaries for distribution. For example, Procter & Gamble (P&G) focuses its resources and expertise on developing new types of FMCG, whereas Sainsbury's core retailing activity is to make P&G's products (and others) available to consumers.

Multichannel Structure

An increasing number of organizations adopt a hybrid, or multichannel, structure to distribute goods and services (Park and Keh, 2003). Here, the producer controls some marketing channels and intermediaries control others. For example, many airlines sell their tickets directly to consumers through the Internet, but also rely on travel agents. Music labels also sell their CDs directly, using catalogues and the Internet, as well as independent music retailers such as Rise on the Clifton Triangle in Bristol. Consider the options for the purchase of a mobile device. This could occur directly from the Samsung website, from a service provider such as EE, or perhaps at Tesco, while picking up some bread and milk. Samsung, Lenovo, and LG Electronics use service providers, electronic retailers, and wholesale discount clubs alongside their own direct Internet and telesales channels to market and deliver their mobile phones.

Research Insight 10.1

To take your learning further, you might wish to read this influential paper.

Rosenbloom, B. (2007) 'Multichannel strategy in business-to-business markets: Prospects and problems', *Industrial Marketing Management*, 36(1): 4–9.

Rosenbloom has written extensively about marketing channels and published several books on the topic. This paper provides an interesting insight into the issues of channel strategy within a B2B context.

 **Visit the online resources to read the abstract and access the full paper.**

The benefits of a multichannel structure include the following.

- *Increased reach*—By utilizing existing direct networks and the relationships of intermediaries, organizations can reach a wider target audience.
- *Producer control*—Producers have greater control over prices and communication, and can reach customers directly.
- *Greater compliance*—Intermediaries can perceive producers to be a competitor and so comply with channel rules.
- *Optimized margins*—Producers can improve margins from the direct channel element and increase their bargaining power as they become less dependent on intermediaries.
- *Improved market insight*—By developing relationships with their direct customers, producers can derive a better understanding of their needs and markets issues.

The use of multichannel strategies has been encouraged by the growth of the Internet, which has increased the efficiency with which consumers and manufacturers can interact (Park and Keh, 2003). At the same time, technologies are increasing the efficiency of information exchange between producers and intermediaries, for example through electronic data interchange (EDI) and extranets. However, the sharing of profits among channel members can be a source of conflict, especially when intermediaries perceive the producer as a competitor as well as a supplier. This structure may also confuse and alienate customers who are unsure about which channel they should use.

Channel Intensity

Sometimes referred to as 'channel coverage', 'channel intensity' refers to the number and dispersion of outlets that an end-user customer can use to buy a particular offering. This decision concerns the level of convenience that customers expect and suppliers need to provide to be competitive. The wider the coverage, the greater the number of intermediaries, which leads to higher costs associated with the management control of the intermediaries.

Intensive	Selective	Exclusive
Distribution through every reasonable outlet in the market	Distribution through multiple, but not all, reasonable outlets in the market	Distribution through a single wholesaling intermediary and/or retailer

Figure 10.5 Intensity of distribution continuum

There are three levels of channel intensity: intensive, selective, and exclusive (see Figure 10.5).

Chocolates and other snacks are typical examples of impulse purchases characterized by intensive distribution.

Source: © Mawardi Bahar/Shutterstock.

- **Intensive distribution** involves placing an offering in as many outlets or locations as possible. It is used most commonly for offerings that consumers are unlikely to search for and which they purchase on the basis of convenience or impulse, such as magazines and soft drinks or confectionery.
- **Selective distribution** occurs when a limited number of outlets are used. This is because, when customers are actively involved with a purchase and experience moderate-to-high levels of perceived risk, they are prepared to seek out appropriate suppliers. Those that best match their overall requirements are successful. Producers determine and control which intermediaries are to deliver the required products and level of services. Electrical equipment, furniture, clothing, and jewellery are categories in which selective distribution is appropriate.
- **Exclusive distribution** occurs when intermediaries are given exclusive rights to market an offering within a defined 'territory'. This is useful where significant support is required from the intermediary, and the exclusivity is thus 'payback' for their investment and support. High-prestige goods, such as Ferrari sports cars, and designer fashion brands, such as Chanel and Gucci, adopt this type of distribution intensity.

Through the Internet, nearly all distribution is intensive because of the massive reach of the web. Even the smallest manufacturer can advertise and sell worldwide, using the same courier services to deliver its offerings as do major firms.

The decision about the number of intermediaries is often driven by cost considerations. The costs of intensive distribution are higher because of the number of outlets that must be served. The implications of these three strategies for distribution are summarized in Table 10.1.

Table 10.1	Intensity of channel coverage		
Characteristics	**Exclusive**	**Selective**	**Intensive**
Objectives	Strong image channel control and loyalty; price stability	Moderate market coverage; solid image; some channel control and loyalty	Widespread market coverage; channel acceptance; volume sales
Channel members	Few in number; well-established; reputable stores	Moderate in number; well-established; better stores	Many in number; all types of outlet
Customers	Few in number; trendsetters; willing to travel to store; brand-loyal	Moderate in number; brand-conscious; somewhat willing to travel to store	Many in number; convenience-oriented
Marketing emphasis	Personal selling; pleasant shopping conditions; good service	Promotional mix; pleasant shopping conditions; good service	Mass advertising; nearby location; items in stock
Examples	Automobiles; designer clothes; caviar	Furniture; clothing; watches	Groceries; household products; magazines

Managing Relationships in the Channel

An important managerial issue concerns channel relationships. Because channels are open social systems (Katz and Kahn, 1978), some level of conflict between channel members is inevitable. Conflict follows a breakdown in the levels of cooperation between channel partners (Shipley and Egan, 1992) and may well affect channel performance. Gaski (1984: 11) defined 'channel conflict' as 'the perception on the part of a channel member that its goal attainment is being impeded by another, with stress or tension the result'.

Channel conflict may involve intermediaries on the same level (tier), for example between retailers or between agents (that is, **horizontal conflict**). It may also occur between members on different levels (tiers), involving a producer, wholesaler, and a retailer (that is, **vertical conflict**).

If strategies to prevent or avoid conflict have failed, it is necessary to resolve the conflict that erupts. The strategies depicted in Table 10.2 vary from selfishness or stubbornness and a refusal to work with other members, through cooperation and compromise, to seeking to accommodate all of the views of other parties, even to the extent of jeopardizing one's own position. The prevailing corporate culture, attitude towards risk, and sense of power that exists within coalitions shapes the chosen strategy.

Visit the **online resources** and read about the conflict that has arisen in the supermarket industry in the UK.

Table 10.2 Conflict resolution strategies

Strategy	Explanation
Accommodation	Modifying expectations to incorporate requirements of others
Argument	Attempting to convince others of the correctness of one's position
Avoidance	Removing self from the point of conflict
Compromise	Meeting the requirements of others halfway
Cooperation	Mutual reconciliation through cooperation
Instrumentality	Agreeing minimal requirements to secure short-term agreement
Self-seeking	Seeking agreement on own terms or refusing further cooperation

Source: Fill and McKee (2012). Used with kind permission.

Market Insight 10.2 **Troubling Power in the Channel**

In modern marketing channels, supermarket chains tend to have a significant amount of power that can sometimes lead to vertical conflict with their suppliers. Tesco, the largest supermarket in the UK, has been the target of criticism from many of its suppliers, especially small and medium-sized businesses, who claimed that it used unfair tactics to foster its own self-interest to the disadvantage of its partners.

The Groceries Code Adjudicator—a government post recently created to police the respect of codes of practice in the retailing industry—launched an investigation into the supermarket that stretched from 25 June 2013 to 5 February 2015. The investigation found Tesco responsible for a number of unfair practices. Arguably the most troubling finding was that Tesco knowingly delayed payments to suppliers to put pressure on them in future negotiations. The debt allowed Tesco to demand harsher terms. In several cases, suppliers felt that they had to waive the debt because they did not want to damage the relationship with one of their most important clients. Complaints from suppliers were

Channel power: Tesco has apologized to its suppliers for the unfair tactics it may have used in the past.

Source: © Darren Grove/Shutterstock.

Market Insight 10.2 (continued)

often dismissed, or simply mismanaged, so that it would take months before a supplier could get a reply.

Recently, Tesco has implemented significant changes to its practices to improve its relationships with suppliers. Dave Lewis, appointed chief executive officer (CEO) in July 2014, apologized for Tesco's treatment of suppliers and worked to restore the company's reputation. In January 2015, it introduced the Tesco Supplier Network, a social media tool to link suppliers, buyers, and producers globally. The Network, together with changes in internal policies, is helping Tesco to rebuild its relationships with suppliers, with the objective of creating better solutions for its customers.

1 **What are the sources of Tesco's power in the marketing channel?**

2 **What sources of conflict can you think of in the relationship between a manufacturer and a supermarket?**

3 **How might Tesco ensure that suppliers are always treated fairly?**

Source: Ruddick (2015); Armstrong (2016).

Supply Chain Management

The second major issue associated with marketing channels concerns the movement of parts, supplies, and finished products. Melnyk and colleagues (2009) believe that 'supply chain management' (SCM) is concerned with the value creation chain of all of the activities associated with physical distribution. This embraces the chain of suppliers involved in providing raw materials (upstream), through the assembly and manufacturing stages, to distribution to end-user customers (downstream). This linkage is now referred to as a 'supply chain', formerly commonly called 'logistics' and, before that, 'physical distribution'.

Integrated SCM refers to the business processes associated with the movement of parts, raw materials, work-in-progress, and finished goods. Unlike marketing channels, which are concerned with the management of customer behaviour, finished goods, and inter-organizational relationships, the goal of SCM is to improve efficiency and effectiveness with regard to the physical movement of products. Supply chain management is essentially about the management of all of the business activities necessary to get the right product, in the right place, for the right customer to access in a timely and convenient way (Fill and McKee, 2012).

Supply chain management comprises four main activities: **fulfilment**, transportation, **stock management**, and **warehousing**. Brewer and Speh (2000) argue that it also seeks to accomplish four main goals: waste reduction, time compression, flexible response, and unit cost reduction (see Table 10.3).

By achieving these four goals, the efficiency of a supply chain is improved and, as a result, end-user customers can experience improved levels of channel performance. Figure 10.6 shows these activities and goals brought together to promote superior supply chain performance.

Management of Asda Wal-Mart's supply chain is based on computerized scanning to inform suppliers very quickly of which products need delivery and in what quantities. More recent

Table 10.3 Supply chain management goals

Goal	Explanation
Waste reduction	By reducing the level of duplicated and excess stock in the chain, it becomes possible to harmonize operations between organizations to achieve new levels of uniformity and standardization.
Time compression	Reducing the order-to-delivery cycle time improves efficiency and customer service outputs. A faster cycle indicates a smoother and more efficient operation and associated processes. Faster times mean less stock, faster cash flow, and higher levels of service output.
Flexible response	By managing the order-processing elements (size, time, configuration, handling), specific customer requirements can be met without causing them inconvenience, and this contributes to efficiency and service delivery.
Unit cost reduction	By understanding the level of service output that is required by the end-user customers, it then becomes possible to minimize the costs involved in delivering to that required standard.

Source: Fill and McKee (2012); adapted from Brewer and Speh (2000).

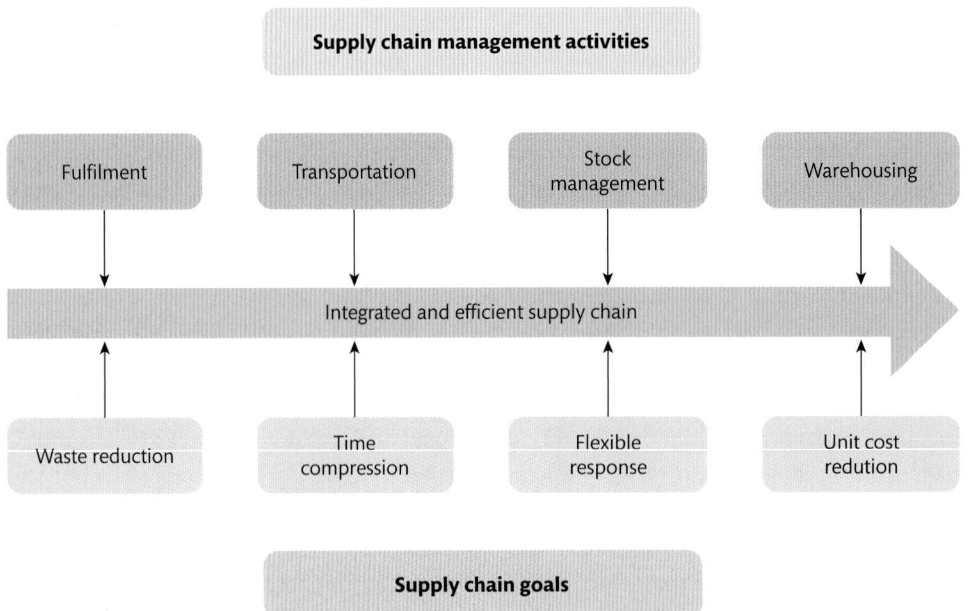

Figure 10.6 Developing high-performance supply chains

developments in electronic technologies, such as radio-frequency identification (RFID) tags, are improving the efficiency and effectiveness with which supply chain activities are managed.

Cost control is a core SCM activity, given that about 15 per cent of an average product's price comprises shipping and transport costs alone. Ikea can sell its furniture 20 per cent cheaper than competitors because it buys furniture ready for assembly, thereby saving on transport and inventory costs. The Benetton **distribution centre** in Italy is run largely by robots, delivering numerous goods to 120 countries within 12 days. Benetton also uses just-in-time (JIT) manufacturing, with some garments manufactured in neutral colours and then dyed to order, with very fast turnaround to suit customer requirements. However, beyond lowering costs, many organizations are increasing their focus on managing activities to improve customer service, meet the explosion in product variety, and harness the improvements in information and communication technology (ICT).

Thanks to its superior supply chain management, Ikea can be significantly cheaper than its competitors.

Source: © Tooykrub/Shutterstock.

Fulfilment

Fulfilment or materials handling is about locating and picking stock, packing and securing it, and then shipping the selected items or bundle to the next channel member. The increasing use of specialist software, IT, and equipment helps organizations to manage a range of fulfilment activities. Intra-warehouse stock movement needs to be minimized, while inter-warehouse movement is optimized (Fill and McKee, 2012). Automated emails are sent out to customers following online purchase of, for example, music from iTunes, a book from Amazon, or a train ticket. Accuracy and speed of billing and invoicing customers is also vitally important, especially for customer relationships.

Transportation and Delivery

Transportation is considered to be the most important activity within SCM. Transportation involves the physical movement of products using, for example, road, rail, air, pipeline, and shipping. Sometimes, transportation is seen only as a way of supplying tangible goods, but it can also be as relevant to many service organizations and the delivery of electronic (or digital) products. Consultants, IT companies, and health organizations have to move staff around, incurring transport and accommodation costs. Management of transport usually involves making decisions between one or more transportation methods and ensuring vehicle capacity. Transportation methods also include electronic delivery modes, such as electronic vending machines, the telephone, the Internet, or EDI.

Stock Management

Stock, or inventory, management involves trying to balance responsiveness to customer needs with the resources required to store stock. The management of both finished and unfinished goods can be critical to many organizations. A balance needs to be achieved between the number of finished goods to be available when customers need it (known as 'speculation') and a store of unfinished goods that can be assembled at a later date or when the stock of finished goods runs low (known as 'postponement').

Warehousing and Materials Handling

Supply chains involved with the exchange of goods usually require storage facilities for the periods between production, transportation, and purchase or consumption. Books, dry goods such as sugar and canned goods, and even clothing all require some level of storage between the time when they leave the producer or manufacturer and that at which they are required to be delivered to end-user customers.

Visit the **online resources** and use the web link to read about how a major retailer has had to redesign and update its warehousing to cope with online sales.

Market Insight 10.3 **Getting it There, on Time . . . : Medicine, IT, and Fashion**

The distribution of medicines by companies such as bioMérieux, Horiba ABX, and NovoNordisk involves a larger number of issues because human lives are at risk. As a result, logistics providers have to guarantee that products such as insulin are delivered not only securely and on time, but also in pristine condition. Warehouses and temperature-controlled trailers use probes and telesurveillance systems to ensure that temperatures are maintained within set parameters during transportation. Speed of delivery is also important, so companies such as XPO Logistics arrange for delivery to be made without breaking the 'cold chain'. The trucks used to transport pharmaceutical products rarely stop and pallet unloading time is minimized. There are systematic controls carried out each time a driver stops, and deviations in temperature and other problems are detected in real time.

In the IT industry, life cycles are only 13 weeks long, so, yet again, on-time delivery is critical. For

The design of the supply chain enables Zara to respond to new fashion trends quickly and efficiently.

Source: © Vytautas Kielaitis/Shutterstock.

companies such as ASUS, production and shipments need to be timed precisely to ensure that the transition between old and new products is smooth, and results in optimal sales and a minimum of old products still on the shelf. An ASUS notebook made

Market Insight 10.3 (continued)

in China takes two-and-a-half weeks to reach North America by ocean freight. In addition, there is a further two weeks taken for it to reach customers' stores. So, when XPO Logistics improved the ocean schedules using faster vessels and an evening crew, to turn the cargo around on the same day, transit times were slashed. This led to a competitive advantage, because ASUS could get new products to market faster than its competitors.

Inditex, whose brands include Zara, Bershka, and Stradivarius, has developed a supply chain built around its customers. The organization can design, produce, and deliver a new garment to its 6,683 stores across 88 countries in just 15 days, and turns orders into delivered items in 24 hours in Europe and 48 hours in America and Asia. This is achieved through a holistic approach to SCM—one that optimizes the entire chain instead of focusing only on individual parts. A single, centralized design and production centre consists of three spacious halls: one for women's clothing lines, one for men's, and one for children's. Separate design, sales, and procurement and production planning staffs are dedicated to each clothing line. Although it is more expensive to operate three channels, the information flow for each channel is fast, direct, and unencumbered by problems in other channels—making the overall supply chain more responsive.

1 **Explore the notion that managers of supply chains should have a greater concern for ethical issues than marketing channel managers.**

2 **How might the Norbert Dentressangle Group (and its competitors) encourage potential clients to use its particular services?**

3 **Make a list of the different issues associated with the transportation of dairy products, computers, cars, and medicines.**

Sources: Ferdows et al. (2004); Hansen (2012); Leob (2015); http://www.inditex.com/documents/; http://www.norbert-dentressangle.co.uk/Client-Success/Case-studies/; http://www.telegraph.co.uk/sponsored/business/.

Warehousing Tangible Goods and 'Digital' Products

For the storage of tangible goods, such as FMCGs, an organization can use either **storage warehouses** or distribution centres. Storage warehouses store goods for moderate-to-long periods (that is, products that have long shelf lives), whereas distribution centres are designed to move goods, rather than only to store them. For products that are highly perishable with short shelf lives, such as fruit and vegetables, distribution centres are more appropriate.

Electronic warehousing systems, or database systems, are increasingly being used for the storage of products (or product components) that can be digitized. For example, emerald-library.com, ABI-Inform, or ScienceDirect are electronic databases accessible through the Internet that store a vast array of documents electronically to facilitate customers' searches for information. In addition, many organizations use data warehousing facilities whereby product information, or even actual products, are stored in digital form awaiting distribution. Apple iTunes is the largest music retailer in the world. By February 2013, the online store had categorized more than 26 million songs, 190,000 television episodes, 45,000 movies, and 1,500 books. This does not include the tens of thousands of games and podcasts stored electronically. Customers can find, download, play, and sync in a fraction of the time it would take them to drive to a store.

We will now look more closely at one particular type of intermediary used in consumer markets: the retailer.

Retailing

Retailing encompasses all of the activities directly related to the sale of products and services to consumers for personal use. Retailers differ from wholesalers, who distribute the product to businesses, not consumers. Whether they are large retailers, such as Lotte (South Korea), Extra (Brazil), or Carrefour (France), or one of the thousands of small owner-run retailers in India, all retailers provide a downstream link between producers and end consumers.

Retailers provide consumers with access to products. As such, it is very important for retailers to find out what consumers actually want if the retailer is to deliver value. Convenience and time utility is the primary concern for most consumers, with people increasingly being 'leisure time poor' and keen to trade off shopping time for leisure time (Seiders et al., 2000). Consequently, convenience drives most innovations in retailing, such as supermarkets, department stores, shopping malls, the Internet, and self-scanning kiosks, in pursuit of providing customer convenience. As noted by Seiders and colleagues (2000), from a customer's perspective, 'convenience' means speed and ease in acquiring a product, and consists of:

- *access* convenience—that is, being easy to reach;
- *search* convenience—that is, enabling customers to easily identify what they want;
- *possession* convenience—that is, ease of obtaining products; and
- *transaction* convenience—that is, ease of purchase and return of products.

These are outlined in more detail in Table 10.4.

Table 10.4 Retailing convenience: A customer's perspective

Element	Description
Access convenience	• Accessibility factors include location, availability, hours of operation, parking, and proximity to other outlets, as well as telephone, mail, and Internet • Convenience does not exist without access • Increasingly, customers want access to products and services to be as fast and direct as possible, with very little hassle • A global trend, e.g. rise of convenience stores in Japan • Direct shopping driven by time and place utility
Search convenience	• Identifying and selecting the products wanted is connected to product focus, intelligence outlet design and layout (servicescape), knowledgeable staff, interactive systems, product displays, package and signage, etc. • Solutions can be provided in the form of in-store kiosks, clearly posted prices, and mobile phones for sales staff linked to knowledge centres • One example of good practice is German discount chain Adler Modemärkte AG, which uses colour-coded tags to help customers to quickly spot sizes

Table 10.4 Retailing convenience: A customer's perspective (*continued*)

Element	Description
Possession convenience	• About having merchandise in stock and available on a timely basis, e.g. clothing store Nordstrom guarantees that advertised products will be in stock • Has limitations for certain channels, e.g. highly customized products • Internet scores highly for search convenience, yet is generally low in terms of possession convenience
Transaction convenience	• Speed and ease with which consumers can effect and amend transactions before and after the purchase • A number of innovations exist here, e.g. self-scanning in Carrefour, Tesco, and Metro • Well-designed service systems can mitigate the peaks and troughs in store traffic, as with the use in Sainsbury's of in-store traffic counters to monitor store traffic • Even with queue design, single queues in post offices and banks differ from those in supermarkets owing to space and servicescape design • A significant issue on the Internet, with pure Internet retailers having problems with returns, and customers not prepared to pay for shipping and handling costs

Source: Based on Seiders et al. (2000). Reproduced with the kind permission of MIT *Sloan Management Review*.

Market Insight 10.4 **Enhancing Channel Experiences**

The rise of digital and mobile marketing, and the growth of online shopping, has put pressure on retailers to reconsider and improve their in-store customer experience. One of the approaches has been to involve music in retail environments, which has been found to encourage customers to stay longer and spend a little more than when there is no music. Sales can also be improved by matching the music with the products being sold. This is referred to as 'directional audio'. For example, research has shown that sales of French wine increase when French music is played and, likewise, sales of German wine increase when German music is played. In a similar study in Sweden, shoppers bought 10 per cent more organic products when

The House of Vans is based in the tunnels under Waterloo station and includes London's only permanent indoor skate park.

Source: Courtesy of House of Vans London.

Market Insight 10.4 (continued)

they could hear the sound of farm animals, with a narrator talking about the various benefits of organic products.

Changes in the luxury retail market have forced retailers to adapt and enhance the in-store experience. Many luxury consumers have been found to be less interested in accumulating possessions and are much more interested in the buying (shopping) experience. One of these involves the use of in-store sales associates to assist luxury customers in their purchase decisions. Whilst the use of personal shoppers in luxury stores is well established, stores such as Bebe, Zara, and Anthropologie now also offer personal styling services in-store.

The role of play within retail stores is becoming an important feature in the drive to create meaningful experiences. Toy retailer Hamleys launched its largest European store in Moscow with a central design feature that provides opportunities for customers of all ages to play. Nine different zones, which include an enchanted forest to explore, motor city with a go-kart track, and a safari section, make the store feel more like a theme park rather than a pure retail outlet. Each zone is designed to stimulate the senses, and achieves this by mixing interactive attractions and entertainment.

Vans, the US clothing and footwear brand, opened The House of Vans in the tunnels under Waterloo station. It offered London's only permanent indoor skate park, along with an art gallery, live music venue, and cinema, featuring events and exhibitions that are changed regularly. The informality of the environment enables brand relationships to develop through soft interaction.

Car manufacturer Audi has developed Audi City in London. This environment encourages visitors to explore and configure their ideal car using touchscreens and multisensory displays. The Lexus Intersect space focuses on the whole Lexus lifestyle, not only cars. By focusing on a range of topics, from food to fashion, Lexus has positioned itself as a cultural hub more than a showroom.

1. **How might a fashion retailer provide memorable in-store experiences?**
2. **Identify those types of retailer that may be more dependent than others on the value-added activities of the marketing channel.**
3. **Visit the websites of a department store (for example http://www.johnlewis.com) and a supermarket. How do they compare? Are there any retailing similarities?**

Sources: Anon. (2014); Regan (2015); Sorin (2015).

Research Insight 10.2

To take your learning further, you might wish to read this influential paper.

Glynn, M. S., Brodie, R. J., and Motion, J. (2012) 'The benefits of manufacturer brands to retailers', *European Journal of Marketing*, 46(9): 1127–49.

In this paper, the authors discuss the key value and benefits that consumers derive from retailing. They consider the key benefit of convenience in retailing strategy from a customer's perspective. They define 'convenience' as meaning speed and ease, and consisting of four key elements: access, search, possession, and transaction.

 Visit the **online resources** to read the abstract and access the full paper.

Types of Retailer

There are numerous types of retailer. These can be classified according to the marketing strategy employed (that is, product, price, and service level) and the store presence (that is, store or non-store retailing).

Table 10.5, although not exhaustive, provides a useful summary of these elements across the differing types of retailing channel.

Table 10.5 Marketing strategy and retail store classification

Type of retail store	Product assortment	Pricing	Customer service	Example
Department	Very broad and deep, with layout and presentation of products critical	Minimize price competition	Wide array and good quality	David Jones Debenhams Harrods
Discount	Broad and shallow	Low-price positioning	Few customer service options	Dollar Dazzlers poundstretcher Poundland
Convenience	Narrow and shallow	High prices	When high quality, can be a competitive advantage	7-Eleven Co-op
Limited line	Narrow and deep	Traditional = avoids price competition; new kinds = low prices	Vary by type	Bicycle stores Ladies' fashion Sports stores
Speciality	Very narrow and deep	Avoids price competition	Standard; extensive in some	Bridal boutiques Athletics shops
Category killer	Narrow and very deep	Low prices	Few to moderate	Ikea Office Works Staples
Supermarket	Broad and deep	Some = low price; others = avoid price disadvantages	Few and self-service	Carrefour (Europe) Tesco plc (UK) Woolworths Ltd. (Australia)
Superstores	Very broad and very deep	Low prices	Few and self-service	ASDA Wal-Mart Tesco Extra

The types of retailing establishment can be further distinguished as follows.

- *Department stores* are large-scale retailing organizations that offer a very broad and deep assortment of products (both hard and soft goods), and provide a wide array of customer service facilities for store customers. Debenhams, for example, has a wide array of products including home furnishings, foods, cosmetics, clothing, books, and furniture, and further provides variety within each category (such as brand, feature variety).
- *Discount retailers* are positioned based on low prices combined with the reduced costs of doing business. The key characteristics here involve a broad, but shallow, assortment of products, low prices, and very few customer services. Matalan in the UK, for example, Kmart in Australia, and Target in the United States all carry a broad array of soft goods (such as apparel), combined with hard goods (such as appliances and home furnishings). To keep prices down, the retailers negotiate extensively with suppliers to ensure low merchandise costs.
- *Limited-line retailers* have a narrow, but deep, product assortment and customer services vary from store to store. Clothing retailers, butchers, baked goods, and furniture stores that specialize in a small number of related product categories are all examples. The breadth of product variety differs across limited line stores and a store may choose to concentrate on several related product lines (for example shoes and clothing accessories), a single product line (for example shoes), or a specific part of one product line (for example sports shoes).
- *Category killer stores*, as the name suggests, are designed to kill off the competition and are characterized by a narrow, but very deep, assortment of products, low prices, and few-to-moderate customer services. Successful examples include Ikea in home furnishings, Staples in office supplies, and B&Q in hardware.
- *Supermarkets*, founded in the 1930s, are large, self-service retailing environments that offer a wide variety of differing merchandise to a large consumer base. Tesco Extra in the UK stocks products from clothing, hardware, music, groceries, and dairy products to soft furnishings. Operating largely on a self-service basis, with minimum customer service and centralized register and transactional terminals, supermarkets provide the benefits of a wide product assortment in a single location, offering convenience and variety. Today, supermarkets are the dominant institution for food retailing.
- *Convenience stores*, or 'corner shops', offer a range of grocery and household items that cater for convenience and last-minute purchase needs. Key characteristics include long opening times (for example 24 hours a day, seven days a week, or '24/7'), being family-run, and belonging to a trading group. The 7-Eleven, Spar, and Co-op are all examples. Increasingly, we are seeing smaller convenience stores threatened by large supermarket chains such as Asda Wal-Mart and Tesco, especially as laws for longer opening times for larger stores are relaxed (such as Sunday trading hours in the UK).

Visit the **online resources** and complete Internet Activity 10.2 to learn more about the variety of Internet retailing sites and the importance of delivery information for the music sector.

Market Insight 10.5 **Programmatic Commerce**

Gone are the days when having a website with an online shopping facility was considered the height of innovation for retailers. Nowadays, most leading companies are aware that they need to aim for a consistent service delivery across a multiplicity of channels, both online and off. This trend is often called 'multichannel', or 'omnichannel', retailing. But as companies adjust to managing the complexity of multiple retailing formats, the next revolution is already taking shape. Some call it 'programmatic commerce' and it is essentially based on the seamless integration of the Internet of Things (IoT)—the idea that devices can increasingly communicate with each other through the Internet—into existing retailing systems.

With 20.7 million devices expected to be connected to the Internet by 2020, it will be possible to let technology make purchase decisions for us on the basis of pre-programmed consumer needs and learned preferences. For example, your coffee maker will know that you have almost run out of your favourite blend of coffee and will automatically update your shopping app with a default choice, or a range of choices. At that point, it will take seconds for you to review the option and confirm the purchase. In fact, you could even completely automate the decision to buy a certain product when it runs out, so that you save time making decisions.

This new model of retailing requires the widespread availability of interconnected devices, as well as consumers feeling comfortable with sharing more of their personal data with organizations they trust. The advantage is an increase in the ease of choice: many decisions that customers need to make every time they buy a product, especially in the FMCG area, will become automatic. Some online retailers such as Amazon are already experimenting with this paradigm, offering discounts for subscriptions to products that consumers routinely purchase.

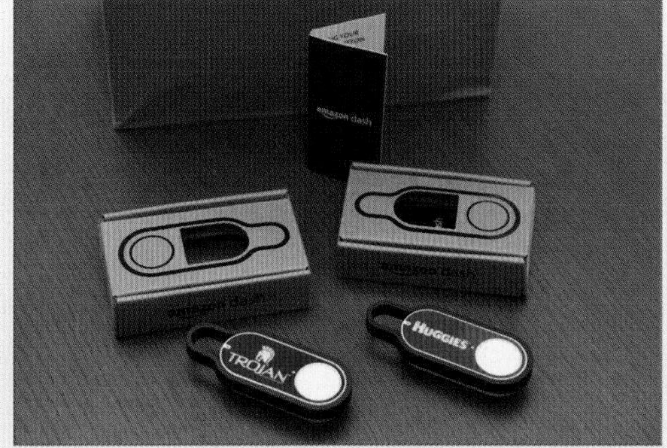

Amazon Dash is a Wi-Fi button that allows customers to automatically reorder their favourite brands.

Source: © Getty / Bryan Bedder / Stringer.

Programmatic commerce would have far-reaching implications. It would improve efficiencies, because consumption patterns would be easier to predict and stocks could be minimized. It would also create important marketing implications, because it would lead to an increase in switching costs. Once a brand of coffee becomes a customer's default choice, competitors will find it increasingly difficult to enter into that customer's consideration set. Marketers should pay attention and start experimenting now to find potential solutions for the challenges that this new environment could pose.

1. **What are the advantages for customers of programmatic commerce?**
2. **How could programmatic commerce affect the relationship between retailers and manufacturers? What are the advantages and disadvantages of this innovation for manufacturers?**
3. **How could we use programmatic commerce to collect useful customer data? What are the ethical implications of the data collection that this form of commerce can generate?**

Sources: Arthur (2016); Temple (2016).

Chapter Summary

To consolidate your learning, the key points from this chapter are summarized below.

- **Describe the nature and characteristics of a marketing channel.**

  Marketing channels are chains of organizations that are concerned with the management of the processes and activities involved in creating and moving particular offerings from producers and manufacturers to end-user customers. Marketing channels enable different types of uncertainty to be lowered by reducing the complexity, increasing value and competitive advantage, offering routinization, and/or providing specialization.

- **Explain the different types of intermediary and their roles in the marketing channel.**

  An intermediary is an independent organization that operates as a link between producers and end-user consumers or industrial users. There are several different types of intermediary, including agents, merchants, distributors, franchises, wholesalers, and retailers. The main role of intermediaries is to reduce uncertainty experienced by producers and manufacturers, and they promote efficiency. The key difference between the various intermediaries is that not all of them take legal title or physical possession of a product.

- **Understand the different marketing channel structures and their core characteristics.**

  There are three main marketing channel structures: a direct channel involves selling directly to end-user customers; an indirect channel involves using intermediaries; and a multichannel involves both. At the simplest level, direct channels offer maximum control, but do not always reach all of the target market. Indirect channels can maximize coverage, but often at the expense of control. This is because intermediaries start adapting the marketing mix and demand a share of the profits in return for their involvement. Multichannel strategies often result in greater channel conflict because intermediaries perceive the manufacturer to be a competitor.

- **Explain the factors that influence the design and structure of marketing channels.**

  When establishing or adapting marketing channels, it is necessary to consider the type of market coverage that is required, the number and type of intermediaries to use, and how the relationships between channel members are to be managed. These choices are important because they can affect the value that is ultimately provided to customers.

- **Describe the main elements that constitute supply chain management.**

  Supply chain management (SCM) concerns the various suppliers involved in providing raw materials (upstream), those that assemble and manufacture products, and those who distribute finished products to end-user customers (downstream). It embraces four main activities—fulfilment, transportation, stock management, and warehousing—which also subsume other important activities, such as order processing and purchasing. Although these are not traditionally marketing management decisions, it is important to understand that they require a marketing focus and marketing insight.

- **Consider the role and function of retailers in the marketing channel.**

  Retailing concerns all activities directly related to the sale of goods and services to consumers for personal and non-business use. Retailers provide consumers with access to products and help to reduce the uncertainty experienced by other intermediaries in the channel, such as wholesalers and manufacturers. This is achieved by taking small quantities of stock on a regular basis, promoting cash flows, and providing demand for their products and services. The different types of retailing establishment can be classified according to two key characteristics: the marketing strategy (that is, product, price, and service) and the store presence (that is, store or non-store retailing).

Review Questions

1. What do we mean by 'marketing channel management'?
2. Why do organizations use intermediaries?
3. What are the key elements of a channel strategy?
4. What are the advantages and disadvantages of the three different marketing channel structures?
5. What are the advantages of using an exclusive, rather than an intensive, marketing channel strategy?
6. Why is supply chain management of increasing importance to marketers?
7. What are some of the reasons for channel conflict?
8. Identify six types of retailer.
9. What does the term 'non-store retailing' mean? Identify the main types.
10. Write brief notes on how the role of intermediaries in marketing channels has changed as a result of the introduction of electronic technologies.

Worksheet Summary

To apply the knowledge you have gained from this chapter, and to test your understanding of implementing the marketing mix, visit the **online resources** and complete Worksheet 10.1.

Discussion Questions

1. Having read Case Insight 10.1, what do you see as the main challenges for Åhléns in developing its online offer? How would you advise Åhléns to deal with them?

2. Discuss the importance of intermediaries. In your discussion, outline the benefits and limitations of three types of intermediary.

3. Select three direct channels and identify two types of product that are best suited to this approach. Identify the benefits of this channel strategy.

4. Convenience has become a critical issue in marketing channel decisions. Assess the arguments for and against focusing on convenience from a customer's perspective.

Visit the **online resources** and complete the multiple-choice questions to assess your knowledge of the chapter.

Glossary

direct channel structure marketing channel whereby the product is delivered directly from the producer to the final customer.

distribution centres facilities designed to move goods, rather than only to store them.

distribution channel *see* **marketing channel**

exclusive distribution distribution whereby intermediaries are given exclusive rights to market the good or service within a defined 'territory', and thus a limited number of intermediaries are used.

fulfilment activities associated with locating and picking stock, packing, and shipping the selected items to the next channel member.

horizontal conflict conflict that may arise between members of a channel on the same level of distribution.

indirect channel structure marketing channel whereby the product moves from the producer, through an intermediary or series of intermediaries, such as a wholesaler, retailer, franchisee, agent, or broker, before being delivered to the final customer.

information utility the provision of information about the product offering before and after sales. It can also provide organizations with information about those purchasing their offerings.

intensive distribution distribution whereby an organization places its product or service in as many outlets or locations as possible to maximize the opportunity for customers to find it.

marketing channel an organized network of agencies and organizations that, together, perform all of the activities required to link producers and manufacturers with consumers, purchasers, and users to distribute product offerings.

multichannel structure marketing channel whereby multiple sales channels provide a variety of customer touchpoints.

ownership utility the immediate availability of goods from the intermediaries' stocks, allowing ownership to pass to the purchaser.

place utility the relocation of an offering to enable more convenient purchase and consumption.

retailing also known as the 'retail trade', all of the activities directly related to the sale of goods and services to the end consumer for personal and non-business use.

selective distribution distribution whereby some, but not all, available outlets for the good or service are used.

stock management activity involving achieving a balance between the anticipated number of finished goods required by customers and a sufficient store of unfinished goods that can be assembled at a later date or when the stock of finished goods runs low.

storage warehouses facilities that store goods for moderate-to-long periods.

supply chain management (SCM) an activity formed when organizations link their individual value chains.

time utility the gap bridged when manufacture, purchase, and consumption might occur at differing points in time.

transportation the physical movement of products using, for example, road, rail, air, pipeline, and shipping.

vertical conflict conflict between sequential members in a distribution network, such as producers, distributor, and retailers, over such matters as carrying a particular range or price increases.

warehousing facilities used to store tangible goods for the periods between production, transportation, and purchase/consumption.

References

Anon. (2014) 'How to create immersive in-store experiences with directional audio', *Retail Customer Experience*, 18 September. Available online at http://www.retailcustomerexperience.com/articles/how-to-create-immersive-in-store-experiences-with-directional-audio/ [accessed 23 July 2015].

Armstrong, A. (2016) 'Five ways Tesco turned the screws on its suppliers', *The Telegraph*, 26 January. Available online at http://www.telegraph.co.uk/finance/newsbysector/retailandconsumer/12122662/Five-ways-Tesco-turned-the-screws-on-its-suppliers.html [accessed 16 May 2016].

Arthur, R. (2016) 'The next big thing in retail: Programmatic commerce', *Forbes*, 24 February. Available online at http://www.forbes.com/sites/rachelarthur/2016/02/24/the-next-big-thing-in-retail-programmatic-commerce/#3cc08bbb3f52 [accessed 16 May 2016].

Brewer, P. C., and Speh, T. W. (2000) 'Using the balanced scorecard to measure supply chain performance', *Journal of Business Logistics*, 21(1): 75–95.

Ferdows, K., Lewis, M. A., and Machuca, J. A. D. (2004) 'Rapid-fire fulfilment', *Harvard Business Review*, 82(11): 104–10.

Fill, C., and McKee, S. (2012) *Business Marketing*, Oxford: Goodfellow.

Gaski, J. F. (1984) 'The theory of power and conflict in channels of distribution', *Journal of Marketing*, 48(3): 9–29.

Hansen, S. (2012) 'How Zara grew into the world's largest fashion retailer', *New York Times*, 9 November. Available online at http://www.nytimes.com/2012/11/11/magazine/how-zara-grew-into-the-worlds-largest-fashion-retailer.html [accessed 1 January 2017].

Katz, D., and Kahn, R. L. (1978) *The Social Psychology of Organisation* (2nd edn), New York: John Wiley.

Kotler, P., and Keller, K. (2009) *Marketing Management*, Englewood Cliffs, NJ: Prentice Hall.

Leob, W. (2015) 'Zara leads in fast fashion', *Forbes*, 30 March. Available online at http://www.forbes.com/sites/walterloeb/2015/03/30/zara-leads-in-fast-fashion/ [accessed 15 July 2015].

Melnyk, S. A., Lummus, R. R., Vokurka, R. J., Burns, L. J., and Sandor, J. (2009) 'Mapping the future of supply chain management: A Delphi study', *International Journal of Production Research*, 47(16): 4629–53.

Park, S. Y., and Keh, H. T. (2003) 'Modelling hybrid distribution channels: A game theory analysis', *Journal of Retailing and Consumer Services*, 10(3): 155–67.

Parker, M., Bridson, K., and Evans, J. (2006) 'Motivations for developing direct trade relationships', *International Journal of Retail and Distribution Management*, 34(2): 121–34.

Regan, J. (2015) 'The art of play is becoming serious business for retailers', *The Guardian*, 28 May. Available online at http://www.theguardian.com/media-network/2015/may/28/play-retail-experiences-brands-marketing [accessed 24 July 2015].

Ruddick, G. (2015) 'Tesco tries to rebuild relationship with suppliers', *The Telegraph*, 22 January. Available online at http://www.telegraph.co.uk/finance/newsbysector/retailandconsumer/11362881/Tesco-tries-to-rebuild-relationship-with-suppliers.html [accessed 16 May 2016].

Seiders, K., Berry, L. L., and Gresham, L. G. (2000) 'Attention retailers! How convenient is your convenience strategy?', *Sloan Management Review*, 41(3): 79–89.

Shipley, D., and Egan, C. (1992) 'Power, conflict and co-operation in brewer–tenant distribution channels', *International Journal of Service Industry Management*, 3(4): 44–62.

Sorin, K. (2015) 'Evolving retail expectations require enhanced experiences in-store: Report', *Luxury Daily*, 2 July. Available online at http://www.luxurydaily.com/evolving-retail-expectations-require-enhanced-experiences-in-store-report/ [accessed 23 July 2015].

Temple, J. (2016) 'Programmatic commerce: The next big thing'. Available online at https://www.salmon.com/en/resources/blogs/programmatic-commerce/ [accessed 16 May 2016].

Part 4

Managing Marketing Relationships

Chapter 11
Digital and Social Media Marketing

Learning Outcomes

After studying this chapter, you will be able to:

- define 'digital marketing' and 'social media marketing';
- explain how digitization is transforming marketing practice;
- discuss key techniques in digital marketing and social media marketing;
- review how practitioners measure the effectiveness of social media marketing; and
- discuss crowdsourcing and explain how it can be harnessed for marketing.

Case Insight 11.1
Spotify

Market Insight 11.1
Who's in Charge?

Market Insight 11.2
Digital Marketing Games

Market Insight 11.3
Searching the Amazon

Market Insight 11.4
Black Milk Clothing: More Virus than Viral

Case Insight 11.1 **Spotify**

What role does social media play and how should organizations incorporate it into their communication campaigns? We talk to Chug Abramowitz (pictured), vice-president of global customer service and social media at Spotify, to find out more.

Spotify's dream is to make all of the world's music available instantly to everyone.

Our streaming service launched in Sweden in 2008 and, as of 2015, we're available in 58 markets, with more than 75 million active users. Of these, more than 20 million are paid users. Today, Spotify brings you the right music for every moment—on computers, mobiles, tablets, home entertainment systems, cars, gaming consoles, and more.

Social media has been an important part of Spotify's growth in two ways: the marketing team has worked with agencies to create social media campaigns that engage customers and attract them to the Spotify brand, while the customer support team has monitored social media channels and used them as tools to help dissatisfied customers.

Lately, we've noticed that the customer support social media team is more effective than our agencies at customer engagement. The agencies are typically less in tune with what Spotify actually stands for and our tone. And while customer service is primarily about reacting to customers' concerns and praise, our reactions help to build the Spotify brand. For example, after solving someone's issue, our customer support social team regularly replies by drafting a message in the form of a playlist. Jelena Woehr, a satisfied customer, shared her experience online of a playlist in which the titles of the songs spelled out the message 'Jelena/You Are Awesome/ Thanks a Lot/For These Words/It Helps Me/Impress/ The Management'. The list quickly went viral.

We call these 'RAKs', which stands for 'Random Acts of Kindness'. This is our way of doing something special

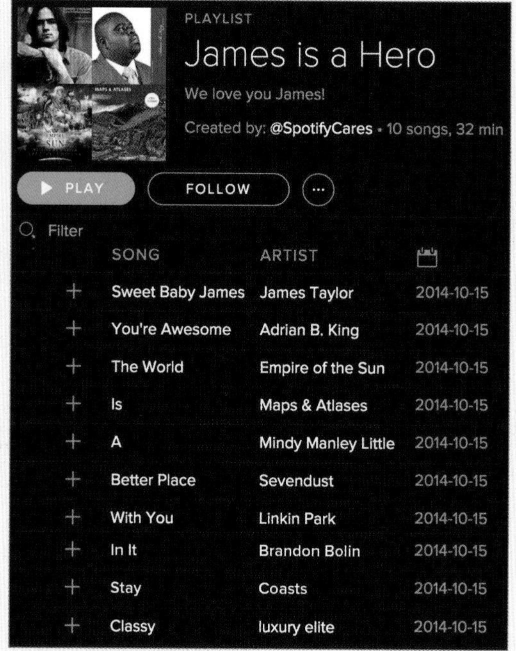

Another example of Spotify's use of playlists as random acts of kindness (RAK).

Source: Courtesy of Spotify.

for our customers that highlights music and our product in a very Spotify way. Our internal support advisers came up with RAKs, which is why I think they nail our tone of voice so well.

My focus now is to devise a strategy that incorporates the spot-on tone our social media support team has in our marketing campaigns. Most likely, campaigns will continue to be agency-created, but they will have to be filtered through the lens of our in-house social media crew. We also need to be

Case Insight 11.1 (continued)

better at using what we already have internally, in terms of both our content and our people. At Spotify, we create tons of content and we're not maximizing its value. Why have an agency make content when internal teams are developing materials that espouse Spotify's brand at its core? On top of that, Spotify's employees love music and go to gigs every week. We're missing an engagement opportunity with tremendous potential to show who we are and our entire company's love of music.

It's clear that social media offers so many possibilities, especially to a brand like Spotify that's centred on music, an integral part of most people's life. Social media offers the potential to show a company's passion for what it does and nobody is fully taking advantage of that yet. There are many brands out there doing interesting things here and there, but no one has been able to put it all together on a consistent basis. We're going to be the ones who do it.

To move forward, Spotify needs to answer the question: how can it combine customer support's great engagement with the type of advance planning and scale needed for marketing campaigns?

See also Griner (2013).

Introduction

Consider for a moment your own personal use of digital technology and social media. How often do you go online? What device do you use? It is most likely that you will notice that your behaviours have changed rather dramatically in the past five years. Devices such as the iPhone and the iPad, now an integral part of many people's everyday lives, were first introduced to the market as recently as 2007 and 2010, respectively. The same is true for many of the services and apps that we use. Airbnb (founded in 2008), Spotify (founded in 2006), and Uber (founded in 2009), which have used digital technology to transform where we stay when we travel, how we listen to music, and how we move around cities, all began their international expansions in the 2010s.

In 2015, the world's most 'networked ready' economy—'network readiness' being a measure of the degree to which economies leverage information and communication technology (ICT) for enhanced competitiveness—was Singapore, with Finland ranking second and Sweden third. The UK ranked eighth, the Netherlands, fourth, the United Arab Emirates (UAE), 30th, China, 51st, and India, 69th, out of 142 countries evaluated, according to a study by business school INSEAD and the World Economic Forum (Dutta et al., 2015). With increasing broadband penetration (largely via mobile devices), the adoption of digital and social media marketing techniques is vital. Apps, blogs, microblogs, social networking sites, wikis, and other multimedia sharing services have become commonplace. The technological development is rapidly changing the way in which consumers behave and marketers need to adapt accordingly.

As people change how they communicate, the marketing profession has turned to digital and social media marketing to complement, and sometimes replace, traditional marketing channels and activities. However, digitization is not only altering consumers' expectations of their interaction with organizations online, but also changing marketing in all forms.

In this chapter, we will focus on **digital marketing** and social media marketing as a tool with which to communicate and interact with consumers. First, we define digital and social media marketing, and track their evolution. We will then move on to discuss key areas of digital marketing communications, Internet advertising, search marketing, email marketing, social media marketing, content marketing, and **mobile marketing**. We then define 'crowdsourcing' and explain how it is used in marketing. Finally, we review some wider considerations in the development of digital marketing strategy.

Digital Marketing

Digital marketing is the management and execution of marketing using digital electronic technologies and channels (for example web, email, digital television, wireless media) and digital data about user/customer characteristics and behaviour. It is an established, and increasingly important, subfield of marketing brought about by advancements in digital media technologies and digital media environments. Digital marketing extends beyond Internet marketing, which is one form of digital marketing specific to the use of Internet-only technologies (such as web, email, intranet, extranets), in that it makes use of a range of different electronic technologies and channels, such as mobile telephony, digital display advertising, and the Internet of Things (IoT).

A variety of terms are used in relation to digital marketing, including 'e-marketing', 'Internet marketing', 'direct marketing', 'interactive marketing', 'mobile marketing', and 'social media marketing', among many others. Whilst these terms are sometimes incorrectly used interchangeably, they each have their own specific meaning (see Table 11.1). Sometimes, 'social marketing' is used as a synonym for 'social media marketing'. This is incorrect, however, because social marketing is an established term referring to the use of marketing to influence the behaviour of a target audience in which the benefits of that behaviour are intended by the marketer to accrue primarily to the audience, or to the society in general (hence are social), and not to the marketer. Social media marketing, meanwhile, is a tool increasingly being used by, for example, non-profits and public organizations to achieve such social benefits.

Visit the **online resources** and follow the web link to the eMarketer website for a comprehensive source of information on marketing in a digital world.

Before looking more closely at different types of digital marketing activity, we will briefly review the evolution of digital and social media marketing.

Evolution of the Internet

Since the early 1990s, the Internet has evolved and, with it, digital marketing. The rise of social media has led marketing to evolve away from a hierarchical, one-sided mass communication model towards more participatory technologies (such as social channels and online communities). These technologies facilitated the practice of user-generated, co-created, and user-shared content with a focus on the active (not passive) user/participant. By facilitating user participation, they contributed to a digital development away from a one-way model of information being 'pushed' through

Table 11.1 Defining digital marketing terms

Term	Definition
Digital marketing	Management and execution of marketing using digital electronic technologies and channels (e.g. Internet, email, digital television, wireless media) and digital data about user/customer characteristics and behaviour.
Direct marketing	'A specific form of marketing that attempts to send its communications direct to consumers using addressable media such as post, Internet, email, and telephone and text messaging' (Harris, 2009: 70).
E-marketing	Process of marketing accomplished or facilitated through the use of electronic devices, applications, tools, technologies, platforms, and/or systems. Not limited to one specific type or category of electronic technology (e.g. Internet, television), but includes both older analogue and developing digital electronic technologies.
Interactive marketing	Marketing that moves away from a transaction-based effort to a conversation (i.e. two-way dialogue) and can be described as a situation or mechanism through which marketers and a customer (e.g. stakeholders) interact, usually in real time. Not all interactive marketing is electronic (e.g. face-to-face sales).
Internet marketing	Process of marketing accomplished or facilitated via the use of Internet technologies (e.g. web, email, intranet, extranets).
Mobile marketing	'A set of practices that enables organizations to communicate and engage with their audience in an interactive and relevant manner through and with any mobile device or network' (MMA, 2009).
Social marketing	'Marketing designed to influence the behavior of a target audience in which the benefits of the behavior are intended by the marketer to accrue primarily to the audience or to the society in general and not to the marketer' (AMA, 2015).
Social media marketing	A form of digital marketing that describes the use of the social web and social media (e.g. social networks, online communities, blogs, wikis) or any online collaborative technology for marketing activities.

to target audiences towards a multichannel and multi-user approach in which web users were empowered to 'pull' down information, and/or to interact with the organization and content, as well as with each other (that is, consumer-to-consumer, or peer-to-peer).

This development means that consumers are increasingly relying on digital tools to guide their behaviours. It also means that consumers are becoming increasingly used to determining what information they want, when they want it, and how they want it. The web enables consumer pull (rather than organization push), ever-greater customer participation, co-creation of offerings (not only mass production), dialogue, and shared control over the form and content of a brand. This, in turn, is changing how marketers communicate, share information, interact, and create (or produce) an offering. The implications for digital marketing will be discussed further later in the chapter.

Evolution of Social Media

Social media has had a significant impact on marketing in the past 15 years. 'Social media' refers to a wide range of online, word-of-mouth forums, including blogs, company-sponsored discussion boards, and chat rooms, as well as consumer-to-consumer messaging services, consumer product or service ratings websites and forums, Internet discussion boards and forums, moblogs (sites containing digital audio, images, films, or photographs), and social networking websites (Mangold and Faulds, 2009). Social media enable individuals and organizations to connect to each other by means of digital devices such as laptops, tablets, and smartphones. Whereas social interactions have always been central to human, and thus consumer, behaviour, social media enables those interactions to expand in time and place. It also enables them to be made visible to more people, marketers included.

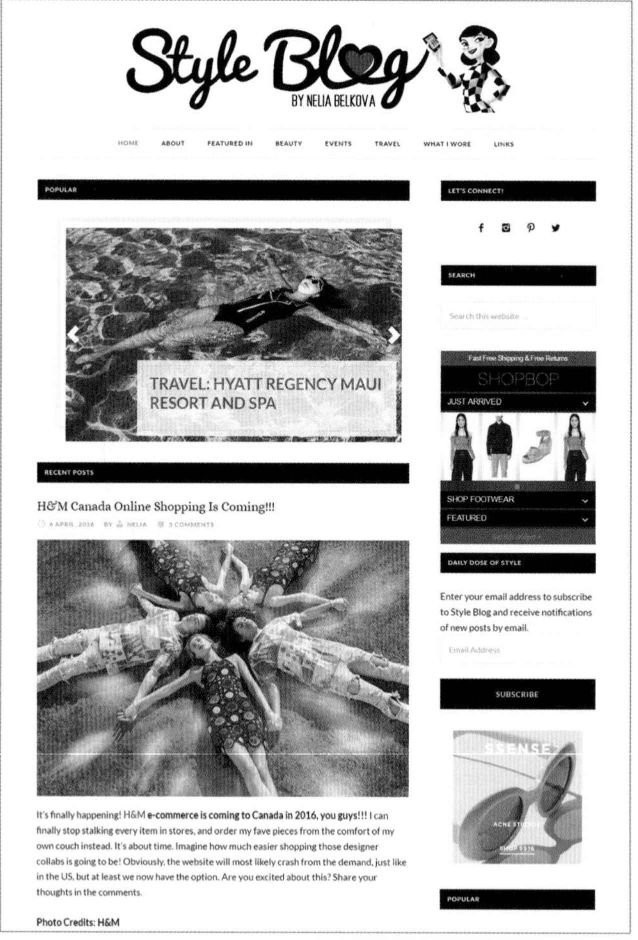

Consumers often consult sites such as Nelia Belkova's style blog before making their purchases.

Source: Property of Nelia Belkova.

In 2015, the global average social media penetration was 29 per cent, with North America having the highest penetration, at 59 per cent. In Europe, just under half of the population has at least one social network account (in Western Europe, 47 per cent; in Eastern Europe, 46 per cent). Social networking sites especially have seen massive growth since their inception. In 2014, Iceland (70 per cent) and Norway (64 per cent) had the largest share of monthly active social media users in Europe, followed by Malta and Denmark (both 58 per cent), and Sweden and the UK (both 57 per cent) (Anon., 2015a). In 2015, 72 per cent of Internet users in the UK had a social media profile, compared with 22 per cent in 2007, and 81 per cent of them use social media at least once a day (Ofcom, 2015). Facebook is by far the world's largest social network, with more than 1,550 million users globally. (For an overview of the top ten largest social media networks in 2016, see Table 11.2.)

Social media has had a major impact on marketing. In fact, many argue that it has turned marketing practice upside-down. Former beliefs no longer hold and marketers are working on adjusting to these changes, of which two are particularly noteworthy.

The first major change has to do with *power*. Social media enable users to generate, share, and comment on content at their own discretion (van den Bulte and Wuyts, 2007). Content in social media is co-created by consumers rather than (as in traditional offline media) primarily created by media companies and marketers. The proliferation of **user-generated content**

Table 11.2 Top ten social media networks in 2016

Social network	Users (millions)
Facebook	1,550
WhatsApp	900
QQ	860
Facebook Messenger	800
Qzone	653
WeChat	650
Tumblr	555
Instagram	400
Twitter	320
Baidu Tieba; Skype (tied)	300

Source: Anon. (2016).

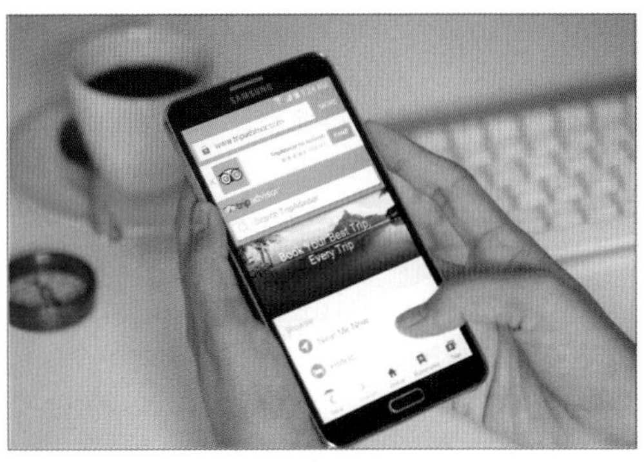

Tripadvisor is only one among a myriad review sites that are a critical source of information for consumers.

Source: © zaozaa19/Shutterstock.

(UGC)—that is, content made available over the Internet, which reflects creative effort, and is created outside professional routine and practices (Wunsch-Vincent and Vickery, 2007)—such as review sites (for example Epinions.com, Tripadvisor.com, and reviews on Amazon.com) and widely shared first-hand feedback about consumer experiences (for example through a picture and comment on Instagram) means that consumers have become increasingly influential. Social media allow consumers to share their experiences with each other at their own discretion, making service and product quality assessments widely available, thereby shifting power from marketers to consumers.

The second shift has to do with *control*. Whereas marketers have traditionally been in charge of the messages they communicate, this is no longer the case. In a computer-mediated environment, consumers not only are able to create and modify content to suit their needs, then share this content with consumers, companies, or third parties, but also have a voice in reacting to product offers and marketing that they do or do not like. As an example, the choice of (very thin or objectified) models used by fashion retailers in their advertisements is frequently debated and questioned in social media (recent examples include H&M and American Apparel), forcing the retailers to rethink the way in which they cast models in all of their marketing communications. With social media come higher transparency and less control for marketers in terms of how their communication is received and passed on.

Visit the **online resources** and complete Internet Activity 11.1 to learn more about how EY uses Twitter to maintain an ongoing real dialogue with its followers.

How Digitization is Transforming Marketing

Digital technology has the potential to transform marketing. According to a study by McKinsey and Co., companies that are integrating digital technology into their businesses perform significantly better financially than those who are not (Alldredge et al., 2015). According to the same study, the key characteristics for such digitally advanced companies are as follows.

- *Strategy*—Some 90 per cent of online leaders have digital initiatives fully integrated into their strategic planning process, not as a bolt-on.
- *Culture*—While 84 per cent of companies indicate their culture to be risk-averse, companies such as Amazon and Google embrace a different mentality: 'We think big and are not afraid to fail' (quoted in Alldredge et al., 2015). Instead of waiting for perfection, digital leaders adopt a fail–fast-forward mindset.
- *Organization*—Leading companies use non-traditional organizational structures, digital talent acquisition, and management to execute their digital vision. Some 65 per cent of digital leaders have an aggregated digital budget and sufficient budget allocation to scale their digital initiatives.

Market Insight 11.1 **Who's in Charge?**

In the past 15 years or so, social media have evolved from a debating ground for the initiated few to a conversational arena for the masses. Nowhere is this more evident than when it comes to discussions about purchases, companies, and brands. Customers taking their negative experiences online cause headaches for many marketing executives. Social media conversations, even in a company's own social media channels, are difficult to control, and if they are handled poorly, they may spin out of control and become issues in their own right. Moreover, the public nature of social media conversations makes such failings available to everyone for a very long time.

One example is the case of US retailer Target and Mike Melgaard. Mr Melgaard, when surfing Facebook one night, discovered that Target had removed gender-based labels on its toys. Anticipating outraged reactions from his more conservative American compatriots (with whom he does not agree on this issue), he quickly set up a fake Facebook account called 'Ask for Help' and included a profile picture similar to that of Target's own bull's-eye logo. Mr Melgaard then began commenting on the many negative posts that were soon piling up on Target's Facebook page as if he were an actual Target customer service representative. Over the course of 16 hours, Mr Melgaard gave humorous and slightly obnoxious replies to almost 50 posts before his fake account was shut down. One such instance included a negative post that began 'I know this means little to Target, but I am tired of all this political correctness . . . ', to which Mr Melgaard replied: 'Actually Gary, it means NOTHING to us that you feel this way. Have a great day!'

Target, when queried about the incident, offered a neutral statement that it is committed to customer service for everyone and that Mr Melgaard clearly did not represent the company. A few days later, however, Target quietly endorsed Mr Melgaard's actions by posting a picture of two toy trolls on its Facebook page, with the caption: 'Remember when Trolls were the kings of the world? Woo hoo! They're back and only at Target stores.' The photo generated more than 30,000 likes. Mr Melgaard—under his own name, this time—commented on the photo saying: 'Target. Seriously, You are AWESOME.' That comment alone generated more than 2,500 likes.

Is Mike speaking for Target? Flows of information are more difficult to control online.

Source: © Getty / Bloomberg / Contributor.

1. **Visit Target's website. In your opinion, what segment does Target consider to be its main target (no pun intended) audience? Considering that audience, do you think Target benefited from Mr Melgaard's actions?**
2. **What do you make of Target's strategy to cope with the situation? Could or should it have done something differently?**
3. **How do you think that Target's decision to quietly endorse Mr Melgaard's actions affected this incident and its core business?**

Sources: Colliander and Wien (2013); Nudd (2015a, 2015b).

This market insight was kindly contributed by Dr Jonas Colliander, Stockholm School of Economics, Sweden.

Research Insight 11.1

To take your learning further, you might wish to read this influential paper.

Kozinets, R. V., de Valck, K., Wojnicki, A. C., and Wilner, S. J. S. (2010) 'Networked narratives: Understanding word-of-mouth marketing in online communities', *Journal of Marketing*, 74(2): 71–89.

This paper develops a theoretical framework for understanding conversations around brands in social media. By means of a qualitative study of social media marketing using bloggers and an extensive review of extant word-of-mouth theory, the article gives insights into how marketers employing social media marketing should plan, target, and leverage social media conversations.

 **Visit the online resources to read the abstract and access the full paper.**

- *Capabilities*—Digital leaders make decisions based on data, and build capabilities that connect people, processes, and technology across all channels that engage with consumers. Some 80 per cent of digital leaders effectively invest in their digital IT infrastructure to support growth. That means moving beyond model building into implementing processes that can bring relevant internal and external resources to take action quickly.

Market Insight 11.2 **Digital Marketing Games**

The digital landscape is said to offer unlimited possibilities for companies to connect and influence their audiences. Social, digital, and mobile are transforming marketing communications. However, clouds are gathering on this clear digital sky as consumer exposure to communications in these channels increases. How can companies succeed in the digital landscape without getting stuck in ad-blockers or fading away in a cluttered environment?

Underwear brand Björn Borg was more than aware of these challenges when launching a new sportswear collection targeted at a young audience. How could it make an underwear campaign that was attention-grabbing, fun, and relevant? And could this campaign merge market communications with e-commerce? Meet 'First Person Lover'—a free online computer game in which players, dressed in their favourite underwear, battle evil forces with kisses and love grenades. To maximize the connection with the audience and to stimulate publicity, the game was filled with Internet jokes and political references. The audience loved it.

International media picked up on the game and, a few days after its launch, YouTube star PewDiePie (with more than 45 million subscribers) praised the game as one of the best of the year.

The results were instant: 512,000 players from 190 countries engaged with the game. Before playing, they were all given the opportunity to dress their characters in their preferred look from the new

Market Insight 11.2 (continued)

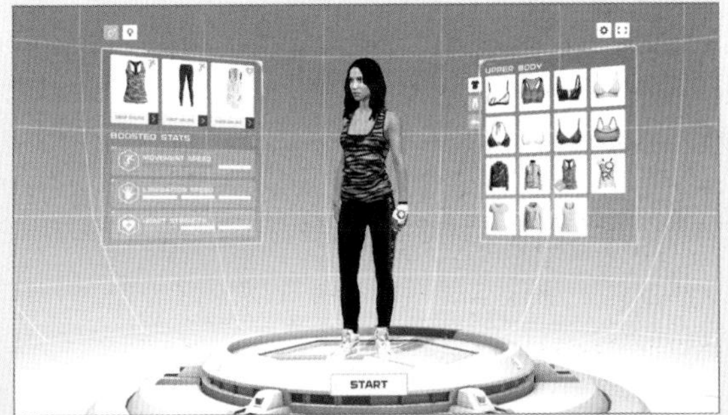

First Person Lover is a free online video game that joins the ability to communicate effectively with an e-commerce environment.

Source: Courtesy of BJÖRN BORG.

collection. The items were also available for purchase directly in the game. Moreover, the game was filled with hidden promotional codes that engaged players could use in Björn Borg's online shop. This led to a 40 per cent increase on online sales.

The digital landscape is filled with new opportunities if new technology is merged with relevant and entertaining communication.

1. **What would you say were the key success factors in the development of Björn Borg's game?**
2. **What benefits and drawbacks can you see of using a game to launch new products?**

Sources: Björn Borg (2015); Wisterberg (2015).

This market insight was kindly contributed by Dr Erik Modig, Stockholm School of Economics, Sweden.

Digital Marketing Communications

Investments in digital marketing communications are growing rapidly. Focus is primarily on communication using Internet-only technologies (such as web, email, intranet, extranet), which are accessed using desktops, laptops, tablets, and/or smartphones, but different types of digital display and tracking device are also increasingly being used to market products and brands.

Whereas traditional media are easily divided into formats based on the logic underlying them, this is not the case for digital marketing communications. The borders between paid ('advertising') media, earned ('publicity' and 'word-of-mouth'), and owned media (for example websites, profiles on social media, emails) are blurry and hard to establish.

In the following sections, we will discuss some of the most frequently used digital marketing communication activities in more detail.

Internet Advertising

'Internet advertising' refers to a form of marketing communication that uses the Internet for the purpose of advertising regardless of what device is being used to access it. Typically, it involves marketers paying media owners to carry their messages on their websites. Payment is either impression-based (for example cost per thousand, or CPM, pricing), performance-based (for example cost per click, sale, lead, acquisition, or application), or straight revenue share (for example percentage commission paid on sale). The aim of Internet advertising is to increase website traffic and/or encourage product trial, purchase, and repeat purchase activity (Cheng et al., 2009), and advertising format and payment should be adapted accordingly.

Table 11.3 offers a list of different Internet advertising formats and their definitions. Internet advertising in the UK totalled £7.194 billion for 2014 and, in the first six months of 2015, it had grown 13.4 per cent over the same period in 2014 (IAB and PwC, 2015a), with much of the growth being driven by mobile, digital video, and social media.

Table 11.3 Types of Internet advertising format

Ad format	Description	Share of Internet ad investments (%)*
Banner advertising	Advertiser pays an online company for space on one or more of the online company's pages to display a static or linked banner or logo.	16
Sponsorship	Advertiser pays for custom content and/or experiences, which may or may not include ad elements such as display advertising, brand logos, advertorial, or pre-roll video.	2
Search	Fees advertisers pay online companies to list and/or link their company site domain names to a specific search word or phrase (includes paid search revenues). Search categories include paid listings, contextual search, **paid inclusion**, and site optimization.	38 (excl. mobile search)
Lead generation	Fees paid by advertisers to online companies that refer qualified potential customers (e.g. auto dealers that pay a fee in exchange for receiving a qualified purchase inquiry online) or provide consumer information (demographic, contact, behavioural) whereby the consumer opts in to being contacted by a marketer (email, postal, telephone, fax). These processes are priced on a performance basis (e.g. cost per action, lead or inquiry), and can include user applications (e.g. for a credit card), surveys, contests (e.g. sweepstakes), or registrations.	4
Classifieds and auctions	Fees paid to advertisers by online companies to list specific products or services (e.g. online job boards and employment listings, real estate listings, automotive listings, auction-based listings, Yellow Pages).	5

Table 11.3	Types of Internet advertising format (continued)	
Ad format	**Description**	**Share of Internet ad investments (%)***
Rich media	Display-related ads that integrate some component of streaming interactivity. Ads often include Flash or Java script, but not content, and can allow users to view and interact with products or services (e.g. scrolling or clicking within the ad opens a multimedia product description, expansion, animation, video or a 'virtual test-drive').	3
Digital video advertising	Advertising that appears before, during, or after digital video content in a video player (i.e. pre-roll, mid-roll, post-roll video ads). Includes television commercials online and can appear in streaming content or in downloadable video. Display-related ads on a page (that are not in a player) that contains video are categorized as rich media ads.	7
Mobile advertising	Advertising tailored to and delivered through wireless mobile devices such as smartphones, feature phones (e.g. lower-end mobile phones capable of accessing mobile content), and media tablets. Typically taking the form of static or rich media display ads, text messaging ads, search ads, or audio/video spots, such advertising generally appears within mobile websites (e.g. websites optimized for viewing on mobile devices), mobile apps, text messaging services (i.e. SMS, MMS) or within mobile search results (i.e. 411 listings, directories, mobile-optimized search engines). Mobile advertising formats include search, display (banner ads, digital video, digital audio, sponsorships, and rich media), and other advertising served to mobile devices.	25
Digital audio	Refers to partially or entirely advertising-supported audio programming available to consumers on a streaming basis, delivered via the wired and mobile Internet.	n/a

*Based on US ad spend, 2014; may not total 100 per cent because of rounding.

Source: IAB and PwC (2015b).

Major considerations arising when using Internet advertising include the following.

- *Cost*—Internet adverts are still relatively cheap compared with traditional advertising.
- *Timeliness*—Internet adverts can be updated at any time, with minimal cost.
- *Format*—Internet adverts are richer, using text, audio, graphics, and animation. In addition, games, entertainment, and promotions can be incorporated.
- *Personalization*—Internet adverts can be interactive and targeted towards specific interest groups and/or individuals.

- *Location*—Using wireless technology and geo-location technology (a global positioning system, or GPS), Internet advertising can be targeted towards consumers wherever they are (for example near a restaurant or theatre).
- *Intrusiveness*—Some Internet advertising formats (such as pop-ups) are seen as intrusive and suffer more consumer complaints than other formats.

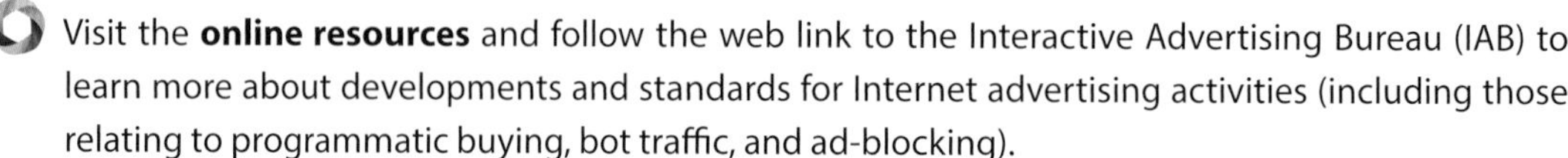

Visit the **online resources** and follow the web link to the Interactive Advertising Bureau (IAB) to learn more about developments and standards for Internet advertising activities (including those relating to programmatic buying, bot traffic, and ad-blocking).

Search Marketing

The growth in digital content available through the web has given rise to a number of interactive decision aids used to help web users to locate data, information, and/or an organization's digital objects (for example pictures, videos). The main two types of decision aid are a **search directory** (web directory) and a **search engine**.

A *search directory* is a human-edited database of information. It lists websites by category and subcategory, with categorization usually based on the whole website rather than one page or a set of keywords. Search directories often allow site owners to submit a site directly for inclusion and editors review submissions for fitness. Examples of search directories are Yahoo Pages and The Open Directory Project (http://www.dmoz.org). Given its large scope, Amazon could also be considered to offer a search directory for shopping.

In contrast, a *search engine* operates algorithmically, or uses a mixture of algorithmic and human input, to collect, index, store, and retrieve information on the web (for example webpages, images, information, and other types of file), making this information available to users in a manageable and meaningful way in response to a search query. Information is retrieved by a web crawler (also known as a 'spider'), which is an automated web browser that follows every link on the site, analysing how it should be indexed, using words extracted from page and file titles, headings, or special fields called 'meta-tags'. The indexed data are then stored in an index database for use in later queries. When a user enters a query into a search engine (typically using keywords), the engine examines its index and provides a search engine result page (SERP)—that is, a listing of webpages ordered according to best match with the input criteria. There are only a few dominant search engines in the market, with Google leading the global market share at 89 per cent, followed by Yahoo! and Bing, both at 4 per cent, and Chinese Baidu at just below 1 per cent (Anon., 2015a).

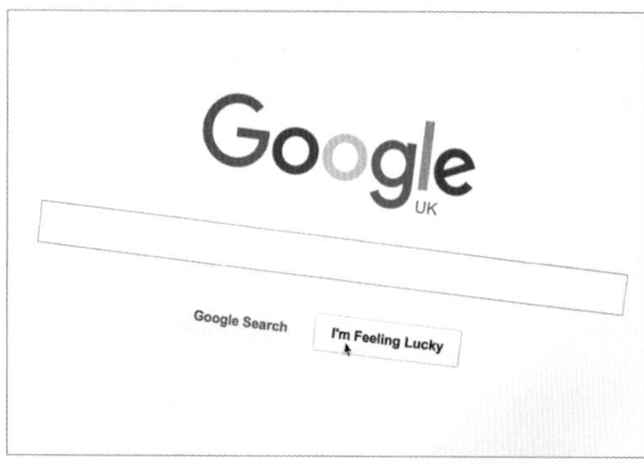

Google makes most of its revenues through Google AdWords, where advertisers bid on keywords relevant to their target market.

Source: © IB Photography/Shutterstock.

Search engines have evolved significantly over the years. Whereas, in the early years of the Internet, searches focused on keywords used, today, semantic analysis ensures that they also take into account previous search behaviour and knowledge about the context in which the search is being made (for example when, where, how, and by whom). An example of contextual adaption is local searches whereby search results are adapted to the location where the search is undertaken.

Given the central role of search in consumer online behaviour, it is not surprising that search is central to most digital marketing strategies. In 2015, 52 per cent of all Internet advertising investments were in search. Search, often referred to as 'search engine marketing' (SEM), is one of the main forms of Internet advertising, with a UK spend of £3.74 billion in 2014, accounting for about 52 per cent of total UK online ad spend (IAB and PwC, 2015a). Its aim is to promote websites by increasing their visibility in SERPs. Search engine marketing methods include the following.

- *Paid listings*—Payments are made for clicks on text links that appear at the top or side of search results for specific keywords. The more a marketer pays, the higher the position the link gets. Marketers pay only when a user clicks on the text link. Paid listings, or **pay per click (PPC)**, typically mean that the advertisers bid on keywords or phrases relevant to their target market, with sponsored or paid search engine listings aiming to drive traffic to the advertiser's own website. The search engine ranks adverts based on a competitive auction and other related criteria (for example popularity, quality). Google AdWords, Yahoo! Search Marketing, and Bing Ads are the three largest ad-network operators, with all three operating under a bid-based model.
- *Contextual search*—This is a form of targeted advertising, with adverts (for example banners, pop-ups) appearing on websites, the adverts themselves being selected and served by automated systems based on the content displayed to the user. A **contextual advertising** system scans the text of a website for keywords and returns adverts to the webpage based on what the user is viewing. Google AdSense was the first major contextual advertising programme. Payments are typically made only for clicks (PPC) on text links that appear in an article based on the context of the content rather than a user-submitted keyword.
- *Paid inclusion*—This occurs when a search engine company charges fees related to inclusion of websites in its search index. Some organizations mix paid inclusion with organic listings (for example Yahoo!), whereas others do not allow paid inclusion to be listed with organic lists (for example Google and Ask.com). Payments are made to guarantee that a marketer's URL is indexed by a search engine (that is, it is not paid only for clicks, as in paid listings).
- *Search engine optimization (SEO)*—This refers to a process whereby a website's structure and content is improved to maximize its listing in organic SERPs using relevant keywords or search phrases. Payments may also be made to optimize a site to improve the site's ranking in SERPs.

Increasingly, there is recognition that SEO and social media are interlinked. Dunphy (2012) argues that:

> [E]very share, like, re-tweet, +1, subscription, and pin means one more endorsement for your website, simultaneously increasing your search creditability. By gaining a massive amount of social shares, you're not just boosting your SEO signals and your site visibility—you're also creating content with value for your customer base.

Email Marketing

Email is one of the most frequently used digital marketing tools. Email marketing includes 'opt-in' and 'opt-out' mailing lists, email newsletters, and discussion list subscriptions. Importantly, with

Market Insight 11.3 Searching the Amazon

Search is a key behaviour online and Google is the go-to place for search—or is it? In 2015, 44 per cent of US consumers stated that they head directly to Amazon when searching for products, up from 30 per cent in 2012. In comparison, 34 per cent go straight to a search engine such as Google, Yahoo, and Bing.

Whereas Google has done its part in making product discovery and search intuitive, convenient, and seamless, Amazon now seems ready to step in and take over. Almost half of US consumers bypass search engines and other websites in favour of Amazon when on a shopping mission. This means that the search bar is increasingly becoming a key asset in Amazon's user experience.

Enabling search not only allows consumers to find the products for which they are looking, but also enables Amazon to collect valuable data on consumer searches and to relate them to actual sales. On-site search queries are clear expressions of user intent. Coupled with reviews from the millions of Amazon customers who have left appraisals on the website, the data are invaluable and Amazon continually leverages that data to intelligently promote products across its website.

Amazon's advanced algorithmic recommendation capability accurately predicts intent and suggests products better than any other website. Now, Amazon is also using its shopping pattern data to derive advantages offline. In November 2015, Amazon opened its first brick-and-mortar bookstore in Seattle, WA. Seattle was chosen for the first physical bookstore because it is close to Amazon's headquarters and because Seattle is a top market for readers.

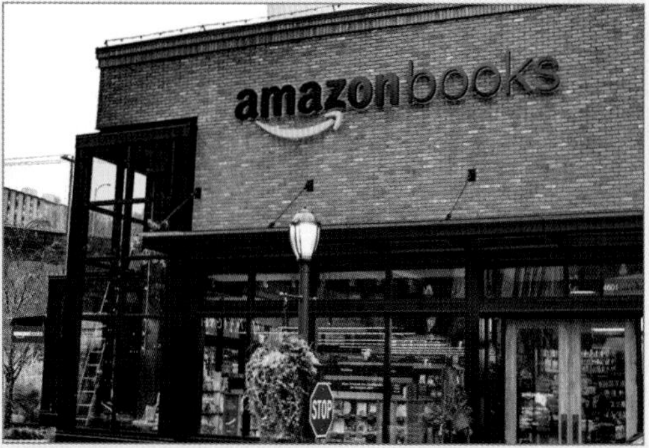

The assortment in Amazon's physical store has been selected using data on online shopping patterns.

Source: © SEA STOCK/Shutterstock.

In opening a bookstore, Amazon is betting that the troves of data it generates from shopping patterns on its website will give it advantages in its retail location that other bookstores cannot match and that using these data to pick titles that will most appeal to Seattle shoppers will allow Amazon to succeed where others have not.

Visit Amazon's website and search for a product in which you are interested.

1. **What options for finding the product do you have? How useful is the directory? How useful is the search engine?**
2. **What type of contextual information does Amazon seem to use to guide the results that are presented?**
3. **How do the search results you get on Amazon differ from what you would get if you were to use Google, Bing, or Yahoo!?**

Sources: Budds (2015); Madov (2015); Miller (2015)

email marketing, the communicator sends the message only to those who have agreed to receive messages. Such **permission-based email marketing** is a highly cost-effective form of digital marketing (Waring and Martinez, 2002; Cheng et al., 2009). As a marketing tool, it is easy to use and costs little to send. Still, cost can be higher when personalizing messages and when a database must be developed or purchased. Nevertheless, email can reach millions of willing prospects in minutes. Unsolicited emails, which clog email servers and use up much-needed Internet bandwidth, are referred to as **spam**.

In designing a successful email campaign, marketers need to think carefully about the target audience and its willingness to receive emails. This means that they should provide a mechanism for list members to opt in or opt out and to choose what type of email offerings they are interested in receiving (for example newsletter, discount offers, and specific updates). As far as possible, emails should be personalized. Using an email system that allows tracking and reporting on all elements of the campaign (including opens, clicks, pass-alongs, unsubscribes, and bounce-backs) allows marketers to closely test and monitor different email marketing strategies in terms of when to send them and how often, as well as what to offer, write, and highlight. The insights gained from such data-mining exercises can be invaluable. For example, one large-scale study of more than 1 billion emails over a two-year period shows that people are 38 per cent more likely to click—and 47 per cent more likely to convert—when they are presented with a percentage-off rather than a money-off offer (O'Brien, 2015). According to the same study, short subject lines (of between six and ten words), visual and personalized messages, and clear calls to action are key to a successful email.

Social Media Marketing

'Social media marketing' describes the use of the social web and social media (for example social networks, online communities, blogs, wikis) or any online collaborative technology for marketing activities (such as sales, public relations (PR), research, distribution, customer service). Social media marketing includes both the creation and curation of corporate and/or brand profiles and content on social media and advertising. 'Social media advertising' (SMA) refers to advertising delivered on social platforms, including social networking and social gaming websites and apps, across all device types.

Marketers are increasingly investing in social networks (for example Facebook, LinkedIn, and QQ in China), video-sharing sites (for example YouTube), image-sharing sites (such as Flickr, Pinterest), blogging platforms (such as WordPress), and microblogs (for example Twitter) for marketing purposes. According to one 2015 survey of chief marketing officers (CMOs), 11 per cent of marketing budgets were invested in social media in 2015 and this share is expected to grow to 24 per cent between 2015 and 2020 (Moorman, 2015). In 2016, the growth rate for social media in Western Europe was expected to be 23 per cent (Anon., 2015b).

The social web does not make conversations happen; it only supports them. Mangold and Faulds (2009) offer the following examples of marketing activities aiming to stimulate conversations:

- networking platforms (for example Sephora's beauty insiders, Nike+);
- blogs and social media tools to engage customers—because customers like to give feedback on a broad range of issues (see 'Content marketing');
- both Internet and traditional promotional tools to engage customers;
- information on, for example, correct or alternative product usage;
- exclusivity—because people like to feel special;

- offerings that are designed from the perspective of consumers' desired self-images and with talking points to make advocacy easier, for example JetBlue, the US budget airline, making leather seats and televisions available to its customers;
- support for causes that people value; and
- memorable stories.

As an example of the last, UK food and beverage company innocent outlines the story of its founding on its website. Innocent has it that three friends set up a stall to sell smoothies at a London music festival. A sign above the stall read 'Should we give up our jobs to make these smoothies?' and people were asked to throw their empties into one of two bins marked either 'Yes' or 'No'. Needless to say, 'Yes' won.

The options available for social media advertising differ between different social media platforms. Moreover, they are constantly subject to change. Visit the **online resources** and complete Internet Activity 11.2 around advertising options on different social media platforms.

Evaluating Social Media

Although marketers agree that social media marketing is key to success in the contemporary marketplace, many marketers are still struggling to identify how to evaluate these activities. In 2015, only 15 per cent of CMOs had been able to prove the impact of those investments quantitatively, while 44.5 per cent had a good qualitative sense of the impact and 41.5 per cent had not been able to demonstrate the impact (Moorman, 2015). This clearly shows that, for marketers, while engaging in social communities provides opportunities, it can also be a challenge.

The process of measuring social media effectiveness requires a detailed sevenfold process, as follows (CIM, 2013).

1. Start by looking at measurement metrics. (Table 11.4 provides a detailed list of the most frequently used social media measures and how their use has evolved.)
2. Review your social media campaign objectives. For example, was your motivation to (a) build traffic on your website, (b) improve brand perceptions, (c) deepen relationships with customers, (d) learn from the community, (e) drive purchase intent, (f) foster dialogue, (g) promote advocacy, (h) facilitate support, or (i) spur innovation? (See Murdough, 2009; Owyang and Lovett, 2010.)
3. Map your campaign—that is, show how the brand is consumed on the web by means of (a) brand-generated content, (b) consumer-generated content, (c) consumer-fortified content (for example by showing online locations where consumers can go to distribute content relating to the brand), and (d) exposure to content consumers (for example favourable product reviews on websites).
4. Choose the criteria and tools of measurement by (a) determining the criteria for assessing effectiveness and (b) selecting the most appropriate software measurement tools.
5. Establish a benchmark (for example by measuring where your company is in relation to some of the metrics in Table 11.4).
6. Undertake the campaign, and then analyse the outcomes, compare the outcomes against your proposal benchmarks to assess the variance between the two, and propose changes.
7. Continue to measure on a daily, weekly, monthly, and quarterly basis.

Table 11.4	Social media measures used by marketers

Rank	Measure	% of total respondents, 2010	% of total respondents, 2014
1	Hits/visits/page views	48	60
2	No. of followers and friends	24	45
3	Repeat visits	35	39
4	Conversion rates (from visitor to buyer)	25	31
5	Buzz indicators (mentions, shares)	16	24
6	Sales levels	18	17
7	Online products/service ratings	8	14
8	Customer acquisition costs	12	14
9	Net promoter score	8	13
10	Revenue per customer	17	13
11	Text analysis ratings	7	12
12	Customer retention costs	8	6
13	Abandoned shopping carts	4	6
14	Profits per customer	9	6

Source: Moorman (2014).

Content Marketing

Content marketing is an approach to marketing communication in which brands create and disseminate content to consumers with the intention that the content will generate interest, engage consumers, and influence behaviour (Stephen et al., 2015). Although branded content has been around for more than 100 years, this marketing activity has accelerated in the digital space.

Marketers are therefore paying increasing attention to creating online content that can benefit their target audiences by adapting traditional journalism and publisher techniques. These activities are often referred to as 'content marketing'.

Table 11.5 Top B2B content marketing tactics, 2015

Rank	Tactic	Use (% of B2B businesses)
1	Social media content	92
2	E-newsletters	83
3	Articles on own website	81
4	Blogs	80
5	In-person events	77
6	Case studies	77
7	Videos	76
8	Illustrations/photos	69
9	White Papers	68
10	Online presentations	65

Source: Pulizzi and Handley (2015).

The aim of content marketing is to create content that has value for the receiver (for example by being useful, educational, or entertaining in and of itself), thereby pulling the consumer toward the brand. Content marketing is common both in consumer and business-to-business (B2B) marketing. For example, Red Bull has transformed its content operations into a fully fledged media house specializing in high-quality coverage of extreme sports. There is thus plenty of opportunity to provide value in a way that can be mutually beneficial for the brand and the receiver.

Mobile Marketing

Mobile marketing is the set of practices that enables organizations to communicate and engage interactively with their audiences through any mobile device or network (MMA, 2009). With the added benefits of store-and-send technology giving the option of message storage, mobile marketing is quick, inexpensive, and reaches markets wherever they are, despite limitations in message content.

Investments in mobile are both through paid (mobile advertising) media and the development of owned media, such as apps. In 2019, global mobile internet ad spending is predicted to hit \$196bn, representing around 70.1 per cent of total digital ad spending and around 26.8 per cent of total media spending (*eMarketer*, 2015).

Current changes in behaviours clearly show that mobile is taking over more and more of consumer online searches, and that marketers need to consider to stay relevant and accessible at

Research Insight 11.2

To take your learning further, you might wish to read this influential paper.

Rosengren, S., and Dahlén, M. (2015) 'Exploring advertising equity: How a brand's past advertising may affect consumer willingness to approach its future ads', *Journal of Advertising*, 44(1): 1–13

This paper investigates what drives consumers' willingness to pay attention to advertising. Based on empirical studies of more than 1,700 consumers and 100 brands in more than 12 different product categories, it shows how adding value in advertising is vital to succeed in a digital environment in which consumers are increasingly in charge of their own media consumption.

Visit the **online resources** to read the abstract and access the full paper.

Market Insight 11.4 **Black Milk Clothing: More Virus than Viral**

Fashion brand Black Milk Clothing (BMC), based in Brisbane, Australia, found out the dangers of viral marketing the hard way. Founded in 2009 by James Lillis, BMC is known for its printed Lycra leggings, dresses, and swimwear. It has become one of Australia's fastest growing clothing companies, with expanding export markets, multimillion-dollar turnover, and a strong reputation for engaging brand communities through effective Facebook postings, and hashtagging of products on Instagram and Facebook. Marketing almost exclusively online to a committed community of self-titled 'Sharkies', BMC routinely opens its virtual doors to followers to participate in corporate decision-making (product development, fabric selection, photographic techniques, and pricing) and has had successful tie-ins with several of the biggest names in blockbuster franchising, including *Harry Potter*, *Lord of the Rings*, *Game of Thrones*, and *Star Wars*.

So what happened on 4 May 2014 when it ran an online promotion to tie in with Star Wars Day ('May the Fourth [force] be with you')? A supposedly tongue-in-cheek comparison between 'sexy geek' (a 'cool'-looking model in a *Star-Wars*-themed dress) and 'nerdy geek' (a picture of *Big Bang Theory*'s Amy Farrah Fowler looking demure in a *Star Trek* uniform) was criticized by the community, including long-term loyal fans. Black Milk responded by censuring fan's angry comments, with a post blaming them for not getting the 'joke' and making a fuss about nothing, suggesting that they like a different page if they still were not happy, and banning community members deemed too negative. The backlash from these actions was swift. As many other companies have learned, what goes on in social media stays in social media (forever), and Sharkies were able to revisit video blogs and past corporate communications, suggesting that BMC had failed to live by its own 'commandments' relating to being 'excellent' to each other and not making critical comments about other women's bodies. What was the result? Loyal and articulate community members felt betrayed, precipitating a drop of thousands in Facebook page likes, the development of an external website dedicated to what the company has done wrong in social media, much unwanted social media coverage, including

Market Insight 11.4 (continued)

unflattering memes, and the possible future loss of consumer spending. Unsurprisingly, the company was forced to apologize for the way in which it had handled the affair.

1. **Why do you think Black Milk got it so wrong given its previous success in social media marketing?**
2. **Aside from never having released the advert in the first place (given that it violated its own 'commandments'), how should BMC have responded in the first instance once it had received criticism of its promotional ads on social media?**
3. **Of what other social media marketing failures are you aware? What happened and how could the company involved have dealt with it better?**

Sources: Huynh (2014); Russon (2014); https://www.facebook.com/blackmilkclothing/posts/797141630304921.

This market insight was kindly contributed by Dr Angela R. Dobele, RMIT University, Australia.

different stages in the consumer decision process. Increasingly, the use of smartphone apps is becoming the default mechanism for such searches. These apps use a combination of barcode scanning and location-based services to provide relevant information, for example showing only stores near to a consumer carrying out a price comparison. These apps are thus suited to deliver context-specific, and hence more relevant, information to consumers.

Location-based marketing has long been expected to be the next big thing in mobile advertising. However, adaption has been slow and location-based still makes up only a small proportion of total mobile investments. In part, this could be explained by technological problems leading location-based assessments to have low accuracy. Location-based marketing is thus expected to pick up the pace in the coming years as the accuracy of mobile technologies improves (Johnson 2014, 2015).

Consumers are increasingly searching for information about products through various digital platforms and devices, but is this the case for all products? Visit the **online resources** and complete Internet Activity 11.3 to find out more about online and offline search.

Research Insight 11.3

To take your learning further, you might wish to read this influential paper.

Edelman, D. C., and Singer, M. (2015) 'Competing on customer journeys', *Harvard Business Review*, 9(11): 88–100.

This article discusses how digital and mobile technology has changed how consumers research and buy products, and how companies need to come up with new tools, processes, and organizational structures to proactively lead digital customers from consideration to purchase and beyond.

Visit the online resources to read the abstract and access the full paper.

Crowdsourcing

A common definition sees 'crowdsourcing' as:

> . . . engaging a large group of people to come up with an idea or solve a problem. Some companies use the process to draw on the knowledge and opinions of a wide body of Internet users to create better products and marketing plans, or solve other problems.
>
> (Vallone, 2011: 5)

Crowdsourcing in marketing is used most commonly in four main categories: routine activities, content, creative activities, and funding (see Table 11.6).

- One example of the crowdsourcing of *routine activities* was reCAPTCHA (which stands for Completely Automated Public Turing test to tell Computers and Humans Apart), the initiative aiming to digitize books by supplying websites with CAPTCHA protection from bots attempting to access restricted sites. The test requires users to retype images of words not recognized by optical character recognition (OCR) machines and, in so doing, helped to digitize the Internet archive and the archives of the *New York Times*.
- iStockphoto and openstreetmap are good examples of companies that crowdsourced *content*.
- Companies that have used crowdsourcing for *creative activities* include InnoCentive and Wilogo, which use crowdsourcing mechanisms for research and development (R&D) projects and to produce logo designs, respectively.

Table 11.6 Forms of crowdsourcing (CS)

Consideration	CS of routine activities	CS of content	CS of creative activities	CS of funds
Role of the crowd	Provision of time; ability to process information	Provision of content (especially information)	Provision of solutions, ideas, knowledge	Provision of monetary recourses
Goal	Division of labour (integrative)	Division of labour (integrative)	Winner takes all (selective)	Raising money
Remuneration	Micro-payments	Micro-payments or voluntary	Micro- to high payments	Equity/loan/reward
Size of the crowd	Very important	Very important	Of little importance	Very important
Diversity of the crowd	Not important	Very important	Very important	Not important
Commercial examples	reCAPTCHA	iStockphoto openstreetmap	InnoCentive Wilogo	FundedByMe

Source: Burger-Helmchen and Pénin (2011) and the authors.

- When it comes to crowdsourced *funding*, there are several different websites offering this possibility to companies. According to a recent report from one of them, the success of crowdfunding campaigns is highly contingent on social media sharing, as well as accuracy and reliability of market assessments and financial forecasts (Lundquist and Gromek, 2015).

Crowdsourcing is increasingly ubiquitous in marketing as organizations seek to use it to reduce their marketing costs, to reduce the time taken to undertake a particular task, to find and use resources (skills, labour, money) that do not exist in-house, to obtain information and market intelligence, to design new products and services, and to design promotional material. One of the key considerations when setting up a crowdsourcing task is how to motivate the crowd to take part. One common rule of thumb suggests that 90 per cent of visitors to the site will consume the content (that is, see the task), 9 per cent will partially engage (that is, read the task and consider taking part or request further information), and 1 per cent will fully engage (that is, provide a submission).

Legal and Ethical Considerations

With the rise in digital resources and their increasing use for marketing activities come complications and changes to legislation and regulated business practices. The types of legal, ethical, and regulatory issue that marketers need to consider include the following.

- *Jurisdiction*—Where does digital marketing activity take place? Commercial law is based on transactions within national boundaries, but digital marketing exposes both individual organizations and the community to information, transactions, and social activity outside these boundaries (for example European Union legislation and Microsoft).
- *Ownership*—Who owns the content that we create and share? Copyright law is a national issue and copyright laws (that is, what can and cannot be used without the originator's permission) differ from one country to another. The value of copyright is also being questioned with the increase in UGC and **co-created content (CCC)**, and the rise of the Creative Commons (CC) free licence system.
- *Permissions*—Do we have the right permissions to upload and share content? Privacy legislation is also national or regional and the right of an individual or organization to use information is subject to this legislation.
- *Security*—How secure are the data and information we share? Information and transaction security, and protection from fraud and identity theft, are other areas of increasing change.
- *Accessibility*—Does everyone who wants access have access? Disability and discrimination legislation also require consideration in this regard. As more services and marketing information are shared digitally, the right to access and usability for all becomes an important agenda item for the dissemination of information and services.

Visit the **online resources** and complete Internet Activity 11.4 to learn more about consumer privacy concerns.

Chapter Summary

To consolidate your learning, the key points from this chapter are summarized below.

- **Define 'digital marketing' and 'social media marketing'.**

  'Digital marketing' is the management and execution of marketing using digital technologies and channels (for example web, email, digital television, Internet) to reach markets in a timely, relevant, personal, interactive, and cost-efficient manner. It is related to, but distinct from, e-marketing, direct marketing, and interactive marketing. 'Social media marketing' is a form of digital marketing, which uses social networking sites to produce content that users will share, which will, in turn, create exposure of the brand to customers and thereby increase or reinforce its customer base.

- **Explain how digitization is transforming marketing practice.**

  The growth of digital technologies is not only changing consumer behaviours, but also changing business. Digital marketing must therefore be considered and adapted more widely than only as a new communication or distribution channel. It can help organizations to create new business opportunities, and enable new relationships with and between (and thereby insights into) consumers.

- **Discuss key techniques in digital marketing and social media marketing.**

  Key techniques in digital marketing include Internet advertising, search marketing, email marketing, social media marketing, content marketing, and mobile marketing. Characteristic of digital marketing, especially that through social media, is that marketers need to give up some control and power to consumers.

- **Review how practitioners measure the effectiveness of social media marketing.**

  To measure the effectiveness of a social media campaign, marketers should follow a seven-step process, which includes: identifying a set of appropriate social media metrics; reviewing the social media campaign objectives; mapping the campaign by highlighting links to brand-generated content, consumer-generated content, consumer-fortified content, and exposure to content(ed) consumers; choosing the criteria and tools of measurement; establishing a benchmark; undertaking the campaign; and measuring it frequently.

- **Discuss crowdsourcing and explain how it can be harnessed for marketing purposes.**

  Crowdsourcing is the process of outsourcing a task or group of tasks to a generally large community ('crowd') of people. It can be used in marketing to outsource routine activities, to obtain content, or to obtain creative input. It can also be used as a way in which to gain access to financial resources.

Review Questions

1. **Describe how digital marketing differs from interactive and Internet marketing.**
2. **How is digitization transforming marketing practice?**
3. **Compare and contrast the difference between 'pull' and 'push' approaches to digital marketing.**
4. **What are the main features of search marketing? In what contexts is search marketing most effective?**

5 **What is social media and how has it changed marketing?**

6 **What is social media marketing and why do marketers use it?**

7 **How can you measure the effectiveness of social media marketing?**

8 **What is content marketing and why do marketers use it?**

9 **How is the growth of mobile devices (for example smartphones) impacting on marketing?**

10 **What marketing activities can crowdsourcing support?**

Worksheet Summary

To apply the knowledge you have gained from this chapter, and to test your understanding of digital and social media marketing, visit the **online resources** and complete Worksheet 11.1.

Discussion Questions

1 Having read Case Insight 11.1, how might Spotify use social media to support its service and build customer loyalty?

2 Do you think that digital resources are redefining marketing?

3 Why are many marketers having difficulties adapting to a situation in which they have to share control and power over a brand with consumers?

4 Privacy and ownership of digital information is increasingly challenged. When participating on Facebook, for example, we think that we control our own data and information—but do we? Discuss.

Visit the **online resources** and complete the multiple-choice questions to assess your knowledge of the chapter.

Glossary

co-created content (CCC) content or applications created by at least two parties, potentially the organization and the consumer.

contextual advertising a form of targeted advertising, on websites, whereby adverts are selected and served by automated systems based on the content displayed to the user.

digital marketing the process of marketing accomplished or facilitated through the application of electronic devices, appliances, tools, techniques, technologies, and/or systems.

mobile marketing the set of practices that enables organizations to communicate and engage with their audiences in an interactive and relevant manner through any mobile device or network.

paid inclusion can provide a guarantee that the website is included in a search engine's natural listings.

pay per click (PPC) advertising that uses sponsored search engine listings to drive traffic to a website, whereby the advertiser bids for search terms and the search engine ranks results based on a competitive auction, as well as other factors.

permission-based email marketing also known as 'opt-in email marketing', a method of advertising by email that the recipient has consented to receive.

search directory a database of information maintained by human editors, which lists websites by category and subcategory, usually based on the whole website rather than one page or a set of keywords.

search engine operates algorithmically, or using a mixture of algorithmic and human input, to collect, index, store, and retrieve information on the web, then make it available to users in a manageable and meaningful way in response to a search query.

spam unsolicited email—that is, the junk mail of the twenty-first century—which clogs email servers and uses up much-needed Internet bandwidth.

user-generated content (UGC) content made publicly available over the Internet that reflects creative effort by users, not professionals.

References

Alldredge, K., Newaskar, P., and Ungerman, K. (2015) 'The digital future of consumer-packaged-goods companies', *McKinsey Insights*. Available online at http://www.mckinsey.com/insights/consumer_and_retail/the_digital_future_of_consumer_packaged_goods_companies [accessed 4 November 2015].

American Marketing Association (AMA) (2015) 'Social marketing'. Available online at http://www.marketing-dictionary.org/ama [accessed 25 February 2016].

Anon. (2015a) 'Worldwide market share of leading search engines from January 2010 to July 2015', *statistica*. Available online at http://www.statista.com/statistics/216573/worldwide-market-share-of-search-engines/ [accessed 8 November 2015].

Anon. (2015b) 'Social network ad spending to hit $23.68 billion worldwide in 2015', *E-marketer*, 15 April. Available online at http://www.emarketer.com/Article/Social-Network-Ad-Spending-Hit-2368-Billion-Worldwide-2015/1012357#sthash.LKObvSEJ.dpuf [accessed 4 November 2015].

Anon. (2016) 'Leading social networks worldwide as of January 2016, ranked by number of active users (in millions)', *statistica*. Available online at http://www.statista.com/statistics/272014/global-social-networks-ranked-by-number-of-users/ [accessed 25 February 2016].

Björn Borg (2015) 'Björn Borg case'. Available online at http://webcollection.se/cannes/2015/fpl/#/ [accessed 28 June 2016].

Budds, D. (2015) 'How Ikea is defining the state of play (with a little help from DreamWorks)', *Design Partnership*. Available online at https://designtothepowerofpartnership.wordpress.com/how-ikea-is-defining-the-state-of-play-with-a-little-help-from-dreamworks/ [accessed 4 November 2015].

Burger-Helmchen, T., and Pénin, J. (2011) 'Crowdsourcing: définition, enjeux, typologie [Crowdsourcing: definition, stakes, typology]', *Revue Management et Avenir*, 41(1): 254–69.

Chartered Institute of Marketing (CIM) (2013) 'How to measure the impact of your social media campaign'. Available online at http://www.cim.co.uk [accessed 17 February 2013].

Cheng, J. M.-S., Blankson, C., Wang, E. S.-T., and Chen, L. S.-L. (2009) 'Consumer attitudes and interactive digital advertising', *International Journal of Advertising*, 28(3): 501–25.

Colliander, J., and Wien, A. (2013) 'Trash talk rebuffed: What can we learn from the phenomenon of consumers defending companies criticized in online communities?', *European Journal of Marketing*, 47(10): 1733–57.

Dunphy, J. (2012) 'SEO and social media get married', *Econsultancy*, 24 December. Available online at http://econsultancy.com/uk/blog/11406-seo-and-social-media-get-married [accessed 1 January 2017].

Dutta, S., Geiger, T., and Lanvin, B. (eds) (2015) *The Global Information Technology Report: 2015. ICTs for Inclusive Growth*. Available online at http://www3.weforum.org/docs/WEF_GITR2015.pdf [accessed 15 October 2015].

Edelman, D. C., and Singer, M. (2015) 'Competing on customer journeys', *Harvard Business Review*, 9(11): 88–100.

eMarketer (2015) *Mobile Ad Spend to Top $100 Billion Worldwide in 2016, 51% of Digital Market*. eMarketer, 2 April. Available online at http://www.eMarketer.com/

Article/Mobile-Ad-Spend-Top-100-Billion-2016-51-of-Digital-Market/1012299 [accessed 9 January 2017].

Griner, D. (2013) 'Spotify thanks customer with custom playlist featuring a secret message', *AdWeek*, 12 July. Available online at http://www.adweek.com/adfreak/spotifys-customer-service-looks-and-sounds-just-about-perfect-151157 [accessed 10 May 2016].

Harris, P. (2009) *Penguin Dictionary of Marketing*, London: Penguin Books.

Huynh, M. (2014) 'Anti-marketing is the new marketing: Black Milk Clothing's hipster philosophy pivotal to its growth', *Start Up Daily*, 11 September. Available online at http://www.startupdaily.net/2014/09/anti-marketing-new-marketing-black-milk-clothings-hipster-philosophy-pivotal-growth [accessed 10 May 2016].

Internet Advertising Bureau UK (IAB) and PricewaterhouseCoopers (PwC) (2015a) *Digital Adspend Study UK*. Available online at http://www.iabuk.net/research/library/h1-2015-digital-adspend-results [accessed 4 November 2015].

Internet Advertising Bureau UK (IAB) and PricewaterhouseCoopers (PwC) (2015b) *IAB Internet Advertising Revenue Report, 2014 Full Year Results*. Available online at http://www.iab.com/wp-content/uploads/2015/05/IAB_Internet_Advertising_Revenue_FY_2014.pdf [accessed 4 November 2015].

Johnson, L. (2014) 'Mobile marketers know who you are and where you've been and what you're reading on your phone', *Adweek*, 24 September. Available online at http://www.adweek.com/news/technology/mobile-marketers-know-who-you-are-and-where-youve-been-158491 [accessed 13 November 2015].

Johnson, L. (2015) 'Are marketers finally getting the hang of location-based mobile ads?', *Adweek*, 28 September. Available online at http://www.adweek.com/news/technology/are-marketers-finally-getting-hang-location-based-mobile-ads-167212 [accessed 13 November 2015].

Lundquist, A., and Gromek, M. (2015) 'Successful equity crowdfunding campaigns: A Nordic review'. Available online at http://www.slideshare.net/MichalGromek/successful-equity-crowdfunding-campaigns3 [accessed 9 November 2015].

Madov, N. (2015) 'DreamWorks creates a magical world for Ikea's new line of toys', *Creativity*, 21 October. Available online at http://creativity-online.com/work/ikea-welcome-to-the-world-of-lattjo/43838 [accessed 27 October 2015].

Mangold, W. G., and Faulds, D. J. (2009) 'Social media: The new hybrid element of the promotion mix', *Business Horizons*, 52(4): 357–65.

Miller, M. J. (2015) 'Play it forward: IKEA taps DreamWorks to bring Lattjo games to life', *BrandChannel*, 26 October. Available online at http://www.brandchannel.com/2015/10/26/ikea-dreamworks-lattjo-102615/ [accessed 27 October 2015].

Mobile Marketing Association (MMA) (2009) 'Buy mobile marketing'. Available online at http://mmaglobal.com/about/content_category/research/10/341 [accessed 22 July 2016].

Moorman, C. (2014) *CMO Survey Report: Highlights and Insights*, August. Available online at http://www.slideshare.net/christinemoorman/the-cmo-survey-report [accessed 4 November 2015].

Moorman, C. (2015) *CMO Survey Report: Highlights and Insights*, August. Available online at http://www.slideshare.net/christinemoorman/the-cmo-surveyhighlightsandinsightsaug2015 [accessed 25 February 2016].

Murdough, C. (2009) 'Social media measurement: It's not impossible', *Journal of Interactive Advertising*, 10(1): 94–9.

Nudd, T. (2015a) 'Man poses as Target on Facebook, trolls haters of its gender-neutral move with epic replies', *Adweek*, 13 August. Available online at http://www.adweek.com/adfreak/man-poses-target-facebook-trolls-haters-its-gender-neutral-move-epic-replies-166364 [accessed 22 July 2016].

Nudd, T. (2015b) 'Target loved the guy who trolled its haters, judging by this genius Facebook post', *Adweek*, 14 August. Available online at http://www.adweek.com/adfreak/target-loved-guy-who-trolled-its-haters-judging-genius-facebook-post-166408 [accessed 22 July 2016].

O'Brien, M. (2015) 'How to construct the perfect marketing email', *ClickZ*, 22 October. Available online at http://www.clickz.com/clickz/news/2431283/how-to-construct-the-perfect-marketing-email [accessed 4 November 2015].

Ofcom (2015) *Adults' Media Use and Attitudes, Report 2015*. Available online at http://stakeholders.ofcom.org.uk/binaries/research/media-literacy/media-lit-10years/2015_Adults_media_use_and_attitudes_report.pdf [accessed 4 November 2015].

Owyang, J., and Lovett, J. (2010) 'Social marketing analytics: A new framework for measuring results in social media', 22 April. Available online at http://www.slideshare.net/jeremiah_owyang/altimeter-report-social-marketing-analytics?qid=b352b96f-d8d3-4e2a-bd91-f28c9c132c53&v=&b=&from_search=2 [accessed 1 January 2017].

Pulizzi, J., and Handley, A. (2015) *B2B Content Marketing: 2015 Benchmarks, Budgets, and Trends*. Available online at http://contentmarketinginstitute.com/wp-content/uploads/2014/10/2015_B2B_Research.pdf [accessed 11 November 2015].

Rosengren, S., and Dahlén, M. (2015) 'Exploring advertising equity: How a brand's past advertising may affect consumer willingness to approach its future ads', *Journal of Advertising*, 44(1): 1–13.

Russon, M.-A. (2014) 'Black Milk geek clothing brand sorry over Star Wars Day Facebook meme', *International Business Times*, 6 May. Available online at http://www.ibtimes.co.uk/black-milk-geek-clothing-brand-sorry-over-star-wars-day-facebook-meme-1447384 [accessed 23 May 2016].

Stephen, A. T., Sciandra, M. R., and Inman, J. J. (2015) 'The effects of content characteristics on consumer engagement with branded social media content on Facebook', Marketing Science Institute Working Paper No. 15–110.

Vallone, J. (2011) 'Crowdsourcing could predict terror strikes, gasoline prices', *Investors' Business Daily*, 29 August, 5.

van den Bulte, C., and Wuyts, S. (2007) *Social Networks and Marketing*, Boston, MA: Marketing Science Institute.

Waring, T., and Martinez, A. (2002) 'Ethical customer relationships: A comparative analysis of US and French organisations using permission-based email marketing', *Journal of Database Marketing*, 10(1): 53–70.

Wisterberg, E. (2015) 'Pewdiepie-effekten lyfter Björn Borgs FPS-spel' ['Pewdiepie effect raises Bjorn Borg's FPS-games'], 2 February. Available online at http://www.dagensmedia.se/marknadsforing/kampanjer/pewdiepie-effekten-lyfter-bjorn-borgs-fps-spel-6090265 [accessed 28 June 2016].

Wunsch-Vincent, S., and Vickery, G. (2007) *Participative Web: User-Created Content*, DSTI/ICCP/IE(2006)7/FINAL. Available online at http://www.oecd.org/internet/interneteconomy/38393115.pdf [accessed 4 November 2015].

Chapter 12
Services Marketing and Customer Experience Management

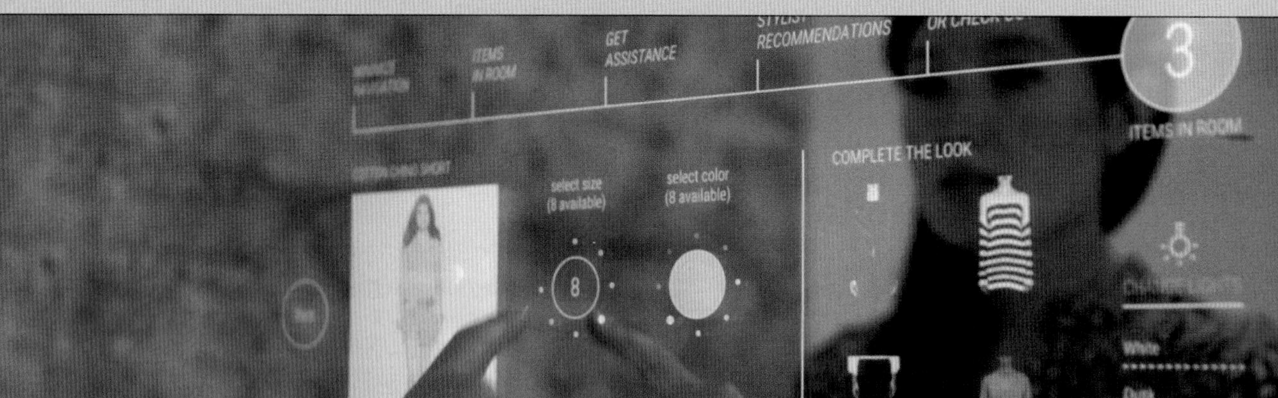

Learning Outcomes

After studying this chapter, you will be able to:

- explain the nature and characteristics of services;
- describe what is meant by the term 'service encounters';
- outline the principles of relationship marketing and the relationships between trust, commitment, and customer satisfaction; and
- define the term 'customer experiences' and explain its dimensions, how it has evolved, and how it might be measured.

Case Insight 12.1
Withers Worldwide

Market Insight 12.1
Purely Products and Purely Services

Market Insight 12.2
Revolutionizing the Shopping Encounter

Market Insight 12.3
Customer Experiences and Environmental Sustainability

Case Insight 12.1 **Withers Worldwide**

Founded in London in 1896, Withers Worldwide has global revenues of over US$200 million, 163 partners, employs more than 1,000 people, has clients in more than 80 countries, and has acted for 42 per cent of the top 100 *Sunday Times* Rich List and 20 per cent of the top 100 of the *Forbes* Rich List. We speak to Laura Boyle (pictured), head of EU marketing and business development, to explore how Withers works to improve the quality of its client relationships.

Predicting the global nature of private capital, Withers set out over a decade ago from its origins as a London-based firm to do something that law firms had not done before—to develop a genuinely international offering for global wealth. Choosing global centres of private wealth, the firm strives to ensure that we match our clients' evolving needs. We are now the largest law firm focused on the needs of private wealth in the world, with 18 offices across the United States, Europe, Asia Pacific, and the Caribbean. Other law firms focused on this market have, up until recently, operated from a domestic base.

As a professional services organization, making sure that our employees understand our strategy and brand is paramount, because they liaise with our clients and embody the **customer experience**. Keeping everyone informed on developments has been challenging given our rapid expansion. In addition to the usual internal communications, such as newsletters, intranet, and leadership briefings, we have developed 'Withers television'; television screens placed in prominent places in our offices. They share daily news updates about clients and our people, so that everyone is in the best position to feel part of the Withers Worldwide brand and know how to talk about it externally. This supports more personal communications too, for example with annual AGM sessions for all staff.

We run standardized inductions for new joiners and each team is assigned a business development manager, who acts like a key account manager for them as internal clients, connecting them to central strategy, the brand, and our best-practice approach.

The **variability** of our service offering worldwide is a real benefit to our clients; it is how we deliver tailored services. We need to have lawyers with associated legal support, operating in different areas of specialism and at differing levels of experience, to deliver a comprehensive service, priced in the best way for clients. Any conversation with a prospective client first considers what their needs are and we then calibrate the input of senior partner time required, together with the support needed from more junior lawyers and paralegals.

We avoid potential issues around variance in **service quality**, through our marketing function, which incorporates client relationship management specialists. We seek feedback from our clients, but also from those who refer work to us and who recommend us to their clients. Our learning and development team delivers a global employee training programme, ensuring that, as we grow and acquire new teams of lawyers, they are brought into the Withers 'way of working'. We also work hard to ensure that our collective and accumulated

Case Insight 12.1 (continued)

knowledge is shared across all offices—by running a global precedent system.

The problem we had as an organization focused on the way in which we sought client feedback. We had always focused on the trusted adviser, client–lawyer, relationship, which involved personal and tailored requests for feedback. But while we had a good idea where we were doing well and where one-off problem existed, we had no central view of how clients perceived our service quality.

The question arose for Withers: how should it develop a more comprehensive system to evaluate the quality of how clients experienced its service offering?

Introduction

Services and products are different. One of the distinguishing dimensions of products is that they have a physical presence. Services do not have a physical presence and they cannot be touched. This is because their distinguishing characteristic is that they are an act or a performance (Berry, 1980). A service cannot be put in a bag, taken home, stored in a cupboard, and used at a later date. A service is consumed at the point at which it is produced. For example, watching a play at a theatre, learning maths at school, or taking a holiday all involve the simultaneous production and consumption of the play, new knowledge, and leisure.

The service industry sector forms a substantial part of most developed economies. Not surprisingly, the range of services is enormous, and we consume services in nearly all areas of our work, business, home, and leisure activities. Table 12.1 indicates the variety of sectors and some of the areas in which we consume different types of service.

Table 12.1 Service sectors

Sector	Examples
Business	Financial, airlines, hotels, solicitors and lawyers
Manufacturing	Finance and accountants, computer operators, administrators, trainers
Retail	Sales personnel, cashiers, customer support advisers
Institutions	Hospitals, education, museums, charities, churches
Government	Legal system, prisons, military, customs and excise, police

The sheer number of services that are available has grown, partly because it is not always easy to differentiate products based only on feature, benefit, quality, or price. Competition can be very intense and most product innovations or developments are copied quickly. Services provide an opportunity to add value, yet not be copied, because each service is a unique experience.

Most products contain an element of service: there is a product–service combination designed to provide a means of adding value, differentiation, and earning a higher return. The extent to which a service envelops a product varies according to a number of factors—that is, the level of tangibility associated with the type of product, the way in which the service is delivered, variations in supply and demand, the level of customization, the type of relationship between service providers and customers, and the degree of involvement with the service that people experience (Lovelock et al., 1999).

Many grocery products have few supporting services—only shelf stocking and checkout operators. The purchase of new fitted bedroom furniture involves the cupboards, dressers, and wardrobes, plus the professional installation service necessary to make the furniture usable. At the other end of the spectrum, a visit to the dentist or an evening class entails little physical product-based support, because the personal service is delivered by the service deliverer in the form of the dentist or tutor.

The Nature of Services

In view of these comments about the range and variety of services, and before moving on, it is necessary to define what a 'service' is. As with many topics, there is no firm agreement, but, for our purposes, the following definition, derived from a number of authors, will be used:

> A service is any act or performance offered by one party to another that is essentially intangible. Consumption of the service does not result in any transfer of ownership even though the **service process** may be attached to a physical product.

Much of this definition is derived from the work of Grönroos (1990), who considered a range of definitions and interpretations. What this definition provides is an indication of the various characteristics and properties that set services apart from products.

Research Insight 12.1

To take your learning further, you might wish to read this influential paper.

Shostack, G. L. (1977) 'Breaking free from product marketing', ***Journal of Marketing*****, 41(2): 73–80.**

This passionately written paper seeks to draw a clear and distinct line between the requirements for marketing products and services. The author states that a marketing mix that is appropriate for products is not suitable for services. A key thrust of the paper is the need for an understanding of the difference between image (for products) and evidence (for services).

 **Visit the online resources to read the abstract and access the full paper.**

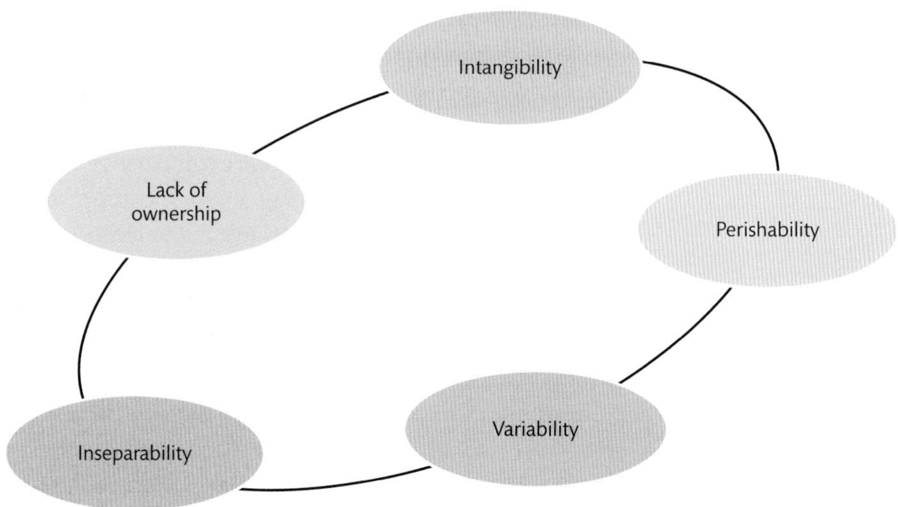

Figure 12.1: The five core characteristics of services

Distinguishing Characteristics

Services are characterized by five distinct characteristics: **intangibility**, **perishability**, variability, **inseparability**, and a lack of ownership (see Figure 12.1). These are important aspects that shape the way in which marketers design, deliver, and evaluate the marketing of services.

Intangibility

The purchase of products involves the use of most of our senses. We can touch, see, smell, hear, or even taste products before we buy them, let alone use them. When purchasing a tablet or smartphone, for example, it is possible to see the physical product and its various attributes such as size and colour, to test its functionality, to feel its weight and touch it. These are important purchasing decision cues, and even if the equipment fails to work properly, it is possible to take it back for a replacement.

If a decision is made to buy additional insurance or support, however, this will be itemized on the receipt, but it is not possible to touch, taste, see, hear, or smell it. Services are intangible, and they are delivered and experienced only post-purchase.

Intangibility does not mean that customers buy services without using their senses. What it does mean is that they use substitute cues to help them to make these purchasing decisions and to reduce the uncertainty, because they cannot touch, see, smell, or hear the service. People make judgments based on a range of quality-related cues. These cues serve to make tangible the intangible service. Two types of cue can be identified: intrinsic and extrinsic (Olson and Jacoby, 1972). *Intrinsic* cues are drawn directly from the 'service product' itself, and are regarded as difficult to change. *Extrinsic* cues, on the other hand, are said to surround the 'service product' and can be changed relatively easily. Brady and colleagues (2005) found that different types of service brand need different types of cue. Financial and investment-based brands prosper from the use of intrinsic cues, which stress objective information sources, such as a strong reputation, industry rankings, and favourable media reviews. The reverse is true for services that have a more tangible element, such as hotels and transport services. In these circumstances, more subjective communication, such as advertising and referrals through word-of-mouth, are more influential.

Perishability

A bottle of shampoo on a supermarket shelf attracts a number of opportunities to be sold and consumed. When the store closes and opens again the following day, the bottle is still available to be sold, and it remains available until purchased or the expiry date is reached. This is not the case with services. Once a train pulls out of a station, or an aeroplane takes off, or a film starts, those seats are lost and can never be sold. This is referred to as 'perishability' and is an important aspect of services marketing. Services are manufactured and consumed simultaneously; they cannot be stored either prior to or after the **service encounter**.

The reason why these seats remain empty reflects variations in demand. This may be the result of changes in the wider environment and may follow easily predictable patterns of behaviour, for example family holiday travel. One of the tasks of service marketers is to ensure that the number of empty seats and lost-forever revenue is minimized. In cases of predictable demand, service managers can vary the level of service capacity—a longer train, a bigger aircraft, or extra screenings of a film (multiplex facilities), for example. However, demand may vary unpredictably, in which case service managers are challenged to provide varying levels of service capacity at short notice.

One of the main ways in which demand patterns can be influenced is by means of differential pricing. By lowering prices to attract custom during quieter times and raising prices when demand is at its highest, demand can be levelled and marginal revenues increased. Hotel and transport reservation systems have become very sophisticated, making it easier to manage demand and improve efficiency, and, of course, customer service. Some football clubs categorize matches according to the prestige or ranking of the opposition and adjust prices to fill the stadium. In addition to differential pricing, extra services can be introduced to divert demand. Hotels offer specialist weekend breaks, such as golfing or fishing and mini vacations, to attract retired people outside of the holiday season. Leisure parks offer family discounts and bundle free rides into prices to stimulate demand.

Variability

As already noted, an important characteristic of services is that they are produced and consumed by people, simultaneously, as a single event. One of the outcomes of this unique process is that it is exceedingly difficult to standardize the delivery of services around the blueprint model mentioned earlier. It is also difficult to deliver services so that they always meet the brand promise, especially because these promises often serve to frame customer service expectations. If demand increases unexpectedly and there is insufficient capacity to deal with the excess number of customers, service breakdown may occur. A flood of customers at a restaurant may extend the arrival of meals for customers already seated and who have ordered their meals; too many train passengers may mean that there are not enough seats: in both of these cases, it is not possible to provide a service level that can be consistently reproduced.

A different way of looking at variability is to consider a theatre. The show may be doing well and the lead actors performing to critical acclaim. However, the actual performance that each actor delivers each night will be slightly different. This change may be subtle, such as a change in the tone

It is difficult to standardize the delivery of services, because each 'event' is unique. This variability of service delivery can be observed in theatre performances.

Source: © Pavel L. Photo and Video/Shutterstock.

of voice or an inflexion, and will pass by relatively unnoticed. At the other extreme, some actors go out of their way to make their performances very different. It is alleged that actor Jane Horrocks once remarked that, during the performance of a certain theatre play, she deliberately changed each evening's show to relieve her boredom.

There has been substantial criticism of some organizations that, in an effort to lower costs, have relocated some or all of their call-centre operations offshore. These strategies sometimes fail because the new provider has insufficient training and local or product knowledge, or, in some cases, simply cannot be understood. This type of service experience will vary among customers and by each customer. The resulting fall in customer satisfaction can lead to increased numbers of customers defecting to competitors.

The variability of services does not mean that planning is a worthless activity. By anticipating situations in which service breakdown might occur, service managers can provide facilities. For example, entertainment can be provided for queues at cinemas or theme parks, to change the perception of the length of the time it takes to experience the service (film or ride).

Inseparability

As established earlier, products can be built, distributed, stored, and eventually consumed at a time specified by the ultimate end-user customer. Services, on the other hand, are consumed at the point at which they are produced. In other words, **service delivery** cannot be separated from or split out of service provision or service consumption.

This event in which delivery coincides with consumption means that not only do customers come into contact with the service providers, but also there must be interaction between the two parties. This interaction is of particular importance not only to the quality of service production, but also to the experience enjoyed by the customer. So, to continue the earlier example of a theatre play, the show itself may provide suitable entertainment, but the experience may be considerably enhanced if the lead actor—Jane Horrocks, Judi Dench, or Scarlett Johansson—actually performs, rather than has the night off because she is unwell. Alternatively, private doctors may develop a strong reputation and, should there be an increase in demand beyond manageable levels, pricing can be used to reduce or reschedule demand for their services.

These examples of service experiences highlight service delivery as a mass service experience (the play) and as a solo experience (the doctor). The differences impact on the nature of the interaction process. In the mass service experience, the other members of the audience have the opportunity to influence the perceived quality of the experience. Audiences create atmosphere and this may be positively or negatively charged. A good production can involve audiences in a play and keep them focused for the entire performance. However, a poor performance can frustrate audiences, leading to some members walking out, and hence influencing the perception others have of the performance and experience of the play.

Interaction within the solo experience (doctor–patient) allows for greater control by the service provider, if only because it can manage the immediate context within which the interaction occurs and not be unduly influenced by wider environmental issues. Opportunities exist for flexibility and adaptation as the service delivery unfolds. For example, a check-in operator for an airline operates within a particular context, is not influenced by other major events during the interaction, and can adapt tone of voice, body language, and overall approach to meet the needs of particular travellers.

Market Insight 12.1 **Purely Products and Purely Services**

Sweden's Tetra Pak revolutionized the food packaging industry, Finland's Huhtamäki Oyj is one of the world's leading manufacturers of paper cups and plates, Danish company Schur Technology is a leading North European total supplier of packaging solutions, and Norwegian company Elopak is a leading global supplier of cartons for liquid food products. Rexam is one of the world's leading consumer packaging groups, supporting the beverage, beauty, pharmaceuticals, and food markets.

What is common to all of these organizations? Their skill and core competence is in packaging. They make tangible products to which, traditionally, there are few service additions.

Packaging is an example of a 'pure product' that cannot be enhanced through extra services.

Source: © Getty / Amy Sussman / Stringer.

Market Insight 12.1 (continued)

Management consulting firms such as PwC offer an extensive range of technical services based on knowledge and intangible expertise.

Source: © Jpstock/Shutterstock.

Alternatively, Bain, McKinsey, Towers Perrin, and PricewaterhouseCoopers (PwC) are some of the leading management consulting organizations. Owned by IBM, PwC offers a huge range of services across many industries and sectors. Its approach to work is said to be about 'connectedthinking'.

All of these organizations do not make or sell any products; they provide knowledge and skills—that is, pure services.

1. **Identify ways in which packaging might influence consumers.**
2. **Think about the role of a marketing consultant and make a list of the different types of knowledge that might constitute 'connectedthinking'.**
3. **Draw the product–service spectrum and place on it various product–service combinations.**

Sources: http://www.elopak.com/; http://www.huhtamaki.com/; http://www.pwc.com/; http://www.rexam.com/; http://www.schur.com/skabeloner/; http://www.tetrapak.com/.

One final aspect of variability concerns the influence arising from the mixture of customers present during the service delivery. If there is a broad mix of customers, service delivery may be affected because the service provider has to attend to the needs of different groups. Such a mixture may dilute the impact of the service actually delivered.

Lack of Ownership

The final characteristic associated with services marketing arises naturally from the other features: services cannot be owned because nothing is transferred during the interaction or delivery experience. Although a legal transaction often occurs with a service, there is no physical transfer of ownership as there is when a product is purchased. The seat in a theatre, or on train, plane, or ferry is rented on a temporary basis in exchange for a fee. The terms associated with the rental of the seat determine the time and use or experience to which the seat can be put. However, the seat remains the property of the theatre owner, rail operator, airline, or ferry company, respectively, because it needs to be available for renting to other people for further experiences.

One last point concerns **loyalty** schemes, such as frequent-flyer programmes and membership clubs, whereby the service provider actively promotes a sense of ownership. By creating customer involvement and participation, even though there is nothing to actually own, customers can develop an attitude based around their perceived right to be a part of the service provider.

Visit the **online resources** and follow the web link to the British Bankers Association (BBA) to learn more about financial services.

Service Encounters

The development of service marketing strategies involves understanding the frequency with and the ways in which customers contact service providers. Once this is understood, strategies can be developed that maintain required levels of service, but the processes and linkages that bring the elements of the services marketing mix and associated systems together can be reformulated. Service marketing strategy should therefore be based on insight into the ways in which customers interact or contact a service. The form and nature of the customer encounter is of fundamental importance.

A service encounter is best understood as a period of time during which a customer interacts directly with a service (Shostack, 1985). These interactions may be short and encompass all of the actions necessary to complete the service experience. Alternatively, they may be protracted, involve several encounters and several representatives of the service provider, and indeed several locations, so that the service experience can be completed. Whatever their length, the quality of a service encounter impacts on perceived service value, which, in turn, influences customer satisfaction (Gil et al., 2008).

Originally, the term 'encounter' was used to describe the personal interaction between a service provider and customers. A more contemporary interpretation needs to include all interactions that occur through people and their equipment and machines with the people and equipment belonging to the service provider (Glyn and Lehtinen, 1995), as set out in Market Insight 12.2. As a result, three levels of customer contact can be observed: high-contact services, medium-contact services, and low-contact services (see Table 12.2).

One of the interesting developments in recent years is the decision by some organizations to move their customers away from high-contact services into low-contact services. Clear examples of this are to be found in the banking sector, with first automatic teller machines (ATMs), then telephone and now Internet banking, all of which either lower or remove personal contact with bank employees. Further examples include vending machines, self-service or rapid checkout facilities in hotels, and online ticket purchases.

Table 12.2 Levels of customer contact

Contact level	Explanation
High-contact services	Customers visit the service facility, so they are personally involved throughout the service delivery process, e.g. retail branch banking and higher education.
Medium-contact services	Customers visit the service facility, but do not remain for the duration of the service delivery, e.g. consulting services, and delivering and collecting items to be repaired.
Low-contact services	Little or no personal contact between customer and service provider, with service delivered from a remote location, often through electronic means, e.g. software repairs, and television and radio entertainment.

Market Insight 12.2 **Revolutionizing the Shopping Encounter**

Digital technologies are increasingly being used to innovate and improve service encounters. The retail clothing industry is seeing the rapid adoption of new technologies that allow consumers to try on new items using 'virtual changing rooms'. Start-ups such as Avametric and Metail have developed digital alternatives that allow customers to see themselves wearing the clothes they are considering purchasing without physically trying them on in a changing room. Although these technologies are often used to improve online shopping, they can also be used to enhance the service encounter in-store.

Virtual changing rooms in-store will work as a kind of interactive mirror that allow customers to see themselves wearing the item of interest. Manufacturers are also interested in this technology because it can generate useful information on which items are attracting consumers' attention. Virtual changing rooms could also aid the integration between online and in-store shopping. Avametric installs digital scanners in physical locations to take precise measurements for each customer. Once the measurements have been taken, the information is then accessible for online shopping as well as shopping in-store.

Ralph Lauren has launched an interactive digital fitting room in its flagship store in New York. It allows customers to try any item available in the collection without leaving the room. Customers can also test how the outfit looks in different settings by choosing different lightning conditions. The image can be saved and stored, as well as shared with friends on social media. If customers have questions on a specific item, sales assistants are alerted via an iPad app.

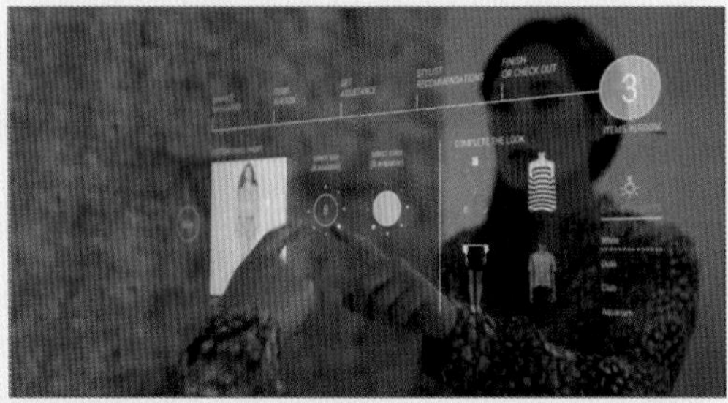

Interactive digital fitting rooms such as those pioneered by Oak Labs are revolutionizing the service encounter in retailing.

Source: Oak Labs, Inc.

Although such innovations are likely to become much more common in our shopping experiences, they need to be carefully integrated into the overall value proposition. In 2012, British retailer John Lewis trialled an early generation of virtual mirrors in a few stores. The experiment, however, was considered unsuccessful, because it did not seem to improve the service encounter significantly, considering the positioning of the brand and the customers it attracts.

1. **How would you classify the virtual changing room as a form of service encounter?**
2. **How might business-to-business (B2B) marketers make use of the information generated by virtual changing rooms?**
3. **How might virtual changing rooms impact on the relationships between retailers and their customers?**

Sources: Burn-Callander (2014); Bain (2015).

Sirianni and colleagues (2013) suggest that, by actively branding service encounters, organizations can reinforce brand meaning and positioning, whilst influencing customers' responses to brands. They define 'branded service encounters' as:

> ... service interactions in which employee behaviour is strategically aligned with the brand positioning. This strategic alignment may be evident in various elements of the employee's presented behaviour, appearance, and manner that can reinforce brand meaning during service interactions with customers.
>
> (Sirianni et al., 2013: 108)

This suggests that branded service encounters should be an integral element of any integrated marketing communication activity.

Key Dimensions of Services Marketing

The marketing of services can be improved by understanding how customers evaluate service performance. This begs the question: how do customers judge the quality of a bank's services, or those of an airline? This is potentially very difficult because complex services such as surgery or stockbroking have few tangible clues upon which to base a judgment about whether the service was extremely good, good, satisfactory, poor, or a disgrace. Customers purchasing physical goods can make judgments about the features, style, and colour, prior to purchase, during purchase, and even post-purchase, returning faulty or otherwise unwanted goods. This is not possible with some types of service—especially people-processing services.

Service performance is regarded as an important contributor to a firm's financial outcomes. Heskett and colleagues (1994) show that superior customer service, within a consumer context, leads to increased financial performance. The notion of service time as an indicator of service performance (Lund and Marinvova, 2014) has also gained increasing attention as service providers in general, and retailers in particular, look to gain competitive advantage.

Zeithaml (1981) determined a framework that categorizes different services, which, in turn, influences the degree to which market offerings can be evaluated, identifying three main properties, as follows.

- *Search* properties are those elements that help customers to evaluate an offering prior to purchase. As mentioned above, physical products tend to have high search attributes that serve to reduce customer risk and increase purchase confidence.
- *Experience* properties do not enable evaluation prior to purchase. Sporting events, holidays, and live entertainment can be imagined, explained, and illustrated, but only by experiencing the performance or sitting in an audience of 100,000 people can a customer evaluate the service experience.
- *Credence* properties relate to those service characteristics that, even after purchase and consumption, customers find difficult to evaluate. Zeithaml (1981) refers to complex surgery and legal services to demonstrate the point.

As demonstrated earlier, most physical goods are high in search properties. Services, however, reflect the strength of experience and credence characteristics that, in turn, highlight their intangibility and their variability.

Garry and Broderick (2007), however, challenge this classification on the basis that it does not entirely reflect contemporary service markets. Whereas the original classification vested expertise in the service provider, emerging research recognizes customer expertise and sophistication. With more information, customers have increasing skills and abilities to make judgments about the quality of service offerings, prior to purchase. According to Garry and Broderick (2007), this increased focus on customer attributes should also be matched with a consideration of the attributes that we associate with service encounters. Here, they consider issues relating to information accessibility, time and interactivity, and the level of customer-centricity present within a customer experience.

Many organizations recognize the importance and complexities associated with the marketing of services. As a result, they often develop and plan their marketing activities in such a way that they help and reassure their customers prior, during, and after purchase. This is achieved through the provision of varying levels of information to reduce **perceived risk** and to enhance the service experience. Two techniques, branding and internal marketing, are instrumental in delivering these goals in services marketing.

Understanding service encounters, customer satisfaction, and associated service measurement techniques, however, fails to lead to an understanding beyond the moment of truth—that is, the point at which the service is actioned. Understanding and measuring the experience that customers take away as a result of an interaction is much more pertinent and insightful.

Principles of Relationship Marketing

Our attention now turns to ideas about **relationship marketing**. First, we look at founding ideas about the exchanges that occur between a pair of buyers and sellers, two main types of which can be identified: **market (or discrete) exchanges** and **collaborative exchanges**.

Market exchanges occur where there is no prior history of exchange, and no future exchanges are expected between a buyer and seller. In these transactions, the primary focus is on the product and price. Often referred to as 'transactional marketing', the 4Ps approach to the marketing mix variables (the 'marketing management' school of thought) is used to guide and construct transaction behaviour. Buyers were considered to be passive and sellers, active, in these short-term exchanges.

The assumption, however, that buyers are passive was soon challenged by the notion that, in reality, buyers are active problem-solvers, seeking solutions that are both efficient and effective. Research into business markets identified that, in practice, purchasing is not about a single discrete event; rather, it is about a stream of activities between two organizations. These activities are sometimes referred to as 'episodes'. Typically, these may be price negotiations, meetings at exhibitions, or a buying decision, but these all take place within the overall context of a relationship. This framed the 'relationship marketing' school of thought—one in which the buyer–seller relationship was the central element of analysis. This meant that the focus was no longer the product, or even the individual buying or the firm selling, but rather the relationship and its particular characteristics over time.

Relationship marketing is therefore based on the principle that there is a history of exchanges and an expectation that there will be exchanges in the future. Furthermore, the perspective is long-term, envisioning a form of loyalty or continued attachment by the buyer to the seller. Price, as the key controlling mechanism, is replaced by customer service and quality of interaction between the two organizations. The exchange is termed 'collaborative' because the focus is on both organizations seeking to achieve their goals in a mutually rewarding way and not at the expense of one another. Table 12.3 offers a more comprehensive list of fundamental differences between transactional and collaborative-based marketing exchanges.

Although market exchanges focus on products and prices, there is nonetheless a relational component, if only because interaction requires a basic relationship between parties for the transaction to be completed (Macneil, 1980).

Dwyer and colleagues (1987) refer to relationship marketing as an approach that encompasses a wide range of relationships, not only those with customers, but also those that organizations develop with suppliers, regulators, government, competitors, employees, and others. From this,

Table 12.3 Characteristics of market and collaborative exchanges

Attribute	Market exchange	Collaborative exchange
Length of relationship	Short-term Ends abruptly	Long-term Continuous process
Relational expectations	Conflicts of goals Immediate payment No future problems (there is no future)	Conflicts of interest Deferred payment Future problems expected to be overcome by joint commitment
Communication	Low frequency of communication Formal communication predominates	Frequent communication Informal communication predominates
Cooperation	No joint cooperation	Joint cooperative projects
Responsibilities	Distinct responsibilities Defined obligations	Shared responsibilities Shared obligations

relationship marketing might be regarded as all marketing activities associated with the management of successful relational exchanges.

Theron and colleagues (2013), amongst others, recognize that the role of collaboration in relationship marketing is important. Many organizations however, maintain a variety of relationships with their different customers and suppliers—some highly collaborative and some market-oriented, or, as Spekman and Carroway (2005: 1) suggest, 'where they make sense'.

Visit the **online resources** and follow the web link to the Association for the Advancement of Relationship Marketing (AARM) to learn more about continuing professional development (CPD) in relationship marketing.

Relationship Trust, Commitment, and Satisfaction

Trust is a key feature of personal, intra-organizational, and inter-organizational relationships, and is necessary for their continuation. Gambetta (1988) argues that trust is a means of reducing uncertainty so that effective relationships can develop.

Cousins and Stanwix (2001) also suggest that although 'trust' is a term used to explain how relationships work, it often actually refers to ideas concerning risk, power, and dependency, and these propositions are used interchangeably. From their research of vehicle manufacturers, it emerges that B2B relationships are about the creation of mutual business advantage and the degree of confidence that one organization has in another.

Trust involves judgments about reliability and integrity, and is concerned with the degree of confidence that one party to a relationship has that another will fulfil its obligations and responsibilities. The presence of trust in a relationship is important because it reduces both the threat of opportunism and the possibility of conflict, which, in turn, increases the probability of buyer satisfaction. It has been claimed that the three major outcomes from the development of relationship trust are satisfaction, reduced perceived risk, and continuity (Pavlou, 2002).

- Perceived risk is concerned with the expectation of loss and is therefore tied closely with organizational performance.
- Trust that a seller will not take advantage of the imbalance of information between buyer and seller effectively reduces risk.
- Continuity is related to business volumes, necessary in online B2B marketplaces, and the development of both online and real-world enduring relationships. Trust is associated with continuity and, when present, is consequently indicative of long-term relationships.

Trust within a consumer context is important because it can reduce uncertainty. RAKBANK, a retail and business bank in the United Arab Emirates (UAE), for example, understood that many of its potential customers distrusted banks because of the hidden annual fees and cynical charges relating to credit cards. Strong brands provide sufficient information for consumers to make calculated purchase decisions in the absence of full knowledge. In a sense, consumers transfer their responsibility for brand decision-making, and hence brand performance, to the brand itself. Through regular brand purchases, habits, or 'routinized response behaviour', develop. This is important not only because complex decision-making is simplified, but also because the amount of communication necessary to assist and provoke purchase is considerably reduced.

The presence of trust within a relationship is influenced by four main factors: the duration of the relationship; the relative power of the participants; the presence of cooperation; and various environmental factors that may be present at any one moment (Young and Wilkinson, 1989). Although pertinent, these are quite general factors, and it is Morgan and Hunt (1994) who established what are regarded today as the key underlying dimensions of relationship marketing. In their seminal paper, they argued that it is the presence of both **commitment** and trust that leads to cooperative behaviour, customer satisfaction, and, ultimately, successful relationship marketing.

Commitment is important because it implies a desire that a relationship continues and is strengthened because it is of value. Morgan and Hunt (1994) proposed that commitment and trust are the **key mediating variables (KMV)** between five antecedents and five outcomes (see Figure 12.2).

According to the KMV model, the greater the losses anticipated through the termination of a relationship, the greater the commitment expressed by the exchange partners. When relationship partners share similar values, commitment increases. Morgan and Hunt (1994) proposed that building a relationship based on trust and commitment can give rise to a number of benefits, including developing a set of shared values, reducing costs when the relationship finishes, and increasing profitability because a greater number of end-user customers are retained as a consequence of the inherent value and satisfaction they experience. Cooperation arises from a relationship driven by high levels of both trust and commitment (Morgan and Hunt, 1994).

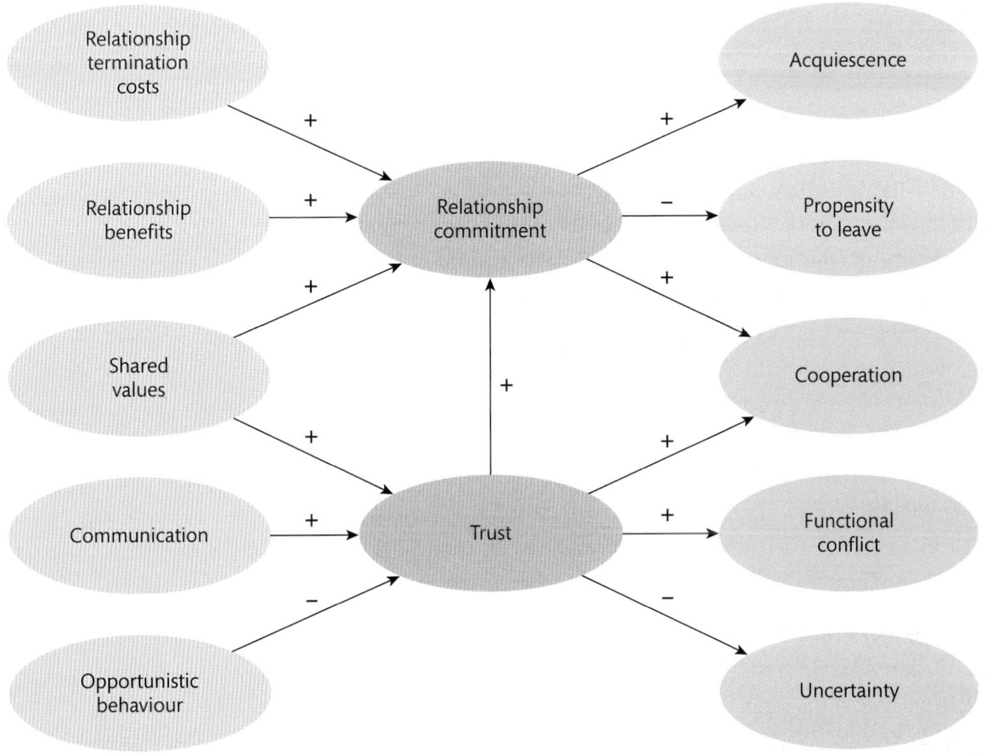

Figure 12.2: The KMV model of relationship marketing

Source: Reprinted with permission from R. M. Morgan and S. D. Hunt (1994), 'The commitment–trust theory of relationship marketing', *Journal of Marketing*, 58(July), 20–38, published by the American Marketing Association.

Ryssel and colleagues (2004: 203) recognize that trust (and commitment) has a 'significant impact on the creation of value and conclude that value creation is a function of the atmosphere of a relationship rather than the technology employed'. Trust and commitment are concepts that are central to relationship marketing.

Research Insight 12.2

To take your learning further, you might wish to read this influential paper.

Morgan, R. M., and Hunt, S. D. (1994) 'The commitment–trust theory of relationship marketing', *Journal of Marketing*, 58(3): 20–38.

This well-known paper examines the role of trust and commitment in buyer–supplier relationships. The authors present the KMV model to explain various behavioural and cognitive aspects associated with exchange partnerships. Using social exchange theory, it is argued that, through mutually beneficial exchanges, trust and commitment develop, which, in turn, leads to longer lasting relationships.

 **Visit the online resources to read the abstract and access the full paper.**

Customer Satisfaction

A natural outcome from building trust and developing commitment is the establishment of customer satisfaction. This is seen as important because satisfaction is thought to be positively related to **customer retention**, which, in turn, leads to an improved return on investment (ROI) and hence profitability. Unsurprisingly, many organizations seek to improve levels of customer satisfaction, with the intention of strengthening customer relationships and driving higher levels of retention and loyalty (Ravald and Grönroos, 1996). The simple equation is: build trust, drive satisfaction, improve retention, and increase profits.

Customer satisfaction is not driven by trust alone, however; customer expectations also play an important role and help to shape a customer's perception of product or service performance. Customers compare performance against their expectations and, through this process, feel a sense of customer satisfaction or dissatisfaction. More recent ideas suggest that the **perceived value** of a relationship can be more important than trust when building customer satisfaction (Ulaga and Eggert, 2005).

If expectations are met, then customer satisfaction is achieved. If Withers Worldwide, for example, can exceed the expectations of its customers, then both parties will be delighted. If expectations are not met, then customers will be said to be dissatisfied. This simplistic interpretation can be misleading, because satisfaction does not always imply loyalty (Mittal and Lassar, 1998): what may be seen as loyalty may be nothing more than convenience, or even inertia—and this means too that dissatisfaction need not result in brand desertion (O'Malley, 1998).

Cumby and Barnes (1998) provide a useful insight into what contributes to customer satisfaction, citing:

- *core product/service*—the bundle of attributes, features, and benefits that must reach competitive levels if a relationship is to develop;
- *support services and systems*—the quality of services and systems used to support the core product/service;
- *technical performance*—the synchronization of the core product/services with the support infrastructure to deliver on the promise;
- *elements of customer interaction*—the quality of customer care demonstrated through face-to-face and technology-mediated communications; and
- *affective dimensions of services*—the subtle and non-core interactions that say something about how the organization feels about the customer.

This is a more useful insight into what it is that drives customer satisfaction, because it incorporates a wide range of factors and recognizes the importance of personal contact. Customer satisfaction and the quality of customer relationships are related, in differing ways, among differing people and contexts. However, one factor that is common to both is the perceived value of the interaction between parties.

Measuring Service Quality and Performance

Measuring the quality of a service encounter is an important factor in managing service-based organizations. Service quality is based on the idea that customer expectations of the service they will receive shape their perception of the actual service encounter. Customers therefore compare perceived service with expected service.

If the perceived service meets or even exceeds expectations, customers are satisfied and much more likely to return in future. However, if the perceived service falls below that expected, they may feel disappointed and not return.

Various models have been proposed to help organizations achieve consistent levels of service, including asking customers to rate the performance of a service encounter, asking customers what is expected from a service against what is delivered and comparing the performance of the different elements that make up a service with the customer's perception of the importance of these elements. Each approach has strengths and weaknesses but the approach that has received most attention is **SERVQUAL** developed by Parasuraman et al. (1988). For some, it represents the benchmark approach to managing service quality.

SERVQUAL is based on the difference between the expected level of service and the actual perceived level of service. This approach assumes that there is a service quality gap overall which breaks down into five sub-variants as follows.

- **GAP 1—the gap between the customer's expectations and management perception.** By not understanding customer needs correctly, management directs resources into inappropriate areas. For example, train service operators may think that customers want places to store bags, whereas they actually want a seat in a comfortable, safe environment.
- **GAP 2—the gap between management perception and service quality specification.** In this case, management perceives customer wants correctly but fails to set a performance standard, fails to clarify it, or sets one that is unrealistic and unachievable. For example, the train operator understands customer desire for a comfortable seat but fails to specify how many should be provided relative to the anticipated number of passengers on each route.
- **GAP 3—the gap between service quality specifications and service delivery.** In this situation, the service delivery does not match the service specification. This may be due to human error, poor training, or a failure in the technology necessary to deliver parts of a service. For example, the trolley buffet service on a train may be perceived as poor because the trolley operator was impolite because he/she had not received suitable training or because the supplier had not delivered the sandwiches on time.
- **GAP 4—the gap between service delivery and external communications.** The service promise presented in advertisements, on the website, and in sales literature helps set customer expectations. If these promises are not realized in service delivery practice, customers become dissatisfied. For example, if an advertisement shows the interior of a train with comfortable seats and plenty of space, yet a customer boards a train only to find a lack of space and hard seating, the external communications have misled customers and distorted their view of what might be realistically expected.
- **GAP 5—the gap between perceived service and expected service.** This gap arises because customers misunderstand the service quality relative to what they expect. This may be due to one or more of the previous gaps. For example, a customer might assume that the lack of information when a train comes to a standstill for an unexpectedly long period of time is due to ignorance or a 'they never tell us anything' attitude. In reality, this silence may be due to a failure of the internal communication system.

Using this GAPS approach five different dimensions of service quality have been established.

1. Reliability—the accuracy and dependability of repeated performances of service delivery.
2. Responsiveness—the helpfulness and willingness of staff to provide prompt service.
3. Assurance—the courtesy, confidence, and competence of employees.

4 Empathy—the ease and individualized care shown towards customers.

5 Tangibles—the appearance of employees, the physical location and any facilities and equipment, and the communication materials.

The SERVQUAL model consists of a questionnaire containing 22 items based around these five dimensions. When completed by customers it provides management with opportunities to correct areas where service performance is perceived to be less than satisfactory and learn from and congratulate people about the successful components. Although SERVQUAL has been used extensively, it is not without perceived problems. Difficulties concern the different dimensions customers use to assess quality, which varies according to each situation. In addition, there are statistical inconsistencies associated with measuring differences and the scoring techniques plus reliability issues associated with asking customers about their expectations after they have consumed a service (Gabbott and Hogg, 1998). Finally, ideas about measuring satisfaction are being overtaken as understanding about customer experience becomes more widely known. This is explored in the next section.

Customer Experiences

The path of this chapter began with an exploration of the evolution of marketing practices related to services marketing, then moved on to consider ideas about customer relationships. This chapter closes with an exploration of customer experiences (Maklan and Klaus, 2011).

The idea that providing a superior customer service might help in the (repeat) purchase decision process is something that several organizations, including Withers Worldwide, now appreciate. For a long time, it was assumed that product quality and pricing were sufficient differentiators. However, product quality is no longer a viable means of establishing competitive advantage, simply because of shortening life cycles and evolving technologies. Service, although difficult to deliver in a consistent way, is very difficult to replicate and has become an important aspect of customer management.

Although generating customer satisfaction is important, it provides an incomplete picture. Of greater interest is 'customer experience'. As Prahalad and Ramaswamy (2004: 137, cited by Iyanna et al., 2012) suggest, the literature on value is no longer embedded in goods and services, or indeed relationships, but 'is now centered in the experiences of consumers'. Customer value is regarded by an increasing number of academics and practitioners as the central marketing activity (Iyanna et al., 2012) and that value is now central to customers' experiences. The implications for marketing are clearly asserted by Meyer and Schwager (2007: 118) when they say that 'customer experience encompasses every aspect of a company's offering—the quality of customer care, of course, but also advertising, packaging, product and service features, ease of use, and reliability'. (For

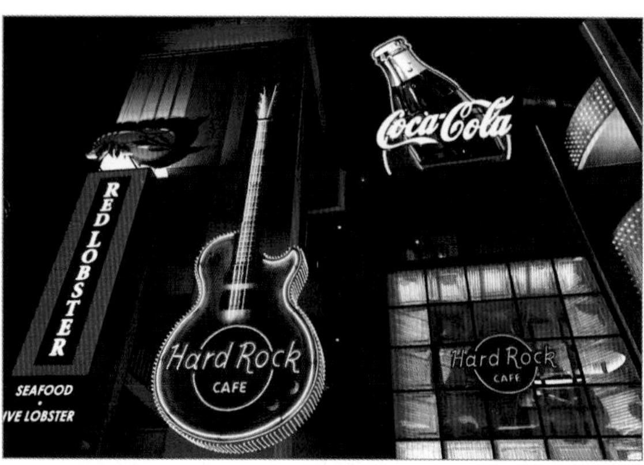

For the Hard Rock Cafe, the iconic brand and associations with music are also part of the customer experience.

Source: © Usa-Pyon/Shutterstock.

a deeper understanding of the issues arising from the adoption of a customer experience perspective, see Research Insight 12.3.)

The importance and significance of customer experience to both individuals and society was first established by Pine and Gilmore (1998) when they referred to the 'experience economy', a term that is used frequently by authors and researchers in this area. Chang and Horng (2010) suggest that themed restaurants, such as Starbucks and Hard Rock Cafe, are prime examples of customer experience. These brands are not only about the consumption of coffee, but also a situation or environment in which the consumption of services occurs and relationships are developed, and in total provide a meaningful or valuable customer experience. Ismail and colleagues (2011) refer to the trend towards creating unique experiences for customers with a view to developing a competitive advantage—something that is sustainable particularly for those in the service sector, because replication is very difficult.

Before exploring the characteristics and issues associated with customer experience, it is helpful to consider how the concept is defined, in which regard there has been little consensus. Some of the more notable attempts are set out in Table 12.4.

There are some similarities across many of these definitions. Customer experience is seen to be an individual event, and as concerning emotional reactions following direct and indirect interaction with an organization. It is also related to events prior to, during, or post consumption. Perhaps one crucial point is that it is not possible for two people to have or to share the same experience (Pine and Gilmore, 1998). As a result, the task of managing and measuring customer experiences is inherently complex.

To help us to disentangle some of this complexity, Pine and Gilmore (1998) derive four distinct realms of experience, based on two dimensions. These dimensions concern a customer's participation in an experience (weak/passive or active/strong) and an individual's connection with the environment of the experience or environmental relationship (from absorption/weak to immersion/strong).

The four realms of experience that emerge from these dimensions are as follows.

- *Educational realm*—This arises when individuals learn and enhance their skills and knowledge as a result of the events unfolding before them (Pine and Gilmore, 1999; Oh et al., 2007).
- *Entertainment realm*—This arises when an individual views a performance, listens to music, or reads for pleasure, during which the experience is absorbed passively (Pine and Gilmore, 1999).

Research Insight 12.3

To take your learning further, you might wish to read this influential paper.

Meyer, C., and Schwager, A. (2007) 'Understanding customer experience', *Harvard Business Review*, 85(2): 116–26.

This paper looks at how firms can benefit from adopting a customer experience perspective. It provides a clear understanding of what customer experience is practically and discusses the managerial issues that can be avoided by utilizing an experience-based view, rather than a relationship-based view. It also contains a useful table showing how customer relationship management (CRM) differs from customer experience management.

 **Visit the online resources to read the abstract and access the full paper.**

Table 12.4 Definitions of experience

Source	Definitions
Csikszentmihalyi (1977: 36)	The individual is experiencing flow when he has: . . . a unified flowing from one moment to the next, in which he is in control of his actions and in which there is little distinction between self and environment, between stimulus and response, between past, present and future.
Holbrook and Hirschman (1982), cited in Carù and Cova (2003)	Experience is defined as a personal occurrence, often with important emotional significance, founded on the interaction with stimuli that are the products or services consumed.
Carbone and Haeckel (1994: 8)	The take-away impression formed by people's encounters with products, services, and businesses, a perception produced when humans consolidate sensory information . . .
Schmitt (1999: 60)	From a customer perspective: Experiences involve the entire living being. They often result from direct observation and/or participating in the event—whether they are real, dreamlike or virtual.
Shaw and Ivens (2002: 6)	. . . an interaction between an organization and a customer. It is a blend of an organization's physical performance, the senses stimulated and emotions evoked, each intuitively measured against customer experience across all moments of contact.
Gentile et al. (2007: 397)	The customer experience originates from a set of interactions between a customer and a product, a company, or part of its organization, which provoke a reaction. This experience is strictly individual and implies the customer's involvement at different levels (rational, emotional, sensorial, physical and spiritual). Its evaluation depends on the comparison between a customer's expectations and the stimuli coming from the interaction with the company and its offering in correspondence of the different moments of contacts or touch-points.
Brakus et al. (2009: 53)	. . . subjective, internal consumer responses (sensations, feelings, and cognitions) and behavioural responses evoked by brand related stimuli that are part of a brand's design and identity, packaging, communications, and environments . . .
Ismail et al. (2011)	Emotions provoked, sensations felt, knowledge gained, and skills acquired through active involvement with the firm before, during, and after consumption

Source: Adapted from Ismail et al. (2011).

- *Aesthetic realm*—This arises when an individual passively appreciates an event or environment, but leaves without affecting or altering the nature of the environment (Pine and Gilmore, 1999; Oh et al., 2007).
- *Escapist realm*—This arises when individuals become completely immersed in their environment and actively participate, so that they affect actual performances or occurrences in the environment (Pine and Gilmore, 1999; Oh et al., 2007).

This approach has subsequently led to research that focuses on the ways in which experiences are produced, narrated, and mediated (Lofgren, 2008).

Various authors have contributed to what might be the key dimensions of customer experience. Of these, Nysveen and Pedersen (2014) used the dimensions highlighted by Brakus and colleagues (2009)—namely, sensory, affective, intellectual, and behavioural—and added a further relational dimension, as determined by Nysveen and colleagues (2013).

- The *sensory* dimension refers to the extent to which a brand appeals to, and makes impressions on, consumers' senses.
- The *affective* dimension refers to how strongly a brand induces consumer feelings and emotions.
- The *intellectual* (or *cognitive*) dimension refers to how much a brand stimulates a consumer's curiosity, thinking, and problem-solving.
- The *behavioural* dimension refers to how strongly a brand engages consumers in physical activities.
- The *relational* dimension refers to how well an experience creates value for customers by driving social engagement, and providing a social identity and a sense of belonging.

From their research, Nysveen and Pedersen (2014) validated the importance of all of these dimensions. They stressed, however, the significance of the relational dimension, and its strong positive influence on both brand satisfaction and brand loyalty.

Visit the **online resources** and follow the web links to see how the Customer Experience Professionals Association (CXPA) supports the industry.

Market Insight 12.3 **Customer Experiences and Environmental Sustainability**

Companies are also adopting the logic of customer experience in the promotion of environmental and/or social causes that are consistent with their overall positioning. In the past, environmental concerns of consumers translated into the development and promotion of more environmentally sustainable, or 'green', alternatives. From this focus on discrete 'green' exchanges, companies are shifting towards relational practices aimed at the promotion of sustainability. Consequently, they are increasingly introducing long-term initiatives that engage consumers over time and are not simply associated with a single purchase.

Some of Patagonia's sustainable practices focus on the reuse of old materials for new clothing items.

Source: © Getty / Bethany Mollenkof / Contributor.

For example, in 2008, Starbucks introduced a website called 'MyStarbucksIdea' on which consumers can interact and discuss issues of social responsibility that are important to them. Over time, the platform began attracting a lot of comments on products and service enhancements that the company could

Market Insight 12.3 (continued)

implement. Today, the website is an open forum for discussion, containing hundreds of thousands of ideas on disparate topics: from environmental and social issues, to new ideas for drinks that the company should consider. The website also allows employees to interact directly with customers, creating an environment ideal for the development of strong experiences consistent with the brand.

Patagonia is an American brand of premium outdoor clothing. As a company strongly committed to environmental protection, Patagonia has been able to leverage its support to environmental movements and grassroots campaigners to reinforce its customer experience and its core brand values. Patagonia organizes local events and national conferences where employees, fans of the brands, and activists can meet to discuss environmental issues and to share best practices. The company has also published a manual, *Patagonia Tools for Grassroots Activists: Best Practices for Success in the Environmental Movement*, aimed at supporting grassroots organizations. These activities are not instrumental; they are motivated primarily by the brand's concern for the environment and long-standing commitment to positive change. Nonetheless, they reinforce customers' experience of the brand, and represent an extension to the sustainability arena of the concept of 'experience economy' popularized by Pine and Gilmore (1999).

1 **To what extent is customer experience capable of being measured?**

2 **Explain the key differences between customer satisfaction and experience.**

3 **Choose a brand with which you are familiar and list the different ways in which it might attempt to improve customer experience.**

Sources: Carr (2016); O'Connor (2016).

Chapter Summary

To consolidate your learning, the key points from this chapter are summarized below.

- **Explain the nature and characteristics of services.**

  Unlike products, services are considered to be processes, and products and services have different distinguishing characteristics. These are based around their intangibility (you can touch a product, but not a service), perishability (products can be stored, but you cannot store a service), variability (each time a service is delivered, it is different, but products can be identical), inseparability (services are produced and consumed simultaneously), and a lack of ownership (you cannot take legal possession of a service). These are important because they shape the way in which marketers design, develop, deliver, and evaluate the marketing of services.

- **Describe what is meant by the term 'service encounters'.**

  A 'service encounter' is best understood as a period of time during which a customer interacts directly with a service (Shostack, 1985). There are three levels of customer contact: high-contact services, medium-contact services, and low-contact services.

- **Outline the principles of relationship marketing and the relationships between trust, commitment, and customer satisfaction.**

  Relationship marketing is based on the premise that retained customers are more profitable than transactional marketing-based customers. There are several key concepts associated with the management of customer relationships, the main ones being trust, commitment, and satisfaction. These are interrelated, and the management of customer relationships should be based on the principles of reducing the influence of power and the incidence of conflict to build customer trust, gain customer commitment, and, through loyalty and retention, generate customer satisfaction. This approach should increase the perceived value of the relationship for all parties.

- **Define the term 'customer experiences', and explain its dimensions, how it has evolved, and how it might be measured.**

  Customers' experience an emotional transition and response through interactions with an organization and its offerings. This individuality of experience implies that there are different types or levels of experience, such as rational, emotional, sensorial, physical, and spiritual. The development of customer experience marketing has been built on evolving ideas concerning service encounters, perceived value, relationship marketing, and customer satisfaction.

Review Questions

1. **Identify the essential characteristics of services and make brief notes explaining how these characteristics affect the marketing of services.**
2. **What are the main types of service process? Identify their key characteristics.**
3. **Explain the term 'service encounter'.**
4. **How does an understanding of the relevant search, experience, and credence properties of a service influence the way in which they are marketed?**
5. **What are the key differences between transaction marketing and relationship marketing?**
6. **Why is trust an important aspect of relationship marketing?**
7. **Describe the key mediating variables (KMV) model and the relationships between its components.**
8. **To what extent does the concept of 'relationship intensity' assist our understanding of relationship marketing?**
9. **Make notes for a short presentation in which you explain the term 'customer experience' and track its evolution.**
10. **Compare and contrast three of the different definitions of customer experience offered in Table 12.4.**

Worksheet Summary

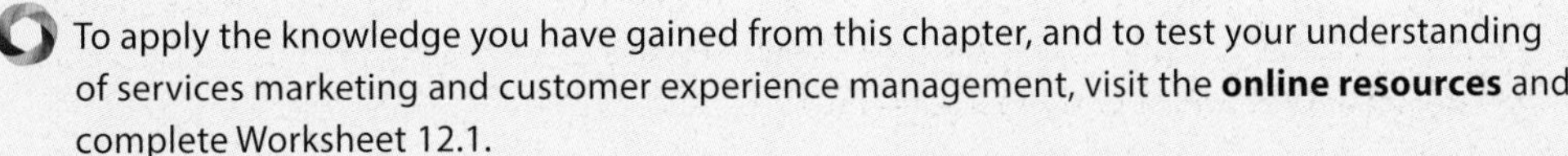

To apply the knowledge you have gained from this chapter, and to test your understanding of services marketing and customer experience management, visit the **online resources** and complete Worksheet 12.1.

Discussion Questions

1 Having the read Case Insight 12.1, how would you advise Withers Worldwide about how best to evaluate the quality of its service offering?

2 To what extent is the traditional marketing mix a useful basis for developing marketing strategies for service organizations?

3 Westcliffe and Sons makes a range of fruit juice drinks. The business falls into two main segments, consumer and business user, such as local councils and catering companies. Recent sales figures suggest that orders from some catering companies are down on previous years and that some have stopped buying from them altogether. The marketing director of Westcliffe has reported that he cannot understand the reason for the decline in business, because product quality and prices are very competitive. Advise the marketing director about the key issues he should consider and discuss how the company should re-establish itself with the catering companies.

4 Using PowerPoint prepare a short presentation in which you explain the meaning of 'customer experience'.

Visit the **online resources** and complete the multiple-choice questions to assess your knowledge of the chapter.

Glossary

collaborative exchanges a series of transactions between a buyer and seller in which the relationship is the main focus.

commitment a desire that a relationship should continue.

customer experience the individual feelings and emotions felt during interactions with an organization and its offerings.

customer retention a stage in a buyer–seller relationship that is stable, and at which levels of trust and commitment are strongest.

inseparability a characteristic of a service, referring to its instantaneous production and consumption.

intangibility a characteristic of a service, referring to its lack of physical attributes, which means that it cannot be perceived by the senses—that is, tasted, seen, touched, smelt, or possessed.

key mediating variables (KMV) the dimensions of commitment and trust used within the Morgan and Hunt (1994) model of relationship marketing.

loyalty the extent to which a customer supports, possibly through repeat purchases, a particular brand.

market (or discrete) exchanges a type of transaction between a buyer and seller in which the main focus is on the product and price.

perceived risk the real and imagined uncertainties that customers consider when purchasing products and services.

perceived value the 'net satisfaction' derived from consuming and using a product, not only the costs involved in obtaining it.

perishability a characteristic of a service, referring to the fact that any spare or unused capacity cannot be stored for use at some point in the future.

relationship marketing marketing activities associated with the management of successful relational (collaborative) exchanges.

service delivery the means through which services are experienced by customers.

service encounter an event that occurs when a customer interacts directly with a service.

service process a series of sequential actions that leads to the delivery of a predetermined service.

service quality the extent to which customer expectations of a service are met through an actual service encounter.

SERVQUAL a model which measures the difference between the expected service and the actual perceived service.

trust a judgment about the reliability, integrity, and the degree of confidence that one party to a relationship has that another will fulfil its obligations and responsibilities.

variability a characteristic of a service, referring to the amount of diversity allowed at each step of service provision.

References

Bain, M. (2015) 'Ralph Lauren's high-tech, futuristic fitting room makes trying on clothes seem legitimately fun', *Quartz*, 19 November. Available online at http://qz.com/554592/ralph-laurens-high-tech-futuristic-fitting-room-makes-trying-on-clothes-seem-legitimately-fun/ [accessed 22 June 2016].

Berry, L. L. (1980) 'Services marketing is different', *Business*, May–June: 24–30.

Brady, M. K., Bourdeau, B. L., and Heskel, J. (2005) 'The importance of brand cues in intangible service industries: An application to investment services', *Journal of Services Marketing*, 19(6): 401–10.

Brakus, J. J., Schmitt, B. H., and Zarantonello, L. (2009) 'Brand experience: What is it? How is it measured? Does it affect loyalty?', *Journal of Marketing*, 73(3): 52–68.

Burn-Callander, R. (2014) 'Virtual fitting room firm raises £7.5m as consumers find new ways to shop online', *The Telegraph*, 16 October. Available online at http://www.telegraph.co.uk/finance/businessclub/11168037/Virtual-fitting-room-Metail-firm-raises-7.5m-as-consumers-find-new-ways-to-shop-online.html [accessed 22 June 2016].

Carbone, L. P., and Haeckel, S. H. (1994) 'Engineering customer experiences', *Marketing Management*, 3(3): 8–19.

Carr, P. (2016) 'My Starbucks idea: The Starbucks crowdsourcing success story', 12 February. Available online at http://smbp.uwaterloo.ca/2015/02/my-starbucks-idea-the-starbucks-crowdsourcing-success-story/ [accessed 10 May 2016].

Carù, A., and Cova, B. (2003) 'Revisiting consumption experience: A more humble but complete view of the concept', *Marketing Theory*, 3(2): 267–86.

Chang, T.-C., and Horng, S.-C. (2010) 'Conceptualizing and measuring experience quality: The customer's perspective', *The Service Industries Journal*, 30(14): 2401–19.

Cousins, P. D., and Stanwix, E. (2001) 'It's only a matter of confidence! A comparison of relationship management between Japanese and UK non-owned vehicle manufacturers', *International Journal of Operations and Production Management*, 21(9): 1160–80.

Csikszentmihalyi, M. (1977) *Beyond Boredom and Anxiety*, San Francisco, CA: Jossey-Bass.

Cumby, J. A., and Barnes, J. (1998) 'How customers are made to feel: The role of affective reactions in driving customer satisfaction', *Customer Relationship Management*, 1(1): 54–63.

Dwyer, R. F., Schurr, P. H., and Oh, S. (1987) 'Developing buyer–seller relationships', *Journal of Marketing*, 51(2): 11–27.

Gabbott, M., and Hogg, G. (1998) *Consumers and Services*, Chichester: John Wiley.

Gambetta, D. (1988) *Trust: Making and Breaking Co-operative Relations*, New York: Blackwell.

Garry, T., and Broderick, A. (2007) 'Customer attributes or service attributes? Rethinking the search, experience and credence classification basis of services', Paper presented at the 21st Service Workshop of the Academy of Marketing, 15–17 November, University of Westminster.

Gentile, C., Spiller, N., and Noci, G. (2007) 'How to sustain the customer experience: An overview of experience components that co-create value with the customer', *European Management Journal*, 25(5): 395–410.

Gil, I., Berenguer, G., and Cervera, A. (2008) 'The roles of service encounters, service value, and job satisfaction in business relationships', *Industrial Marketing Management*, 37(8): 921–39.

Glyn, W. J., and Lehtinen, U. (1995) 'The concept of exchange: Interactive approaches in services marketing', in W. J. Glyn and J. G. Barnes (eds) *Understanding Services Management*, Chichester: John Wiley, 89–118.

Grönroos, C. (1990) *Service Management and Marketing: Managing the Moment of Truth in Service Competition*, Lexington, MA: Lexington Books.

Heskett, J. L., Jones, T. O., Loveman, G. W., Sasser, S. E., Jr., and Schlesinger, L. A. (1994) 'Putting the service-profit chain to work', *Harvard Business Review*, 72(2): 164–7.

Holbrook, M. B., and Hirschman, E. C. (1982) 'The experiential aspects of consumption: Consumer fantasies, feelings and fun', *Journal of Consumer Research*, 9(2): 132–40.

Ismail, A. R., Melewar, T. C., Lim, L., and Woodside, A. (2011) 'Customer experiences with brands: Literature review and research directions', *The Marketing Review*, 11(3): 205–25.

Iyanna, S., Bosangit, C., and Mohd-Any, A. A. (2012) 'Value evaluation of customer experience using consumer-generated content', *International Journal of Management and Marketing Research*, 5(2): 89–102.

Lofgren, O. (2008) 'The secret lives of tourists: Delays, disappointments and daydreams', *Scandinavian Journal of Hospitality and Tourism*, 8(1): 85–101.

Lovelock, C., Vandermerwe, S., and Lewis, B. (1999) *Services Marketing: A European Perspective*, Harlow: FT/ Prentice Hall.

Lund, D. J., and Marinova, D. (2014) 'Managing revenue across retail channels: The interplay of service performance and direct marketing', *Journal of Marketing*, 78(5): 99–118.

Macneil, I. R. (1980) *The New Social Contract*, New Haven, CT: Yale University Press.

Maklan, S., and Klaus, P. (2011) 'Customer experience: Are we measuring the right things?', *International Journal of Market Research*, 53(6): 771–92.

Meyer, C., and Schwager, A. (2007) 'Understanding customer experience', *Harvard Business Review*, 85(2): 116–26.

Mittal, B., and Lassar, W. M. (1998) 'Why do consumers switch? The dynamics of satisfaction versus loyalty', *Journal of Services Marketing*, 12(3): 177–94.

Morgan, R. M., and Hunt, S. D. (1994) 'The commitment–trust theory of relationship marketing', *Journal of Marketing*, 58(3): 20–38.

Nysveen, H., and Pedersen, P. I. (2014) 'Influences of co-creation on brand experience', *International Journal of Market Research*, 56(6): 807–32.

Nysveen, H., Pedersen, E. E., and Skard, S. (2013) 'Brand experiences in service organizations: Exploring the individual effects of brand experience dimensions', *Journal of Brand Management*, 20(5): 404–23.

O'Connor, M. C. (2016) ' "Tools for grassroots activism" is Patagonia's guide to saving the World', 25 February. Available online at http://www.outsideonline.com/2058051/patagonias-guide-saving-environment [accessed 10 May 2016].

O'Malley, L. (1998) 'Can loyalty schemes really build loyalty?', *Marketing Intelligence and Planning*, 16(1): 47–55.

Oh, H., Fiorie, A. M., and Jeoung, M. (2007) 'Measuring experience economy concepts: Tourism applications', *Journal of Travel Research*, 46(2): 119–32.

Olson, J. C., and Jacoby, J. (1972) 'Cue utilization in the quality perception process', in M. Venkatesan (ed.) *Proceedings of the Third Annual Conference of the Association for Consumer Research*, Toronto, ON: Association for Consumer Research, 167–79.

Parasuraman, A., Zeithaml, V., and Berry, L. L. (1988) 'SERVQUAL: A multiple-item scale for measuring consumer perceptions of service quality', *Journal of Retailing*, 64(1): 5–37.

Pavlou, P. A. (2002) 'Institution-based trust in interorganisational exchange relationships: The role of online B2B marketplaces on trust formation', *Journal of Strategic Information Systems*, 11(3–4): 215–43.

Pine, B. J., and Gilmore, J. H. (1998) 'Welcome to the experience economy', *Harvard Business Review*, 76(4): 97–105.

Pine, B. J., and Gilmore, J. H. (1999) *The Experience Economy: Work is Theatre and Every Business a Stage*, Boston, MA: Harvard Business School Press.

Prahalad, C. K., and Ramaswamy, V. (2004) *The Future of Competition: Co-creating Unique Value with Customers*, Boston, MA: Harvard Business School Press.

Ravald, A., and Grönroos, C. (1996) 'The value concept and relationship marketing', *European Journal of Marketing*, 30(2): 19–33.

Ryssel, R., Ritter, T., and Gemunden, H. G. (2004) 'The impact of information technology deployment on trust, commitment and value creation in business relationships', *Journal of Business and Industrial Marketing*, 19(3): 197–207.

Schmitt, B. H. (1999) *Experiential Marketing*, New York: Free Press.

Shaw, C., and Ivens, J. (2002) *Building Great Customer Experiences*, New York: Palgrave Macmillan.

Shostack, G. L. (1977) 'Breaking free from product marketing', *Journal of Marketing*, 41(2): 73–80.

Shostack, G. L. (1985) 'Planning the service encounter', in J. A. Czepiel, M. R. Solomon, and C. F. Surprenant (eds) *The Service Encounter*, Lexington, MA: Lexington Books, 243–54.

Sirianni, N. J., Bitner, M. J., Brown, S. W., and Vlandel, N. (2013) 'Branded service encounters: Strategically aligning employee behavior with the brand positioning', *Journal of Marketing*, 77(6): 108–23.

Spekman, R. E., and Carroway, R. (2005) 'Making the transition to collaborative buyer–seller relationships: An emerging framework', *Industrial Marketing Management*, 35(1): 10–19.

Theron, E., Terblanche, N. S., and Boshoff, C. (2013) 'Building long-term marketing relationships: New perspectives on B2B financial services', *South African Journal of Business Management*, 44(4): 33–45.

Ulaga, W., and Eggert, A. (2005) 'Relationship value in business markets: The construct and its dimensions', *Journal of Business-to-Business Marketing*, 12(1): 73–99.

Young, L. C., and Wilkinson, I. F. (1989) 'The role of trust and co-operation in marketing channels: A preliminary study', *European Journal of Marketing*, 23(2): 109–22.

Zeithaml, V. A. (1991 [1981]) 'How consumer evaluation processes differ between goods and services', in J. H. Donnelly and W. R. George (eds), *Marketing of Services*, Chicago: American Marketing Association, 186–90.

Index

C

D

F

G

H

I

J

L

Q

R